**CRIMINAL
JUSTICE
VOCABULARY**

CRIMINAL JUSTICE VOCABULARY

By

JULIAN A. MARTIN, B.S., M.S., J.D.
Professor Emeritus, Department of Criminal Justice
Louisiana State University
Baton Rouge, Louisiana

and

NICHOLAS A. ASTONE, Ph.D.
Chairman, Professor of Criminal Justice
Department of Criminal Justice
Alabama State University
Montgomery, Alabama

CHARLES C THOMAS • PUBLISHER
Springfield • Illinois • U.S.A.

Published and Distributed Throughout the World by
CHARLES C THOMAS • PUBLISHER
Bannerstone House
301-327 East Lawrence Avenue, Springfield, Illinois, U.S.A.

This book is protected by copyright. No part of it
may be reproduced in any manner without written
permission from the publisher.

© *1980, by* CHARLES C THOMAS • PUBLISHER
ISBN 0-398-03987-9
Library of Congress Catalog Card Number: 79-22231

With THOMAS BOOKS careful attention is given to all details of manufacturing and design. It is the Publisher's desire to present books that are satisfactory as to their physical qualities and artistic possibilities and appropriate for their particular use. THOMAS BOOKS will be true to those laws of quality that assure a good name and good will.

Martin, Julian A
   Criminal justice vocabulary.

   1. Criminal justice, Administration of—Dictionaries. I. Astone, Nicholas A., joint author. II. Title.
HV6017.M37   364'.03   79-22231
ISBN 0-398-03987-9

Printed in the United States of America
M-3

ACKNOWLEDGMENTS

The authors are grateful for the research assistance provided by Miss Mary Lou Burkett, Mr. Gary Corbin, and Mr. David Bordelon. The following publishers have granted permission to cite a limited number of terms and definitions, which has added to the comprehensiveness of the *Criminal Justice Vocabulary:*

Geary, David Patrick: *Community Relations and the Administration Of Justice.* John Wiley and Sons, Inc., New York, New York, 1975.
Radelet, Louis A.: *The Police and the Community.* Macmillan Publishing Co., Inc., New York, New York, 1973.
Juris, Harvey A. and Feuille, Peter: *Police Unionism: Power and Impact in Public-Sector Bargaining.* D. C. Heath and Co., Lexington, Massachusetts, 1973.
Newman, Donald J.: *Introduction to Criminal Justice.* J. B. Lippincott Co., Philadelphia, Pennsylvania, 1975.
Houts, Marshall: *From Arrest To Release.* Charles C Thomas, Publisher, Springfield, Illinois, 1958.

J.A.M.
N.A.A.

CRIMINAL JUSTICE VOCABULARY

A

Abandon (a *ban* den). Legal term: To discard; to rid one's self of possession; to relinquish or give up possession of something with intent of never again resuming one's right or interest. "Abandoned property may be obtained legally by an officer and used as evidence without it being involved in a search and seizure problem."

Abandonment (a *ban* den mint). A criminal offense wherein minor children, animals, or pregnant wives are deserted.

Abate (a *bait*). To put an end to; to diminish, to lessen in degree of intensity or nullify something. (Used frequently in legal phraseology.)

ABC Sheet. Gambling term: Also known as **ABC Marker.** A ruled, professional-type marker. The three center columns represent win, place, and show.

Abdomen (*ab* dough men). That part of the body between the lower ribs and the pelvis.

Abduction (ab *duck* shun). Criminal law: The offense of taking away a wife, child, or ward by fraud and persuasion or open violence.

Abet (a *bet*). To actively instigate and/or encourage someone to do something; to aid in the accomplishment of a criminal undertaking. "He abetted the accused in the crime."

Abettor (a *better*). One who abets. (This is used frequently in legal terminology.)

Abeyance (a *bay* ons). Inactivity; suspension. "I will hold the matter in abeyance until I receive instructions."

Abide (a *bide*). 1. To await; to wait for something to occur. 2. To obey instructions or endure conditions without objection. "Regardless of my personal feelings, I will abide by your instructions."

Ab iniatio (ab e *nish* eo). Latin: From the beginning; also see *de novo,* another term closely related in meaning. "The act was wrong *ab iniatio.*"

Abjure (ab *jur*). To renounce or abandon on oath.

Abode (a *boad*). Place where one lives. "We visited his place of abode."

Abolish (a *boll* ish) (boll as in doll). To do away with; extinguish; destroy. "Slavery was abolished in this country."

Abolitionism (a bo *lish* in ism). The radical support of the ceasing of slavery.

Abortifacient (a *bor* te *fa* shent). A drug or medicine capable of or used for producing an abortion.

Abortion (a *bor* shen). Miscarriage; premature birth or expulsion of a fetus at a stage too young to live (nonviable). "The crime of abortion is the illegal procuring of a miscarriage." Under most circumstances the act of abortion on the part of the one bringing it about has been illegal except under very restricted circumstances. As of 1970 there was a movement to liberalize the legal aspects of the situation in some states.

Abortive Trial (a *bor* tiv). A trial in which no verdict has been reached, through no fault of the parties involved.

Abortus (a *bor* tus). The fetus produced by an abortion.

Above. Gambling slang: The amount of earnings shown openly on the books for official purposes; contrasted with "below."

Abrasion (a *bray* zhen). The change (usually damage) of something by friction, generally by a wearing, grinding, or rubbing away. "The traffic accident victim suffered from abrasions but no broken bones." Photographic term: Markings on the emulsion surfaces of photographs, appearing as lines or scratches. Rubbing, rough handling, or weight against the emulsion may cause them.

Abridge (a *brij*). To reduce or contract; usually spoken of written language. In practice: To shorten a declaration or count by taking away or severing some of the substance of it (*Black's Law Dictionary*).

Abrogate (*ab* roe gait). To render inoperative or annul through authoritative action; to abolish. "The court abrogated the provisions of the contract."

Abscond (ab *skond*). To leave secretly and conceal oneself; to flee to avoid arrest. "He absconded with the money, and no one has heard from him."

Absent Without Leave (AWOL). A military term: To absent oneself from one's place of assignment without taking official leave.

Absolve (ab *zolve*). To relieve or free from accusation; to relieve of responsibility to perform an obligation. "Investigation absolved the suspect from guilt of the crime."

Absorption of Alcohol (ab *zorp* shun). The process of alcohol being absorbed into the bloodstream.

Abstain (ab *stane*). To refrain from doing something on a voluntary basis. "Although he enjoyed drinking, he abstained from the use of alcoholic beverages when driving an automobile."

Abstainer. One who does not drink alcoholic beverages.

Abstinence (*ab* ste nens). The voluntarily abstaining from doing something, such as eating or drinking.

Abstinence Syndrome. The characteristic mental distress and physical pain symptoms of a drug or narcotic addict during and after withdrawal from the use of the cause of addiction.

Abuse. The mistreatment of an individual, particularly a child. When applied to a female it usually refers to sexual molesting.

Abyssinian Polo (ab e *sin* ee an). Slang: A dice game.

Academic (ack e *dem* ick). Related to a school, especially one of higher learning (college or university).

Academician (*ack* e dem *ish* en). A teacher or researcher in an institution of learning (usually a college or university); one learned in a field who teaches. "The lecturer in our training program is an academician."

Academy Training. The formal training and education through which newly accepted employees of the criminal justice system are put.

Acapulco Gold. Slang: A term for marijuana.

Accelerant (ack *sell* er ant). Something that hastens or accelerates. "In the act of arson an accelerant is used at times to accelerate the burning."

Accelerate (ack *sell* er ate). To increase speed; to go from a slower to a faster speed; to "pick up" speed;

VOCABULARY

to move faster. "The car did not accelerate well."

Acceptance (ak *sep* tens). Approval; approving reception; an express or implied act by which one accepts an obligation, offer, contract, etc., together with all its legal consequences.

Accessory (ack *sess* or ree). One who assists in a crime; one who assists in or instigates the commission of an offense but is not present at, nor does he participate in, the actual commission of the crime. Some states have abolished the accessory categories, and persons involved in such activities are charged as principals.

Accessory After the Fact. One who assists, harbors, or conceals a person, knowing such person has committed a crime; the accessory was not present at nor a participant in the crime so committed. Some states have abolished this charge and charge the "accessory" as a principal in the crime.

Accessory Before the Fact. One who aids, counsels or directs another in the commission of a crime prior to its commission and was not present when it was committed. Some states have eliminated this charge and consider one in this position as a principal.

Accident (*ack* se dent). An unforeseen event that occurred from unawareness, carelessness, ignorance or unavoidable causes, usually resulting in damage or injury. "Some experts say there is no such thing as an unavoidable accident." The most commonly encountered accident in law enforcement involves traffic, in which it is a major cause of death or injury.

Accidental (ack se *dent* al). A fingerprint pattern that does not fall into one of the three basic patterns. This is a "catch-all" pattern. This pattern contains two or more characteristics of the other patterns but does not include the plain arch with two or more deltas. In classifying fingerprints it is classified as a whorl.

Accidental Criminal. A person unintentionally engaged in some form of criminal behavior.

Accidental Killing. A killing that is legally done under a reasonable belief that no harm is possible. Note: "Involuntary manslaughter" is the result of an illegal act.

Accommodation Arrest (a kom oh *day* shun). An arrest that is previously arranged between the arrestee and the police in order to make it appear that the police are doing their job. This is also called a stand-in arrest.

Accommodation Paper. A bill, note, or draft endorsed by one person without requiring collateral or a fee in order to let another person raise money or obtain credit.

Accomplice (a *kahm* ples). A confederate in a crime; an associate or fellow-criminal. "We arrested one of the burglars in the act, but his accomplice escaped."

Accord and Satisfaction (a *kord*; sat ess *fak* shun). An agreement between two persons whereby one who has a right of action against another accepts something different from what might be legally enforced.

Accrue (a *crew*). To accumulate; to reach a state of existence by addition or increase. "He has accrued a substantial bank account."

Accuse (a *kyuze*). To charge with a crime or misdeed. "The indictment in effect accuses a person of an offense."

Accused. One charged with a crime; the defendant in a criminal action. "The accused is scheduled for a trial on the fifteenth."

Ace. 1. Narcotics slang: A sentence of one year in jail or prison; marijuana; a friend or pal. 2. The (one) spot on a die (singular of dice).

Ace in the Hole. Slang: Something of importance held in reserve until needed for the success of an undertaking.

Aces. Slang: A person considered to be "A-1," "tops" or the best at something. Also refers to things that are best.

Achieved Status (a *cheevd; stat* ess). Status assigned to a person on the basis of his/her individual achievements, effort or merit.

Acid. 1. Narcotics slang: LSD, LSD-25 (lysergic acid diethylamide). 2. A substance that, on dissociation, releases hydrogen ions (H+); the opposite of a base.

Acidhead. Slang: Frequent user of LSD.

Acid Test. Party at which LSD has been added to the punch.

A.C.L.U. (ACLU). American Civil Liberties Union.

Acoustics (a *koos* tiks). The qualities (physical features) of a room or enclosure that govern the clarity of audible sounds. "The acoustics of the auditorium are excellent. One can hear the speaker from any location."

Acquiesce (ak wee *ess*). To admit the truth of a statement or accusation by remaining silent.

Acquire (a *kwire*). Slang: To steal.

Acquit (a *kwit*). To legally free an accused person. To find an accused person not guilty.

Acquittal (a *kwit* el). The freeing of or the finding of innocence of an accused person.

Across the Board. In horse racing (or other racing), to bet the same amount on a participant to win, place, or show. The same amount bet for win, place, or show.

Across the Tracks. Juvenile slang: Boundaries of juvenile gangs.

Act. Something done voluntarily by a person for which he is legally responsible.

Acting Crowd. A crowd gathered for some common reason, generally of a hostile nature.

Action. 1. Law: A suit at law; legal proceedings. 2. Slang: Activity; place of activity. "Let's go where the action is." 3. Gambling slang: The gambling activity. 4. Firearms term: Firearm mechanism.

Actionable (*ak* shun a bull). Those facts which permit legal action to be taken, i.e. those which constitute a specific criminal offense.

Act, Legislative. A law passed by the legislature; statute.

Actual Violence. An assault in which actual physical force is used. The term *violence* is used interchangeably with *physical force*.

Acute (a *kyute*). Sharp on the end; having a drastic effect on the senses: "acute pain." Serious in nature—a crisis; critical or crucial.

A.D. Latin: Anno Domini. In the year of our Lord.

Adamism (*adam* ism). Nude exhibitionism; a person exposing himself in the nude.

Adam's Ale. An alcoholic beverage derived from apples.

Adanon (ada *non*). Methadone.

Addict (*a* dikt). One who has developed an addiction to drugs. One who gives in to or surrenders to

VOCABULARY

something; one who obsessively acts due to habit, such as the use of drugs.

Addiction (a *dick* shun). Physical dependence upon a drug or narcotic.

Additive. Initiate; to add; additional information.

Ad Hoc (add *hock*). For a specific and limited purpose at hand. "An *ad hoc* committee was appointed to draft a set of rules, which will then be studied by the organization."

Ad Infinitum (add in fi *nigh* tum). Latin: Without end; indefinitely.

Adipocere Formation (*add* e po *seer*). An occurrence in which the fat of the body (corpse) turns into a wax. This may happen where the body has been buried a long time or immersed in a liquid.

Adjective. The part of a law that defines who will have the power to enforce the law.

Adjourn (a *jern*). To suspend a meeting or activity until a certain time or indefinitely. "Let's adjourn the meeting until 9 AM tomorrow."

Adjourned Summons (a *jern* ed). A summons that is first taken in a judge's chambers and then brought into a court to be argued by the counsels.

Adjournment (a *jern* ment). Temporarily postponing the business of a court, legislative body, or meeting.

Adjudge (a *judge*). To judge; to reach a decision upon a matter that is under consideration; to judicially find guilt as to an accused. "The accused was adjudged guilty by the court."

Adjudication (a jude e *ka* shen). The determination of the facts of a case by a court and the reaching of a decision or judgment of such facts. The disposition (sentence) then follows. The term is used frequently in juvenile court proceedings.

Adjudicatory Hearing (add *jude* e ca *tory*). The juvenile proceeding equivalent to the adult criminal trial.

Adjutant General. 1. The commanding officer of the state or territory national guard or militia. 2. In the United States Army the Adjutant General's Department is headed by the Adjutant General, who has charge of the records of the Army.

Administrator (ad *men* is tra tor). One having the legal authority and responsibility to handle the affairs of an estate; one who directs and supervises (administrates) the operations of an organization. "The Chief of Police is a capable administrator."

Admiralty (*add* mirel tee). Matters pertaining to maritime affairs; those laws handled in an admiralty court.

Admiralty Courts (*add* mire tee). Courts dealing with controversies relating to the sea, civil or criminal.

Admissible (add *miss* i bul). Legally entitled to be admitted into the court record as evidence.

Admonish (ad *mon* ish). To reprimand gently and in a friendly and sympathetic manner for something that has been done incorrectly. "The sergeant admonished the patrolman on his manner of dress."

Adolescence (add o *less* ens). That period in life between puberty and adulthood which legally ends when a person reaches the age of majority.

Adopt. 1. Law: To legally and voluntarily take one (child) as a member of the family. 2. To accept and use practice or procedure as one's own. "I adopted the procedures used in your department."

A.D.T.C. (ADTC). American District Telegraph Company.
Adult (a *dult*). One of full legal age.
Adulterine (a *dull* te rin). A child born of adulterous intercourse.
Adulterous Bastard (e *dull* ter us). A child conceived through illegal sexual act of two people who at the time were not legally entitled to be married as one or both were then married to someone else.
Adultery (a *dull* te ry). In common law: Sexual relations with the husband or wife of another. It has been made a crime in some states by statute.
Adultery, Open and Notorious. Openly and publicly living in adultery within a community that knows that the parties are not married.
Ad Valorem (add ve *low* rem). Latin: According to value; a percentage imposition of rate based on value. "An ad valorem tax on property is commonly used."
Adversary (*add* ver say ree). An opponent; one who opposes or resists; an enemy. "We use the adversary system in the trial of criminal cases, which may not be without faults but is believed to be the best method to bring out the facts."
Adversary System. A legal system that entails a contest between two opposing parties under a judge who acts as an impartial umpire. (In the United States the accused is considered innocent until proven guilty beyond a reasonable doubt by the pleadings and evidence introduced in court.)
Adverse (add *vurse*) (vurse as in purse). Unfavorable; in a contrary direction; not in accord with one's interest. "The investigating committee submitted an adverse report as to the operations of the department."
Adverse Possession. A method of acquiring a title by possessing it for a statutory period under certain conditions.
Advise (ad *vize*). To give advice; to inform someone; to warn. "Prior to questioning an accused who is in custody we must advise him of his rights."
Advocate (*add* vo kate). One who assists another in a court of law; a counselor; one who pleads the cause of another at a hearing or trial.
Aerosol Irritant Projectors. Nonlethal chemical irritant device used by police to subdue or temporarily disable a person.
A Fair One. Juvenile slang: A fair fight between gangs or gang members.
Affective Insanity. A comprehensive term describing all forms of insanity that relate to emotions.
Affiant (a *figh* ant). The person who makes a written statement under oath. Used synonymously with "deponent."
Affidavit (af i *day* vit). A written sworn statement given under oath before a judicial officer who is legally authorized to perform such acts, i.e. a magistrate (judge or justice of the peace).
Affirm (a *furm*) (furm as in worm). 1. To make a positive statement. 2. Law: To uphold the judgement of a lower court. "The Court of Appeals affirmed the judgement of the District Court."
Affirmation (*af* fur *may* shun). A statement or declaration made before a legally recognized government officer (judge, justice of the peace, notary public, etc.) in place of and having the legal effect of an oath. The Fourth Amendment of

VOCABULARY

the Bill of Rights says in part "and no warrants shall issue but upon probable cause, supported by oath or affirmation."

Affirmative Action Programs. Programs that insure minorities and ethnic groups of having even or better chances of getting admissions into schools, employment, promotion, etc., when competing with majority groups.

Affirmative Defense. The assertion by the defendant of new matter over and above a general denial of guilt, which would relieve him of criminal responsibility if found true, e.g. insanity is an affirmative defense.

Affray (a *fray*). 1. Fracas, brawl, noisy incident. "He joined the affray and got a bloody nose." 2. A sudden unpremeditated fight or brawl in public that involves two or more persons.

A Force. Of necessity.

Aforethought (a *for* thot). Premeditated; planned. The term is most frequently found in definitions of murder: "Murder aforethought."

A Fortiori (a *for* she *or* ee). Latin: Of greater force. A term used in logic to indicate that one conclusion is stronger or more persuasive than another.

A.G. (AG). Attorney General.

Age. 1. The time in a person's life calculated from date of birth. It is an important item in description of a person. In getting information about the age of a person it is good to obtain and record the date of birth (DOB). 2. The age of maturity (legal) majority. "He is of age" = He has reached majority, which is determined by the law of the state.

Agent. Short for special agent, the title of investigators of some government and private agencies. "He is an agent of the FBI."

Age-specific Birthrate. The number of births from women of a certain age group per 1000 women.

Agglutination (a *glue* ti *nay* shen). A reaction in which red blood cells suspended in a liquid collect into clumps; usually occurs in the presence of a specific antibody.

Agglutinin (a *glue* ti nen). Antibody substance in the blood that will cause a pulling together or clumping of blood cells or bacteria in liquid suspension. This principle is used in a crime laboratory in blood typing.

Aggravated Assault (*ag* ra vay tid a *salt*). An unlawful attack by one person upon another for the purpose of inflicting severe bodily injury, usually accompanied by the use of a weapon or other means likely to produce death or serious bodily harm.

Aggressive Patrol. A controversial police practice usually involving the saturation of a high-crime area with policemen who stop, question, frisk, and search pedestrians and motorists, almost at random, in an effort to prevent crimes and confiscate weapons.

Agitate. To cause trouble; to do things to make people angry; to disturb. "The extremist group did things to agitate the police."

Agitator. Slang: A prisoner who is constantly causing trouble and arousing the other inmates to cause trouble and revolt.

Agreement. Legal document: Mutual promise.

Ahead. Gambling slang: The amount of money a player has won. "He's ahead $10" means he is ten dollars over the amount he started with.

Aid and Comfort. To help or encourage. The constitutional definition of treason uses the term "aid and comfort."

Aim, Dead. Carefully aiming or sighting a firearm at a target.

Airplanes, Stolen. Stolen aircraft constitutes a violation of the state law of theft or larceny. If the craft is transported from one state to another, there is also a violation of federal law.

Al-Anon, Al-Anon Family Groups. An Alcoholics Anonymous program for the family of an alcoholic in order to help them deal with this problem.

Alarm. A device that signals a message, usually of danger, when activated by movement, sound, temperature or other specific factors (such as time). "The burglar alarm went off at 11:45."

Albastone (al *bass* tone). A commercially prepared material for casting footprints, etc. Used by some instead of plaster of Paris.

Alateen. An Alcoholics Anonymous program for rehabilitating teenage alcoholics.

Alcohol (al co hol). A sharply odored, colorless liquid with a burning taste. Two kinds: 1. Ethyl, grain, ethanol (C_2H_5OH), obtained from fermented grain or fruits. 2. Methyl, methanol, wood alcohol (CH_3OH). Very poisonous.

Alcoholic (al ko *hall* ick). 1. Pertaining to alcohol. 2. A person who drinks alcohol excessively and regularly; one addicted to alcohol.

Alcoholic Dementia (de *men* she ah). A form of mental malfunction occurring in persons in the late stages of chronic alcoholism.

Alcoholics Anonymous. An organization made up of alcoholics who are refraining from drinking. The members aid one another and also assist alcoholics who are not members of the organization. Their purpose is to aid themselves and others in the treatment of alcohol addiction. Chapters of the organization are found in principal cities. The members are most dedicated to the goals of the organization.

Alcoholism (*al* ko *hall* ism). Disease of drunkenness; caused by long and frequent use of alcoholic beverages.

Alcohol Poisoning. The poisoning of body tissue due to excessive ingestion of alcohol.

Alias. An assumed name; a name other than one's own; otherwise called. "Jones used the alias of Ralph Smith."

Alibi. The claim of being at a place other than at the place of the commission of a crime at the time it occurred.

Alibi Store. A skill game in which the player has little or no chance to win. Played at fairs and carnivals.

Alidade (*al* i daid) (daid as in aid). A device for determining direction, consisting of a rule having connecting with it a simple or telescopic sight. Used in sketching, especially large outdoor areas.

Alien (*ail* ee yen). Foreign, i.e. not belonging to or a citizen of the country where one is located. "He is an alien in the United States."

Alienate (*ail* ee yen ate). To transfer to another, as property; to transfer affection or devotion from one to whom it belonged.

Alienist (*ail* yen ist). A specialist in mental diseases.

Alimony (*al* i moe nee). Divorced wife's allowance (payment of money or property).

Aliunde (*a* lee *un* dee). From an-

VOCABULARY

other place, e.g. proof of the corpus delicti by evidence other than the defendant's confession.

Allege (a *lej*). To state something as a fact; to affirm.

Allen Case. Illinois v. Allen, 397 U.S. 337 (1970). Concerns disruptive defendants.

All In. Slang: Tired out; exhausted.

All Lit Up. Narcotics slang: Under the influence.

Allocution (al low *kew* shen) (kew as in pew). A demand of a person convicted of a felony or treason that he state why the court should not proceed to a judgement against him.

Allot (uh *lot*). To assign or distribute by shares.

All Out. Going to the limit or pushing as hard as one can to win.

Alloy (*al* oi; a *loi*). A combination of metals fused together.

All Shook Up. Slang: Disturbed; excited.

All Wet. Slang: Wrong; misinformed; mistaken in his statements. "His theory is all wet."

Alpha Ray (*al* fah). A positively charged nuclear particle, identical with the nucleus of a helium atom, moving at high speed due to radioactive emission.

Also-Ran. Slang: One who seeks an objective but fails to reach it; one who is a failure in an undertaking.

Altercation (all tur *kay* shen). A fracas, fuss, noisy quarrel.

Alternatives. Options; courses of action; other ways of doing the same thing.

Alternative Society. Hippie term: A society or mode of life outside the modern conventional society. The commune is the main support system of the alternative society.

Alveolar Air Breath Alcohol System. Trade name of a device to test the breath to determine blood alcohol content.

AM. Radio term: Amplitude modulation. A type of radio transmitting wave. This is the conventional type of transmitting wave and is more susceptible to static interference than is FM, frequency modulation, which has little or no static problems.

Ambulance Chaser. Slang: A lawyer whose ethics are questionable, especially as pertains to getting clients. The expression originated from situations where lawyers followed ambulances to the scene of accidents to offer their services to the injured.

Amend (a *mend*). To correct, change, add to or delete a part. "The resolution was amended to add one sentence."

Amendment (a *mend* ment). A change or alteration. In relation to legislative or parliamentary procedure, any proposed or actual change in an act, bill, statute, constitution, or other official documents. For the first ten amendments to the United States Constitution see **Bill of Rights.**

Amentia (a *men* she ah). A total lack of intelligence, reason, or mental capacity.

Amercement (a *merss* ment). A penalty of a pecuniary nature imposed by a court. It differs from a fine in that a fine is fixed at a certain sum by statute whereas an amercement is an arbitrary assessment of the court.

American Bar Association (ABA). A national professional organization of lawyers.

American Bar Foundation (ABF). A research wing of the ABA.

American Civil Liberties Union (ACLU). A nationwide organization with goals to defend constitutionally guaranteed individual rights and liberties. National headquarters: 156 Fifth Avenue, New York, New York 10010.

American District Telegraph Company (ADTC). A company operating nationally in the burglar alarm field. It utilizes various protective devices on business houses to detect unauthorized entry into premises and activate alarms.

American Law Institute (ALI). A national association of prominent lawyers and legal scholars who voluntarily draft model laws, such as the **Model Penal Code**.

American Society for Industrial Security. 404 NADA BUILDING, 2000 K Street N.W., Washington, D.C. 20006. Telephone: (202) 338-7676. National organization of industrial security officers.

Amicus Curiae (*a* mi kus *ku* ree ay). Law; Latin: Friend of the court. One who enters a litigated matter and assists the court. See **Friend of the Court**.

Amidone. Slang: Methadone.

Amino (a *mee* no). With intent.

Amnesia (am *nee* zhe). Loss or impairment of memory. May be the result of organic or physical causes or due to psychological factors.

Amphetamine (am *fet* a meen). Name of benzedrine sulfate. A synthetic drug; central nervous system stimulant; causes local constricting effect on mucous membranes. Can be taken orally as a white powder or by injection when in solution. Slang names: benny, pep pill, and many others.

Amping; Over-Amping. Slang: Overdose of drugs, usually referring to heroin.

Amplify (*am* pli fie) (fie as in pie). To enlarge in scope; increase in strength or volume.

A.M.T. (AMT). Slang: DMT.

Analgesic (an el *jee* zek). A drug that relieves pain or kills pain.

Anarchy (*an* are kee). A condition of society where every person is free of restraints against any actions he desires to perform, i.e. there is no power to enforce the law. A condition of chaos exists. "The current activities by extremists against the establishment could lead to anarchy."

Angel. 1. Slang: The victim of a thief or swindler. 2. The male-playing homosexual who provides things for his partner.

Angina Pectoris (*an* ji na *peck* tor iss). A heart disease, manifested by pain in the chest accompanied by a feeling of suffocation. It is caused by contraction of the smaller arteries that supply blood to the heart muscles. Pain may occur in the chest, left shoulder, and/or the inner side of the left arm. In addition to pain there may be shortage of breath, fear, and sweating. If the victim has medication for the condition, he should take it. Medical treatment should be made available quickly. This condition is brought on by any of several factors, including stress.

Angle. Slang: A scheme or plan to accomplish or obtain something by illegal or unethical means—cheating, trickery, fraud, etc.

Angling. Card slang: A prearranged deal between two players to split the pot or to not bet against each other.

Angstrom (*ang* strem; ang as in hand). A minute unit of linear measurement, used to measure wavelengths of light.

Anguish. Mental pain and suffering.

Anilingus (anna *ling* us). Licking the

anus of another person, producing sexual excitement.

Animal. Gambling slang: A professional strong-arm man who keeps his boss's employees in line and collects overdue gambling losses.

Animated Ivories. Dice slang: A pair of dice.

Annihilate (a *nigh* e late). To absolutely destroy; totally destroy. "The animals were annihilated."

Anno Domini (*an* oh *dom* e nigh). Latin: The year of our Lord.

Annulment (a *nul* ment). Abolition; invalidation; the rendering void of something that has been done.

Antagonize (an *tag* o nize). To make one feel unfriendly; to create an enemy; to arouse ill feeling.

Ante (*ann* tee). Gambling slang: An amount of money that must be placed into the pot before a player is eligible to play the game.

Anterior (an *tear* e ur) (tear as in pier). The front part of a living being; in man it is the front side contrasted to the back side, or posterior. It is used in conjunction with many other words; for example, anterior pituitary means the front part of the pituitary gland.

Anthropometry (*an* throw *pom* e try). The science that involves measuring the human body and its parts.

Anthropophagy (an thre *pof* e je). Sex deviation term: Eating the flesh of another, either bitten off or sliced from the body.

Antibiotic (*an* tie by *ah* tik). A substance produced by or derived from living organisms, such as yeast or molds, which will kill or slow the growth of germs (bacteria).

Antibody (*an* tie body). A globular protein in the body that reacts with a specific antigen and destroys it.

Anticipatory Socialization (an *tis* i pay *tory*). Modeling your behavior after persons who occupy the roles you wish to occupy in the future.

Antigen (*an* tie gin). A protein or carbohydrate substance that triggers the production of an antibody.

Antiserum (*an* tie se rum). A serum containing specific antibodies.

Antisocial Personality. See **Psychopath.**

Antitheft Devices for Motor Vehicles. Devices built into a vehicle that prevent its starting and/or being moved when the ignition key is removed.

Antithesis (an *tith* a sis). Contrasting or opposing idea; directly opposite. "His idea is the antithesis of that of his associate."

Antitrust Law. Federal and state law that forbids the formation and operation of monopolies and combines that adversely affect commerce.

Anvil. Firearms term: A piece of metal in the primer cup of a cartridge, which when struck by the firing pin activates the priming material.

Anxiety (ang *zi* e ty). A condition of being worried about something; uneasy of mind because of a problem (real or imaginary).

Apalachin Meeting. A meeting of high officials of the Cosa Nostra held at Apalachin, New York, in 1957. The meeting was interrupted by law enforcement officers, who obtained the identity of several persons in attendance. Reference: Salerno, Ralph and Tompkins, John S.: *The Crime Confederation.* Garden City, New York, Doubleday, 1969.

Apathy (*ap* a the). Indifference to matters; complacence; showing no interest or feeling. "Due to the apathy of people, certain groups are destroying our society."

Ape. Slang: Thug or strong-arm man.

A *Posteriori* (*a po* stir e *or* e). Latin: A term in logic describing the process by which one reasons from the effect or end result back to its cause. If one knows the end result, he can determine its cause.

Apparent Danger. As related to the doctrine of self-defense, a term meaning such overt actual demonstration, by conduct and acts, of intent to take a life or do great bodily harm, that would make a killing an apparent necessity.

Appeal (a *peel*). Law: The request that a higher court review the findings and/or rulings of a lower court with a view of correcting error or injustice; the removal of a legal matter from an inferior court to a superior court for purposes of review and actions on the law and/or facts (some appeal courts only have jurisdiction to rule on the law, while others may review the case and rule on the law and the facts).

Appeal Bond. The bond posted by the party that appeals (appellant), guaranteeing to pay damages and costs if he fails to go forward prudently with the appeal.

Appearance. Law: The coming into court of either of the parties to a lawsuit or legal action.

Appellant (a *pell* ant). The party who appeals a case to a higher court; one who appeals. The other party is the appellee (respondent).

Appellate (a *pell* ate). Having authority and jurisdiction to consider and rule on cases on appeal. "The District Court has no appellate jurisdiction."

Appellate Review. A comprehensive rehearing of a case in a court other than the one in which it was previously tried.

Appellee (a pell *ee*). The respondent; the party in a lawsuit against whom an appeal is taken. Contrasted with appellant.

Applejack. An alcoholic beverage made from fermented apples.

Apple-Polish. Slang: To gain favor with superior or someone of importance through flattery or by rendering special favors. Synonyms: Ass-kiss, brownnose.

Applied Research. Knowledge generated by research which can be applied practically.

Apprehend (ap pre *hend*). To seize; take into custody; arrest. "I will apprehend the violator."

Approver. An accomplice in a crime who is admitted as a witness against his companions.

Appurtenance (a *pur* te nans). That which belongs to an estate or property.

Arbitration (ar be *tra* shen). The settlement of a dispute by a person chosen to hear both sides and come to a decision.

Arch. A fingerprint pattern. The ridges come in from one side, do not recurve, and go out the other side. The ridges make an upward thrust at or near the center of the pattern. There are two kinds: plain arch, where the upthrust is smooth and gradual, and tented arch, where the upward thrust is sharp.

Are You Straight? Juvenile slang: Are you one of the gang? Are you prepared?

Argue (*are* gu). To quarrel. To present reasons to support a thought or point of view. "The lawyers argued the case in court."

Armor, Body. See **Body Armor.**

Arms. Weapons; firearms.

VOCABULARY

Around the Turn. Narcotics slang: Having gone through the withdrawal period.

Arraign (a *rain*). To call or bring an accused before a court (judge) to answer to a criminal charge (usually an indictment or information) against him. The accused is called before the judge and the charge (against him) is read to him, after which he is called upon to plead guilty or not guilty. This plea is entered on the record.

Arraignment (a *rain* ment). The act or process of being arraigned. "He appeared for arraignment."

Arrest (a *rest*). Law: The taking of one person into custody by another for violation of the law.

Arrest of Judgement. Staying or suspending the execution of a judgement.

Arrest Warrant. A document issued by a court ordering law officers to arrest a specified individual.

Arsenic (*are* sen ik). A poisonous chemical element that, in combination with other chemical elements, makes poisonous drugs. White arsenic (arsenic trioxide) is one such compound. Arsenic under proper conditions and in specified amounts is used in medicine. Arsenic has been used to cause death.

Arterioscleroses (are *tee* ree o skle *row* sis). A hardening and thickening of the artery walls, usually associated with advanced age.

Artery (*are* te ry). 1. A blood vessel that carries blood from the heart to various parts of the body. 2. A means of transportation, such as a main highway.

Artillery. Slang: 1. Underworld term for gun or guns, pistols, or other weapons. 2. Equipment for injecting drugs.

Artist. Slang: A skillful criminal or con artist who has gained the respect of his peers.

A'S. Slang: Stimulant drugs—amphetamines.

ASA. American Standards Association. This organization has arrived at numerical ratings for film emulsion. Most light meters (exposure meters) use this rating in calculating their devices. "The ASA rating of the film is 200."

Ascetism (e *set* e siz em). Sex deviation term: Refraining from sexual involvement.

Asleep at the Switch. Slang: Not alert; inattentive; not concentrating on the task at hand.

Asphyxiate (as *fik* see ate). To suffocate.

Aspirin-Hound. Slang: Person addicted to aspirin.

Asportation (as pour *tay* shun). The act of carrying away goods. This is one of the elements in the crime of larceny.

Assassination (a *sass* i *nay* shun). Killing by treacherous means; killing by surprise or by secret attack. The word comes from "hashshashin"—those addicted to hashish. It originally meant a member of a secret order of Mohammedans, who committed secret murders while under the influence of hashish.

Assault (a *salt*). An intentional, unlawful offer of corporal injury to another by force, or force unlawfully directed toward person of another, under such circumstances as create well-founded fear of imminent peril, coupled with apparent present ability to execute attempt, if not prevented (*Black's Law Dictionary*). An attempted battery. There are usually different grades of assault, i.e. aggravated assault—where a dangerous weapon is used, and simple assault—where no dangerous weapon is used. There may be further specific kinds of assault, such as assault with intent to commit manslaughter, rape, or robbery. It varies among states.

Ass-Backwards. Slang: Hind part before; reversed; confused.

Assemble (a *sim* bel). To meet together as a group. "The vice squad will assemble at 8 AM in room 100."

Assignation, House of (as ig *nay* shun). Bawdy house; whorehouse; house of prostitution.

Assimilation (a sim i *lay* shun). The cultural blending of two or more people.

Assise, Assize (a *siz*). The circuit courts and their judges in England.

Ass-Kisser. Slang: One who seeks favor with superiors by flattery, servility, or willfully being humiliated. Synonyms: Apple-polisher, brown-noser.

Associate (a *sow* she at). Fellow worker; partner, companion. "The suspect is an associate of Smith, a known burglar."

Associative Evidence (a *sow* she tive). See **Evidence, Associative.**

Assumpsit (a *sump* sit). Suit incurred through the breach of a simple contract.

Assumption of the Risk. An action where a plaintiff assumes the consequences of injury occurring through the fault of a defendant, third person or fault of no one.

At Bar. Before the court; or within the railing of the courtroom.

Atom. The smallest particle of an element that can exist either alone or in a combination.

Atomic Mass Number. The mass of any atom, which is equal to the number of protons and neutrons in the nucleus.

Atomic Number. The number of protons in the nucleus of an atom, unique to that type of atom.

Atropine (*at* ro pin). A poison found in the nightshade plant and in the seeds of the jimson weed. Respiratory paralysis is the cause of death.

Attache (at a *shay*). A member of the diplomatic staff of his nation, by reason of expert qualifications, stationed in a foreign country.

Attachment. A legal document issued by a court commanding a seizure of something. "He served the writ of attachment."

Attainder (a *tane* der). A procedure used in England from the eleventh to the nineteenth centuries, which was somewhat similar to the ancient practice of outlawry. The criminal who was convicted of treason or a felony suffered forfeiture, corruption of blood, and the loss of all civil rights. The person was declared "attainted." The procedure became synonymous with "civil death." Reference: Vanderbilt Law Review: The collateral consequences of a criminal conviction. *Crim L Bull,* Sept. 1971, 577.

Attainder, Bill of. Laws that provide for attainder. Such were prohibited in the United States by the Constitution, Article 1, Section 9, which states, "No Bill of Attainder . . . shall be passed."

Attainted (a *tane* ted). Under English law: One who was convicted of treason of felony. See **Attainder.**

Attempt. A crime: A person having a specific intent to commit a crime does or omits an act for the purpose of and tending directly toward the accomplishing of his object. The

VOCABULARY

planning of a crime and doing an overt act toward its commission.

Attest (a *test*). To bear witness to; to bear witness to a fact; to affirm to be true or genuine; to act as a witness to; to certify; to certify to the verity of a copy of a public document, formally by signature; to make solemn declaration in words or writing to support a fact; to signify by subscription of his name that the signer has witnessed the execution of the particular instrument (*Black's Law Dictionary*).

Attestation (a test *tay* shun). The act of witnessing the signature or execution of a deed or some other kind of an instrument and the showing of the name of such witness as testimony of such witnessing.

Attorney, United States. The chief law officer (federal) in the Federal Judicial District. He represents the United States government in civil and criminal matters. He is under the direction of the United States Attorney General, who heads the United States Department of Justice. The United States Attorney usually has assistants who aid him in performing the duties of the office.

Attorney General, State. The chief legal officer of the state, representing the state in civil and, under certain circumstances, in criminal matters. He furnishes legal advice to the governor and state departments.

Attorney General, United States. As a member of the President's Cabinet, he heads the United States Department of Justice. He is appointed by the President. He is the chief legal officer of the federal government, representing the national government in civil and criminal matters. He also gives legal advice to other federal agencies and the President.

Attorney-in-Fact. One legally authorized to act for another; an agent.

Auburn System. A prison system or procedure first started in Auburn State Prison in New York in 1816. It demanded silence on the part of the inmates. The prisoners were assigned to individual cells at night and forced to work in silence during the day.

Audio Surveillance (*aw* de o). A surveillance by listening. This may be by wiretapping or the use of electronic eavesdropping equipment to pick up conversations of persons. The courts have put restrictions on these types of activities. Reference: Katz v. U.S., 389 U.S. 347 (1967), on use of electronic eavesdropping.

Aunt. Slang: 1. An old prostitute or madam of a house of prostitution. 2. An aged homosexual. 3. An elderly Negro woman.

Aural (*aw* ral). Having to do with the sense of hearing or the ear.

Authority (aw *thor* ity). One with the right to command; one in command. A government or law enforcement agency and its personnel. "I learned from the authorities that the man is wanted."

Authorized Emergency Vehicles. Any of the designated public service vehicles used in times of emergency, e.g. ambulances, fire trucks, police vehicles.

Autoeroticism (auto e *rot* e siz em). Sex deviation term: Self-induced sexual gratification or feelings, such as by masturbation.

Automatism (auto *mat* ism). An illegal act arising from a reflex action or without conscious intent.

Automobile Theft. The stealing of an automobile or motor vehicle. Under state law it is theft or theft of a motor vehicle. Under federal law it is a violation to transport, or cause to be transported, from one state to another, knowing the vehicle has been stolen.

Auto Races. Gamblers' slang: A gambling game. See **Razzle Dazzle**.

Autosadism (auto *say* diz em). Sex deviation term: Sexual satisfaction obtained by pain to one's self, self-inflicted.

Avow (a *vow*). To state openly; acknowledge; openly admit membership or association with something. "He is an avowed Communist."

A.W.O.L. (AWOL). Military term: Absent Without Leave.

Axiom (*ak* see um). In logic, a truth that is self-evident.

Ax Rap. Slang: Murder conviction.

B

B.A. (BA). Bachelor of Arts degree.
Babbling Brook. Slang: A criminal.
Babo. Malline used to treat narcotic poisoning from heroin, methadone, or morphine. It is called "Babo," since it "takes the user to the cleaners."
Babysit. Slang: To guide a person through his drug experience.
B.A.C. (BAC). Blood alcohol content.
Backboard. Gambling term: A board or other hard barricade against which the dice must be rolled in a game of dice so that the dice cannot be controlled.
Backer. Gambling term: The person who puts up the money (bankroll) for the gamblers.
Back-Gate Parole. Prison slang: The death of a prisoner from natural causes.
Backstrap. Gambling term: An unauthorized telephone extension.
Back-to-Back Betting. Gambling term: Stud poker. Two cards of the same denomination consisting of the hold card and the first dealt upcard.
Backtrack. Slang: To withdraw the plunger of a syringe before injecting drugs to make sure the needle is in the proper position.
Back Up Man. An associate in crime who stays in the background.
Backwards. Slang: A term applied to tranquilizers.
Badge. Underworld term: Police officer.
Badge Bandit. Slang: Used among youngsters to denote a motorcycle police officer.

Badger Game. Blackmail achieved by putting the victim in a sexually embarrassing situation and the blackmailer then finding him in such plight. The blackmailer threatens exposure unless the victim complies with his demands.
Bag. Slang: 1. A woman of loose morals; a prostitute. 2. Packet of drugs.
Bag, Finding Your. Slang: Doing what seems best to you.
Bag, In the. Slang: Assured of success; everything is under control; all OK.
Bagged. Caught in the act of cheating or stealing.
Bag Man. 1. One who collects illicit or illegal money. In kidnapping it is the one who collects the ransom. In other illegal operations it is the middleman, who collects or delivers bribe money. One who collects the money for the "powers" who afford the protection. 2. A drug supplier.
Bail (bale). Bond to insure the appearance in court or other legally designated place at a certain time of a person released from custody; security furnished by the arrestee or person being detained, or by someone else, to insure the appearance in court or other place at a designated time. "The man was released from custody on bail."
Bail Bondsman. A person who, for a fee, will post cash or a security required to meet the bail set for an arrested person.
Bailee (bale ee). The one for whom bail or bond is furnished.

Bailiff (*bay* leff). An officer assigned to the court to maintain order and perform other duties as the judge directs; may be a deputy sheriff or constable.

Bailiwick (*ba* li wik). The geographical jurisdiction of a bailiff.

Bailment. 1. The providing of bail for an arrested person. 2. The delivering of goods by one party to another to be held in trust for a specific purpose and returned when that purpose is ended.

Bailor (*bale* or). The one who furnishes or puts up bail.

Bait. Slang: 1. Male or female person who, because of being attractive, receives the unsolicited attention of homosexuals. 2. Someone or something placed and kept under surveillance where criminals may be apprehended while committing a crime. "The policewoman was used as bait to catch the pursesnatcher."

Ball. Slang: Absorption of stimulants and cocaine via genitalia. 2. A blast, gas—a party; a good time.

Balling. Slang: Having a good time.

Ballistics (ba *lis* ticks). The science or study of the flight of projectiles; for example, bullets fired from a pistol or rifle.

Balloon. A rubber balloon used for storing or delivering narcotics.

Balloon Test. A test to measure alcoholic content in the breath in which the subject must blow up a balloon.

Ballyhoo. Slang: Loud and noisy conversation.

Bamboo. Underworld slang: An opium pipe.

Bammies. Narcotics slang: Poor quality marijuana.

Bang. Slang: 1. Narcotic injection; injection of drugs. 2. To have sexual relations. 3. Underworld slang: To shoot.

Banger. Underworld slang: A hypodermic needle; an addict.

Bangtail. Slang: A racehorse.

Bang to Rights. Slang: Used to describe a "fair cop" who has a perfect case against someone.

Bang-Up. Slang: A bang-up job is one done very well or with great success.

Bang Up. Gambling slang: The closing of a casino or a card game voluntarily.

Banish (*ban* ish). To deport or expel one considered undesirable by a government.

Banishment. The sending of a convicted criminal away from a given geographical area.

Bank. Gambling term: 1. In a banking game it is the house; in a numbers game it is the headquarters. 2. Money used to finance a gambling operation. 3. One who finances a gambling plan.

Bank Craps. A dice game where the house takes all the bets.

Banker. Gambling term: One who furnishes the finances for a gambling operation. The banker in a dice game.

Banking Game. A gambling operation where the players wager all bets against the house.

Bank Robbery. The robbing of a bank by force, threats, or intimidation. This is a specific federal violation if the bank is a national bank, a member of the Federal Reserve System, or is insured by the Federal Deposit Insurance Corporation. Bank robbery is covered by state statutes on armed robbery in some states.

Bankroll Man. Gamblers' slang: The one who puts up the money (finances) for a gambling operation.

Bankruptcy. Insolvency; inability to pay debts as fall due in the usual

VOCABULARY

course of business, allowing a person's creditors to administer and distribute assets between them.
Bar. A drinking establishment that sells alcoholic beverages to be consumed there.
Barbiturate (bar *bi* tue rate) (tue as in due). Any one of several derivatives of barbituric acid. May be used as a sedative or hypnotic drug. The possession or sale of the drug is usually illegal unless obtained by prescription. These drugs are depressants and are addictive.
Barbs. Slang: Depressant drugs—barbiturates.
Barfly. A frequenter of bars; a person who "hangs out" at bars; a person who begs drinks at a bar.
Bargain, Implicit. A sentencing practice by which the defendent pleads guilty and throws himself on the mercy of the court, with the implied understanding that he will receive a lighter sentence than if he pleaded not guilty and demanded trial.
Bargain Justice. Slang: A "deal" made with the accused to plead guilty to a lesser charge, thus removing the need for trial.
Barometer (ba *rom* e tur). An instrument for measuring air pressure.
Barratry (*bare* ah tree). The illegal practice of stirring up litigation and spurious legal claims.
Barrel (*bear* el). 1. The part of a firearm (rifle, pistol, or shotgun) through which the projectile (bullet, slug, or shot) is discharged (fired). The barrel may have a smooth bore—having no spiralled raised ridges. It may be rifled—having spiraled lands and grooves (depressions between the ridges). The purpose of the rifling is to cause the projectile to spin in flight. 2. Slang: To drive fast. See **Over a Barrel**.

Barrel-House. Slang: A run-down bar or a combination of a bar, a house of prostitution, and rooming house.
Barrel-House Bum. A person who hangs around bars and gambling establishments in hopes of getting free drinks or handouts.
Barrel Time. Firearms term: Time of the movement of the bullet from the time the hammer falls until the bullet reaches the muzzle of the gun.
Barricade (*bear* a kade). 1. To put up some obstruction or otherwise prevent or slow down passage or travel along a road, street, highway, or walk; a means of preventing passage along a way of travel. "After the robbery, a barricade was set up on each road leading out of town." 2. To take refuge in a structure or place and secure the means of entry to prevent, or slow down, persons from entering. "The gangsters barricaded themselves in the building and shot at the officers."
Barrier (*bear* ee ur). Something that acts as a barricade or that separates people or things; an object or structure that restricts the free movement of people. "A barrier of rope was put up around the crime scene to keep people out."
Barrister (*bear* iss tur). In England, a lawyer who tries cases in court and argues motions before the judges. He has progressed professionally beyond the rank of attorney or solicitor, who are still basically office lawyers and who are not yet ready to go into court on their own.
Base. A substance that can accept a hydrogen ion (H+).
Base Dealer. Gambling term: A card shark who deals off the bottom of the deck.
Basic (*bay* sick). Fundamental; elementary; serving as the starting

point. "Each new officer must take the basic training course."

Bastard (*bass* terd) (bass as in ass; terd as in herd). A derogatory term for a despised person of either sex but generally limited to a male. A person born out of wedlock.

Bastardy Proceeding. The legal process by which a man becomes the legal father of an illegitimate child.

Bastille, The (bass *teel*). 1. A Paris fort exploited as a prison. When destroyed during the French Revolution, it was a symbol of oppression. 2. Underworld slang: A state or federal prison.

Bat. Slang: 1. A homely woman; a prostitute; a streetwalker; a promiscuous female; a screwball. 2. Criminal trial; to go to bat is to be tried for a criminal offense. 3. A drinking bout; to go on a bat, on a spree.

Bathtub Gin. Gin made by bootleggers during Prohibition.

Batman. Juvenile slang: Highway patrolman.

Baton (ba *ton*) (ton as in bon). A law enforcement officer's nightstick; a "billy stick."

Battered Child Syndrome. Deliberate injury of children by adult brutality. The majority of victims are under three years of age. Injury caused by parents or custodians.

Battery (*bat* er e). The intentional use of force or violence upon the person of another; or the intentional administration of a poison or other noxious liquid or substance to another. It is action prohibited by law. The definition varies among states. "He was charged with aggravated battery in that he used a dangerous weapon when he attacked the victim."

Battery. Horse racing term: A device used by jockeys in a horse race to give a horse an electric shock.

Bawdy House (*bawd* e) (bawd as in fraud). A place used for purposes of prostitution or other illicit sexual relations.

B & E. Breaking and entering—a criminal law violation.

Beak. Slang: A magistrate, as in up before the beak; being on trial by a magistrate.

Beam Test. A microscopic examination of crushed marijuana as a means to identify it.

Beans. Slang: Amphetamines.

Bearer. A person presenting a check, draft, or security for payment.

Beast, The. Slang: LSD.

Beat. 1. The area usually assigned to a foot patrolman to cover and be responsible for. 2. Slang: To avoid the consequences of an action.

Beatnik (*beat* nick). Slang: A person whose appearance, demeanor, and speech does not conform to the standards of the times. Characterized by unusual and slouchy dress and unkempt appearance; seldom regularly employed. This term was coined in 1957 by a columnist for the *San Francisco Chronicle,* Herb Caen.

Beat Pad. Slang: A marijuana hangout or place where such is sold.

Beat the Chair. Slang: To escape the death penalty by any means.

Beat the Gong. Narcotics slang: Smoke opium.

Beat the Rap. Slang: To be found innocent of criminal charges. Implies use of influence, legal trickery, or payoff to avoid conviction.

Bedbugs. Narcotics slang: Fellow addicts.

Beef. Slang: A complaint; to complain; to turn state's evidence.

Beefer. Slang: Someone who turns state's evidence; a person who complains.

VOCABULARY

Been Had. Slang: Arrested; cheated out of something.
Beer. Alcoholic beverage made from hops and barley.
Beer Blast. Student slang: A party in which those involved get drunk solely on beer.
Behavior. Way in which an individual or group acts. The word carries no sense of moral or other values.
Behavioral Laws. The accepted norms, principles, and customs regarding behavior.
Behavioral Motivations. Influence of goals, even if unconsciously.
Behavioral Norms. Conforming to accepted standards, expectations.
Behavioral Patterns. Observable modes of individual or group action.
Behavioral Probabilities. As according to the evidence available.
Behavior Clinics. Clinics designed for the expert study and treatment of children presenting problems of behavior.
Behaviorism (Theories of). Biologic nonconscious response to stimuli (stimulus-response conditioning).
Behavior Modification. A psychological therapy in which "good" behavior is reinforced and "bad" behavior goes unreinforced. In some cases it has the effect of shaping deviant behavior into socially acceptable behavior.
Belch. Underworld slang: To inform on someone.
Belladonna (bell ah *don* na). Drug obtained from a plant, *Atropa belladonna*. Has been used in medicine for a long period to stimulate heart and breathing, relieve pain, induce sleep, and treat spasms.
Bellyfull. Slang: Enough or too much of something.
Belly Gun. A handgun (revolver) having a short barrel, the principal use of which is for close-range firing.
Belly Joint. Slang: A dishonest carnival game where the operator leans against a platform to control a wheel.
Belongs. Narcotics slang: On the habit.
Below. Gambling term: The profits from the gambling business that are not shown on the books or officially reported.
Bench. 1. To place a firearm, not in use, on a bench, table, or other suitable object. "Unload your pistol and bench it." 2. The place where the judges sit in court; the collective body of judges sitting as a court.
Bench Warrant. A warrant of arrest issued by a judge while court is in session, directing that the accused be arrested and brought into court. Usually issued on an indictment but can be issued on other grounds.
Bend (Cards). Slang: To fold a card to help a cheat.
Bending and Bowing. Narcotics slang: Under the influence.
Benefit of Clergy. A special plea in the early common law courts that would permit the accused, after conviction, to be transferred to the ecclesiastical courts for punishment.
Benny (Bennie). Narcotics slang: Benzedrine or any other amphetamine pill. 2. Slang: An overcoat.
Bent. Juvenile slang: Intoxicated.
Benzedrine® (*ben* ze dreen). A trade name for a chemical that causes shrinkage of nasal cavity membranes. It is one trade name for amphetamine, which is also a stimulant.
Benzidine Test. A preliminary chemical test for blood. If the test is negative, the presence of blood is eliminated. If it is positive, the stain may be blood, but the laboratory

should conduct further tests to determine definitely if blood is present.
Bequeath (be *queeth*). To give personal property by will.
Bequest (be *quest*). The gift of property by will or testament.
Berries. Slang: Money.
Bertillon System (*ber* ti lawn). A system of identification based on accurate measurements of parts of the body coupled with determining the color of the eyes and other body characteristics; the recording of such data by a code. The system was developed by Alphonse Bertillon (1853-1914), French anthropologist. It has been replaced as an identification system by fingerprint classification and its accompanying identification system.
Best Evidence Rule. One coming into court must bring the best evidence available to prove the questions involved in the case. If a written document is involved, it is the best evidence and must be produced unless it is shown it has been lost or destroyed.
Bestiality (bees che *al* i tee). Sex deviation term: Human sexual act upon an animal—sodomy; sexual relations with an animal; actions or behavior befitting an animal (beast).
Bet. A wager. The pooling of money contributed by two or more persons on the condition that upon the happening of some event or the proof of the existence of some proposition one person shall take it all.
Beta Ray (*bait* ah). A fast-moving negatively charged particle, identical to an electron, emitted due to nuclear radiation.
Betting Commissioner. A British term for a bookmaker.
Bevels. Dice that have one or more edges rounded, which allows the crooked dice to roll over more easily on these sides than they do on the square sides.
Beyond a Reasonable Doubt. A legal term used relative to proof by evidence. In cases where the state (prosecution) uses direct evidence (in whole or part) as proof of the offense, the evidence must convince the jury (the judge if no jury is used) of the guilt of the accused "beyond a reasonable doubt." See **Reasonable Doubt**).
B-Girl. Slang: A girl, who may or may not be a professional prostitute, who works in bars to encourage customers to buy drinks. Some B-girls do not receive pay from the bar but do the work for the privilege of soliciting.
Bias (*by* us). Favor or support of a given point of view; preference or prejudice.
Bible. Juvenile slang: Rules and regulations.
Bicycle. Every device propelled by human power upon which any person may ride, having two tandem wheels, either of which is more than twenty inches in diameter.
Bifurcation (by fur *ka* shun). The dividing or forking of one line into two or more branches. A term used in describing fingerprint patterns. See **Fingerprints**.
Bigamy (*big* a me). The act of marrying someone while still legally married to another.
Big Bitch. Criminal jargon for the law providing that the third felony conviction brings an automatic life sentence.
Big Bloke. Narcotics slang: Cocaine.
Big Cage. Slang. A penal establishment (penitentiary or reformatory).

VOCABULARY

Big Cough. Slang: Explosion; bomb blast.
Big D. Slang: LSD.
Big Dick. In a dice game, the point of ten.
Big Drop. Gambling term: A headquarters where numbers game runners and controllers bring the day's money earned.
Big Harry. Slang: Heroin.
Big House. Slang: A state or federal prison or penitentiary.
Big John. Slang: The police.
Big Order. Gambling slang: A bet made on a sports event.
Big People. Slang: Older members of the gang.
Big School. Slang: Penitentiary.
Big Shot. A leader of a gang of henchmen or underlings.
Big-Timer. One recognized in his field as a "big operator" or a "big shot." This is used by the gambling group to denote a professional.
Bike. Motorcycle; motorcycle police officer; bicycle.
Bilateral. Two sided.
Bilateral Contract. A contract in which both of the contracting parties are bound to fulfill obligations reciprocally towards each other.
Bill of Exceptions. Law: A written statement of objections or exceptions taken by either side (or party) on the court's rulings or instructions during a trial. These are used as an integral part of the record when the case is appealed and are used by the appellate court in reaching its decision. "When the judge ruled against the motion of the defense attorney, he reserved a bill of exceptions."
Bill of Exchange. A written order to pay a certain sum of money to another person named or to his account.
Bill of Indictment (in *dite* ment). A document, usually prepared by the prosecutor, charging a person with the commission of a crime, which is furnished the grand jury for their consideration. If the latter finds there is sufficient grounds to support the charge, they return it with the endorsement "true bill," if not, they endorse it with the words "not a true bill."
Bill of Lading. A contract issued to a shipper by a transportation agency, listing the goods shipped, acknowledging their receipt, and promising delivery to the person named.
Bill of Rights. The first ten amendments to the United States Constitution.
Bill of Sale. A formal instrument for the conveyance or transfer of title of goods and chattels.
Billy. A policeman's nightstick or baton.
Bindle. Pocket of narcotics, folded as an envelope. A bindle of heroin.
Bind-Over. The order of a committing magistrate that an accused shall be held for trial or grand jury action in a court of general trial jurisdiction.
Binge (binj). Slang: A drunken escapade; a spree.
Bingle. Slang: 1. Narcotics. 2. A seller of narcotics.
Bingler. Slang: A seller of narcotics.
Bingo Machine. Gambling term: A pinball machine built and equipped for gambling.
Binny. Slang: A large garment worn by a shoplifter (booster) for concealing stolen items.
Bird. Slang: 1. Canary—an informer. 2. A sucker. Also pheasant, chippy, chump. 3. "Do bird" is to "do time" in prison.
Birdcage. 1. A jail or penitentiary cell. 2. Gambling term: A device

shaped like a cage, used in a gambling house, in which the dice are shaken to insure against cheating in the rolling of the dice.

Bird Dog. Slang: One who finds or locates people; a plainclothes officer who ferrets out information to locate someone. To trail, observe, or follow close behind.

Birthmark. A disfiguration, discoloration, or abnormal blemish on the skin at the time of birth.

Bisexuality (by *sex* you *al* i tee). Playing the role of the male and female simultaneously. A person often does not consciously realize the roles being played. It has been said that no one is completely free of this dual role playing.

Bit. Slang: 1. Prison or penitentiary sentence. 2. Portion or share of proceeds from any criminal activity.

Bite, The. Slang: The asking for money. "I put the bite on him for five dollars."

Biweekly. Happening every two weeks. Occurring at two-week intervals.

Biz. Slang: Equipment for injecting drugs.

Blab Off. Slang: A person who talks too much; one who does not keep a secret.

Black. Slang: Opium.

Black and White. Slang: A police car.

Black Code. State laws that intended to keep Negroes in an inferior position by making interstate travel difficult.

Blacklist. To put someone's name on a list of, or to otherwise associate a person's name with, a group of people with a bad reputation.

Blackmail. Extortion by threats to expose some derogatory information about the victim, a member of his family, or someone held dear to him, which would tend to harm or destroy reputation or social standing. The definitions vary among the states and with the federal criminal law. Some states have the violation as a part of the law on extortion.

Black Man. In common use it refers to people who are descendants of the African Negro, but it may include any dark-skinned people. Synonyms: Negro; colored man.

Black Maria. Slang: Van used to transport prisoners; the "paddywagon."

Black Market. Illegal, questionable, or unethical sales, including sale of stolen or government-rationed items or items that are in great demand and in short supply.

Black Panther Party. A racially oriented extremist group organized in the late 1960s whose goals are to bring about change in the American society through violent activities.

Black Powder. A gunpowder made of potassium nitrate, carbon, and sulfur, usually in the ratio 75/15/10, respectively.

Blank. Slang: Extremely low grade narcotic.

Blanket Party. Prison slang: To cover the head of a prisoner and subject him to punishment or abuse such as beating or sexual attack.

Blanket Roll. A term used in the game of craps: Rolling dice on a surface, such as a blanket, that affects the control of the dice.

Blast. Slang: 1. Strong effect from a drug. 2. To shoot. 3. To smoke marijuana.

Blasted. Slang: Under the influence of drugs.

Blasting Cap. Detonator; an explosive device for detonating explosive charges. They can be activated by a

VOCABULARY

fuse or electric charge (depending on the type of detonator). They are small cylinders made of brass or aluminum. Blasting caps are dangerous. They have enough force to cause injury or death.

Blast Party. Slang: A party of drug addicts; a group of marijuana smokers; a party at which narcotics users are present.

Bleed. Slang: To obtain money from a person or corporation by some plan or by unethical or illegal means. Usually the procedure extends over a period of time.

Blemish (*blem* ish). A defect or abnormality evidenced by disfiguration, particularly of the skin. Synonyms: Blot, stain.

Blind. Slang: Intoxicated beyond control.

Blind Bet. Gambling term: A bet that is made before a card player looks at his cards.

Blind Pig. Slang: An unlicensed saloon. Place where illegal whiskey is sold.

Blisterfoot. Slang: A police officer in uniform; a foot patrolman.

Blockout Work. Gambler's term: Marking playing cards by changing the appearance of the designs on the backs slightly so as to be able to identify the cards from the designs of the backs.

Blood. Juvenile slang: Port wine.

Bloodless Emergency. An emergency situation confronting a police officer where the subject is not involved in violence such as accidents, shootings, or fights. Bloodless emergencies may be responses to mental cases, victims of drugs or alcohol, or suicidal patients. Reference: Adams, Michael F.: The bloodless emergency. *Law & Order*, June 1971.

Blood Money. 1. A sum paid by the murderer to the relatives of a homicide victim in partial compensation for the loss of the victim. 2. Money that was very hard to win, get, or earn.

Bloomer. Slang: Mistake; miscue, criminal effort yielding no loot.

Blotter, Police. The record of arrests by the police agency per day; the "book."

Blow. Slang: 1. To reveal the identity of an informant. 2. To inform against someone; to betray someone. 3. To perform fellatio or cunnilingus on someone. 4. To get away; to leave town or the place where a person is. 5. To open a safe with explosives.

Blow a Parole. To do some act that causes a revocation of parole.

Blow a Pot. Narcotics slang: Use marijuana.

Blow a Stick. Narcotics slang: Use marijuana.

Blow Charlie. Narcotics slang: Sniff cocaine.

Blower. Slang: Telephone.

Blow Horse. Narcotics slang: Sniff heroin.

Blow Job. 1. Safe burglary term: The opening of a safe with explosives. 2. Cunnilingus or fellatio.

Blow Snow. Narcotics slang: Sniff cocaine.

Blow the Whistle. Slang: To tell what is known about someone—to inform; to make known a scandal.

Blow Your Cool. Slang: To lose your temper or self-control.

Blow Your Mind. Slang: 1. To get high on drugs. 2. To be amazed.

Blow Your Top. Slang: To lose your temper.

Blue Bands. Slang: Pentobarbitol sodium.

Blue Birds. Slang: Sodium amytal.

Blue Cheer. Narcotic slang: A type of LSD.

Blue Devils. Slang: Depressant drugs—barbiturates.

Blue Flu. Slang: Numerous police officers reporting in sick at the same time or on the same shift. It is a form of strike. Reference: *The Police Chief*, December 1969, p. 40.

Blue Funk. Slang: A condition of deep emotional depression; "down in the dumps."

Blue Heaven. Slang: Depressant drugs—barbiturates.

Blue Man. Slang: A law enforcement officer in uniform.

Blue Sky Law. Legislation to protect innocent people from being sold securities (stock) by fraud.

Blue Ticket. Slang: An army discharge that is not honorable nor dishonorable—in between.

Blue Velvet. Slang: Paregoric® (camphorated tincture of opium) and Pyribenzamine® (an antihistamine) mixed and injected. Also refers to a mixture of Pyribenzamine and sodium amytal.

Board. Slang: The Pardon Board (see **Pardon Board**).

Boat Race. Slang: Fixed horse race.

Bobby. Slang: Policeman, especially in England. Believed to have originated after Sir Robert Peel reorganized the Metropolitan Police in the London area during the first half of the nineteenth century.

Bobtail Jury. Slang: A "five-man" jury.

Body. Slang: A woman who is attractive physically.

Body Armor. Equipment to protect the wearer against attacks from blows, hurled objects, knives, bullets, and other weapons.

Body Fluids. Fluids of the body, including blood, urine, saliva.

Body Guard. A device to protect occupants of the driver's seat in a car from attack by persons in the rear of the vehicle. See **Driver Protection**.

Body Snatch. Underworld slang: A kidnapping.

Bogart. Slang: To "bogart a joint" is to either salivate on or to retain (and not pass around) a marijuana cigarette.

Bogus (*bow* gus) (bow as in row). Not genuine; fake; false; not what it purports to be.

Bohunk (*boe* hunk). Slang: A central European native living in the United States (derogatory).

Boilermaker. Slang: A strong intoxicating drink.

Bolero. Gambling game. See **Razzle Dazzle**.

Bolita. A numbers game—gambling operation.

Boliver. Slang: A pistol, such as a revolver.

Boloney (bo *lo* nee). Slang: Bull, ridiculous, not true; bunk; nonsense; statement that is believed invalid.

Bolshevik (*bowl* she vick). From the Russian word meaning majority. In 1903, at a meeting in England of the Congress of the Russian Social Democratic Labor Party, a dispute arose over whether membership in the movement should be limited to the fully dedicated revolutionaries (idea sponsored by V.I. Lenin) or be opened to all who were in sympathy with the movement. Lenin's group constituted the majority; thus they became known as the Bolshevik Party, which under Lenin's guidance overthrew the Russian government and came to power as the Communist Party on November 7, 1917.

Bomb. 1. Nonmilitary or homemade infernal machine. Bombs follow no

VOCABULARY

definite plan of construction and are extremely dangerous; they may be detonated by one or more of several means. First consideration should be to clear the area of people who would be hurt by the explosion and then give attention to doing something to prevent property damage. The army has trained personnel who are qualified to cope with the problem. 2. Slang: An automobile that has been "souped-up."

Bombed. Slang: Intoxicated on drugs or alcohol.

Bombido. Slang: Stimulant drugs—amphetamines.

Bomb Mattress. The name given to a bomb suppression device sold by Federal Laboratories, Inc.

Bona Fide (*bone* a fide). Latin: In good faith; genuine.

Bond. See **Bail**.

Bond Method. The Premium Bond Lottery of England. Only the 4 percent interest goes into the lottery. Prizes are tax-free.

Bonehead. Slang: A dull-witted or stupid person.

Bones. Slang: Dice.

Bonnet. Slang: Detonator cap used in blowing a safe.

Boo. Slang: Marijuana.

Boob. Slang: A stupid person; simpleton.

Booby Hatch. Slang: Insane asylum or other institution for the treatment of the mentally ill.

Booby Trap. Slang: Infernal machine; a hidden, secreted, or disguised explosive device.

Boodle. Slang: Counterfeit, bribe, or payoff money.

Book. 1. Betting operation, "making book," operated by a "bookie." 2. A document in a jail or law enforcement agency on which information is recorded concerning persons who have been arrested—"police blotter." 3. The act of entering information on the "police blotter" or book.

Book, The. 1. To receive the full penalty allowable. 2. One who gambles or places bets on horses. 3. To receive the penalty of life in prison.

Bookie. Person who operates a racing "book"; one who takes illegal bets on horse races.

Bookie Joint. Slang: A place where bets on horses are taken by a bookie.

Bookmaker. 1. A bookie. 2. One who takes bets on sporting events and races.

Boomer. Slang: An itinerant, transient worker who changes jobs frequently.

Boondocks. Slang: A rural or isolated place.

Booster. Slang: One engaged in shoplifting; a thief; a narcotic drug injection.

Boot, The. Slang: Loss of a job or position; getting fired.

Bootleg. Slang: Non-tax-paid liquor.

Bootlegging. 1. Selling illegal alcoholic beverages or other contraband. 2. Racetrack term: Transmitting information from the track to confederates outside in order to "beat the bookies," i.e. the confederates may place bets on races, the results of which are known, before the "bookie" gets the results.

Booze. Slang: Whiskey.

Boozed Up. Slang: In a drunken condition.

Booze-Fighter. Slang: A habitual heavy drinker of alcoholic beverages; a drunkard.

Boozer. Slang: A drunkard; a public house.

Bopping Clubs. Slang: Juvenile clubs made up of gangs who have the reputation of fighting.

Bore. Firearms term: The gun barrel diameter. Same as the gauge.
"Born Criminal" Theory. An early theory of deviance holding that criminals can be identified by their physical characteristics.
Borrow. Slang: To steal.
Borstal System. The halfway house in Europe. Devised there and used to reorient persons recently released from prison or hospital (for drugs or alcohol, etc.).
Boss. The head of a "family" in the Cosa Nostra. He has absolute authority on matters within the jurisdiction of his family. He is also known as the Old Man, the Don, and other names. See **La Cosa Nostra**. Reference: *The Challenge of Crime in a Free Society*. Washington, D.C., U.S. Government Printing Office, 1967, p. 182.
Boss Man. Gambling term: One who stands at a gambling table and places the house winnings in a locked box under a slot in the table.
Both Hands. Slang: A prison sentence of ten years.
Bottle Dealer. Slang: A person who sells drugs, in 1000 tablet or capsule bottles.
Bottle Man. Slang: A habitual drunkard; a heavy drinker.
Bottom Dealer. See **Base Dealer**.
Bounce. Slang: The return of a check that is not honored by the bank on which it is drawn. "The check bounced."
Bounce, The. Slang: Physical eviction from a public place or a gathering place, private or public; being thrown out of a place.
Bouncer. Slang: An employee of an establishment who removes disorderly or unwanted persons from the premises.
Boundaries (*bound* a reez). The limits by which groups determine who is a member of the group and who is not.
Bourgeoisie (boor zhwah *zee*). By Communist definition, this means the "capitalist" class—the wealthy and the middle class. The Communist plan calls for the destruction of this class. Reference: Hoover, J. Edgar: *Masters of Deceit*. New York, Henry Holt, 1958.
Bow (bough as in how). The front end of a ship.
Bow Street Runners. A unit of the police force as organized in the London metropolitan area in the last half of the 1700s by John and Henry Fielding. They were also known as "Thief Takers." They operated out of the Bow Street station. Some called this unit the first detective squad, as their function was to get to the scene of the crime quickly and investigate the case.
Box. 1. Criminal slang: A safe. 2. A public or private fire alarm box. 3. Call box formerly used in police work.
Boxcars. Slang: The throwing of two sixes with dice.
Boxed. Slang: In Jail.
Box Man. Slang: Safecracker; safe blower.
Boy. A derogatory (intentional or not) form of addressing a minority group member.
Boys, The. 1. Inveterate gamblers. 2. Racketeers.
Brainwash. To change a person's thinking, outlook, attitudes, or philosophies by teaching, indoctrination, propaganda, or other means. "He was a sound thinker, but he has been brainwashed." A technique developed by Pavlov, a Russian scientist, who found that by exhaustion (resulting in confusion), togeth-

er with subjection to physical pain and fear, an animal or human could be forced into a mental breakdown, after which he could be oriented in his thinking to suit the purposes of the brainwasher. Reference: Schwarz, Fred: *You Can Trust the Communists to Do Exactly as They Say*, Englewood Cliffs, New Jersey, Prentice-Hall, 1961, p. 127.
Bracelets. Slang: Handcuffs.
Brains. Slang: The director or leader of a gang who makes plans for the gang.
Brainstorm. Slang: A new, innovative idea that suddenly occurs to a person.
Brain Teaser. Juvenile slang: Schoolteacher.
Brass. Slang: Top official or top officials as a group.
Brawl. Slang: A dance or party where the people become loud, unruly, or engage in fighting; a noisy fight or quarrel.
Breach (breech). Violation of an obligation or of the law.
Breach of Prison. The offense of breaking out of prison.
Bread. 1. Slang: Money. 2. Narcotics slang: Money obtained illegally so narcotics may be bought.
Breadbasket. Slang: The stomach.
Breadbox. Slang: A cheap safe.
Break. Slang: 1. To solve a case by law enforcement officers. "They were able to break the case." 2. Prisoner who escapes or attempts escape. 3. A lucky event that happens to someone. "I got a break on the market."
Breakage. Gambling term: As used at the pari-mutuel tracks, it denotes the fractions of a cent on each payoff less than a full penny, plus the odd pennies over five or ten, usually kept by the track operators.

Breakage to a Nickel or Dime. Racetrack term: Where the odd cents on a two dollar mutuel ticket are eliminated so the amount comes to a five or zero. Some racetracks break to a dime, others to a nickel.
Break-in. Slang: Burglary.
Breaking Jail. A prisoner escaping from jail.
Breath Alcohol. The alcohol content in the breath, used to measure the alcohol content in the bloodstream.
Breathalizer®. Name of a commercial product (device) to test the breath of a suspected drinker and arrive at a determination of the blood alcohol content of the person.
Breath-Testing Equipment. Equipment designed to test the breath of a person to determine the blood alcohol content of the person. There are several such devices manufactured commercially. Some of the manufacturers of such equipment may be determined from trade publications.
Breech. The rear end of the gun barrel; the place where the ammunition is loaded into the barrel.
Breechblock (*breech* blok). The steel block against which the barrel or bore of a breech-loading gun closes to prevent the escape of the explosive charge. The firing pin functions through the breechblock. Imperfections (marks and small ridges) on the face of the breechblock are imparted to the softer metal of the cartridge case or shell when the gun is fired, thus making identification possible by a laboratory examination to establish that such cartridge or shotgun shell was fired in a particular weapon.
Breech Face. The face or flat surface of the breechblock.
Breech Loader. An early-developed

rifle of the United States. A gun where ammunition is inserted in the barrel at the breech end as contrasted to the muzzle loader, where the ammunition is loaded through the front end or muzzle of the barrel.

Briars. Slang: Small hacksaws.

Bribery (*brye* burr ee). The definition of bribery varies among the states. It is essentially the offering, soliciting, giving, or taking of anything of value to influence actions of an official; or in the performance of an official duty, corruptly influencing another.

Brick. 1. Gambling term: A die that has been altered in shape so it is not an exact cube; to make crooked dice. 2. A kilo of marijuana in compressed brick form.

Bricks. Slang: Altered or crooked dice.

Bricks, Hit the. Slang: 1. To walk or patrol on foot; to leave a building and walk on the street. 2. To be released from prison.

Bridge. 1. Fingerprint ridge pattern or configuration where two main ridges are joined by a connecting ridge. 2. See **Roach Clip**.

Brief. The written or printed argument of an attorney on points of fact and law.

Brig. Slang: A jail or prison.

Brig Rat. Slang: A prisoner, especially a serviceman.

Broad. Slang: A woman; a woman of questionable reputation.

Broadsman. Slang: A professional card cheat.

Broke. Juvenile slang: Arrested.

Broken Family. Conjugal unit in which parents have been separated by fact, decree, divorce, or death.

Broncho. Slang: A spy sent out by safecrackers to locate a job.

Brothel (*broth* el). Primarily a European term: A place used as a house of prostitution.

Brother. Slang: One of similar nature, group, or philosophy.

Brotherhood, The. A movie concerning an Italian criminal family (1969).

Brownie Points. Slang: 1. Acts that operate toward gaining favor with someone, usually a superior. 2. The favor gained in such a manner.

Brown-Nose. Slang: To gain favor with a superior or a teacher.

Brown Shoes. Slang: Name for "squares."

Bruh (Bruzz). Juvenile slang: Close male friend.

Bruise. Medical term: A contusion; an injury on the body of a person that does not break the skin.

Bruiser. Slang: A big, strong male, especially one with a rough appearance or manner.

Buccal Intercourse (buckle intercourse). Sex deviation term: Act of using the mouth on the sex organs.

Buccal Onanism (buckle *oh* nen *iz* em). Sex deviation term: Penis sucking; fellatio.

Buck. Slang: A dollar.

Buck, A. Prison slang: A riot or general disorder.

Buck, Pass the. Slang: To pass on to another a job or responsibility.

Bucket-Shop. Slang: 1. A saloon, bar, or lounge. 2. Place where questionable or worthless stocks are sold.

Buff, Police. A person interested in police, police cars and equipment, police departments, and operations.

Buffer, The. A position in the Cosa Nostra family. The Buffer is a staff position on the same level as the Underboss. He is an administrative aide to the Boss and his function is to protect the Boss. He acts as "go-be-

VOCABULARY

tween" as concerns the Boss and those below in the organizational structure. Reference: Salerno, Ralph et al.: *The Crime Confederation*. Garden City, New York, Doubleday, pp. 91, 100.

Bug. Slang: 1. Electronic surveillance (electronic listening devices). 2. A police officer's badge. 3. A metal device used in a slot machine that makes it impossible for certain combinations to hit. 4. A clip apparatus fastened beneath a gambling table that holds cards clandestinely removed from the deck. 5. Annoy, pester. 6. A person who is insane or of low intelligence.

Bug Boy. Racetrack term: Apprentice jockey.

Bug Doctor. Slang: A psychologist or psychiatrist, as one employed in the field of corrections.

Bugged. Slang: To be sent to an institution for the insane or the criminally insane.

Bugged Joint. Slang: A place suspected of having a listening device installed.

Buggery (*bug* e ree). Sodomy; crime against nature.

Bughouse. Slang: 1. An insane asylum; an institution for the mentally deranged. 2. Insane, imbecilic.

Bug-Out. Slang: 1. To leave suddenly or withdraw. 2. Retreat from a place or position.

Bug-Test. Slang: A psychiatric test for insanity.

Build. Pertains to the general body structure of a person being described, i.e. heavy, slender, etc. A feature used in recording the description of a person.

Buildup. An act put on in order to arouse a player's gambling spirit. It can also be called a pitch or "con act."

Bulb. Photographic term: A setting for the shutter of the camera where the shutter remains open when the button is pressed and stays open until the button is released. On most cameras it is marked "B."

Bulging (*bulj* ing). A section of a gun barrel that is more swollen than the rest.

Bull. Slang: 1. A law enforcement officer; 2. Idle talk; nonsense; to talk much about inconsequential things; 3. To deceive by lying or stretching the truth. Something useless or offensive.

Bulldyke (bull dike). Slang: Female homosexual who has masculine physical traits and who plays the masculine role with other women.

Bullet (*bull* it). A projectile made for firing in a rifle or pistol. It is that part of a cartridge which is discharged or fired from a firearm. It is usually made of lead. The types of bullets include 1. Connelures: has grooves around it for lubricant or for crimping. 2. Flat-point: has a flat nose. The "wadcutter" used for target practice is of this type. 3. Hollow-point: has hollowed nose, which causes the bullet to flatten or mushroom on impact. 4. Metal-cased: has a jacket of metal covering the nose. 5. Softpoint: has a metal case except for the nose, which is of lead.

Bulletproof Equipment. Equipment in the nature of armor, shields, or garments that protect the user from firearms bullets. Much research has been done in recent years to develop such equipment. The International Chiefs of Police Association has arranged with the National Bureau of Standards to operate a testing laboratory to test police equipment. Information on the merits of equipment can be obtained through this source.

Bullpen. Slang: A room in jail or prison to confine persons in custody while awaiting transfer.

Bull's-Eye. The center portion of a "ringed" target. A hit in the center portion of such a target.

Bullshooter. Slang: One who talks nonsense or talks much about trivial matters.

Bum. Slang: 1. One who begs, asks for, or solicits for things from people for free. 2. A hobo, tramp or person of ill repute. 3. False, unfounded, invalid. "He gave me a bum steer."

Bum Beef. Slang: An unfair complaint; a groundless complaint.

Bummer. Narcotics slang: An overdose of narcotics; bad experience with psychedelics. A bad experience.

Bum Move. Gambling: A move made by a player in a game that looks very suspicious to other players. An obvious or clumsy cheating move.

Bump Off. Underworld slang: To kill or murder.

Bump or Raise. Gambling: A bet made by a player that increases the amount of the bet by the preceeding bettor.

Bum Rap. Slang: A charge of crime that is not founded; a false charge against a person.

Bum's Rush. Slang: Unexpected advance; ejection of a person from a public place or room; any obvious or discourteous method of getting rid of a person.

Bum Steer. Slang: Incorrect information; a false lead furnished to an investigator.

Bum Trip. Slang: Bad experience with psychedelics (LSD).

Bunco (Bunko). Slang: A swindling, cheating, or fraudulent game. "He conducted a bunco game."

Bunco Artist. Slang: A professional swindler or confidence man.

Bunco Steerer. Slang: An accomplice in a confidence game (bunco game).

Bundle. Slang: A large amount of money, usually paper currency, especially as used in gambling or in a con game.

Bundook (Bandook). Slang: A rifle used in World War I.

Bunk. Slang: Nonsense, untruth, unreliable information.

Bunk You. Juvenile slang: I'm not thinking of you.

Bunny. 1. A female passive partner for a lesbian; a male passive partner for a male homosexual. 2. A person who is mixed up (mentally), such as a "dumb bunny."

Burden of Proof. Law: The obligation on the part of the state in a criminal case to convince the judge or jury of the defendant's guilt beyond a reasonable doubt. The task or responsibility of proving alleged facts in a judicial proceeding. Generally the burden of proof is upon the person alleging the existence of a fact. In criminal proceedings the prosecutor has the burden of proof to establish guilt beyond a reasonable doubt.

Bureaucracy. A complex formal organization with a highly structured hierarchical system depending on job specification, a set of rules and standards designed to promote uniformity, and on an attitude of impersonal impartiality.

Bureau of Narcotics and Dangerous Drugs (BNDD). Formed April 8, 1968, by a merger of the Bureau of Narcotics of the United States Treasury Department and the Bureau of Drug Abuse Control of the Department of Health, Education, and Welfare. It is a part of the United States Department of Justice. The

VOCABULARY

address is Bureau of Narcotics and Dangerous Drugs, United States Department of Justice, Washington, D.C. 20537. BNDD has regional offices and laboratories strategically located throughout the nation. Reference: BNDD. *The Police Chief*, January 1970, p. 26.

Burglar (*bur* gler). One who commits burglary.

Burglar Alarms. Devices used in buildings and structures to set off an alarm when anyone enters without authority.

Burglary (*bur* gla ree). The unauthorized entry into a dwelling, other structure, or moveable, with intent to commit a felony or a theft. The definition varies among the states. Some require a forceable entry. Some divide the crime into nighttime and daytime. Some have the crimes of aggravated burglary and simple burglary.

Burglary, Safe. The illegal entry of a safe. Several methods are used by safe burglars: "blowing"—the use of explosive; "peeling"—peeling the safe back until entry is gained, usually by manipulating the locking device; "punching"—the use of a punch to force the locking mechanism; "ripping"—using a device working on the principle of a can opener and ripping open parts of the safe; "drilling"—drilling holes in the safe at pertinent points and either forcing the locking mechanism or actually gaining access to the inside chamber of the safe by reaching through the hole; and "burning"—gaining entry by use of a flame cutting torch or thermal burning bar.

Burglary Tools. Tools that are suitable for gaining illegal entry to a safe. The possession of such tools is illegal in many states, but the intent to use them to commit a crime must also be shown. The courts have held that it is immaterial that the tools might also be used for lawful purposes.

Burgle. Slang: To commit a burglary.

Burn. Slang: 1. To be executed in the electric chair. Synonyms: Hot seat, the chair. 2. To be cheated or disappointed by dealing with a person or persons. "I got burned once by following his advice." 3. To burn—to kill. 4. Juvenile slang: To shoot, murder, or die by gunfire. 5. To gain entry to a safe by a flame cutting device such as an oxyacetylene torch or a thermal burning bar. 6. To alert the subject by investigation.

Burn a Card. Gambling: Taking a card out of play during a card game.

Burn Baby Burn. A slogan used by some extremists during the late 1960s, implying the burning of the property of others.

Burned. Narcotics slang: Received phony narcotics. Slang: Identified; identity of an informant revealed.

Burned Out. Slang: The sclerotic condition of the vein present in most conditioned addicts.

Burnese (Bernice, Bernies). Slang: Cocaine.

Burning Bar. See **Thermal Burning Bar**.

Burn the Midnight Oil. Underworld slang: To smoke an opium pipe.

Burn the Road. Slang: Drive a car fast.

Burrhead. Slang: A Negro.

Bus. Any public or private vehicle designed for carrying more than ten passengers.

Bush Parole. Slang: Escapee from a

penitentiary, especially a prisoner who was working outside the institution.

Bushwhack. Slang: To ambush someone, as in a purse snatching.

Business, The. 1. Slang: Rough treatment; a reprimanding; an intentional rudeness; a beating; murder. 2. Narcotics slang: The materials and instruments necessary for giving oneself an injection of narcotics.

Business District. The center of economic and social activity, which is usually the oldest part of any urban area.

Business Fire. Arson fire related to trade conditions. Also called "trade fires." Arson committed in order for the owner or manager of a business to gain from the fire.

Businessman's High. Slang: Dimethyltriptamine (DMT).

Bust. Slang: Police raid; the arrest of a person or persons. To strike a person.

Bust a Cap. Juvenile slang: Shoot a gun; reach a degree of intoxication.

Busted. Slang: Arrested.

Busters. Gambler's term: A pair of misspotted dice, also called "tops."

Bust Out. Slang: 1. To break out of a place of confinement, such as a jail or penitentiary. 2. The point in a swindle or confidence game where the victim surrenders his money or other valuables. This is the crux of the affair—the "pay off." 3. Disposal of merchandise of a business by bankruptcy fraud—also called "scam." Reference: Gressy, Donald R.: *Theft of a Nation.* p. 105.

Bustout Game. Slang: A setup to take a sucker. A fixed game.

Bustout Man. Gambler's term: One who is adept at switching dice in and out of a crap game, particularly where "tops" dice are substituted for others periodically.

Bust Outs. Gambling slang: Dice that have been altered, especially "loaded."

Butch. Slang: Female homosexual who assumes the role of the male.

Butter Up. Slang: To seek favor through flattery.

Button. Slang: A police officer's badge.

Buttons. The sections of the peyote cactus.

Buy. 1. Slang: To accept a proposition or business deal. To believe in something. "I'll buy that idea." 2. Narcotics slang: To make a purchase of drugs.

Buy, A. The purchase of illegal narcotics, contraband or stolen property by officers or informers in order to gain evidence of law violations.

Buy, Make a. To purchase narcotics or other illegal or contraband goods, usually for the purpose of obtaining proof of a crime.

Buyer. Slang: A fence; one who buys stolen or "hot" merchandise from criminals.

Buzzer. Slang: 1. A pickpocket. 2. A law enforcement officer's badge.

Buzzon. Slang: To feel good.

C

C. 1. Slang: One hundred dollars. 2. Narcotics slang: Cocaine. 3. Gambling term: When appearing on a policy slip indicates a number to be played in combination. Usually written 317-C-50¢.

CA. Abbreviation for Circuit Court of Appeals, Federal. The letters are followed by the designation for the Circuit, i.e. CA5 = 5th Circuit; CADC = The District of Columbia Circuit Court.

Cabal (ka *bal*). A small group of conspirators.

Cabbage. (Slang): Paper money.

Cache (cash). A hidden quantity of materials or items. "The soldiers found a cache of enemy weapons."

Cackle the Dice. Gambling term; To hold the dice in the hand so they will not change position but go through the motions and sound of the dice being rattled.

Cacodaemonomania. A type of schizophrenia where the person believes the devil is controlling his actions.

Cadaver (ke *dav* er). The body of a dead human; a corpse.

Cadaveric Spasm (ka *dav* e rick). A condition of muscle contractions just prior to a person's death that usually shows up in the hand grasp.

Cadet. 1. A newly hired young officer who is being taught law enforcement. 2. Slang: One who is beginning as a narcotic addict. 3. A prostitution pimp.

Caesarean Section or Operation (see *sair* e an). The taking of a baby from the uterus of its mother by cutting through the abdominal wall and the wall of the uterus. Its name is derived from the belief that Julius Caesar was delivered by this means.

Cagey (cagy). Slang: Sly, cunning.

Cake-Cutter. Slang: Circus use—one who short-changes the public (customers).

Calaboose (*kal* a boose). A small jail or room for detaining persons under arrest; used mostly in small towns in the South.

Calculator (*kal* cue lay tor). Gambling slang: One who works in the racetrack sections where the odds are computed.

Caliber (*kal* i bur). Firearms term: The size (diameter) of a rifle or pistol barrel. The bore diameter is measured in hundredths of an inch. Twenty-two caliber is a gun barrel measuring 22/100 of an inch in diameter. This term is similar to gage which is used in shotguns but the latter is arrived at in a different manner. Reference: Soderman, Harry *et al.*: *Modern Criminal Investigation*, 5th ed. New York, Funk and Wagnalls, 1962, p. 200.

Call Bet. Making a bet without putting up money.

Called-for Services. Any activity of the police that is initiated by a citizen; such as a call to report a barking dog.

Call-Girl. Slang: A prostitute who is connected with a house or agency where arrangements are made by telephone for the woman to meet the man at a designated place.

Call House. Slang: 1. A house of prostitution where appointments are made with the prostitutes by telephone 2. A brothel where prostitutes may be called upon by the clients at any time to do anything.

Call Letters. The letters and/or numbers assigned to police radio transmitters and/or transceivers, fixed or mobile. "What are the call letters for your station?"

Call Signals. Coded signals used by law enforcement to transmit short messages by radio or other means of communication where speed and confidentiality are needed. See **Signal, Ten-Dash.**

Calumny (*kal* en ne). False accusation.

Campus Disorders. Misconduct, unruly demonstrations, riots on campuses, or damage to life and property on campuses of colleges, universities, or other schools. This has constituted a very real problem to law enforcement in recent years.

Campus Security. The agency or person employed by a college or university to maintain security—law and order—on the campus. This activity has become more important in recent years with increased campus violence and other undesirable activities.

Can. Slang: 1. Jail. 2. Rest room or toilet. 3. Buttocks. "He got knocked on his can." 4. Narcotics slang: 1 or 2 ounce tin of marijuana ready for cigarettes.

Canary. Slang: Stool pigeon; one who "sings" i.e. tells police what he knows about a crime.

Cancel (*kan* sel). To render null and void; to stop something from being effective. "Cancel order #10."

Cancellation Deleting all or part of an agreement, thereby changing its legal effect.

Candy. Slang: Depressant drugs—barbituates.

Can-House. Slang: A house of prostitution.

Cannabis Sativa. Marijuana

Canned. Slang: Drunk, intoxicated, soused, fired; employment termination.

Cannon. Slang: A pickpocket; a firearms weapon such as a handgun or other type.

Canon (*kan* un). A standard or principle accepted as fundamentally true and in conformity with good usage and practice.

Canons of Police Ethics. Standards, principles and policies governing the conduct of law enforcement officers. It was adopted by the IACP at its 1957 conference. It embraces the following areas of conduct:

    Article 1. Primary Responsibility of Job.
    Article 2. Limitations of Authority.
    Article 3. Duty to Be Familiar With the Law and With the Responsibility of Self and Other Public Officials.
    Article 4. Utilization of Proper Means to Gain Proper Ends.
    Article 5. Cooperation With Public Officials in the Discharge of Their Authorized Duties.
    Article 6. Private Conduct.
    Article 7. Conduct Toward the Public.
    Article 8. Conduct in Arresting and Dealing with Law Violators.
    Article 9. Gifts and Favors.
    Article 10. Presentation of Evidence.
    Article 11. Attitudes Toward Profession.

Reference: Germann, A. C. et al.: *Introduction to Law Enforcement and Criminal Justice.* Springfield, Thomas, 1970, p. 260.

VOCABULARY

Can Opener. Slang: Kit of burglar tools; tool for opening safes.
Cap. Slang: Capsule of narcotics.
Caper. Slang: A criminal escapade; a job; offense; wrongdoing.
Capital. Pertaining to the head or to life, i.e. capital punishment is punishment calling for the penalty of death.
Capitalism (*kap* i tel ism). According to the Communists it is an economic system grounded on the private ownership of property, private ownership of the means of production, and accumulation of wealth. It is opposite to the system of socialism or Communism; therefore, they say it must fall. The Communists say that capitalism replaced feudalism and capitalism will be succeeded by socialism, which in turn will result in a world communist society. Reference: Hoover, J. Edgar: *Masters of Deceit*. New York, Henry Holt, 1958. The free world definition: An economic system of private enterprise and competition in which capital plays a principal part and the ownership of property and natural wealth, the production, distribution, and exchange of goods are thus directly affected.
Capital Offense (*kap* i tel). A crime that is penalized by death.
Capital Punishment. Death penalty resulting from conviction for a crime.
Capon (*kay* pon). Slang: A man with feminine characteristics, usually a homosexual.
Captain (*kap* tin). An administrative title or rank, above lieutenant and below major. Depending on the organizational structure of the agency, the captain usually has command over a company, shift, special operation, or detail. "Captain Smith is in charge of the Auto Theft Section."
Carbon Copy. Slang: A license plate that has been stolen.
Carbon Monoxide (*kar* bon mo *nox* ide). Symbol: CO. Chemical composition: One atom of carbon combined with one atom of oxygen. A colorless, odorless, highly poisonous gas when breathed. Results from incomplete burning of organic fuels such as gasoline and other petroleum products. It is present in exhaust fumes from internal combustion engines.
Car Clout. Slang: Larceny of an automobile.
Card Mechanic. Gambling slang: One who cheats by special handling of the cards.
Card Mob. Gambling slang: Two or more persons working as a team to cheat other persons.
Career (ka *rear*). The life work, profession, or occupation of a person. "A career in law enforcement offers a great opportunity for service to people."
Cargo. Slang: A load or supply of narcotics or drugs.
Carnal (*kar* nel). Pertains to "actions of the flesh"; sensual, sexual.
Carnal Knowledge. Sexual intercourse of a human male with a female. In some states it is a crime, with the consent of the female, where she is of or under a prescribed age, such as when under age seventeen, if she is unmarried.
Carny (*kar* nee). Slang: A person who works with a carnival.
Carouse. To drink liquor freely or deeply.
Carpet Place. Gambling term: High class gambling establishment.
Carrie. Slang: Cocaine.

Carrying. Slang: In possession of a drug.

Cartridge (*kart* rij). A "round of ammunition"; a shell. The metal, paper, or plastic case, primer, explosive charge, and projectile (bullet or shot) for a gun or firearm.

Cartwheel. Slang: 1. Silver dollar. 2. Amphetamine tablet (round, white, double scored).

Case. 1. The investigation of a criminal matter; violation of the law under investigation or in court. "The case of armed robbery at 9th and Main was assigned to Detective Jones." 2. Criminal charges against specific individuals, as they pertain to court action. "The case of State v. Jones is being appealed to the Supreme Court." 3. (Slang) To inspect or study a place with the intent to burglarize, rob, or commit some other crime there. "He cased the bank before the robbery." 4. "A case"-a thief or shoplifter's associate; the one on a criminal gang who spots or cases the places to be "hit."

Case, Active Status of. Refers to a case that is presently being investigated or is in the process of being solved.

Case, Close Status. Refers to a case in which no further investigation will be undertaken.

Case, Pending Status. Refers to an unsolved case in which no further investigation will be undertaken.

Case Law. A body of law formed from previously adjudged cases.

Case Load. The number of parolees or probationers under the supervision of a parole or probation officer.

Case Study. A method of research consisting of an in-depth investigation of a single social unit or given phenomenon.

Case the Deck. Gambling: The ability to remember what cards have been played during a card game.

Case the Joint. Slang: To inspect, examine, or learn the facts about a place of business or other place, by a person with a view of robbing or burglarizing it at a later time.

Cash Room. Gambling term: A place where bets can be placed and results determined.

Casing. Firearms term: The metal holder, generally made of brass, that holds the primer, gunpowder, and bullet.

Casino Manager. The person in charge of a casino. He settles all disputes between the house and the players.

Cast. 1. To mold; to take the impression of certain objects and markings by use of a substance that will harden and retain its shape. Used in law enforcement to record in physical form such things as footprints in soil, tire impressions, tool marks, etc. Many casting materials are used. Plaster of Paris is one commonly used for casting impressions in soil. A material called "moulage" is used where fine detail is needed and the surface is rigid. "We will cast the impression." 2. The physical object or reproduction made by casting. "The officer made a cast of the heel print."

Caste (kast). A society in which all class, status, and power are ascribed. An individual is born into his social class, and because this social system is extremely rigid, the individual has no opportunity to move in or out of a given class.

Castigatory (*kas* ta ga tor ee). An old device used to punish women, such as a ducking-stool.

Casting. In field of moulage: The process whereby a reproduction of

VOCABULARY

an object is secured by introducing a suitable hardening material into a mold or impression.

Castration Complex (cass *tray* shun). The belief that erotic desires are forbidden and that the center of fear is in the genitals.

Casual Criminal. A person who does not commit criminal acts very often.

Cat. A whip for flogging people. Also called a cat-o'-nine-tails.

Catalepsy (*kat* e lep see). An abnormal condition where a physical posture is maintained and the muscles become rigid; usually the subject looses consciousness. This is common in cases of hysteria and schizophrenia.

Catch. To locate and apprehend; to detect someone in the act of doing something. "I did not catch the burglar in the act of burglarizing."

Catcher. Gambling term: One stationed outside a racetrack whose job it is to receive signals from inside the track.

Catch One "Dead-Bang." Slang: To catch in the act.

Catch Out. Prison slang: An inmate's inability to survive in the particular location in which he finds himself; to get out, or escape, in order to prevent himself from being "turned out."

Catheter (*kath* e tur). A slender flexible instrument used to insert into body passages to examine or drain. Usually refers to the instrument used to pass through the urethra to drain urine from the bladder.

Cat House. Slang: A house of prostitution.

Caucasoid (*kaw* ke saw id). Of the white race; having physical features of the white race. "Caucasoid is a standardized descriptive term used for the white race."

Causation (cause *a* shen). That element of a crime which requires a causal relationship to exist between the offender's conduct and the harm or injury sustained.

Cause. The matter for decision in the court.

Cause, Challenge of Jurors for. Each side in a trial (prosecution and defense) has the right, prescribed by law, to challenge prospective jurors (veniremen) for cause, such as prior convictions, unsound mind, kinship to one of the parties, bias or prejudice, etc. If the court agrees with the challenge, the prospective juror will not be allowed to serve on the jury. See **Challenge of Jurors**.

Cause of Action. The right by which a party seeks a remedy against another in a court of law.

Caveat (*kay* ve at). A warning or caution. "The caveat given by the officers prior to questioning the suspect stated that anything he said could be used against him in a court of law."

Caveat Emptor (*kay* ve at *emp* tor). Latin: Let the buyer beware.

Caveat Venditor. Latin: Let the seller beware.

Cecil. Slang: Cocaine.

Cell Block. A group of individual cells or multiple-inmate cells in a prison or institution of some kind.

Cellmate. One who occupies a jail or prison cell with another.

Censure (*sin* chur). To reprimand, condemn, or express disapproval. "Jones received a letter of censure for his actions."

Census. A counting of things (persons, houses, etc.).

Census Family. U.S. Census definition: A minimum of one parent or guardian and one dependent child.

Centigrade (*sin* te grade). A system

of measuring temperature. Under this scale, water boils at 100 degrees (at normal atmospheric pressure). Fahrenheit is the other scale. To convert to Fahrenheit from Centigrade use the following formula: Centigrade reading x 9/5 plus 32.
Central Pocket Loop. A fingerprint pattern. It consists of at least one recurring ridge or an obstruction at right angles to the line of flow, with two deltas, between which, when an imaginary line is drawn, no recurving ridge within the pattern area is cut or touched. It is classified as a whorl.
Cents. Slang: CC's—cubic centimeters.
Century. Slang: A hundred-dollar bill or a hundred dollars.
Certified Check. A check issued by a bank that insures that the account on which it is drawn has sufficient funds to cover the check, i.e. the bank certifies the check will be honored.
Certiorari (*sir* she *rah* ree). An order (writ) from an appellate court instructing a lower court to send up a record of its proceedings so they may be reviewed.
C-4. "Plastic" explosive; a high explosive.
Chain Gang. A number of prisoners chained together while they are outside confinement quarters. "The chain gangs are largely a thing of the past."
Chain of Command. The administrative arrangement (order) of officials of an agency through which orders or instructions are passed (downward or upward). "The chain of command in the department was from the chief, to the captain, to the lieutenants, to the sergeants, to the patrolmen."
Chair, The. Slang: The electric chair.
Chalk. 1. Slang: A horse figured to win a race; a betting favorite. 2. Methamphetamine.
Chalk Bettor. Gambling term: See **Chalk Eater.**
Chalk Eater. Slang: One who bets only on the horses that are favored to win.
Challenge (*chal* enj). To interpose an objection.
Challenge of Jurors. Action on the part of either side of a trial by jury of the prospective jurors (veniremen) to prevent the veniremen from serving on the jury. There are two kinds: Peremptory—no reasons must be given for objecting to the prospective juror—the number allowed to each side is fixed by law; and Challenge for Cause—the reason for objecting to the person as a juror must be given (such as prior conviction, kinship to parties, bias or prejudice, etc.). No limit is placed on the number to be so challenged.
Chamber (*chaim* burr). Firearms term: The end of the gun barrel into which the ammunition is placed for firing.
Chambers. The judge's office where he conducts legal business not carried on in open court. "The judge heard the matter in chambers."
Chambers v. Maroney, 399 U.S. 42 (1970). A United States Supreme Court landmark case on searches of automobiles, holding that if the officer has probable cause to believe that a car contains evidence of crime and the car is mobile, he may search the car at the scene or move it to the police station and search it there, in both instances without a warrant. If he impounds the car he should obtain a search warrant.
Champ. Slang: A drug abuser who will not reveal his supplier—even under pressure.

VOCABULARY

Champerty (*cham* purr tee). The purchase of a contingent interest or share of a lawsuit. The party purchasing this interest undertakes to finance the suit in the hope of winning a share of the property or amount recovered.

Chancery (*chan* sir ee). The courts of equity or that body of law known as equity.

Change of Venue (chainj; *ven* you). A change in place where a trial will be held, ordered by the court, either on its own motion or on request of one of the parties. The basis is usually that a fair trial could not be obtained in the place of regular venue. See **Venue**.

Channel. Slang: A vein, usually in the crook of the elbow or the instep, into which narcotic addicts inject drugs.

Chaos (*kay* oss). Great confusion and/or disorder. "The explosion caused great chaos in the building."

Character (*care* ak ter). 1. Prison slang: Refers to one's self or another inmate (used by more mature criminal inmates). 2. A ground for attacking or discrediting a party or witness in a lawsuit by showing that his standing or reputation in the community is bad.

Character Evidence. In a criminal trial, evidence introduced to show good or bad character of the accused. Stress is on the moral qualities of the person. The law in some states provides that no matter how good the character of an accused is it will not in itself be a bar to conviction if the violation is proven beyond a reasonable doubt.

Characteristic (*care* ek ter *iss* tick). Whatever distinguishes one person or thing from another; special distinguishing features. "The charac-teristic of the native is the tendency to fight."

Charge. 1. To accuse. 2. Slang: An injection of narcotics or the "kick" a user gets from the narcotic. 3. Marijuana.

Charging. The process of formal criminal accusation, usually involving the prosecutor and sometimes a grand jury. The term is also used to mean the judge's instruction of a jury on matters of law.

Charismatic Authority (*care* iz *mat* ick). An authority with special spiritual powers or personal appeal that gives the individual influence over large numbers of people.

Chart. A drawing or sketch showing the location of objects and items and the relationship one to another in a crime scene or other place pertinent to an investigation. "A chart was made of the crime scene."

Charter. Written grant or privilege.

Chaste (Chaist). Pure in sexual morality; virtuous; decent.

Chattel (*chat* el). Moveable or immovable property, except in real estate.

Chauffeur (show *fur*). Every person who is employed by another for the principal purpose of driving a motor vehicle, and every person who drives a school bus transporting school children or any motor vehicle when in use for the transportation of persons or property for compensation.

Chauvinism (*show* ven izm). 1. Extreme and unfounded patriotism. 2. Believing one's self superior to others. Communist Party members apply the term against fellow members as a critical indication of error against the accused. Reference: Hoover, John E.: *Masters of Deceit*. New York, Holt, 1958. p. 167.

Cheaters. 1. Gambling term: Past posters of races. 2. Marked cards or loaded dice used to cheat in gambling. 3. Slang: Eyeglasses.

Cheating. Gambling term: Using any trick or device to deceive, such as marked cards, crooked dice, etc.

Check Bouncer. Slang: One who passes worthless checks, either on nonexisting banks or on banks where he does not have an account or where he has an account but insufficient funds to cover the checks.

Check Cop. Gambling term: Device used for stealing poker chips.

Check Out. 1. Slang: To die; to give up on or abandon a plan or project. 2. Prison slang: To leave a prison by any means, i.e. transfer, parole, escape, execution, etc. 3. To investigate, explore a matter to determine if information received is true and correct. "I will check out his story."

Checks, Fraudulent or Worthless. Bank checks that are not honored (paid) by the bank on which drawn, usually because of insufficient funds that the maker or drawer has on deposit. There are "NSF" (not sufficient funds) checks and "no account" checks (where the maker does not have an account at the bank). In such cases the law usually requires that fraudulent intent be shown. This may be proven by the method of operation of the check passer. In "NSF" cases it may be established by writing the maker of the check a registered letter demanding that the check be made good. If the check is not redeemed within a specified number of days, the presumption of fraudulent intent is created by law. Many techniques are used by "professional" worthless check passers. Their operations are widespread, and their annual "take" runs into the millions of dollars. See **Paper Hanger; National Fraudulent Check File. Checks, Hot.** Worthless checks.

Check-up House. Gambling term: Place where the talley sheet is prepared and money and slips are counted.

Cheek. Slang: Brashness, "gall," audacity, "guts."

Cheesy. Juvenile slang: Traitorous.

Chef (shef). Underworld slang: An expert in the proper use of the opium pipe.

Chemical Transportation Emergency Center. See **CHEMTREC**.

CHEMTREC. Chemical Transportation Emergency Center, operated by the Manufacturing Chemists Association. For information involving hazardous chemicals in an accident information may be obtained by dialing (toll-free) (800) 424-9300. District of Columbia callers dial 483-7616.

Cherry. Slang: Hymen.

Chicago Seven, The. The trial of David T. Dellinger, Thomas E. Hayden, Rennard C. Davis, Abbott Hoffman, Jerry C. Rubin, Lee Weiner, and John R. Eroines on the charge of crossing state lines to incite riots in 1968 (at the time of the Democratic National Convention). On February 18, 1970, the first five listed persons were found guilty. All seven, plus two attorneys, were sentenced on contempt of court due to their actions during the trial. References: *U.S. News and World Report*, March 2, 1970, and *Life*, February 27, 1979.

Chicano (chi *cah* no). A Mexican-American. One living in the United States who is of Mexican descent.

Chick. 1. Prison slang: Penitentiary

VOCABULARY

food. 2. Slang: A good-looking young woman.

Chicken. Slang: Expression used by teenagers to denote one who exhibits cowardice or loss of "nerve." A game played by brash young people whereby two cars drive toward one another on a collision course. The one who turns aside first is called "chicken."

Chicken Powder. Slang: Amphetamine powder used for injection.

Chief. Head of an organization or agency, such as the Chief of Police.

Chief, Case in. The case in chief is the principal cause of action against a person. The main body of evidence used for the purpose of proving a defendant guilty.

Chief, Declaration in. A statement for the principal cause of action.

Chief, Examination in. The first questioning of a witness by the side that called him as a witness.

Chief Justice. Eldest or principal judge of a court of justice; presiding judge.

Chief (The). Slang: LSD.

Child Abuse. The intentional abuse of children. It is a crime in most states. See **Battered Child Syndrome.**

Childbirth, Emergency. See **Emergency Childbirth.**

Child Molester (moe *less* ter). One who injures or has questionable sexual dealings with a child. The child molester who is a sex deviate is called a pedophile. The molested child may be subject to rape, sodomy, indecent exposure, or murder. The pedophile is a relentless hunter of children. See **Pedophilia.**

Chill. Gangster term: To kill.

Chilled Shot. Firearms term: Hard shot (for shotguns, etc.) made with lead and antimony alloy.

Chimel v. California, 395 U.S. 752 (1969). A landmark case on searches in a residence. The court held the officers could search only within the areas of the reach of the arrestee without search warrant.

Chin. Slang: To talk.

Chinese Tobacco. Slang: Opium.

Chink. Derogatory slang: Chinese person.

Chip, Check. Gambling term: A token, usually a plastic coin, used in place of money for betting purposes.

Chippie. Slang: 1. A promiscuous woman or delinquent girl; originally a prostitute, dance-hall girl, female bartender. 2. To trifle with the use of narcotics.

Chipping. Slang: Taking narcotics occasionally.

Chisel. Slang: To cheat or obtain something by taking advantage of someone or by questionable or unethical means.

Chiva (*shee* va). Heroin.

Chloral Hydrate (*klor* al *high* drait). Compound $CH(OH)_2$, used as a sedative or hypnotic.

Chloroform (*klor* oh form). A volatile liquid, the fumes of which are an anesthetic. Not presently used much for this purpose by the medical profession. Composed of chlorine, hydrogen, and carbon. Now used as a constituent of liniments. Overdose of the vapors is poisonous.

Choke. 1. To stop breathing by stricture or pressure on the throat. 2. Firearms term: The muzzle end of the gun barrel of a shotgun is made smaller than the remainder of the barrel so as to regulate the density of the shot pattern—control the spread of the shot as they travel through and leave the gun barrel. The common types are the following: full choke, modified choke,

Chokey, (Choky). Slang: A prison.

Cholly. Slang: Cocaine.

Chopper. Underworld slang: A machine gun, or one who uses a machine gun in connection with gang activities.

Choppers. Slang: A person's teeth or mouth.

Choreic Insanity (ko*ree* ik in*san* i tee). A nervous disease resulting in insanity.

Chow. Slang: Food.

Christmas Tree. Slang: A red and blue capsule. A barbiturate (tuinal), which is a combination of equal parts of seconal and amytal, that results in a rapidly effective, moderately long-acting hypnotic or sedative drug.

Chromatograph (kroe *ma* toe graf). A machine or device used in a crime laboratory to analyze gaseous substances or compounds that can be readily converted into gases. "The laboratory has a gas chromatograph."

Chromosome (*kroam* oh zoam). One of the linear nucleoprotein-containing basophilic bodies of the cell nucleus, made up of chromatids.

Chuck-a-Luck. Gambling game played with several dice; the winning roll is the highest poker hand.

Chuck Horrors. A drug addict's avoidance of food, especially during withdrawal.

Chump. Gambling slang: A gambler with little or no experience. He can also be called sucker, mark, and greenie.

Cider (*sigh* der). A sweet, slightly fermented liquid derived from a fruit.

Cigarettes, Untaxed. Cigarettes on which federal and/or state taxes have not been paid when the cigarettes are sold to the users. This is illegal in most states, and it is a federal violation to transport such cigarettes in interstate commerce (from one state to another).

Cinder Dick. Slang: A railroad law enforcement officer.

Cipher (*sigh* fur). A secret writing whereby letters or symbols are substituted for letters intended in the message; may also consist of a transposition or rearrangement of numbers or letters by a prearranged plan or system.

Circuit Court (*sir* kit kort). A jurisdiction of courts extending over several counties or districts.

Circuit Court of Appeals. A part of the judicial system of the United States (federal courts) known as the United States Court of Appeals. There is one for each of eleven districts in the United States.

Circular Insanity (*sir* ku ler in *san* i tee). Another name for the psychological term manic-depressive.

Circumstantial (sir kum *stan* shel). Depending upon incidents other than the main fact; pertaining to circumstances.

Circumstantial Evidence. Evidence of collateral facts from which the case may be arrived at by inference or deduction.

Citation (sigh *tay* shun). A court-issued writ ordering the person named therein to appear before the court at a designated time.

Citation of Authority (si *ta* shun uv a *thor* i tee). The descriptive matter that shows where a case or legal reference can be located.

Cite (sight). To order or summon one to appear at court or at an official hearing; to officially notify a person of legal action against him and order his appearance to answer same.

Citizen (*sit* i zen). An individual,

VOCABULARY

naturalized or native, who is entitled to protection by a state and who owes allegiance to it.

Citizen's Arrest. The arrest of a person by a citizen (not a law enforcement officer) for a felony, without a warrant. A citizen is not authorized to make an arrest by means of a warrant of arrest. In some common law states (if not changed by statute) an arrest for a breach of the peace commited in his presence can be made by a citizen.

City Courts. Lower courts of original jurisdiction concerning city ordinances.

Civil. Distinguished from criminal; pertaining to a legal matter, pertaining to something noncriminal in nature. Pertaining to the personal or private rights of an individual; pertaining to the legal action in court to enforce private or personal rights. "Proceedings in court are usually criminal or civil." "A suit for personal injury is a civil action."

Civil Action (*siv* el *ak* shun). The legal suit or claim of a private party as distinguished from a criminal action, which is brought in the name of the state.

Civil Code. The code of laws covering only personal or private rights and wrongs; one individual on another.

Civil Courts. Courts concerned only with civil suits, not with criminal suits.

Civil Disobedience. The disobedience of a law by persons for the reason, among others, that they do not believe it just and they are willing to suffer the penalty in order to bring it to the attention of the people.

Civil Disorder. Disturbance of the peace by a person or persons evidenced by refusal to obey or comply with the law. Many participants are motivated by moral causes or convictions, and their actions are symbols of resistance to existing laws and government. Frequently the acts are in violation of criminal laws. Some have called the violent acts "criminal disorder" or "criminal disobedience."

Civil Liberties. The freedoms guaranteed under the Constitution, particularly the first ten Amendments (speech, worship, trial by jury, etc.)

Civil Process. Official orders and documents issued by or under the authority of a court when handling civil matters, such as summons, subpoenas, injuctions, eviction orders, etc. The police officer should be familiar with these, as he may be called upon to aid in serving.

Civil Rights. Analogous to constitutional rights. The rights of a citizen guaranteed by the amendments to the Constitution, particularly the first eight of such Amendments and the Thirteenth and Fourteenth; also numerous statutes enacted by Congress. The state constitutions and statutes also contain "civil rights" for the citizens.

C-Joint (see joint). Slang: A place where cocaine is sold.

Claiming Race. Horse racing term: A horse race where, before the race, a price is set for each horse in the race, and any other entrant in the race is entitled to buy the horse at the price so fixed.

Clamp Down. Slang: To strictly enforce laws or regulations. "The police clamped down on the pinball machine operators."

Clam Up. Slang: Do not talk; stop talking to anyone, especially the police or a judge.

Clandestine (klan *des* tin). Done in secret, usually for a questionable or illegal purpose.
Clang the Door. Juvenile slang: Lock a prisoner in a jail cell.
Clap (Clapp) (klaps). Slang: Venereal disease; especially syphilis or gonorrhea.
Clash. A hostile meeting; a conflict.
Class A. Prison slang: Drugs classified as class "A" by the legal manufacturer.
Class Consciousness (klas *kon* shus ness). Awareness of a common characteristic, situation, philosophy, or niche among people that gives them a sense of solidarity as a group .
Classification Committee. A group that determine programs and treatment in prisons.
Claw on, Put the. Slang: To apprehend; to take into custody; to point out another for purposes of arrest and detention.
Clean. Slang: Found to be unarmed when searched; not implicated in a suspected crime.
Clean. 1. To remove stems and seeds from marijuana. 2. Refers to an addict who is free from needle injection marks. 3. Not holding or possessing any narcotics.
Clear, In the. 1. Free of debt. 2. Innocent of any wrongdoing.
Clearinghouse. Banking term: A place where there is conducted the business of clearing checks and drafts for banks and adjusting balances between such banks.
Clearing Point. Gambling term: Place where a lookout is stationed to watch for cars delivering players to a gambling game and determine if the cars are being followed.
Clear Up. Slang: To withdraw from drugs.
Clemency (*klem* in se). Leniency; compassion or mercy toward offenders.
Clerk of the Court. An officer of the court who handles much of the routine paperwork associated with the administration of the court.
CLETS. California Law Enforcement Telecommunications System.
Client (klient). One who consults an attorney.
Client Role. A recipient of role behavior .
Clinical Conditions (*klin* i kal). Medically approved facilities of a hospital, clinic, laboratory, or doctor's office, and activities carried on by approved medical personnel. In the Scmerber case the court held that the taking of a blood specimen from an unwilling subject so it could be tested for alcohol content was satisfactory, inasmuch as it was done under clinical conditions.
Clinical Tests. Observations of a patient by a physician without outside influence, such as drugs or instruments.
Clink. Slang: A prison.
Clip. Slang: To cheat or swindle someone.
Clip-Joint. Slang: A public place, usually a place of entertainment, where customers are prone to be cheated, swindled, or robbed.
Closed (Closed Up, Closed Down). Slang: A place of business carrying on illegal activities that has stopped or decreased its activity because of law enforcement action or because of fear of such. A community where vice and gambling laws are rigidly enforced by the police.
Closed Shop. A situation where the employer, by agreement, hires only union members in good standing as employees. If no such union members are available at a given time, also

VOCABULARY

by agreement, the employer may hire nonunion workers on condition they apply for and become members of the union immediately.

Closet Queen. A homosexual who refuses to consciously admit to himself or others that he is a homosexual.

Clot, Blood. Blood that has coagulated, i.e. changed from a liquid state to a semisolid state.

Cloture (*klo* cher). The process of stopping or limiting debate in legislative bodies.

Clout. Slang: To commit theft or to grab something.

Clouter. Slang: A person who snatches money or other property and runs with it.

Club Hopping. Juvenile slang: Changing sides.

Clue (klu). A thing or information that is apparently pertinent to the solution of the case (crime).

CN. A lacrimator chemical most commonly used in "tear gas" and in aerosol irritant projectors. The chemical name is chloroacetophenone.

C-Note. Slang: A hundred-dollar bill.

Coast Guard. See **United States Coast Guard.**

Coasting. Slang: Under the influence of drugs; not of need of further drugs at the time.

Cobra-Venom Reaction. A method of serum diagnosis of insanity from haemolysis (breaking up of the red corpuscles of the blood).

Cocaine (ko *kaine*). A stimulant drug obtained from the coca leaves, it is a white, bitter crystalline substance. It is rigidly controlled by the law. Slang names: C, corrine, coke, cecil, carrie, choll, burnese, bernice, bernies, gold dust, happy-dust, dust, heaven dust, stardust, the leaf, dynamite, snow, and others.

Cocktail. Slang: A partially smoked marijuana cigarette placed into one end of a regular cigarette.

Code (kode). 1. A system of secret communication where words or other symbols are substituted for words in an arbitrary fashion. 2. Letters, numbers, or a combination of them, used in a law enforcement communication as a time saver and for security used in radio messages, teletype, and telephone conversations.

Code, International. A code of words, used in law enforcement, to clarify letters of the alphabet when spelling orally as by telephone or radio. For example, D—Delta, E—Echo, G—Golf, etc.

Code, The. Cosa Nostra or Mafia rules and regulations (internal) by which the organization operates, inside the families, between families, and throughout the organization.

Codefendants (*ko* dee fen dants). More than one person jointly charged for the same crime.

Codeine. A derivative of opium. It is similar to morphine but not as strong in its effect. It is a crystalline alkaloid.

Code of Ethics. Written rules, regulations, and/or standards of conduct for members of groups of people engaged in given professions or occupations. Doctors, attorneys, and others have these. One of the codes of ethics for law enforcement is the Law Enforcement Code of Ethics, which was adopted by the IACP at its 1957 conference. It has also been adopted by many other law enforcement associations and other organizations.

Codicil (*cod* e sil). An addition to a will.

Coding. Categorization of information for tabulation and easy reference.
Coercion (ko *er* chen). Improper persuasion. Actual coercion may result from acts or words intended to persuade improperly. Implied coercion may result not from specific acts or words but rather from the situation as a whole.
Coffee Grinder. Slang: A female showgirl who strips and goes through suggestive motions. A woman of ill repute.
Coffee Habit. Narcotics slang: Novice in the use of narcotics.
Cognizance (kog ni zans). Judicial notice of a matter; recognition or notice; the power or jurisdiction given to courts by law. "The court took judicial cognizance of the fact that our state borders on certain other states."
Cognomen (kog *no* men). The family or last name.
Cohabitate (ko *hab* i tate). To live together as husband and wife.
Cohesion (ko *hee* zhun). Attraction that unites bodies.
Coitus (ko *i* tis). The act of sexual intercourse.
Coitus A Tergo. Coitus from the rear.
Coitus Inter Femora. Sexual act performed between the thighs of the participant.
Coke. Slang: Cocaine.
Coke Head. Slang: One addicted to cocaine.
Cokie. Slang: Cocaine addict.
Cold. Slang: An investigative lead that is nonproductive.
Cold Balling. Gambling Term: Chilling one of the Bolita balls to be used to fix the game.
Cold Deck. Gambling slang: A deck of cards in which the cards have been fixed so that they may be dealt in a certain order. The object is to substitute this deck for the one in use at the appropriate time.
Cold Hand. Card gambling game term: The cards are dealt out, and the winner is determined without any additional cards being dealt or drawn. In a regular poker game, only five cards are dealt.
Cold Poke. Slang: An empty or worthless pocketbook.
Cold Prowl. Slang: Ransacking a house while the occupants are away.
Cold Turkey. Slang: 1. To be taken off the use of narcotics entirely, usually during a medical cure of the narcotics addiction, or to quit voluntarily. The addict goes through much physical discomfort in the process. The term comes from the "goose-flesh" condition, which resembles the skin of a cold-plucked turkey. 2. In need of narcotics; a fix.
Cold Water Ordeal. An ancient trial where people were thrown into a river to see if they would sink. The guilty persons were rejected by the river and would float.
Collar. Slang: An arrest.
Collateral Issue (ko *lat* er el *ish* oo). A side of an issue that has no direct bearing on the main issue in a controversy.
Collective Behavior. Unpatterned and unstructured behavior during rapid social change when norms are in transition. Behavior that occurs in a riot or in a mob.
Collector. Gambling term: One who accepts bets from players in a "policy" game.
Collusion (ko *lu* zhun). Wrongful secret agreement; a secret understanding for a wrongful purpose.
Colorimeter (kul e *rim* e tur). A device used to determine the exact

VOCABULARY 51

color of a substance, especially when compared with known standards. It is used in the police labratory in color analysis.

Color of Authority. A legal term describing the effects of implied or expressed authority.

Color of Title. The appearance, semblance, or simulacrum of title.

Coma (ko ma). A state of profound unconsciousness caused by disease, injury, or poison.

Comatose (ko me tos). Similar to a coma; afflicted with a coma.

Comb. Slang: Combination of any safe.

Combination (kom bi *nay* shen). 1. A combination lock, especially the outward portion of it. 2. Gambling term: Gambling organization; confederation. 3. Gambling term: In a "policy" game, the transposition of numerals within a three-digit number.

Combination of Vehicles. Any group of two vehicles, however joined together, that are drawn or propelled by a single motor vehicle.

Combination Ticket. Gambling term: A mutual win-place-show ticket, purchased at a racetrack.

Combustion (kom *bus* chun). A chemical process (as in oxidation) accompanied by the evolution of heat and light.

Come-along. Slang: Device in opening a safe.

Come-Along Hold. A technique in defensive tactics where the person to whom it is applied can be forced to come with the one who applies the technique.

Come-Back. Racetrack gambling slang: A procedure used by bookies for controlling betting odds and for hedging losses.

Come-Back Money. Racetrack gambling slang: Off-track bookie money that is placed (bet) at the tracks for the purpose of changing odds in a race.

Come Clean. Slang: To tell all the facts to law enforcement officers.

Come-On. Slang: A method where a victim is led into a swindle.

Come Out. Gambling term: The first throw of the dice.

Coming Down. Slang: Recovering from a trip (narcotics).

Comity (*kom* e tee). The situation where one court will, out of deference and respect, give effect to the judicial decisions of another. This is followed between federal and state courts as well as between courts of different states.

Command. 1. To order. 2. The person or persons in authority or directing an activity.

Commend (ko *mend*). To compliment, praise, or express pleasure concerning another's actions or deeds.

Commendation (*kom* in *day* shen). The act of praising or complimenting.

Commercial Establishment. An economic unit, generally at a single physical location, where business is conducted or where services or industrial operations are performed, e.g. a factory, mill, store, hotel, movie theatre, bank, or sales office. Note: A place of business that is not recognizable as such from the outside is included in the victimization survey rather than in the commercial survey.

Commercial Incident. Crimes of burglary, attempted burglary, robbery, and attempted robbery at commercial establishments are considered commercial incidents.

Commie. Slang: Member of the

Communist Party or a Communist sympathizer.
Commission, The. The National Council of the Cosa Nostra. It governs conditions that will exist between and among families as well as between the Cosa Nostra and others.
Commissioner (ko *mish* in or). The collector of revenue.
Commission Man. Gambling term: One who handles the "come-back money."
Commit (ko *mit*). 1. To violate the law. "He committed burglary." 2. To officially order the admission for safekeeping of an insane person to a jail or mental institution. "The accused was committed to the mental hospital for observation."
Commitment (ko *mit* ment). A court order or warrant issued by a court, ordering an officer to place a person in jail or prison. The legal authorization for holding one in jail or prison, usually issued by a court or judicial official. 2. To promise; pledge or assign one's self to a particular course.
Common Carrier. A person or company in the business of transporting passengers or goods for a fee.
Common Law. Traditional or general law that receives its force from long and universally accepted use. England developed the common law, and many states in this country have adopted it.
Common-Law Marriage. A marriage in which the couple is not legally married but is living together as husband and wife.
Common Pleas Court. In most jurisdictions, a court of inferior trial jurisdiction.
Communicate (ko *mu* ne kate). To talk; to convey messages from one person to another; to transmit information in such fashion as to be understood by people receiving it; to make one's self understood.
Communication (ko mu ne *ka* shen). Exchange of information or opinions; to transmit and receive.
Communications System (ko mu ne *kay* shens). A system or device for transmitting information. See **CLETS: Computer Systems.**
Communism (*kom* u nizm). Historically, all the theories and doctrines that would provide for common ownership of all property, or at least where all the means of production and distribution are owned and managed by the government. In the twentieth century, the doctrines and operations of the Communist Party as it was created in Russia and other countries where communists have come to power and rule the government. Using socialism as a vehicle the Communist Party, avowedly, seeks to overthrow other forms of government and rule the world. They plan to do this by revolution, by political action, or by a combination of the two. References: Churchill, Winston S.: Winston Churchill on revolution. *Readers Digest,* February 1971, p. 195. Hoover, J. Edgar: *Masters of Deceit.* New York, Henry Holt, 1958.
Communist Front (*kom* u nist). An organization, which ostensibly is not a part of the Communist Party but which is directed by CP members or sympathizers, who adopt a program sponsored by the CP. The membership may be made of many people who have no knowledge or sympathy for the CP. Their function is to act a "transmission belts" to attract noncommunists to the doctrines and activities of the Communist Party. The organization of the front is

VOCABULARY

described as follows: "First, a number of sympathizers who are close to the party, and whom the party knows can be depended upon to carry out party orders, are gotten together and formed into a nucleus which issues a call for the organization of a particular front organization which the party wants to establish. And generally after that is done a program is drawn up by the party, which this provisional committee adopts. Then, on the basis of provisional program, all kinds of individuals are canvassed to become sponsors of the organization, which is to be launched in the very near future. A provisional secretary is appointed before the organization is launched and in every instance in our day the secretary who was appointed was a member of the Communist Party. And as president of the organization we would put up some prominent public figure who was willing to accept the presidency of the organization, generally making sure that, if that public figure was one who would not go along with the communists, he was of such a type that he would be too busy to pay attention to the affairs of the organization....On the committee that would be drawn together, a sufficient number of communists and Communist Party sympathizers, who would carry out the party order, was included, and out of this number a small executive committee was organized....which carried out the affairs of the organization. And this small committee and the secretary are the instruments of the Communist Party, with the result that when manifestos or decisions on campaigns are made, those campaigns are ordered by the Communist Party." References: Testimony of Benjamin Gitlow. *Hearings of the Special Committee on Un-American Activities.* Vol. 7, pp. 4716-4718; *Guide to Subversive Organizations and Publication.* Washington, D.C., U.S. Government Printing Office, 1961.

Communist Party-United States of America (CPUSA). CPUSA was organized June 21, 1919, when the National Conference of the Left Wing of the Socialist Party in New York met, at which time the Left Wing Manifesto was adopted. It was admitted to the Communist International (comintern), a Russian communist organization for worldwide direction and control of communists groups, in 1921. The CPUSA is still active and agressive. See **Communist Fronts; Extremist Groups.** References: Hoover, J. Edgar: *Masters of Deceit.* New York, Henry Holt, 1958. Skousen, W. Cleon: *The Naked Communist* and *The Communist Attack on the U.S. Police.* Salt Lake City, Ensign.

Community (ko *mu* ne te). 1. Residents of a limited area having social relationships, as in a village or town. A larger city would be a community of communities, or neighborhoods—areas whose residents, because of their economic, ethnic, or racial character, may seek local control of their schools, police, etc. The community constitutes the audience that reacts to official actions or statements of policy. 2. A social group of any size whose members reside in a specific locality, share government, share a common membership, and have a cultural and historical heritage.

Community-based Corrections. The location and operation of correctional services in offenders' neighborhoods or other places outside the prison as the result of public proceedings.

Community Leaders. May either be well-known office holders or, more realistically, the less visible persons to whom neighborhoods turn for effective leadership.

Community Property. Property acquired during marriage by either husband or wife or both, except that which is acquired as separate property by either spouse.

Community Relations. The sum total of individual contacts by members of an organization; working with and being a part of the community. It is organizationally a nonline function. Although some departments have a public relations section or department, such work would not be limited to the personnel of that section or department.

Community Service Officer. A field employee, not sworn as a police officer, often assigned duties in community relations and community services.

Commutation (kom u *tay* shun). The reduction in the penalty imposed by the court, such as a commutation of sentence. "The Governor granted a commutation of sentence."

Commute (ko *mute*). The reduction of a prison or jail sentence.

Comparison Microscope (kom *pare* i son *mi* kro scope). A microscope having two objectives, i.e. the part of the microscope nearest the object being viewed. Each objective views a different object, the images being magnified and by prisms brought into focus in a single (or double) eyepiece. It is usually found in a crime laboratory and is used, among other things, for examining markings on bullets to determine if the markings on two bullets can be matched so as to determine if they were both fired from the same weapon. Reference: Soderman, Harry *et al.*: *Modern Criminal Investigation*. New York, Funk and Wagnalls, 1962, p. 204.

Compensation (kom pen *say* shun). Recompensense; to pay for debt owed or for damage caused.

Competent. In the law of evidence, that which is legally acceptable.

Competent Evidence. See **Evidence, Competent.**

Complainant (kom *plain* ant). The person who makes the complaint against someone in a criminal case, usually the victim, person injured, or a relative or friend of such injured party; the one who furnishes information, generally in the form of an affidavit, before a magistrate, upon which criminal charges are instituted. A law enforcement officer may be the complainant, based upon information obtained by him during an investigation.

Complaint. 1. A form for filing a greivance of a citizen versus police. 2. A form filing a petition in a court.

Complaint Desk. The position where complaints and requests for assistance are received.

Complex (*kom* plex). Mental process patterns and man's environmental reactions. It involves instincts as a basis for man's reaction to the environment about him.

Complexion (kom *pleck* shun). The color of the skin, especially of the face, used as a factor in describing a person, i.e. complexion: ruddy.

Comply (kom *ply*). To carry out orders; to act according to instructions. "The officer did not comply with the orders of his superior."

Composition of Creditors. An agreement between an insolvent debtor and his creditors whereby the latter agree to accept a dividend less than the whole amount of their claims.

Compound (*kom* pound). 1. To have knowledge of the actual commission of a crime by another person and, for a consideration or reward, aid in concealing the crime, forbear to assist in prosecution, or allow the offender to escape. "He was charged with compounding a felony." 2. A substance formed by the chemical union of two or more ingredients in definite proportion by weight.

Compounding a Felony. The offense of the victim of a crime entering into an agreement with the criminal not to have him prosecuted provided the victim is paid a sum of money or given restitution by the criminal.

Compromise (*kom* pro mize). Making concessions for the sake of achieving a greater goal.

Compulsion (kom *pul* shen). An abnormal urge to execute an act without the desire to do it. The individual cannot stop it at his will. It is based on an underlying unconscious motive.

Compulsive Neurosis (new *row* sis). Obsessive ideals and desires to do complicated and senseless acts, manifested by pyschoneurosis.

Compurgation (kom per *ga* shen). An early method of finding an accused innocent by the use of his friends and neighbors who would vouch for him under oath.

Compurgator (kom per *ga* tor). A neighbor or friend of the accused who swore that he knew the accused to be a good, honest man who could be believed under oath and who could not be guilty of the crime charged against him.

Computer (kom *pew* ter). A type of machine equipped electronically for the processing of large volumes of coded material and recording facilities for high-speed handling of mathematical problems.

Con (kon). Slang: 1. A convict or an ex-convict. 2. To persuade, inveigle or talk someone into doing something; to swindle or defraud.

Con Artist. Slang: A deceitful person who tricks victims by smooth talk, manipulation, or a sad story in an attempt to get money or something of value.

Concave (con *kave*). A surface that is hollowed out or curved inward. Think of a cave, and this term will not be confused with convex, which is just the opposite.

Conceal (kon *seal*). To hide or cover up.

Concept Role. Set of expectations held by a role incumbent regarding the behavior and attributes of his role, and the behavior and attitudes of a role reciprocal.

Conclusive (kon *kloo* siv). Not permitting proof to the contrary.

Conclusive Presumption. See **Presumption, Conclusive.**

Concreteness (kon *kreet* nes). The process of being specific.

Concur (con *kur*). To agree.

Concurrent (kon *kur* ent). To operate or run at the same time. When used in reference to sentences imposed upon one convicted of a crime, it means he serves all sentences simultaneously or at the same time. If he should be sentenced on two charges and receive five-year sentences on each charge, to run concurrently, he satisfies both after five years imprisonment. As it pertains to jurisdiction of investigative agencies or the courts, it means each has joint jurisdiction, i.e. each agency has jurisdiction over the matter or subject.

Concussion (kon *cush* shun). Injury to some part of the body caused by a blow or fall resulting in the body striking an object.

Condemn (kon *dim*). To declare one to be guilty of a crime.

Conditional Behavior. As modified by environmental factors, etc.

Conditional Release. The release of a prisoner (usually a convict serving time) on the condition that he comply with certain requirements. If the person does not adhere to such requirements, he may be put in prison or jail again.

Condone. To overlook certain things being done or said. To tacitly agree with things done or said. "The parent condoned the fact that his children smoked."

Cone (kone). The section of the gun barrel where the chamber joins the bore and where the diameter of the barrel reduces.

Confabulation (kon *fab* u *lay* shun). The telling of experiences as having actually happened when as a matter of fact the experiences were imaginary—found in pyschopaths.

Confederacy (kon *fed* e ra see). A conspiracy.

Confederate (kon *fed* er it). An accomplice, associate; one engaged in activities with others.

Confederation, The. The name used to signify the national criminal cartel—organized crime, dominated by the Italian Cosa Nostra.

Confess (kon *fess*). To make a statement against interest, involving one's self in crime or other misconduct.

Confession (kon *fesh* un). A statement, usually recorded, by a person who admits violation of the law; an admission of criminal violations. A confession must be given voluntarily, without force, threats, promises, or coercion being used by the officer receiving the confession. Under the Miranda ruling, the person being interviewed must be specifically warned of his specific constitutional rights, and the suspect must specifically and intelligently waive such rights before incriminating statements, made by him in response to questions, can be admitted in evidence.

Confessions, Voluntary. Confessions that are given voluntarily by a suspect.

Confidence Game. A scheme carried out by taking advantage of persons who place confidence in the swindler (operator). There are many confidence games or tricks being used by swindlers.

Confidential (*kon* figh *din* shel). Not freely divulged. In government service: Information and material, particularly as pertains to defense, the disclosure of which could be against the best interests of the nation.

Confidential Informant. Informant.

Confidential Relationship (kon fi *den* chal). A judiciary relation, requiring the utmost degree of good faith between the parties.

Confinement (kon *fine* ment). The incarceration of a person in a place of detention. This may be one accused of crime or one who is believed to be a necessary party to a criminal action, such as a material witness. In its broadest sense it may apply to depriving a person of his freedom of action.

Conflict of Laws. That branch of jurisprudence arising from the di-

VOCABULARY

versity of the laws of different jurisdictions which reconciles the inconsistency or decides which law or system is to govern in the particular case.

Conflict Resolution. Adjustment of differences between persons or groups.

Conflict Role. Exposure to and awareness of conflicting expectations in connection with either single or multiple role incumbencies.

Confrontation (kon fron ta shun). 1. The meeting or coming together of opposing forces. The term is frequently used by radical groups as a goal to their encounters with law enforcement officers. 2. Being real; telling it like it is.

Con Game. Slang: Confidence game; swindle.

Congenital Insanity (kon *jen* i tal). A form of insanity caused by a congenital defect.

Conjugal (*kon* ju gal). Pertaining to the state of marriage or marital relations. "Conjugal visiting in prison is a topic of much controversy."

Conjugal Rights. The right of one spouse to the love, comfort, and affection of the other.

Conjugal Visiting. Visiting of one spouse with the other for purposes of marital relations. The matter of allowing conjugal visiting by the spouses of convicts in or near the place of incarceration is a problem widely discussed by administrators of correctional institutions.

Con Man. Slang: A confidence man; a swindler; one who wrongfully takes money or property by means of trickery or a swindle.

Connect. 1. Slang: To buy drugs. 2. To meet with someone and enter into an agreement with him.

Connection. Slang: 1. Drug supplier (pusher); a person who handles stolen property or who can furnish such goods or narcotics. 2. One in a position to render assistance to a criminal and who can and will deliver favors or assistance for a price. 3. A person with a wide acquaintance of public officials and who is willing to make introductions of such officials to persons in control of vice and gambling operations.

Consanguine Family (kon *san* gwin). Family that includes persons related by blood plus their nuclear families.

Conscientious Objector (*kon* she *en* shuss). One who claims a real opposition to war or military service by reason of an intense moral or religious aversion to either or both.

Consecutive (kon *seck* you tive). One following another; one after the other; successive. In the sentencing of a criminal offender for more than one offense the court may make the sentences consecutive, i.e. to operate consecutively. In such a situation the offender must complete one sentence before he starts the next. Three five-year consecutive sentences means an ultimate prison term of fifteen years (unless, of course, he is paroled or otherwise released).

Consensual (kon *sen* shu el). By common agreement.

Consent (kon *sent*). The voluntary yielding of the will to a proposition made by another.

Consent, Implied. Consent that is not expressly given but that is inferred from actions or which is prescribed by law. Several states have laws that provide that when the operator of a motor vehicle obtains a driver's license he waives his right to object to an intoxication test if he should at a later date be charged with driving while intoxicated. This is generally referred to as the "Implied Consent" Law.

Consent Search. Voluntary consent on the part of the legal possessor of premises or movables for such to be searched. A person, place, or movable may be lawfully searched by an officer of the law if the possessor gives his free and voluntary consent. By possessor is meant the owner if he possesses the premises to be searched or the person who has the legal right to possess same. The owner of a hotel cannot give consent to search the room of one who is renting the room. It is good procedure to obtain such consent in writing.

Consideration (kon *sid* er *ay* shun). Law: Inducement for making a contract.

Console Slot Machine. A large slot machine that accomodates more than one player simultaneously.

Conspiracy (kon *speer* eh see). Law: Two or more persons plan the commission of an offense or crime and one, or more, does an overt act (does something toward carrying out the unlawful act).

Constitution (*kon* sti *too* shun). A written document creating a government and authorizing (and restricting) its powers, deriving its authority from the governed.

Constitutional Law. The basic law of the land, as interpreted by courts.

Constitutional Officer. Any law enforcement officer specifically and expressly provided for in either the Constitution of the United States or each state constitution. The offices of sheriff, constable, and coroner are constitutional officers in several states.

Constitutional Rights. The rights of citizens as guaranteed by the United States Constitution.

Construction (kon *struk* shun). Interpretation, as of the Constitution; strict, according to the literal wording, or loose, as implied.

Constructive Contempt. A contempt committed out of the presence of the court and which does not involve a failure to comply with an order to appear in court or other official judicial body as ordered by the court.

Constructive Intent. Transfer of intent. If a person intends to do an illegal act and in attempting to carry it out he injures someone else, it is said to be constructive intent.

Contact. One who is known to the officer and from whom information or services may be expected; a source of information.

Contact High. Slang: A feeling of being on drugs or "high" from merely being in contact with someone or something reminding one of drugs.

Contact Print. A photographic print on which the image or picture is the same as on the negative from which it is made; a one-to-one size photograph. It is made by placing the light-sensitive print paper against the negative and exposing the negative to light.

Contact Surveillance. The use of tracer preparations (dyes, fluorescent chemicals) that will adhere to the hands, clothing, etc. of a suspect when he comes in contact with it.

Contemporaneous (kon *tem* por *ay* nee us). Occurring at the time of the happening of something else. In an arrest it is something that happens at the time of the arrest, or that occurs soon thereafter as part of a contin-

VOCABULARY

uous, uninterrupted lawful investigation.

"Contempt of Cop" Arrest. An arrest that, although basically legal and correct, probably would not have been made had the arrestee not been antagonistic to the arresting officer.

Contempt of Court. Willful acts that interfere with the orderly conduct of the court; any act that obstructs the court in its administration of justice, hinders its functions, or any act or omission tending to obstruct or interfere with the orderly administration of justice or to impair the dignity of the court or respect for its authority. There are two kinds of contempt—one committed in the presence of the court and one that does not involve orders to appear in court.

Contingent Beneficiary (kon *tin* jent ben a *fish* ee air eee). The second party named to receive benefits from an insurance policy should the primary beneficiary be deceased before the execution of the policy.

Continuance (con *tin* you enss). Adjournment or postponement of a case or action before the court to a certain date or indefinitely. "The defendant was granted a continuance to March 15th."

Continue (kon *tin* you). Law: To retain the matter on the calendar, for decision or action at a later date.

Continuous Crime (kon *tin* you us). A crime consisting of continuous violations, such as possession of stolen property or carrying a concealed weapon. The statute of limitations does not begin to operate on such a crime until the person discontinues the acts constituting the violation.

Contraband (*kon* tra band). Property that may not be lawfully possessed, such as narcotics.

Contraceptive (kon tra *sep* tiv). A means of preventing pregnancy.

Contract (*kon* tract). Underworld slang: An agreement between a leader in crime with someone for the killing of a person; to pay or offer to pay for the death or injury of certain individuals. It may be an agreement for a certain person to perform the deed, or it may be an "open contract" where anyone will be paid a specified sum to do the job.

Contravention (kon trah *ven* shun). 1. Scotch law: The violation of a court order. 2. French law: An act that violates the law.

Contrectation (kon treck *tay* shun). Preliminary sex play.

Contributory Negligence. In a civil case, negligible actions of the plaintiff resulting in damages and thus relieving the defendant from responsibility to pay.

Control. A factor introduced into a model or equation to help determine the cause and effect relationship between two other variable factors.

Controlled-Access Highway. Every highway, street, or roadway in respect to which owners or occupants of abutting lands and other persons have no legal right of access to or from the same except at such points only and in such manner as may be determined by the public authority having jurisdiction over such highway, street, or roadway.

Controller. Gambling term: The "middle management" man in an organization operating a numbers game. Boss of the collectors. They turn their collected slips in to him.

Contumacious (*kon* too *may* shus). Disobedient in a stubborn manner.

Contusion (kon *too* zhen). A bruise

on some part of the body; an injury where the skin is not broken.
Convene. To assemble or come together in a meeting. "The court will convene at 3 PM."
Conversation (kon vur *say* shun). A talk to or with other people.
Conversion (kon *ver* zhen). Acceptance of another individual or group's ideas or ways.
Convex (kon *vex*). Curved outward.
Convey (kon *vay*). Law: To pass title to property.
Conveyance (kon *vay* ence). A means of transportation, such as an automobile, taxi, or bus. Law: A written instrument transferring property or title to property between persons.
Convict. (*kon* vikt). 1. A sentenced criminal; one who has been found guilty of a crime. 2. (kon *vikt*) To find a person guilty of a crime.
Conviction (con *vik* shen). The act of finding one guilty of a crime.
Convict Labor. The leasing of convicts for work outside the prison.
Convoy (*kon* voy). An escort; to accompany others. "In police work the high official is given a convoy so as to hasten his trip and offer protection."
Cook. Underworld slang: One who tends the opium pipe for the smokers.
Cooker. Slang: Bottle cap for heating drug powder with water.
Cook up a Pill. To prepare opium for smoking.
Cool. Slang: 1. Composure, calm temperament, not upset or obviously excited. 2. No law enforcement officers are near. 3. Juvenile slang: An uneasy armistice.
Cool Cat. Slang: A person who is the essence of the standard of the group.
Cooler. Slang: Jail or prison.
Coolie. 1. A cheap oriental laborer. 2. Slang: One who does not belong to any particular juvenile gang.
Cooling-Off Period. A statute requiring striking workers to return to work for a short period while negotiations continue.
Cool It. Slang: Quiet down; stop talking; stop what you are doing; be patient; be calm.
Coon. Slang: Negro.
Cooperative Training Centers (koe *op* er ah tiv). Training centers maintained jointly by many criminal justice agencies for the purpose of training their members.
Coordinate Method (koe *or* din et). A system commonly used in sketching (crime scene, etc.) to show the relative positions of one spot to another.
Coordinates (ko *or* din ets). Lines and points used in drawing and charting to show the locations of objects in the crime scene. See **Coordinate Method.**
Cop. Gambling slang: 1. Stealing or cheating. 2. Winning.
Cop a Deuceway. Slang: To buy a two-dollar pack of marijuana cigarettes.
Cop a Plea. Slang: To plead guilty in court to a criminal charge.
Cope. Slang: To handle one's self effectively while under the influence of drugs.
Copilots. Slang: Stimulant drugs-amphetamines.
Copper. Slang: A police officer.
Coprolalia (kope roe *lay* lee ah). Sex deviate term: Obscene language used as a form of sexual excitement.
Coprophilia (kope roe*feel* ee ah). Sex deviation term: Defecation involved in producing sexual gratification; interest in feces in an abnormal way.
Copy Out. Slang: Plead guilty. Ad-

VOCABULARY

dict term: quit, take off, confess, defect, inform.

Coram Nobis. (Latin:) Writ of error. A petition to the original court of conviction to set aside that conviction on the basis of an alleged error that does not appear in the record.

Core. A formation or character detail in fingerprints used in classifying the pattern. It is the approximate center of the pattern area. It is placed upon or within the innermost looping ridge.

Corine. Slang: Cocaine.

Corker. Gambling term: A gambler who is different, out of the ordinary, or strange. He may be good or bad.

Cork the Air. Underworld slang: To sniff cocaine.

Corn. Slang: Corn whiskey; illegal whiskey.

Coroner's Jury. A panel of citizens hearing evidence as the result of an investigation of a coroner into a death.

Corporal Imbecility. A physical inability to have sexual intercourse.

Corporal Punishment. Punishment of the body by physical means, such as whipping, flogging, or death, as the result of a legal order.

Corpus Delicti (*kor* pus dee *lick* tie). Law: The substance of the crime—composed of two elements: 1. the act and 2. the criminal agency producing the act. In a homicide case it must be shown that a human was killed (the act) and that the killing was done illegally (criminal agency). In a suicide or accidental death the proof of corpus delicti is not satisfied.

Correctional Institution. Institutions, such as jails and prisons, given custody of persons' sentences (making some attempt to rehabilitate such persons.)

Corrections (kor *eck* shuns). The area or discipline in the field of Criminal Justice involved in operations of prisons, rehabilitations services, and probation and parole matters.

Correlations (Behavioral). Measurable relations between behavior patterns.

Corrine. Slang: Cocaine.

Corroborate (ko *rob* o rate). To confirm, to "back up" someone's statement; to make it stronger.

Corroborating Evidence (ko *rob* o rating). See **Evidence, Corroborating.**

Corrosion (ko *row* zhun). Firearms term: Damaging change inside the gun barrel caused from chemical reactions of the residue of ammunition fired in the gun or from other chemicals. Proper cleaning and oiling will prevent much of this.

Corrupt (ko *rupt*). To break the morals and character of someone; to make the honest dishonest.

Cosa Nostra (*kos* a *nos* trah). A highly structured section of organized crime.

Cotics. Slang: Morphine, other opiate derivatives, cocaine, and drugs generally.

Cottons. Slang: Bits of cotton saturated with narcotic solution used to strain foreign matter when drawing solution up into a hypodermic syringe or eyedropper. These cottons are often saved by addicts for an emergency, as they contain a residual amount of the drug.

Cough Syrup. Slang: Money paid as a bribe in order to prevent someone from talking about information he has.

Counsel (*koun* sel). Legal assistance from one trained in law; an attorney.

Counseling and Release. The juvenile proceeding where an offender is

counseled and released into the custody of an adult without entering into the court system.

Count. Legal term: One charge contained in an indictment.

Counterclaim. An opposing claim; a claim, as against a plaintiff in a lawsuit, to offset another claim.

Counterfeiting. The making of imitation money and obligations of the government. Counterfeiting of the above is a federal violation of the law. Primary investigation jurisdiction is in the United States Secret Service, Department of the Treasury.

Countersurveillance. See **Surveillances.**

Counting Room. Gambling term: A locked and heavily guarded room where the winnings from the tables are counted at the end of each shift of operations.

Count-Out. A prison privilege for some trustees to remain out of their cells after regular prisoners have been locked up.

Country Club. Slang: A jail, reformatory, or industrial school for juvenile delinquents.

Count Store. Gambling term: A carnival game that requires a player to score a specified number of points in order to win. This score can be miscalculated, thus cheating the player. It can also be called an Addup Joint.

County (*koun* ty). A geographical and political division of the state, in all states except Louisiana, where such is called a parish.

County Court. An ordinary court having jurisdiction for trials under a jury.

County Mountie. Slang: A local policeman.

Coup (coo). A French word used in the United States by baccarat and chemin de fer players. It means "bet."

Courses of Action. To proceed, to progress; a sequence of events.

Court. The judicial branch of the government. The official body or agency that dispenses justice. The meeting of persons, by authority of the law, for administration of justice.

Court, Inferior. A court of primary and/or limited jurisdiction. It tries cases of a minor nature. It is generally not a court of record, i.e. no record of the proceedings is made (unless worked out by the parties). It usually tries only misdemeanor cases and holds preliminary hearings or examinations. It acts as a committing agency for higher courts. Such courts include Justice of the Peace, Police Courts, Mayor's Courts, and Municipal or City Courts.

Court, Out of. See **Out of Court.**

Court, Supreme. The court of last resort—highest court, found in the federal system and in each state as a part of the state system. In the states it is preceded by the name of the state.

Courteous (*kur* te us). Polite, considerate. This is an important trait for a law enforcement officer to have.

Courtline. A committee for discipline in a prison. An institutional court.

Court Martial. A military court, operating under the Uniform Code of Military Justice, for trying offenders of military law who are members of the military.

Court of Appeal. An intermediary court in both the state and federal systems. In some states it is the court of last resort—the highest court. The United States Courts of Appeal operate in numbered circuits, each circuit having jurisdiction over a

VOCABULARY

designated geographical area consisting of certain states. There are eleven Circuit Court districts in the United States.

Court of Chancery (*chan* sir ee). A court of equity. Formerly existed in England and still exists in some states in the United States for those courts having general equity powers.

Court of Equity (*ek* wi tee). A court, the principal function of which is trying cases following the procedures of equity.

Court of General Jurisdiction. A court of original jurisdiction. A trial court (usually a court of record) having jurisdiction over most criminal and civil matters arising in the territorial jurisdiction.

Court of Last Resort. The last court that may hear a case. The United States Supreme Court is a court of last resort for many kinds of cases.

Court of Limited Jurisdiction. See **Court, Inferior.**

Court of Original Jurisdiction. Trial court. Court of the general jurisdiction; usually has jurisdiction to try all cases brought before it. It often hears cases appealed to it from an inferior court—such appeals are heard de novo, i.e. all over again.

Court of Non-record. A court that does not make a written record of the trial.

Court of Primary Jurisdiction. A court that has the authority to hear (try) cases at the point of origin.

Court of Record. A court that makes a record of the procedures and the testimony of the trial.

Court Reporter. That member of the court's staff who maintains verbatim records of what transpires at a trial.

Courtroom Demeanor. Actions and statements of a person while in court. This includes testimony, conduct, and personal appearance in the courtroom. It is important for the officer to give thought and preparation to this part of his work. He should—
1. Know the facts of the investigation conducted by him—review notes and reports prior to trial.
2. Dress appropriately.
3. Talk at a voice level so as to be heard by all in the courtroom.
4. Be frank and truthful in his testimony.
5. Maintain poise and composure.

Courtroom Disruptions. Courtroom misconduct that disrupts the orderly proceedings of the court. The United States Supreme Court has ruled that the judge may take one or more of the three steps to insure orderly conduct in court:
1. Warn the defendant (if he is the unruly one) and then exclude him from the courtroom and proceed with the trial.
2. Bind and gag him.
3. Cite him for contempt of court.

Courtroom Misconduct. See **Courtroom Disruptions.**

Court Trial. A trial in which a judge decides the verdict without a jury present.

Covenant. Legal undertaking or promise.

Cover (*cuv* er). 1. Something behind which a person may place himself so as to be less visible and also be protected from gunfire or other means of injury. 2. Gambling slang: To accept a bet. 3. **Cover up:** To alibi or lie for another in order that he may escape punishment or detection.

Covert (*kuv* ert). Hidden or secret. Law: Sheltered, protected, as of a married woman.

Coverture (*kuv* er tur). Legal status of a married woman.

Cowboy. Gambling slang: A gambler who bets fast, carelessly, or recklessly.

CPS (Current Population Survey). A continuing national household interview survey of the civilian noninstitutional population of the United States, conducted each month by the U.S. Census Bureau since 1943. It is the basis for estimates of employment, unemployment, income, and many other characteristics of the population.

Crabs. Body lice.

Crack. Slang: 1. To break emotionally, as under stress or strain. 2. To force open a safe by tools or explosives. 3. To solve a case by the police. "He cracked the case." 4. An insulting, tasteless remark.

Crackers. Slang: LSD, in Boston (from animal crackers).

Crack-Up. Slang: 1. A major automobile accident in which the vehicle is badly damaged. 2. A mental breakdown.

Crap (krap as in rap). Slang: 1. In a game of dice to throw a seven. 2. Boloney; not true, incorrect; "bull" 3. Taboo: voided excrement. 4. Something foolish; something valueless or useless.

Crap Dealer. Gambling: The employee of the house at a crap table who pays winners and collects from losers for the house.

Crap Game. Dice game.

Crap Hustler. Gambling: A player who places crap bets at lower than the correct odds.

Crap Out. Slang: To lose in dice by throwing seven while trying to make a point.

Craps. Gambling: The game of dice.

Crash (krash as in rash). Slang: To gain entry to a building or place by use of force; to enter a place or event without an invitation; a police raid. Drug user term: The effects of stopping the use of amphetamines.

Crash Out. Slang: To break out of prison or jail; a jail or prison break.

Crash Pad. Slang: Place where the user withdraws from amphetamines.

Crash Truck. Specialized firefighting apparatus designed to handle fire and accidents involving aircraft. May also refer to special apparatus used to control serious vehicle fires on highways.

Craze. A manner of dress, architecture, decor, etc., reflecting the interests, values, and motives of a given society or group within it, which is short lived, irrational, and obsessive in character.

Crazy. Slang: Exciting, in the know, enjoyable.

Credibility (kred i *bill* i ty). Trustworthiness, believability; the dependability of the testimony. "The credibility of a witness may be attacked by the side opposing the side that offered him."

Credible (*kred* i bul). Believable, trustworthy, reliable.

Credit Card. A card issued by a company authorizing the named holder to purchase merchandise and/or services on credit and pay later. Stolen and altered credit cards offer problems to the work of the police.

Credit Manager. The casino employee who extends or denies credit.

Creditor Beneficiary. A third person, to whom performance of a promise comes in satisfaction of legal duty.

Creek. Juvenile slang: Prison.

Creeper. A crooked carnival wheel

VOCABULARY

whose spindle or arrow spins slowly and is easily controlled.

Creep Joint. Slang: A mobile gambling operation or other illegal operation that moves from place to place to avoid police action.

Cretinism (*creet* i nism). A form of idiocy with physical degeneracy.

Crib. Slang: Residence; sleeping quarters; "pad"; house; room.

Crime (krime). An act or failure to act that is defined as criminal by the law of the state or nation; an act or failure to act forbidden by law and which is punishable upon conviction.

Crime, Federal. 1. An act that is in violation of the laws of the United States; the criminal law of the United States is generally found in the United States Code (USC). 2. Slang: Something unduly exaggerated in importance. "He tried to make the incident a federal crime."

Crime, Infamous. A crime that is particularly evil.

Crime, Quasi. An offense that is against the public but not written as a law. It would not include any indictable offense but could include those crimes in which a fine would result.

Crime Against Humanity. A crime that is so serious that it is answerable only to humanity in general and not to a specific state.

Crime Against Nature. Sodomy or buggery.

Crime Against The Other (husband or wife). A statute stating that one spouse cannot be a witness against the other spouse.

"Crime Commission." The President's Commission on Law Enforcement and Administration of Justice, which was established to make recommendations in the administration of the Justice system.

Crime Control Digest. A biweekly publication reporting current items of interst in the field of criminal justice published by SCI/Tech Digests, Inc., National Press Bldg., Washington, D.C. 20004.

Crime Index. Another name for a "modus operandi" file. The method of the crime is described.

Crime Insurance. The Housing Act of 1970 provides government assistance (financial) to those in high crime areas who cannot otherwise buy crime-loss insurance at reasonable rates. Reference: Crime insurance hard to get? United States aid is on the way. *U.S. News & World Report,* January 18, 1971, p. 18.

Crime Laboratory. See **Laboratory, Crime.**

Crimen Falsi (*kry* men *fall* sy). Indicates the class of offenses that involve the perpetration of a falsehood, e.g. forgery, perjury, counterfeiting, etc.

Crime of Passion. A crime committed in a sudden fit of rage, hatred, emotion, etc., when the offender was incapable of rational reflection and with no premeditation.

Crime Prevention. An attempt by law enforcement agencies to reduce intent to commit wrongful acts rather than reduce the opportunity to commit them.

Crime Prevention Police. As by use of detection, task forces, PCR programs.

Crime Reports, Uniform. See **Crime Statistics.**

Crime Repression. An attempt by law enforcement agencies to reduce the opportunity to commit wrongful acts rather than reducing the intent to commit them.

Crime Scene (seen). The place or area where a crime was committed.

It is important that certain things be done as soon as possible concerning a crime scene after the police arrive:
1. It should be protected to avoid disturbance or damage to evidence.
2. Photographs should be made if practical.
3. It should be sketched and charted.
4. It should be systematically and thoroughly searched.
5. Detailed notes should be taken of all facts.

Crime Scene Sketching. The drawing and charting of a crime scene, showing the relative positions of objects, one to another.

Crime Statistics. A nationwide compilation of crime statistics, based on law enforcement information furnished by local agencies, is prepared and published annually by the FBI in *Crime in the United States*. Uniform Crime Report, Government Printing Office, Washington, D.C. 20402.

Crime Victim Compensation. Payment by the government of losses to victims of crime.

Criminal (*krim* i nal). One who violates the law.

Criminal, The Situation. A person that knowingly commits a crime but believes it is the right thing to do under the circumstances.

Criminal Act. A willful act against the law.

Criminal Behavior. As defined by laws.

Criminal Charge. An accusation of a crime, formulated in a written complaint, information, or indictment and taking shape in a prosecution. (Black's Law Dictionary)

Criminal Conversation. Adultery; illegal sexual relations with a married person.

Criminal Intelligence. Information concerning alleged criminals that is not necessarily substantiated by a determination of guilt or the result of public proceedings.

Criminal Intent. The intent to do an act the results of which are a crime or violation of the law. There is general intent and specific intent. Some statutes require the existence of specific intent, some require only general intent, and if no intent is set forth in the description of the crime by law, no intent is required but the doing of the act is sufficient. The usual traffic violation does not require the presence or proof of intent.

Criminalist (*kri* mi na *list*). A scientist trained to perform crime laboratory functions and relate the findings to criminal investigations.

Criminalistics (krim i na *lis* ticks). The work of the crime laboratory or police laboratory. "The application of science in the police laboratory is a great help to the investigator of a criminal matter—this is called criminalistics.

Criminalization. Classifying and assessing crimes. "Overcriminalization" means to include offenses not thought by some to be crimes (drug addiction, drunkenness, homosexuality).

Criminal Justice. The broad field of law enforcement including police, courts, and corrections.

Criminal Justice, Costs of. $8.6 billion per year (1970).

Criminal Liability. A person's responsibility for criminal behavior.

Criminally Receiving. A crime where a person receives, withholds, buys, or conceals any stolen property.

Criminal Procedure, Law of. The

law dealing with all facets of the procedures followed in taking an offender into custody through the final court proceedings. Arrest, search and seizures, methods of legally charging the offender with crime, arraignment, trial, and sentencing are included.

Criminal Psychology. The study of psychology and its relation to crime and criminal behavior.
Also called forensic psychology.

Criminogenic Encephalosis. A personality disorder that includes nail biting, lack of ability to concentrate, slow learning, behavior disorders, and phases of diurnal torpor.

Criminologist (krim i *nol* o gist). One who studies the knowledge relative to crime and criminal behavior as a social phenomenon.

Criminology (krim i *nol* o gee). The field of scientific study relative to crime and criminal behavior; the body of knowledge concerning crime as a social phenomenon.

Crimp. Gambling: 1. The bending of one or more cards in a deck so that a person would cut those cards (knowingly or unknowingly) in a desired spot. 2. To bend a card in a deck.

Crimping. Firearms term: The cartridge case or shotgun shell is crimped inward at the end holding the bullet or shot, so as to hold it in position.

Critical Stage. A stage of the criminal justice process that the courts have determined to be a crucial point capable of affecting the outcome of a criminal case.

Criticize (krit i size). To make a statement of a critical nature concerning something or someone. It may be a person or a thing. It may be constructive or destructive criticism.

The Circuit Court of Appeals, Washington, D.C. on June 19, 1970, ruled in the case of Minard v. Mitchell that an officer has the constitutional right to criticize the operations of his department and no punitive action could be taken against him for it.

Croak. Slang: To die or kill.

Croaker. Slang: A doctor.

Crooked. Dishonest, fraudulent, false. "Crooked gambling devices are used by swindlers."

Crooked Letter. Prison slang: A letter that is gotten out of a jail or prison by devious means that circumvent censorship. Same as **Flying a Kite.**

Cross. Slang: Double-cross.

Cross Complaint. A countercharge by the defendant to the plaintiff in response to the plaintiff's charge.

Cross Examination. Questioning a witness who was offered by and who testified for the opposing side in a trial.

Cross Projection (pro *jek* shun). A method of sketching the details of a room where the walls and the ceiling are shown (drawn) as if they were on the same plane as the floor. This method gives a clear understanding of the scene, especially if evidence is found on the walls or ceiling.

Cross Roader. Gambling term: A cheating gambler.

Cross the Palms. Slang: To pay for something "under the table," i.e. unethically or illegally; a "payoff" for a favor, service, or goods received; bribery.

Crosswalk. A distinctly marked area on a street indicated for pedestrian crossing.

Crotch Worker. Slang: A thief or shoplifter who places the stolen merchandise between the legs.

Croupier (*kru* pe er). In a gambling

game; the person who works at a gaming table and who pays off to the winners and collects from the losers.

Crowd. A temporary collection of people in the same place at the same time responding to the same stimuli.

Cruel and Unusual Punishment. The Eighth Amendment guarantees freedom from cruel and unusual punishment; however, the term's definition has rested with the courts. In recent years, the U.S. Supreme Court has revised various sentences as unconstitutional and set certain standards for their lengths and conditions.

Cruelty. The intentional and malicious infliction of physical suffering.

Cruise. Slang: To ride the streets looking for a sex partner to pick up; usually refers to teenagers, homosexuals, and prostitutes.

Crutch. Slang: 1. A device used to hold marijuana cigarette when it has burned to the point where it will burn the fingers—usually a half of a paper match book; also called a roach clip. 2. A container for a hypodermic needle.

Crystal. Slang: Methedrine (methamphetamine), "speed," or other amphetamines.

Crystals. Slang: Amphetamine powder for injection.

CS. A chemical agent used as tear gas. Chemical name is orthochlorbenzalmalononitrile. It is newer than CN and has replaced the latter in some instances.

CUBA. Gambling term: A type of numbers lottery operation.

Cube Head. Slang: Frequent user of LSD.

Cubes. Slang: 1. LSD; morphine pills. 2. Dice.

Cuffs (kuffs). Slang: Handcuffs.

Culpable (kul pay bul). Blameable; at fault. "His acts were culpable."

Culpable Negligence (neg li gens). Acts of negligence, where the doing or failure to do results in injury or death to persons and for which the person is held criminally responsible; an act that is done carelessly and would forseeably result in death or injury to other persons. No intent needs to be proven in such cases.

Culprit (kull prit). One who has violated the law but has not been convicted. He may still be sought for the crime or may have been legally charged with the crime but not tried.

Cult. Groups of followers clustered around a leader whose teachings differ substantially from the doctrines of a church or denomination. They are the least conventional and institutionalized form of religious organizations.

Cultural Alternatives (kul chu rul). A choice of cultural patterns (armed versus unarmed police).

Cultural Anonymity. Lacking identity in a group.

Cultural Change. Shift from previously accepted beliefs or patterns.

Cultural Complex. Cultural traits that make up a large pattern of behavior.

Cultural Conflicts. Friction within or between cultures.

Cultural Constructs. Established patterns of doing or believing.

Cultural Continuities. Persistent customs, patterns, and ideas as versus discontinuities, disruptive changes in these.

Cultural-Contracultural Conflicts. Challenging patterns within or between groups.

Cultural Determinism. Behavior is determined by cultural factors only.

Cultural Differences. Variances from normally accepted patterns, or contrasts in characteristics of groups.

VOCABULARY

Cultural Diffusion. Spread of culture traits from one group to another.
Cultural Distance. Degree of difference between culture groups.
Cultural Ethnocentrism. Belief that one's own group's ways are best.
Cultural Insularity. Isolation of a group from other groups.
Cultural Integration. Fusion of groups or of group's norms.
Cultural Interaction. Implemented communication between groups.
Cultural Invention. Innovative ability of a group: technical, artistic, philosophical.
Cultural Lag. Differential rates of change within or between cultures.
Cultural Loss. Disappearance of traits as a result of contacts with other groups.
Cultural Marginality. Conflicting allegiances to two or more groups; A black working in a white society. Double marginality: Black policeman on a white force in a black neighborhood (suspect by both groups).
Cultural Minority Group. Ethnic or racial group with limited rights and privileges, regardless of its size.
Cultural Myths. Traditions and beliefs that a people cherish.
Cultural Pluralism. Idea of a culture comprised of multiple recognized elements (ethnic, racial, economic, political).
Cultural Prejudice. Ill-founded, generally negative attitude toward groups, concepts, etc.
Cultural Prejudice Bias. Tendency to favor or oppose without sound reasons.
Cultural Prejudice Bigotry. Obstinate devotion to one's own ideas, causes, etc.
Cultural Separatism. Belief that certain groups should remain apart.

Cultural Shock. The anxiety a person experiences when his culture has been altered considerably or when he must confront a new culture.
Cultural Specialties. Particular tasks in a larger process: a dishwasher in a cafe, a wheelmounter on an assembly line.
Cultural Sterotype. Baseless but persistent image of persons or groups.
Cultural System. A system of beliefs, attitudes, and values.
Cultural Transmission Theory. A theory that attributes deviant behavior to conformity to social beliefs and to norms of a deviant cultural group to which an individual belongs.
Cultural Universal. A way of behaving common to all cultures or to all persons within a culture.
Cultural Universe. All those in a given category, e.g. bachelors.
Cultural Values. Conceptions of desirable states of affairs in a social system or culture group.
Cultural Visibility. Degree to which ethnic or racial traits are apparent.
Culture (*kul* chur). A state or condition of civilization, especially as related to standards of education, morals, attitudes, and intellect.
Cunnilingus (*kun* i *ling* us). Licking, sucking, or mouthing the female sex organ by a male or female.
Cure, Take the. Slang: Submit to medical treatment, usually at a hospital or sanatorium, to be cured of alcoholism or drug addiction.
Cursive Writing (*kur* sive). Handwriting, contrasted to hand printing.
Curtilage (*kur* te lij). The open space surrounding a dwelling that an average person would consider a part of the dwelling or living area, such as a yard surrounding the dwelling that is enclosed by a fence.
Custodial Officer (kus *tow* di al).

One charged with the keep, safety, and/or detention of persons in a prison, jail, or hospital. "The custodial officer is authorized by law to perform his tasks."

Custody (*kus* to de). Legal safekeeping.

Custom (*kus* tum). Practices or conventions of a group's actions. "Custom is to a group what habit is to an individual."

Cut. Slang: 1. Dilute drugs by adding milk sugar or another inert substance. 2. A share or percentage of money or property; commission. "The racketeer got a cut of all the earnings." 3. Gambling slang: To take a certain amount or percentage from a gambling game, such as a dice game. "The house took a cut."

Cut a Deal. Slang: The covert reaching of an agreement between the prosecutor and the defense that for a guilty plea the defendant will be charged with a less serious offense; secret plea bargaining.

Cut-Edge Dice. Gambling slang: Dice on which some of the edges have been cut at a greater degree than others. This will influence the roll of the dice.

Cuter. Slang: Prosecutor; a prosecuting attorney.

Cutout Card Markings. Gambling slang: The design on the back of the cards has been altered by chemical or mechanical means so that a different appearance is achieved, which can be detected by the cheat who knows about it.

Cutting. Gambling term: Taking a fixed fee or proportion of the amounts wagered while operating a card game.

Cut up the Score. Gambling slang: To divide the winnings.

Cyanide (*sigh* a nide). See **Potassium Cyanide.**

Cyanide Gun. A device used for propelling hydrocynic acid into the face of a murder victim. The acid vaporizes, causing death quickly, which resembles a heart attack. It has been used by some foreign secret agents. Reference: Salerno, Ralph et al.: *The Crime Confederation.* Garden City, New York, Doubleday, 1969, p. 372.

Cybernetics (*sigh* bur *net* iks). The field of science dealing with the principles of communication and control as applied to the operation of complicated machines and the actions of organisms. For example, the application of modern scientific management analysis technology and utilization of integrated information systems.

Cycle. A recurrence of procedures or events.

Cy-Pres Doctrine. As near as possible. A rule for the construction of instruments in equity, by which the intention of the party is carried out as near as it may be when it would be impossible or illegal to give it lateral effect.

D

D. Slang: LSD.

D.A. District Attorney. May also be called prosecuting attorney, prosecutor, or county prosecutor. This official is elected to office by the people of his district. He represents the people (state, county, etc.) in prosecution of criminal offenders.

Dabble. Slang: To take small amounts of drugs on an irregular basis.

Dactyloscopy (dack til *os* ko py). Fingerprints as a means of identification; the study of fingerprints and their use as a means of identification.

Daffy (*daf* e). Slang: Goofy, nonsensical, mentally deranged.

Dago Red. Slang: Any Italian red wine.

Daguerre's Process (da *gere*). The first photographic method used in criminal investigations. The system used wet plates. Each exposure required several minutes, and not more than one print could be made from each photograph.

DaGuerrotypes. Photographs printed on a copper plate covered with silver.

Daily Double. Horse racing term: A single bet is made on specified horses in designated races, which pays off if the particular horses win.

Daily Reports. A report, made daily, recording the work done by the officer during the day.

Daisy. Slang: A male homosexual, usually assuming the female role.

Daisy Chain. Slang: Several persons, usually sex perverts, having sexual relations with one another simultaneously.

Damages. 1. Money paid by, or ordered paid to, a person to compensate for injury, loss, etc. 2. The loss in value that is caused by an unlawful or wrongful act.

Damnify. To cause damage or hurt.

Damn Yankee. An expression formerly commonly used in the South referring to a person from the North. Originated during the Civil War.

Damper. Slang: Cash register.

D and D. Drunk and disorderly.

Dangerousness. The term designating the ranking of offenders and offenses along some sort of seriousness of violent process continuum. Generally denotes physical threat or harm rather than theft or property damage.

Dangerous Weapon. A weapon that is inherently dangerous, such as a firearm, or an instrument that, although not inherently dangerous, can be used to inflict death or serious injury.

Dapp, To Be. Juvenile slang: To be in style.

Dark. Secret, concealed, kept confidential. "I was kept in the dark about the matter."

Data Collection. Electronic data processing term: Incoming data. It is either added to a file on a real time basis or is stored for later file update on a batch basis.

Daub (dob as in cob). Gambling: A liquid or a paste that is used by a player to mark cards during play.

Dauber. Slang: A person who paints for a living.

Davis v. Mississippi, 394 U.S. 721

(1969). A landmark case holding that fingerprints taken as a result of an illegal arrest were inadmissible in evidence. Reference: Law enforcement legal commentaries. *Police.* May-June, 1971, p. 73.

Dawdle (*daw* del). To linger; loiter; waste time; to devote an unnecessary amount of time in doing something. "He dawdled at the dinner table."

Daydreaming. Idly indulging in fantasy during wakefulness. Part of one's fantasy life; an unsatisfied unconscious desire.

Day House. Gambling term: Daily playing of the Bolita game in the daytime.

Daytime. That part of the day when there is enough light to see by. Law: A "rule of thumb" criteria is that is is daytime when there is enough natural light to recognize a person's features at a distance of ten yards. This becomes important in connection with searches where the law and the search warrant specifies search during the daytime.

Daytop Village. A program for rehabilitating drug addicts. See **Therapeutic Community**.

Dead Body. A human corpse.

Dead-Born. An infant born dead. Legally such a child is considered never to have existed.

Deadline. Slang: Line beyond which a known criminal must not pass.

Deadly Weapon. A weapon that is likely to produce death.

Dead on Arrival (D.O.A.). Dead on arrival at a hospital.

Deadpan. Slang: No expression on the face.

Dead Pigeon. Slang: One who is finished; one in a situation where there is no hope; one who is defeated.

Dead Ringer. Slang: One who is similar in appearance to another.

Dead to Rights. Slang: Caught in the wrongful act or having overwhelming evidence that an act was committed.

Deal (deel). 1. To distribute cards to the players in a card game. 2. Slang: The reaching of an agreement. 3. The making of a secret or clandestine agreement.

Dealer. 1. Slang: Drug supplier. 2. Gambling slang: The person dealing. 3. Gambling slang: An operator of a game.

Death. Condition of being dead; permanent stopping of the functions of the vital organs. With the advent of vital organ transplants by surgery, the point of death has become a legal question upon which there is much discussion.

Death, Violent. A death caused by other than natural causes.

Death Penalty. The penalty for particular crimes, such as first degree murder or rape, is the loss of life of the offender.

Death Warrant. A written order issued by the legally authorized executive official (usually the governor) setting the place and time for executing one sentenced to death by the court.

Death Watch. Special guarding of a prisoner condemned to die, to prevent his escape or suicide.

Debauchery (dee *baw* sher ee). Overindulgence of the sexual appetites or activities; sensuality; sex orgy.

De Bene Esse. Latin: Conditionally; on condition.

De Bonis. Latin: Of goods or money.

Debris (dee *bree*). Trash, rubbish; worthless fragments or parts resulting from the destruction of something.

VOCABULARY

Debs. Juvenile slang: Girl affiliates of gang boys.
Debt. Something owed; an obligation.
Debtor (*de* tur). One who owes another; mortgage debtor—one who gives a mortgage on property to secure a debt owed to another.
Debtor's Prison. A prison during Revolutionary times for people who had accumulated debts. The debtors in prison were unable to take steps to liquidate their debts.
Decapitate (dee *dap* i tate). To behead; to cut off the head.
Decedent (dee *see* dent). One who has died, especially one recently dead.
Deceit. The act of representing as true what is known to be false.
Deceive (dee *seeve*). Mislead; defraud; cheat.
Decelerometer (dee *sel* e *rom* e tur). A device for measuring deceleration in connection with brake testing.
Decentralization. A style of police organization that is disguised for greater localized authority of the police.
Decipher (dee *sigh* fer). To determine the meaning of; to decode; to arrive at the meaning of secret characters.
Decision (dee *sizh* un). A court order, decree, or judgment on a question of law or fact. It differs from an opinion in that the latter is the basis of the decision.
Deck. Slang: Packet of narcotics.
Declaration of Intention. A necessary step in the procedure of an alien becoming an American citizen. In this step he renounces allegiance to his native country and expresses his intention of becoming a citizen of the United States.
Declaratory Judgement (dee *klare* a tow ry). A judgement that simply declares the rights of the parties or expresses the opinion of the court on the question of law, without ordering anything done. Its distinctive characteristics are that no executory process follows as a matter of course, nor is it necessary that an actual wrong, giving rise to the action for damages, should have been done or be immediately threatened.
Decline (dee *kline*). To refrain; turn down a proposition; refuse.
Decoy (*dee* koy). One whose role it is to lure a person into a situation where he may be the victim of a crime; one who assumes a role to divert attention away from another; to lure.
Decree. Legal order; judicial decision.
Dedbana. Saxon law: A homicide or manslaughter.
Deduce (dee *doose*). To reach a conclusion or arrive at an answer by reasoning.
Deed. A document under seal, which, when delivered, transfers a present interest in property.
Deeda. Slang: LSD, in Harlem.
Deem. To consider; to make. "The statute deems the act a crime."
Deface. To disfigure, mar, or alter the face or surface of something; to obliterate, alter, or destroy such things as inscriptions, writings, etc.
De Facto (dee *fak* tow). Latin: In fact, whether right or wrong.
De Facto Segregation. Actually existing as by residence distribution; as compared to *de jure*—in conformity with legal factors.
Defamation (deaf a *may* shun). The act of defaming another. Generally it is a violation of the criminal law and is the grounds for a civil action.
Defame (dee *faim*). To make slander-

ous statements about someone; to maliciously publish or express to any person, other than the one defamed, anything that tends to (1) expose any person to hatred, contempt, or ridicule or (2) expose the memory of one deceased to such things; to injure the good name or reputation of another. The legal definition of defamation will differ among the states.

Default (dee *falt*). 1. Fail to appear in court at an appointed or certain time. 2. Failure to pay a debt or obligation when due.

Defect. Something that makes any item inadequate for its proper use.

Defendent. One sued at law in a civil matter or prosecuted in a criminal action as a law violator.

Defense (dee *fence*). 1. The party (or his attorney) against whom an action in court is brought—civil or criminal. Under the adversary system used in our judicial system the two parties in a criminal action are the prosecution and the defense. 2. That which is offered or pleaded in denial of the charge against the accused.

Defense, Department of. Headed by the Secretary of Defense, it is an executive branch of the United States Government.

Defense Counsel. Counsel for the defendant; an attorney who represents and aids the defendant. The courts have held in recent years that the defendant has the right to counsel, either employed by the defendant or appointed by the court, to represent the defendant at each critical stage of the prosecutive procedure, as guaranteed by the Sixth Amendment of the United States Constitution.

Defensive Behavior. Reacting to outside forces.

Defensive Driving. Driving a motor vehicle so as to avoid accidents even though the other drivers may be at fault.

Defensive Tactics. Knowledge and skill in techniques used to defend one's self against physical injury. This is a most important area of knowledge and skill for an officer.

Defer (dee *fur*). Put off; postpone; delay to a future date.

Deferred Sentencing. A system in some states, provided by law, where the person convicted of a crime may be placed on probation immediately following the conviction or after he has served a term of imprisonment.

Deficiency Judgement. A creditor's claim against a debtor for that part of a judgement debt not satisfied by the sale of the mortgaged property.

Defile. To corrupt a woman of previously chaste character.

Defloration. Seduction or debauching.

Defraud. To cheat someone in a business transaction; to swindle; to deprive a person of anything of value by trickery or deceit.

Degenerate (de *jen* e rit). One who is morally degraded; morally bankrupt.

Degree (dee *gree*). 1. A relative ranking of things or events; relative quantity or importance. In criminal law, the ranking of crimes according to seriousness. 2. A scholastic rank of attainment.

Dehorn. Slang: Common alcoholic bum.

De Jure (*dee jure*). Latin: Legally right; by right.

Delay (dee *lay*). Law: Continue; postpone; put off, as in the action of the court or its orders.

Delegate. To give someone authority to represent the giver in performing certain acts.

VOCABULARY

Deliberate. 1. To consider a matter carefully; to discuss with others and carefully weigh the facts. 2. Not sudden, impulsive, or done on the "spur of the moment." Thought carefully prior to acting.

Delineate (de *len* e ate). To illustrate or explain by sketching, drawing, or charting.

Delinquent Child. A young person of less than a specified age who violates the law or who is incorrigible.

Delinquency (de *ling* kwen see). Wrongful deeds or acts; the condition of being a law violator; the failure to live up to specified standards.

Delirium Tremens (dee *lear* e um *tree* menz). Violent temporary spells of mental disturbance, manifested by disordered speech, confusion, trembling, and/or hallucinations. Caused by prolonged heavy use of alcoholic beverages, usually liquors.

Deliver. 1. To rescue or set free. 2. To aid in the birth of a baby.

Delta (*del* ta). A formation or character detail in fingerprints used in classifying the pattern. It is that point on a ridge at or nearest the point of divergence of two typelines and is located at or directly in front of the point of divergence.

Delusion (dee *lu* zhun). A belief or attitude that, although erroneous, is not corrected by reason.

De Malo. Latin: Of sickness; of infirmity.

Demand. To seek legal relief. Also, the relief sought.

Demented. Mentally deranged; insane; crazy.

Dementia (dee *men* shia). Mental deterioration, having symptoms of apathy, impairment of memory, confusion, and lowering of willpower and reasoning power.

Dementia Praecox. An outdated term for schizophrenia.

Demerol® (*dim* e rall). A synthetic equivalent of opiate drugs. Controlled by federal law.

De Minimis. Latin: Very small or trifling matters the law does not care for, or take notice of.

Democracy. A form of government in which the nation's (or state's) power resides in the people. If it is participated in directly by all the people it is a pure democracy. If the people give the power to representatives to speak for them it is a representative democracy.

Demographic (dee mow *graf* ick). Pertaining to the statistical study of the dynamic changes in population, such as births, deaths, marriages, health, etc.

Demography (de *mog* gra fee). The study of human population, birth and death rates, and migration.

Demonstration. A display of feelings, manifested by parades, meetings, exhibiting placards, shouting, speeches, sit-down actions, etc.

Demonstrative Evidence. Evidence that speaks for itself, such as real or physical evidence. Evidence that the jury can see and use in arriving at a conclusion without the necessity of explaining the nature of the evidence.

Demotion (de *mow* shen). A reduction in rank or position.

Demurrer (dee *mur* rer). A legal procedural pleading to the effect that, granting the other side's pleadings are true, they do not constitute a good cause of action.

Demur (de *mur*). Object; take exceptions.

Denounce (dee *now* unz). Attack or

condemn; accuse someone of wrongdoing; to inform on someone.
De Novo. Latin; Law: As new; anew; all over again. When an appellate court reviews a case of an inferior court, the case is heard de novo, i.e. it is tried again in its entirety.
Density (*den* si tee). The quantity per unit volume, unit area, or unit length.
Deny (de *ni*). Refute; claim a statement is untrue; contradict.
Department. The department of highways.
Depersonalization (dee *purse* na li *zay* shun). The condition of one losing his identity; the state of a person believing he is someone else.
Deponent. The person who deposes and makes a written statement under oath; an affiant.
Deport (dee *port*). To eject on from a country; to send one from the country.
Deposition (dep o *zish* un). Law: Sworn testimony obtained out of court.
Depraved (dee *praved*). Wicked; perverted.
Depressant (dee *press* ent). A drug that has a calming effect on the nervous system of a person; a sedative; a tranquilizer. The barbiturate family of drugs is most frequently encountered in this category. Some of the slang names for depressants are down, barbs, redbirds, yellow jackets, goofballs, blue heavens, etc.
Deprive (dee *prive*). To take away something a person has the right to; to dispossess.
Depth Perception. The ability to determine the distance of things seen with the eyes.
Deputy Sheriff. Under-sheriff; an officer duly commissioned who is appointed to work for and under the direction of the sheriff.
Derangement (dee *rainj* ment). Unsoundness of mind (except in the case of an idiot).
Derby. Cockfighting: A free-for-all cockfight in which four to eight cocks are matched and put in the pit.
Derivative Evidence (de *riv* a tiv). Evidence obtained as the result of information obtained by a pervious act or statement, such as search of premises which furnished leads upon which the later evidence was found. The same would hold where a statement or confession is the basis of obtaining the derivative evidence. If the first acts were illegal then the derivative evidence comes into the "fruits of the poisonous tree" category and is inadmissable. See **Fruit of the Poisonous Tree.**
Dermal Nitrate Test. Also called the Paraffin Test; determines whether an individual has recently fired a weapon.
Derogatory (de *rog* a tor ee). Bad; degrading; disparaging. "He spoke in a derogatory manner about the man."
Derrick. Slang: A thief who steals very valuable items.
Description (de *skrip* shun). Information related in words, obtained by means of the senses of sight, hearing, feeling, smelling, and taste; an account of things, persons, or events. "The ability of description is of vital importance to an officer."
Desecrate (*dess* eh krate). To desanctify; to profane; to degrade something sacred.
Desert (de *zert*). To abandon; to leave one's post of duty without authority or permission. "He will not desert his wife and children."
Desertion (de *zer* shun). 1. Law: The

VOCABULARY

foresaking or abandonment of one's wife and children. 2. Military law: The unauthorized leaving or abandonment of one's place of duty or assignment, with the intention not to return, by one who is a member of the military organization.

Deshonra. Spanish law: The seduction of a woman.

Designer. Slang: A term used by counterfeiters for the person who does the counterfeiting.

Desist (dee *sist*). To cease doing something. "The person disturbing the peace was ordered to desist in his actions."

Desperado (*des* per *ah* doe). A criminal; a lawbreaker; generally denotes a dangerous outlaw—one who is desperate enough to cause harm if encountered.

Detail (*dee* tale). Law enforcement: A group of officers assigned to a certain task; a specified assignment. "I was assigned to the worthless check detail."

Detain (dee *tane*). To stop someone and prevent his freedom of action for a period (usually a short period) of time; to interfere with one's freedom of movement or actions.

Detainer (dee *tane* ur). Law: A request placed with authorities of a jail or prison asking that a named person incarcerated in such jail or prison not be released until the requesting authority is notified, inasmuch as the requesting authority seeks custody of such person. This may be in the form of a letter only or a letter accompanied by formal documents supporting the charge against the prisoner.

Detection. The discovery of a crime.

Detective (dee *tek* tiv). A person who detects; usually a law enforcement officer, but there are many private (nonpolice) detectives (private eyes). Many detectives work in civilian dress and therefore are commonly called plainclothes officers. Usually the more experienced officers work as detectives.

Detention (dee *ten* shun). The state of being detained. See **Detain**.

Detention, Preventive. See **Preventive Detention**.

Detention Center. A correctional institution where juveniles are held until their hearing.

Detention in a Reformatory. A short-term confinement for juveniles.

Deterrence, General (dee *turr* ence). The threat of punishment, which is directed to all members of society and which seeks to restrain them from engaging in criminal conduct.

Deterrence, Specific. The preventive effect of actual punishment on the offender, so that he does not repeat his crime.

Detonating Cord (*det* oh nay ting). A highly explosive cordlike object containing PETN.

Detonator (*det* oh nay terr). See **Blasting Cap**.

Detoxification, Alcohol (dee *toks* i fi *day* shun). The process of becoming sober after having been extremely intoxicated.

Detoxification Center. A facility equipped to detain and treat alcoholics (drunks) with medical services and therapy by psychologists and psychiatrists and to provide for aftercare of such patients.

Deuce. Slang: 1. In card playing, a two. 2. Two spots on a die, or two ones on a pair of dice. 3. A two-dollar bill. 4. A two-year prison sentence. 5. Devil; hard luck.

Deuce and a Quarter. Slang: Buick Electra 225.

Deuce Bag. Slang: A two-dollar container of a drug.

Develop. 1. To work out by steps and in detail. "The case developed slowly." 2. To create or bring into being. "I will develop him as a confidential informant." 3. To process exposed film. "The laboratory will develop the film for you."

Deviate (*dee* vee et). A person who is abnormal or different from the usual person. "A sex deviate is a person with an abnormal sex problem."

Divided Highway. Any highway divided into roadways by a median, physical barrier, or clearly indicated dividing section so constructed as to impede vehicular traffic.

Devil on the Neck. An instrument used to torture persons in order to obtain confessions.

Devise. A gift of real property by will.

Dexedrine® (*dex* oh dreen). A stimulant used by the medical profession for weight reducing. Considered potentially dangerous but not addicting if taken as prescribed.

Dexies. Slang: Stimulant drugs; amphetamines (Dexedrine®).

Dextroamphetamine Sulfate (*dex* tro am *fet* a mean *sul* fate). A stimulant—a member of the amphetamine drug family. In orange-colored, heart-shaped tablets known as hearts, oranges, or dexies.

Diabetes (die a *bee* teez). A disease characterized by frequent and excessive urination. Sugar diabetes is the most dangerous form. This is caused by improper secretion of the pancreas, resulting in the inability of the body to properly utilize sugars. The condition may result in a semiconscious or dazed condition or becoming fully unconscious (diabetic coma). The officer may confuse a person in this condition with one in a state caused by intoxication with drugs or alcohol.

Diabetic Coma (die a *bet* ik). Unconsciousness resulting from sugar diabetes.

Dial (Safe). A graduated circular moveable plate, which is an outward part of a combination lock used on "combination" padlocks and safe locks.

Dialectics. The process of debate or reason that follows the premises of logic.

Dice. 1. Two die—cubes with spots on each of six sides numbered from one to six, used in playing dice, craps, and other games. 2. A gambling game played with dice, usually found in gambling establishments.

Dice are Off. Gambling term: Dice that have been altered in some way that has made them untrue.

Dice Degenerate. Gambling term: A crap player who has become compulsive to a point where he can no longer control the urge to gamble.

Dice Hustler. Slang: Professional crap shooter.

Dice Mob. Gambling term: A group of people operating a crooked dice game.

Dichotomy (die *kot* oh mee). A division into two parts or lines. In charting the organizational structure (chain of command) of a police agency from the chief downward, there is a dichotomy when line and staff are shown.

Dick. Slang: A law enforcement officer.

Dictum (*dik* tum). Law: A statement, observation, or opinion made by a judge or court that does not necessarily pertain to issues being tried in the case at hand. It does not have the

VOCABULARY

force of law but shows how the court thinks on such matters.

Die (dye). A tool or instrument, usually made of steel or other hard substance, with which letters or numbers are stamped on objects made of metal or other hard material. They are usually used to identify such items through the letters or numbers.

Diethyltryptamine (dye ethel *tript* a mean). A hallucenogenic drug, chemically prepared, known by the slang name of DET.

Differential Association Theory. A theory of criminal behavior linking criminal behavior to primary groups, reference groups, and subcultures. This theory holds that deviance is learned from deviants.

Differential Treatment. Applying different degrees or types of enforcement at different times and places, or upon the same people at different times, as in the selective enforcement—on every fifth violator, or on youth only, or on certain days—Or in discretionary use of police power by command, or invested in the officer himself, or in "saturation patrols" in crime areas.

Dig. Slang: Understand.

Digital Communication. A communication system that includes a device installed in the radio console of a patrol car, which contains prearranged messages that can be transmitted by pressing special keys on the radio console.

Digits. Juvenile slang: Numbers racket.

Dike (dyke). Slang: Bulldyke—a large, masculine woman.

Dilatory (*dill* a tow re). 1. For the purpose of delay; causing delay or postponement. 2. Law: for the purpose of causing delay or to gain time.

Dilatory Exceptions. Those exceptions and motions filed for the purpose of retarding progress of the case but which do not tend to defeat the charges.

Dildock. Cards: A person who uses a crooked deck of cards.

Dime. 1. Professional gamblers' word for a bet of $1,000.00. 2. Gambling term: Betting term for ten dollars.

Dime Bag. Slang: Ten-dollar package of narcotics.

Dimethyltrytpamine (die methel *tript* a mean). DMT—a hallucinogenic drug.

Dinero. 1. Slang: Money. 2. The Spanish word for money.

Diplomatic (dip lo *mat* ic). Having tact or skill in dealing with people.

Diplomatic Immunity. The immunity from ordinary processes of our laws enjoyed by members of the diplomatic corps (ambassadors, consuls, etc.) and their staffs.

Dipsomania (dip se *may* ne uh). The uncontrollable urge or desire for alcoholic drink or other intoxicants.

Dipsy-Doodle. Slang: Deception; trickery; craftiness.

Direct. 1. Gambling term: Relates to the type of bet made prior to the arrest when the arresting officer makes the play with the bookie or his runner. 2. To supervise; to order things done through vested authority.

Direct Contempt of Court. Any contempt committed in the presence of the court or the failure to comply with a summons, subpoena, or order to appear in court.

Directed Verdict. An order or verdict pronounced by a judge during the trial of a criminal case where the evidence presented by the prosecu-

tion clearly fails to show the guilt of the accused.
Direct Evidence. See **Evidence, Direct.**
Direction Line. One of the elements in the walking picture. It is the indication of the direction in which the walker is moving. See **Walking Picture.**
Director. A member of the board chosen to direct the affairs of a corporation or an institution.
Dirk. A knife.
Dirt Horse. Racetrack slang: A horse on which one has received a tip; a "hot" horse.
Dirty. Slang: Possessing narcotics; liable to arrest if searched.
Discharge. 1. Law: To release one from contractual or other legal obligation; to release one from a situation. 2. The release of someone; the dismissal of one from his employment. 3. The shooting of a firearm.
Discharge in Bankruptcy. An action by which the insolvent party is released from the obligation of all his debts.
Disciplinary Procedures. Can be internal (within the department) or external, as by a civilian review board, or it can be the result of an inquiry by an ombudsman.
Discipline. 1. Order or obedience as a result of training. 2. A particular field of education or learning. 3. To punish.
Discourteous. Rude; ungentlemanly; not polite.
Discovery. Any disclosure that a defendant is compelled to make, as of facts or documents.
Discreet (dis *kreet*). Diplomatic; prudent; tactful.
Discretion (dis *kresh* in). The opportunity to use one's own judgement in a matter; to act as seems best by the actor.
Discretionary Funds. Action funds (15% of total action grant appropriation under section 306) of the Omnibus Crime Control and Safe Streets Act of 1968, which the Law Enforcement Assistance Administration can allocate to grantees by discretion.
Discrimination (dis crim i *nay* shun). 1. Actions taken as a result of racism, sexism, etc. 2. The ability to understand what is being said.
Disenfranchisement. The taking away of the right to vote from a person who otherwise would be entitled the right.
Disguise (dis *guys*). To change appearance so as not to be recognized; alter the usual appearance of something.
Dishonest. Not honest; prone to cheat, lie, or steal.
Dishonor. To refuse or fail to pay a check, draft, bill of exchange, etc.
Disinter (dis in *tur*). To remove from the grave; exhume.
Dismiss (dis *miss*). Law: To end the case in court; to terminate the charges against the accused.
Disorder (dis *or* der). Riotous behavior; confusion of actions; disturbance of the peace.
Disorderly Conduct. Action, defined by statute, pertaining to the disturbing of the peace and which is contrary to the law; that which offends the public sense of morality. A demonstration by a group may fall into this category if it goes beyond the First Amendment rights to peaceably assemble and petition for grievances.
Disorderly House. A house that is bad for public morals, such as a

house of prostitution or a gambling house.

Disorderly Persons. A term for people who disturb the public peace and welfare.

Disparagement. Statements or insinuations used to discredit or to lower in esteem; to depreciate.

Dispatcher. Gambling slang: Improperly marked dice.

Disperse (dis *purse*). To scatter; to drive away; make people go away.

Dispersion (dis *per* shun). The separation of light waves into their component wavelengths.

Disposition. The outcome or culmination of a criminal case, i.e. charges dismissed, found not guilty, guilty, the sentence pronounced, etc.

Disqualification. Depriving one from participating in a proceeding due to a condition or some irregularity. A juror, because of prejudice or bias, may be disqualified from serving on the jury. A judge may disqualify himself from conducting a trial because of some interest in the case, because of personal relationship to one or more of the parties, or because of bias or prejudice.

Disruptive Defendant. See **Courtroom Disruptions**.

Dissent (dis *sent*). The opinion of the judge, or judges on a multijudge court, giving a minority view of all or some part of the majority holding in the case being decided. The expression of the judge who does not agree with the verdict of the majority of the court.

Dissident. Differing; not in accord with existing policy, rules, or laws; opposing; dissenting. One who disagrees with existing policies, etc.

Dissolve. Legal term: To annul or set aside an order such as an injunction.

Dissuade. A law against advising a person not to do an act. For example, persuading someone not to testify.

Distance Meter. See **Range Finder**.

District Attorney. See **D.A.**

District Court. In the federal court system it is the court of original criminal jurisdiction and a court of record. One such court is located in each federal judicial district, and the court has jurisdiction over matters of that district. Several states have district courts, which are state courts of original jurisdiction. The district over which they have jurisdiction may be composed of one or more counties. They are similar to county courts in other states.

District Court of Appeals. The first appellate court beyond the superior court level.

District Judge. A judge of a United States District Court or a state district court.

Disturb (dis *turb*). Agitate; disarrange; create disorder; upset the peace and tranquility.

Disturbing the Peace. A criminal charge for interfering with the peace, quiet, orderliness, and tranquility of a community.

Dive. Joint, flophouse; jungle; hangout.

Diversion. A program providing for treatment of an arrested person rather than a jail or prison sentence by diverting him out of the criminal justice system and into a treatment program. Also refers to halting or suspending, before conviction, formal criminal proceedings against a person on the condition or assumption that he or she will do something in return.

Diversion Programs. Programs designed to prevent defendants from being convicted and incarcerated or from reaching the trial state by providing them with specialized treatment resources.

Diversity (die *ver* sity). A plea by a prisoner in court that he is not the same one that was attained.

Do. Slang: To swindle or cheat.

Docimasia Pulmonum. Medical term: A test to determine if a child was born alive or dead.

Doctrine of Parene Patriae. See **Parens Patriae**.

Dolophine®. Methadone.

Domestic (do *mess* tik). Household; home.

Domicile (*dom* i sile). Residence; place of permanent residence.

Domineering (*dom* i neer ing). Arrogant; haughty; despotic.

Dominicide. The act of killing one's lord or master.

Domino. Slang: To purchase drugs.

Don, The. Synonymous with the "Boss" in the Cosa Nostra.

Donnegan Workers. See **Toilet Workers**.

Door Shaker. Slang: Police officer; night watchman; police officer whose job it is to check doors at night—usually of business establishments.

Dope. Slang: Any narcotic or drug.

Dope Fiend. Slang: A narcotics addict; an addict to any drugs.

Doper. Slang: Person who uses drugs regularly.

Dorian Love. Sex deviation term: The love for young males.

Dorsal. Anatomy term: The back or spine portion of the body.

Dose. Slang: A venereal disease, especially gonorrhea or syphilis.

Dot. 1. A very short ridge in fingerprint pattern. 2. See **Microscopic Dot**.

Do Them Up In. Juvenile slang: Soundly thrash someone.

Do Time. Slang: To serve time in a prison or jail on a criminal conviction.

Dotting. Slang: Placing LSD on a sugar cube.

Double Action. Firearms term: The operation of the revolver where the weapon is cocked and fired with one pull of the trigger.

Double Adultery. Adultery where both parties are married to others.

Double-Base Powder. A powder where the explosive ingredients are nitrocellulose and nitroglycerine.

Double-Cross. Slang: To be treacherous; to be double dealing; to do other than that promised. Also can mean double-scored amphetamine tablets.

Double Dealing. Slang: Unethical, insincere dealings.

Double Indemnity. A clause in life insurance policies providing for the payment of twice the face value of the contract in case of accidental death.

Double Jeopardy. Being prosecuted more than once for the same offense. The time for the beginning of jeopardy differs among the states.

Double Loop. A fingerprint pattern. Also known as twin loop. It contains two separate and distinct sets of shoulders and two deltas.

Double Park. To park a vehicle alongside another that is in a space specified for parking.

Double Sawbuck. Slang: A twenty-dollar bill.

Double the Line. Gambler's term: Bookmaker's payoff at double the rate as an inducement to a customer.

Double Trouble. Narcotics slang: Amobarbital sodium combined with secobarbital sodium in red and blue capsule form.

VOCABULARY

Double-Up. Gambling game. See **Razzle Dazzle**.

Doubt, Reasonable. "A 'reasonable doubt' is such a doubt as would cause a reasonable and prudent man in the graver and more important affairs of life to pause and hesitate to act upon the truth of the matter charged. But a reasonable doubt is not a mere possibility of innocence, not a caprice, shadow, or speculation as to innocence not arising out of the evidence or the want of it" (*Black's Law Dictionary;* see this source for other definitions). See **Beyond a Reasonable Doubt**.

Dough. Slang: Money.

Doup. Slang: Smoke a joint or take an injection of heroin.

Dove. Slang: One who was opposed to the United States war activities in South Vietnam (1969).

Down. Slang: Aftereffects of marijuana.

Downers. Slang: Depressant drugs—barbiturates. See **Depressant**.

Down Stud. Slang: An OK fellow; a close friend.

Draconian Code (dray *kone* ee en). An early Greek code of laws, which meted out very harsh penalties (usually death) for most offenses.

Draft. 1. Law and commerce: A bill of exchange; a written order to a person, bank, etc., for the payment of money to another; a check. 2. Military: Selection of men for compulsory military service through the United States Selective Service System. 3. Juvenile slang: An ultimatum—join the gang or get beaten up.

Drag Factor. See **Friction, Coefficient of**.

Dragging. Juvenile slang: Harassing.

Dragnet (*drag* net). Maximum facilities utilized to catch a criminal.

Drag Race. Slang: A race to test acceleration, generally by two cars competing over a measured distance.

Dramamine® (*dram* e mean). Drug used to relieve or prevent motion sickness.

Drawing and Charting. See **Sketching**.

Dreamer. Slang: Morphine.

Dreams. Slang: Opium pellets for opium eating.

Drifter. Slang: 1. One who wanders from place to place. 2. Member of the underworld who is without prestige among his peers.

Drift Method. Safe burglar's technique for opening a safe. A tool known as a drift punch is used to drive the lock spindle into the safe.

Driver. A person who controls a motor vehicle.

Drivers. Slang: Stimulant drugs—amphetamines. See **Stimulants**.

Driver's Seat. Gambling term: To have the best hand showing in stud poker. To have won most of the money in a game of poker.

Driver Training, Police. Training to equip a police officer with the ability to drive a vehicle more effectively and safely regardless of his prior driving experience.

Driving While Intoxicated (DWI). Driving while under the influence and effect of alcohol.

Dromomania. A compulsion to wander combined with restlessness.

Drop. Slang: 1. To swallow a drug. 2. To murder someone. 3. In a numbers game it is the apparently legitimate business place that is used as a front for illegal activities. 4. A bookie establishment or an operator working for a booking business. 5. Firearms term: The degree to which the stock of a gun is bent downward from a line with the barrel.

Drop a Dime. Juvenile slang: Give me a dime; implicate; inform.

Drop Box. Gambling: A locked cash box under a roulette, crap, or blackjack table, where the money buying the chips is placed through a slot in the table.

Dropped. Slang: Arrested.

Drop Shot. Firearms term: Soft shot, usually made with lead.

Drown. To suffocate as the result of liquids in sufficient quantities gaining entry to the breathing passages to produce a lack of oxygen to the vital organs of the body.

Drownproofing. A technique for water safety whereby a person allegedly can avoid drowning for a long period of time without overexertion. Developed by Fred R. Lanque.

Drug. Medicine; narcotic; dope. A substance (not a food) that produces a change in the body. If beneficial it is a medicine; if harmful to the body it is a poison.

Drug Abuse. The improper use of legal drugs; the use of illegal drugs.

Drug Addict. One who has become addicted to the use of drugs. See **Addiction**.

Drug on the Market. Slang: Something that is too abundant to have much sales demand.

Drugs, Controlled. The drugs that are subject to legal restrictions, such as provided by Drug Abuse Control Amendments of the Food, Drug, and Cosmetic Act (federal). They are known as depressant, stimulant, and hallucinogenic drugs. This category is also covered by state legislation.

Drugs, Dangerous. Drugs, other than the hard narcotics, that have proven harmful if used other than as prescribed by a reputable physician. These drugs have been regulated by law—federal and state. See **Depressants, Stimulants, Hallucinogens**.

Drum. Slang: A jail cell.

Drunk. Intoxicated.

Drunk Drivers. Automobile drivers driving while intoxicated.

Dry-Fire. To go through the actions of firing a weapon without it being loaded; to practice firing a gun while it is empty. "We will dry-fire the pistol before we start target shooting."

Dry Heaves. Painful simulation of vomiting, but in which nothing is in the digestive tract to vomit; often caused by acute intoxification.

Dual Citizenship. Citizenship both of the United States and of a state. The Fourteenth Amendment of the United States Constitution says, "All persons born or naturalized in the United States, and subject to the jurisdiction thereof, are citizens of the United States and of the State wherein they reside."

Dual Court System. The courts of the United States can be conceptualized as belonging to one of two court systems: state or federal.

Dubbe. Slang: Negro slang for a marijuana roach.

Dubois Clubs, W.E.B. (doo *boys*). An organization for young people founded in San Francisco in 1964 and called the W.E.B. Dubois Clubs of America. It allegedly was founded and is financed by the Communist Party.

Dude. Prison slang: Another inmate (term used by many younger inmates).

Due Care. The suitable amount of care a reasonable man would take in

VOCABULARY

order to avoid harm to himself or to things.

Due Process of Law. Law: The right of every person to have legal proceedings according to the rules and principles that have been established in our system of law and jurisprudence for the enforcement and protection of private rights. The rights are given through the Fifth and Fourteenth Amendments of the United States Constitution. Commonly called "due process."

Duffer. Slang: Bread.

Dukes. Slang: Hands or fists.

Dum Dum. Slang: A gang strong man.

Dummy. Slang: Purchase that did not contain narcotics.

Dummy Up. Slang: Refuse to answer incriminating questions.

Dump. Slang: To get rid of something; to abandon an idea or an object.

Dumper. Sport gambler's term: A fixed game.

Duncan Case. A decision of the United States Supreme Court [Duncan v. Louisiana, 88 S.Ct. 1444 (1968)], holding that where state statutes provided maximum penalties of two years imprisonment and/or a fine of up to $300.00, it was serious enough to entitle the defendant to a jury trial, even though the offense was a misdemeanor and did not involve imprisonment at hard labor.

Dunsky. Slang: A victim.

Duquenois Reaction. A chemical test for identifying marijuana.

Duress (doo *ress*). Compulsion; coercion to do something unwillingly. A confession cannot be introduced in evidence if duress was used in obtaining it.

Durham Rule. A legal rule or test dealing with the mentally ill and their responsibility for crime. Under this rule, handed down by a United States Circuit Court [Durham v. United States, 214 F. 2d 862 (D.C. Cir. 1954)], a person is not held responsible for his criminal act if a mental disease caused him to commit the crime.

Dust. Slang: Cocaine, heroin.

Dusted. Juvenile slang: Beaten up.

Duster Door. Slang: Second or inner door of a safe.

Dyer Act. The federal law dealing with the interstate transportation of stolen motor vehicles; more commonly referred to as the ITSMV: Interstate Transportation of Stolen Motor Vehicles.

Dying Declaration. A statement, written or oral, obtained from a person who is the victim of the fatal injury caused by the person on trial for the offense that resulted in the death of the victim. The person giving the statement must be in extremis (at the point of death), must realize his dying condition, and must have given up all hope of recovery. If living, the victim (declarant) would have been a competent witness. The statement must only pertain to the circumstances that produced the condition resulting in death. The victim must have died as the result of the injury caused by the accused. The dying declaration is admissible as an exception to the hearsay rule, on the theory that a person who realizes he is dying will speak the truth. See **In Extremis, Hearsay Rule.**

Dynamite (*die* na might). 1. An explosive material consisting of nitroglycerin impregnated into some inert material. It is generally made in "sticks" and is of different strengths, depending upon the percentage of nitroglycerin as compared with inert material. It is classified as "high" explosive. 2. Slang: Cocaine; a mixture of cocaine and heroin.

Dyspareunia. Medical term: Incapacity of a woman to have sexual intercourse.

E

Ear. Gambling term: A folded corner of a playing card used to identify or locate it in the deck.

Ear Print. The imprint of the ear, showing its structure and contour. Can be made by inking the ear, as in fingerprinting and pressing cardboard or paper against it, thus transferring the print.

Earshot. Distance a sound can be heard. "He could not hear us calling because he was out of earshot."

Easement (*eez* ment). A right or privilege that a person may have in another's land, as the right to pass through.

Easterner. A term used to describe one from the eastern part of the United States.

Easy. Slang: To be easy is to be easily influenced or easy to get money or favors from.

Easy Mark. Slang: A person who is easily victimized; easily fooled or swindled.

Easy Money Guy. Gambling term: A person who gambles and spends money freely, without restraint.

Ea-Tay. Slang: Marijuana.

Eavesdropping (*eevz* drop ping). Clandestine (usually secret) hearing of a conversation that was not intended for the hearer. Wiretapping and the use of electronic "bugs" to hear (and/or record) private conversations, is often referred to as "electronic eavesdropping" or "electronic surveillance."

Eccentricity (ek sen *triss* it ee). Personal peculiarities of a person's mind that make him different from the average person but not enough to be considered insane.

Ecchymosis (ek i *moe* sis). Discoloration under the skin; a black and blue spot.

Ecclesiastic (ek *lee* zee *ass* tik). Pertaining to the Church (body of members or the physical plant).

Ecouteur (eh koo *tur*). A person who gains the most sexual pleasure through the audio senses.

Ecstasy Intoxication (*ek* stess ee). The period of time when a sadist attains the peak of his emotional reaction from his acts.

Edge Markings. Gambler slang: Also known as edge work; marks placed on playing cards between the edge and the design. The locations of the markings designate the card, i.e. ace, king, etc.

Edge Work. Gambling term: Card marking. See **Edge Markings**.

Eed-Waggles. Slang: Marijuana.

Eed-Way. Slang: Marijuana.

Eel. Slang: Elusive individual; one who eludes detection or apprehension by the police.

Effectiveness. The extent to which the criminal justice process (or any agency or individual functionary therein) achieves its objectives in a manner consistent with its long-range responsibilities. Effectiveness requires clear objectives and the capacity to achieve them.

Effeminate (ef *fem* in net). Womanly, having womanly traits, sissy.

Effeminated Man. Sex deviation term: Homosexual male who plays the passive role. Such a person feels and acts in the role of a woman.

Efficiency Report (ef *fish* en see). A performance evaluation report; personnel performance report.

Egg. 1. Gambling term: Sucker. 2. The female gamete in the reproductive system.

Ego Games. Slang: A deprecative term applied by LSD users to social conformity and to normal activities, occupations, and responsibilities of the majority of people.

Egress (ee *gres*). To go out of a structure or building. The means of exit from an enclosure, such as a building.

Eighty-Sixer. A tightwad victim.

Ejaculation (ee *jak* you *lay* shun). Emission of seminal fluid; sexual climax by the male.

Ejectment (ee *jekt* ment). Dispossession; expulsion; removal.

Ejector (ee *jek* tor). Firearms term: A device for ejecting used cartridges or shells from the gun barrel. "The crime laboratory examines the ejector markings on a cartridge case."

Elector (ee *lek* tor). One who is legally qualified to vote; a voter. One who has been chosen by the people to be a member of the Electoral College and thus to formally elect the president and vice-president of the United States.

Electric Dice. Magnetically controlled dice; dice that have been loaded with metal so as to be attracted and controlled by an electric magnet located under the surface on which the dice are rolled.

Electrocute (ee *lek* troh cute). To kill by means of electricity.

Electron (ee *lek* tron). The negatively charged particle of an atom.

Electronic Eavesdropping (ee lek *tron* ik). Listening and/or recording sounds (conversations) clandestinely or where such information or conversations may be pertinent to an investigation. A type of audio surveillance.

Electronic Surveillance (sir *vail* ens). Electronic eavesdropping.

Electron Microscope. An optical device that produces a greatly magnified image of small particles by using a beam of electrons.

Eleemosynary (el i *moss* en ay ree). 1. Of or for charity or alms; charitable. 2. Supported by or dependent upon charity.

Element. A compound consisting of atoms all with the same atomic number and structure.

Elevator. Slang: A holdup man.

Elinquation (ell in *kway* shun). Being punished by having one's tongue cut out.

Elongated Bullet. A bullet that is longer than it is wide. The opposite of a round bullet.

Elude (ee *lood*). To escape, dodge, or slip away from. "The criminal eluded the police."

Embalm (em *balm*). To chemically treat a corpse to prevent decay.

Embassy (*em* bas see). The official residence or official establishment of an ambassador in a foreign country.

Embezzle (em *bez* el). To convert to one's own use, by fraud or trickery, property (money or securities) entrusted to the offender's care or custody; to steal something (money or securities) entrusted to the care of the person stealing it. "The cashier at the bank embezzled the money."

Embolism (*em* boe lizm). Blocking of a blood vessel by a mass, such as a clot or other substance.

Embraceor (im *bray* sur). A person who commits the crime of embracery.

Embracery (im *brace* er ee). Attempting to influence a juror by using some corrupt means.

Emergency Childbirth. The birth of a child under emergency conditions,

VOCABULARY

such as in a police car while the mother is being rushed to the hospital. Officers should know the fundamentals of handling such situations.

Emetic (ee *met* ik). Drug or treatment that causes vomiting.

Emigrate (*em* i grate). To leave one's country or region to take residence in another country or region.

Emission. Medical term: The secretion of any fluid matter from the body, e.g. sweat, urine, etc.

Emission Spectrum (*speck* trum). Light that is shone through a medium and broken up into its various frequencies.

Emmenagogue (eh *men* ah gog). Medical term: A type of medicine that produces the menstrual discharge. It is sometimes used to produce abortions.

Emotional Insanity. A mental condition caused by violent excitement, causing normal reasoning to become impaired.

Empathy (*em* path ee). Understanding of another's feelings and motives.

Empirical (em *peer* i cul). Based on experience and observation; based on established facts.

Emplead. To accuse.

Emulsion (ee *mull* shun). Light-sensitive coating on camera film.

Emulsion Speed. Photographic term: The speed of an emulsion (sensitivity) in reacting to light. It is usually stated as a factor or number, either by ASA rating or values assigned by the light meter (exposure meter) manufacturers.

Enact (en *act*). To legislate; to make into law by a legislature or other such body.

Enclosure (en *kloe* zher). A fingerprint term describing a ridge line separation (bifurcation) that later meets again to form an enclosure.

Encumbrance (en *cum* brens). A lien, charge, or claim attached to the real or personal property of another, such as a mortgage.

End. Gambling term: A share; how much you can win after a game, race, etc. is over.

Endanger (en *dane* jer). Cause danger to.

Ending Ridge. A ridge, in a fingerprint pattern, that ends abruptly.

Endorse (Indorse) (en *dors*). Write one's name and/or instructions on the back of a check; to approve of something or a person.

Energy. The ability of a system to do work.

Enforcer, The. In the organizational structure of the Cosa Nostra, the one who uses force or fear to maintain internal discipline and security and who threatens or uses physical force against persons in order to achieve goals of the organization. The "strong-arm" man.

Engine, The. Underworld slang: The opium pipe and paraphernalia.

Ensel. Slang: Morphine.

Entrapment (en *trap* ment). The act of a law enforcement officer, or his agent, inducing a person to commit a crime not planned by him, or in a case where the person would not otherwise do so, in order to prosecute him for the crime.

Entry. Horse racing term: All horses of one trainer or one stable.

Entry, Illegal. The unlawful entering of any house, building, or structure with the intent to commit a crime.

Enuresis (en you *ree* sis). An involuntary discharge of urine caused by mental problems.

Eonism (*ee* oh nizm). The desire to wear clothing of the opposite sex.

Epidermis (ep eh *der* mis). The outer layer of skin.

Epilepsy (ep i *lep* see). A somewhat common nervous disorder, which manifests itself by recurring convulsions. The seizures are classified as grand mal, involving severe convulsions and loss of consciousness, or petit mal, involving a brief loss of consciousness or a brief period of confusion. The petit mal may last only a few seconds, whereas the grand mal may last several minutes. The officer should protect the victim against self-injury especially if convulsions are involved. Obtain medical assistance after rendering first aid.

Episode (*ep* e sowed). An incident or a series of incidents closely related.

Equalizer. Slang: Gun.

Equal Protection. The constitutional principle asserting that the law must be applied equally and impartially to all, regardless of race, economic class, sex, and so on.

Equipment for Law Enforcement, Testing. See **Laboratory, Law Enforcement Standards.**

Equity (*ek* we tee). Justness, fairness; justice according to ethics and fairness; natural right or justice. Law: Dispensing judgements according to the rules of ethics and fairness, rather than by the rules of common or statutory law. There are courts of equity in our judicial system. They do not handle criminal cases.

Equuleus (*eh* kwuh loos). A rack used to torture persons in order to extort confessions from them.

Ergo. Therefore; hence.

Erosion (ee *row* zhun). Firearms term: The wearing away of the inside of the gun barrel from repeated firing of the weapon.

Erotic. Involved with sexual love; arousing sexual love.

Erotomania (ee rot oh *may* nee ah). Medical term: A type of nymphomania, applied to both sexes. An excessive sexual craving.

Erratic (e *rat* tick). Irregular, unpredictable, not according to the usual or expected.

Erythrocyte (e *rith* row *site*). A red blood cell.

Escape. To get free from custody, confinement, or control; to avoid apprehension or capture. Some states have the crime of aggravated escape, where the escape involves danger to human life, and simple escape, where there is no danger to human life. Assisting escape is a crime on the part of an officer who intentionally permits a person in his custody or care to escape.

Escobedo (es ko *bee* do). A "landmark case" concerning confessions, holding that where a case has reached the accusatory stage the accused has the right to have an attorney present.

Escrow. A written agreement, such as a bond or deed, put in the care of a third party and not delivered or put into effect until certain conditions are fulfilled.

Espionage (*es* pea e nahge). The act of spying; the practice of agents of one country obtaining secret information about another country. Usually pertains to wartime activities of this nature.

Espionage, Industrial. Agents or paid representatives of one company or industry who obtain secret information about another. This may be accomplished by putting an agent into another company as an employee. This practice reportedly is common in some industries.

Espionage Act (1917). A law intended to discourage traffic with the enemy.

VOCABULARY

Espirit de Corps (es *pree* dee *core*). Morale; a feeling of enthusiasm among the personnel of an organization that results in teamwork for the betterment of the group or organization.

Esquire. A term of respect used in this country to designate an attorney at law, a judge, justice of the peace, or anyone directly associated with the administration.

Establishment. 1. An organization or agency. 2. Militant group term: The present order of society-government, agencies, organizations; the system.

Esteem. The opinion or judgement of merit one person has for the other without regard to the person's rank in the hierarchy.

Estop. Law: To legally stop someone from doing something.

Estoppel. The prevention of a person from making an affirmation or denial because it is contrary to a previous affirmation or denial he has made.

Et Cetera. And so forth; and other things.

Ethanol (*eth* a nall). Grain alcohol, ethyl alcohol, the alcohol in alcoholic beverages.

Ethics (*eh* thics). Standards of moral and official conduct; a system of morals.

Ethnic Group (*eth* nick). A group characterized by its cultural differences from the majority.

Ethnic Pluralism. A relationship in which no group is dominant, there is freedom of movement between groups, and all groups retain their ethnic identity.

Ethyl Alcohol. Grain alcohol; the kind of alcohol used in drinking.

Eunuch. A castrated human male.

Evacuate. To bodily vacate a place or structure; to move out of.

Evasive. Elusive; acting to avoid capture or injury.

Even-Up, Even-Up Proposition. Gambling term: A bet that gives the players an even chance to win (a fifty-fifty chance).

Ever-Widening Circle Search. A method of searching a crime scene where the searcher starts at a focal point, at or near the middle of the area, and searches the area by traveling in widening circles. This may be used in an indoor or outdoor crime scene.

Evict (ee *vict*). To legally expel one from a place or structure, such as a tenant.

Eviction. Expulsion of a tenant.

Evidence. Law: All the means by which an alleged fact is proved or disproved.

Evidence, Associative. The establishment of a link between the accused and the crime scene by information obtained from the physical evidence found at the crime scene and that found on the accused or in places traceable to him.

Evidence, Circumstantial (sur kum *stan* shel). Evidence that does not directly prove pertinent facts but from which the pertinent facts can be inferred or deduced.

Evidence, Competent. Evidence that is furnished by a person competent to testify. Examples of incompetent persons include infants, insane people, and laymen seeking to testify in areas of specialized knowledge where they have no expert knowledge.

Evidence, Corroborating (ko *rob* o rate ing). Evidence that strengthens or supports other evidence; evidence that corroborates other evidence.

Evidence, Derivative. See **Derivative Evidence**.

Evidence, Direct. Evidence that proves the facts in dispute directly, without an inference or presumption being drawn from any other set of circumstances.

Evidence, Hearsay. "Secondhand information"; facts that the witness did not personally acquire through his five senses but are what another witness told him. It is generally not admissible in court, but there are exceptions.

Evidence, Inflammatory. See **Evidence, Prejudicial**.

Evidence, Material. Material evidence must relate to the facts at issue and must also be important enough to warrant its use. Materiality of evidence pertains to its importance.

Evidence, Opinion. Conclusions drawn from a set of facts or circumstances that is offered in trial by a witness. It is usually inadmissible when given the layman. There are exceptions, one of which is testimony by an expert after he has been duly qualified before the judge.

Evidence, Physical. Concrete evidence from a crime, such as skin, blood, or fingerprints.

Evidence, Prejudicial. Evidence that is so shocking to the senses of a juror that it may unduly sway his/her attitude toward one of the parties in a criminal trial; inflammatory evidence.

Evidence, Relevant. Relevant evidence is that which relates to or bears directly upon the fact at issue in a case and proves or tends to prove the truth or untruth of the fact.

Evidence Rule, Best. See **Best Evidence Rule**.

Evidence, Rules of. Rules that regulate the type of evidence that can be presented during a trial. For example, there are rules against leading questions and hearsay evidence.

Evidence, Trace. Something that could have been attached to a suspect or have been left at the scene of the crime by a suspect.

Evidentiary Items. Items connected with a crime but not as contraband, fruits or instrumentalities of the crime, or weapons.

Evil Eye. Slang: Superstition—a viewing of one which allegedly will bring misfortune, injury, or death.

Examination (eg zam i *nay* shun). The initial question-and-answer session between the defense or the prosecution and a witness during a trial.

Exception. Law: The formal notification of the court that the party objects to its action, during a trial, in ruling on a request or objection of the party taking the action.

Excessive Bail. More bail than is necessary to keep a person from evading the law.

Exclusionary Rule (ex *kloo* shun ery). Legal prohibitions against the prosecution (government) using evidence illegally obtained (as by illegal search and seizure). Prior to *Mapp v. Ohio*, several states, by law, had exclusionary rules that precluded the use of such evidence.

Ex-Con. Slang: Someone who has been convicted of a felony and has served time in prison.

Exculpate (ex *kull* pate). To exonerate; to clear of blame and guilt; to prove innocent.

Exculpatory (ex *kull* pe to ry). Tending to clear from guilt, blame, or involvement in an offense; non-incriminating.

Excusable. That which prevents the

VOCABULARY

attachment of legal liability, e.g. excusable homicide.

Ex Delicito. Latin: From a crime or civil wrong.

Execute. To carry out; to put into effect; to inflict the death sentence.

Execution. 1. A writ or order, issued by the court, giving authority to put a judgement into effect. 2. The act of carrying out the provisions of such a writ or order.

Executioner. One who puts convicted criminals to death.

Executions, Gangland. Killings that are ordered and carried out by gangsters; hits; murders. A common procedure in the Cosa Nostra.

Executive Branch. That segment of government responsible for the administration, direction, control, and performance of government, e.g. the President of the United States, state governors, city mayors. The police and correctional subsystems are under the executive branch.

Executive Clemency. Authority and power given to certain executive authorities of the government, such as the governor, to set aside a court judgement or sentence. This power is granted by law, usually the Constitution.

Executor. Law: One who is appointed by will to carry out the provisions of the will left by a testator.

Executory Process. Law: Proceedings whereby, by previous agreement of the parties involved, mortgaged property may be seized and sold without going through the procedure of citing the mortgage debtor into court and obtaining a judgement against him. It is an expeditious way of foreclosure and sale of property on which a mortgage or privilege exists.

Exemplar (eg *zem* plar). A known specimen of evidence to be used by experts for comparison with other (questioned) evidence.

Exemplary Damages (eg *zem* plah ree). Damages awarded the plaintiff that exceed exact compensation in order to set an example.

Exhaust (ig *zaust*). To use up; to develop fully and completely.

Exhibit (ig *zib* it). Law: An item of evidence; an item obtained in an investigation, particularly one that is to be used as evidence; a physical object offered in evidence during a trial.

Exhibitionism (*ek* se bish in *iz* em). The exposing of one's body or sex organs (private parts) to obtain sexual gratification.

Exhume (ig *zoom*). Disinter; to recover a dead body that has been properly buried.

Exit. Gambling: To stop playing or to leave the game.

Ex Officio (ex e *fish* e o). Latin: By virtue of an office or position.

Exonerate (ig *zon* e rate). To prove not guilty; acquit; to clear of blame or fault.

Ex Parte (ex *par* tee). Latin: One sided. Law: From the side of one party only; requested by and/or done for one party only. This means the court did not have an adversary hearing before issuing the order. The court only heard one side of the question or matter before issuing the order.

Expert. Law: One who is especially qualified in a field or subject matter. This may be the result of education, training, or experience.

Expert Evidence. Testimony given by an expert concerning a matter that is so complicated the ordinary person does not fully understand it.

Expertise (eks purr *tease*). Special

knowledge concerning a thing or subject. Expertness in a special field.
Expert Testimony. Law: Introduction of evidence by one qualified as an expert; testimony by an expert.
Expert Witness. Law: One who, because of his special knowledge, testifies as an expert.
Expire (eks *pire*). To come to an end, as in a lease contract; to die.
Explicit (ik *splis* it). Plainly shown; spelled out in detail; not vague.
Explode. To detonate; to set off explosives.
Explorers Club. Slang: A group of acid heads.
Explosives. Any chemical compound or mechanical mixture that is commonly used or intended for the purpose of producing an explosion and that contains any oxidizing and combustive units or other ingredients in such proportions, quantities, or packing that an ignition by fire, by friction, by concussion, by percussion, or by detonator of any part of the compound or mixture may cause such a sudden generation of highly heated gases that the resultant gaseous pressures are capable of producing destructive effects on contiguous objects.
Ex Post Facto **Law.** A law, passed after an act is committed or done, which makes the act illegal, unlawful or which changes the legal status of the act. Such laws are constitutionally prohibited.
Exposure (eks *po* zhur). 1. Act of exposing. In photography, the time and extent of light entering the lens (lens opening) in relation to the illumination of the subject (exposure time). 2. Sex crime: See **Indecent Exposure.**
Exposure Meter. Photographic term: A device for measuring and registering the amount of light and correlating this information so as to show the correct exposure for the film being used. It is sometimes called the light meter.
Expression. Manner of making known; to speak or show.
Expressive Crowd. A crowd gathered for the purpose of expressing feelings.
Expropriation (*eks* pro pre *a* shun). Action by the state, under its sovereign power, to take over property for the use of the people. This is under the power of eminent domain. Reasonable compensation must be made for the property so appropriated.
Expulsion (eks *pull* shun). The forceful removal of one group of people by another; for example, the expulsion of the American Indians.
Expunge (ex *spunge*). The act of physically destroying information—including criminal records—in files, computers, or other depositories.
Extended Family. A household consisting of a large or small number of blood relatives living together with their partners and children.
Extent. Gambling slang: The amount of bets the "bookie" will take without laying off or closing the book.
Exterior (eks *tear* e er). The outward side of a body or structure.
Exterminate (eks *term* i nate). To kill; to eradicate by killing.
External. Outside; exterior.
Extinguish. To put out a light or fire; to cause a fire to go out.
Extortion. A threat to do physical harm or property damage, coupled with a demand for something of value.
Extractor (eks *track* ter). Firearms term: That part of the gun which

VOCABULARY

pulls (extracts) the cartridge or shell from the chamber (barrel) of the weapon.

Extradition (*eks* tra *dish* un). A legal procedure whereby a person, taken into custody in one state, is delivered to the authorities in another state where he is charged with crime; to surrender or deliver one to another state or country. Most states have adopted the "Uniform Extradition Act," which, among other things, provides that one must go before a judge in the state of asylum before being transferred to the state where he is charged with crime. In such states the arrestee cannot be returned to the state where he is charged with crime by signing a waiver of extradition before a law enforcement officer.

Extraordinary Bailment. Bailment exceeding the usual, average, or normal bailment.

Extremist Group. A group or organization, the avowed purpose of which is to bring about change in government functions and in society by radical, disorderly, and/or violent methods.

Eyeglass Prescription. The prescription for eyeglass lens prepared by a doctor (optometrist, oculist, eye specialist). Such information is important in tracing a wanted person if he used glasses.

Eye Openers. Slang: Stimulant drugs—amphetamines.

Eyepiece. That part of a microscope, containing the lens, which is nearest the eye.

Eyeshot. A distance where things can be seen; range of sight for the eyes.

Eyewitness. A witness who saw the things happen about which he is testifying; one who witnessed the crime or event.

F

F.A.A. (FAA). Federal Aviation Administration.

Fabricated Evidence (*fab* re kated). Evidence that is falsely arranged for a deceitful purpose.

Face. Face saving; the preservation of dignity, respect, prestige, and/or honor. It is a thing of great importance to Orientals and, to a somewhat lesser degree, to Italians. It is an important factor in the Cosa Nostra in that it aids in the maintaining discipline inside and outside the organization.

Face Value. The value shown on the face. In the case of a bond, the nominal value. The apparent value of a statement.

Facilitation (fass ill i *tay* shun). A process by which something is made easier.

Facsimile (fack *sim* e le). A like copy or reproduction. A method of transmitting messages and photographs by wire and radio. Research is being done to achieve transmittal of fingerprint images by this method. It is already being used by New York State Identification and Intelligence System.

Fact. A crime or unlawful act. Reality; a thing done contrasted with deduction, conclusions, or surmise.

Factor. A person legally appointed to take care of forfeited or sequestered property.

Factors. Something that actively contributes; advantages and/or disadvantages.

Factory. Slang: Equipment for injecting drugs.

Factum. Latin: With respect to change of domicile, factum is important, essential fact upon which an argument rests.

Fad. Something done for a period of time because it is "the thing" to do; a craze.

Fade. 1. Slang: To cover the shooter's bet in a dice game. 2. To go away or lose from sight slowly.

Fade-Out. Disappear from sight or sound. A term used in motion pictures when the close-up scene disappears.

Fading Dice. Gambling term: Dice that are loaded.

Fag. Slang: A gay person or a homosexual.

Fag Bar. Slang: A bar that caters to homosexuals and where pornographic material is sold.

Fagged Out. Slang: Tired out; exhausted.

Faggot. Slang: A fag.

Fahrenheit (*fair* en hite). A scale for measuring temperature where water freezes at 32 degrees and boils at 212 degrees under normal atmospheric conditions.

Faint. 1. Swoon, "pass out"; lose consciousness. 2. Timid, cowardly.

Fairbank. Gambling term: A move made to help a player in a card game win so that he will continue to play or increase his bet.

Fair Dice. Gambling term: Dice that have not been altered; honest dice.

Fair Trade Agreement. A contract between manufacturers of certain trademarked commodities and the distributors, whereby a minimum price is fixed for the retail price.

Fairy. Slang: A homosexual.

Fake. Fraudulent; fictitious; forged.
Fall. Slang: To be arrested or convicted for a crime. Also, to be misled or tricked by a false story.
Fall Dough. Slang: Money set aside for defense in case of arrest.
Fall For. Slang: To be made a sucker of; to be gullible.
Fall Guy. Slang: The one who takes the blame for the commission of a crime. A person who is easily victimized.
Fall Money. Money reserved by criminals to be used when a member is arrested, tried, or convicted.
Fallout. Narcotics slang: Addict who nods or sleeps after an injection.
False. Not true; not real.
False Arrest. Illegal deprivation of one's liberty or freedom of movement by physical restraint imposed by another.
False Cut. Gambling term: Manipulating the cards as if they were being given an ordinary cut but the cards remain in the same position as before.
False Front. Falsely pretending to be something or someone else, other than what is fact.
False Impersonation. Also called personation. To falsely impersonate another and to demand or obtain something of value for one's self or someone else is a federal and a state violation.
False Imprisonment. Illegal restraint of one against his will; illegal detention of a person without legal cause.
False Pretenses. Conditions whereby a person lies in order to obtain another's money or goods.
Falsi Crimen. Latin: Any crime involving fraud or dishonesty.
Falsify (*fall* se fi). To make false statements or representation; to lie.

Falsus in Uno. Comes from the Latin rule that a jury may disregard an entire witness testimony if one part of that testimony was found to be deliberately false.
Famacide (*fam* ah side). A person who slanders.
Family, The. A major segment, in the organizational structure of the Cosa Nostra, directed by the "Boss."
Family Disturbance. Domestic quarrel, fight, or noisy problem.
Fanatic (fe *nat* ik). Overly enthusiastic; one who exhibits an abnormal zeal about certain things, especially religion.
Fanned. Slang: Searched.
Farce. Hoax; mockery; something pretentiously done.
Fare. The passenger in a taxicab; a passenger in a public or semipublic conveyance.
Farm Tractor. Every motor vehicle designed and used primarily as a farm implement, for drawing plows, mowing machines, and other implements of husbandry.
Farol Bank. Carnival term: Letting players win a few times to keep them interested.
Fascism (*fash* iz m). An autocratic form of centralized government that oppresses opposition and rigidly controls finance, commerce and industry.
Fashion. A manner of dress, architecture, decor, etc., that tends to reflect the interests, values, and motives of a given society or group within it.
Fast. 1. Slang: Having loose morals; sexually aggressive. 2. Conditions that facilitate quick action.
Fast Company. Gambling slang: Gamblers who are very good, gamblers who have been gambling for a long time.

Fast Count. Counting fast in order to miss or to conceal one or more numbers or in order to short-change someone.

Fast Pill. Horse racing slang: An illegal stimulant that causes horses to run faster.

Fat. Slang: Describing someone who has a good supply of drugs.

Fatal. Causing death; deadly; resulting in death.

Fatality (fay *tal* i ty). The death of a person.

Fat Backs. Juvenile slang: Rock 'n' roll musical recordings.

Father. Helper characteristics that illustrate the initiative conditions in a helping relationship.

F.B.I. (FBI). Federal Bureau of Investigation.

FBI Laboratory. The crime laboratory of the Federal Bureau of Investigation. The facilities are available, without charge, to all duly constituted state, county, and municipal law enforcement agencies of the United States and its territorial possessions. Examinations are made with the understanding that the evidence is connected with an official investigation of a criminal matter and that the laboratory report will be used only for official purposes related to the investigation or a subsequent criminal prosecution.

FBI National Academy. A training school for law enforcement officers (other than FBI personnel) conducted by the Federal Bureau of Investigation through its Washington, D.C., headquarters. It was started July 29, 1935, as the Police Training School of the Federal Bureau of Investigation.

F.C.C. (FCC). Federal Communications Commission.

F.D.A. (FDA). Food and Drug Administration.

F.D.I.C. (FDIC). Federal Deposit Insurance Corporation.

Feasance (*fee* zance). Performance of an act; a doing.

Featherbedding (*feh* thur bed ing). The unfair labor practice of limiting output or requiring extra workers, as by union contract in order to provide more jobs and prevent unemployment.

Feces (*fee* sees). Stool; fecal matter; excrement.

Federal Aviation Act. A law enacted by Congress in 1968. Paragraph 902 of the act makes it a crime for persons to board an aircraft operated by an air carrier with a concealed weapon. Certain law enforcement officers, such as municipal state, and federal, are exempted.

Federal Aviation Administration. Formerly the Federal Aviation Agency, it is an agency of the United States Department of Transportation. Its functions are to issue and enforce safety regulations of airmen as well as the manufacturing and operations of aircraft and air navigation facilities.

Federal Bank Robbery Act. A law, passed on May 18, 1934, that made robbing a bank insured by the Federal Deposit Insurance Corporation a federal offense.

Federal Bureau of Investigation. One of the investigative agencies of the United States Department of Justice. It has jurisdiction over federal violations not specifically assigned to other agencies and several that have been designated by Congress.

Federal Communications Commission. An independent federal agency that regulates interstate communications and their facilities, i.e. telephone, cable, radio, and television.

Federal Crimes. Acts that are violations of federal laws.

Federal Deposit Insurance Corporation. A federally created corporation established under the Banking Act of 1933 to provide insurance for deposits in member banks. Banks insured by FDIC are under federal jurisdiction where crimes are involved relative to the bank. Thus such crimes as bank robbery, embezzlement, and theft are federal criminal violations.

Federal Food, Drug and Cosmetic Act. A law passed on June 25, 1938, mainly designed to prevent deception in the sale of foodstuffs.

Federalism. A government system in which sovereignty over an area is divided between more than one agent of the government.

Federal Jurisdiction. The legal authority of the federal government, or its agencies, to deal with matters. In the field of law enforcement it pertains to criminal matters.

Federal Kidnapping Act. A law, passed on June 24, 1936, that made carrying someone away against his will a federal offense.

Federal Offense. A violation of a rule, law, or dictate established by a federal government.

Federal Question. Cases that directly involve or challenge some portion of the U.S. Constitution, U.S. statutes, or U.S. treaties.

Federal Reserve Board. A federal agency, created by and operating under the Federal Reserve Act of 1913. It conducts the affairs of the Federal Reserve System. It is composed of seven members.

Federal Reserve System. A banking system created by the Federal Reserve Act of 1913, its functions are to maintain a sound currency and to regulate the national banking resources.

Federal Trade Commission. A federal agency that administers and enforces federal laws pertaining to price fixing, monopolies, and unfair trade practices.

Federation. A formal group of persons, organizations, or governments loosely united for a common purpose.

Feds. Slang: Federal law enforcement agents or officers.

Fee. Payment for services or special privileges; estate of inheritance; property; a charge.

Feeling. To be conscious of an inward impression, state of mind, or other condition.

Feigned Accomplice (fained ah *kom* pliss). A person who pretends to be an accomplice for the purpose of gaining evidence against the other parties involved.

Fellatio (fe *lay* she o). Sex deviation term: The attaining of sexual gratification by sucking the penis. It is practiced by males in homosexuality or by females who suck the penis.

Fellator (fe *lay* tor). Sex deviant term: A male who practices fellatio.

Fellow Traveler. One who agrees with and adopts the ideology and/or program of a group or organization, such as the Communist Party, without being a member. Such persons usually give support and aid to the movement.

Felo-De-Se. A person who commits suicide.

Felon (*fell* on). 1. One who has committed a felony; a criminal. 2. A person who commits a felony.

Felonious (fe *lone* e us). Showing

intent to commit a crime, specifically a felony; malicious.

Felonious Homicide. The killing of someone without justification or excuse.

Felony. A heinous or capital crime; a crime that carries the death penalty or imprisonment at hard labor or imprisonment for more than a year. The definition varies among the states. The federal definition may not be the same for a state.

Felony Murder. Murder committed during another crime, such as armed robbery or burglary.

Felony Murder Rule. The rule of law that states that all killings committed during the commission of a felony will be considered to be first-degree murder.

Femicide (*fem* i side). The killing of a female.

Fence. One who receives or buys stolen property.

Fertility (fur *till* eh tee). The actual rate of childbearing in a population.

Fetal. Pertaining to a fetus; in the stage of a fetus.

Fetish (*fe* tish). Something (an object) that allegedly has magic powers that benefit the possessor.

Fetishism (*fe* tish izm). A mental abnormality and sexual perversion where the sexual desire is abnormally fixed on one part of the body (hand, foot, etc.) or on pieces of the wearing apparel.

Fetters. Chains or shackles for the feet.

Fetus (*fee* tus). A unborn animal or human in the womb. In humans the developing child is referred to as a fetus from the end of the third month until birth.

Feud (fewd). 1. Prolonged quarreling between groups of people, usually existing between families, tribes, or clans. 2. Any continuing contention or quarrel between persons.

Fever. Gambling slang: Habitual gambling that has become a problem.

Fiction. 1. Nonfactual writings; novels. 2. Law: The assumption of a thing as being factual, regardless of its truthfulness.

Fictitious (fick *tish* us). 1. A type of fiction; false; counterfeit. 2. Imaginary; nonexistent.

Fictitious Checks. See **Checks, Worthless**.

Fiduciary (fi *do* she ery). One who acts as trustee; one who holds property in trust for another.

Field Training. Supervised training of new law enforcement officers where principles and techniques are practiced.

Fiend (feend). Slang: Narcotic addict.

Fifth. Slang: 1. A bottle of whiskey containing one-fifth of a gallon. 2. To claim the privilege against self-incrimination guaranteed by the Fifth Amendment of the United States Constitution.

Fifth Column. Originated during the Spanish Civil War. It refers to subversive elements (spies and saboteurs) inside the territory defended by the enemy during war.

Fifty-Fifty. Slang: Half and half; divided equally.

Filch. To steal, especially small items or amounts, one at a time.

File. Preservation of documents or papers. Court record of cases for presentation and reference.

File Charges. To formally and officially bring criminal charges against someone.

Filly. Slang: A young woman.

Film Pack. Photographic term: A

VOCABULARY

container that holds several films, which are so arranged that they are changed by pulling out paper tabs.
Film Pack Adapter. Photographic term: A device that holds the film pack in a camera. Sometimes referred to as the adapter.
Fin. Slang: Five dollars.
Finagle (fe *nay* gle). To cheat; to use trickery in order to obtain something; to accomplish something by devious plans.
Final. A term used in classifying fingerprints. In the classification formula it appears at the extreme right on the classification line and above the line. It is determined by ridge counts in the little finger. The right is used if it has a loop; if not, the left is used if it has a loop. If neither have a loop but both have a whorl, a ridge count between delta and core is made in the right hand.
Final Argument. Concluding arguments in a trial to the jury on the facts of the case.
Final Decision. 1. Decision leaving the parties with nothing left to dispute. 2. Concluded subject matter of suit until it is reversed or set aside. 3. Also, decision from which no writ of error or appeal can be taken.
F.I.N.D. (FIND). Fugitive Interception Network Design.
Finder. One hired by a professional store burglar to locate desired sales or merchandise and so advise the burglar.
Finding. The result of investigations or examinations dealing with court proceedings.
Fine. An assessment of money as a penalty or punishment for violation of law.
Fine Stuff. Slang: Finely cut marijuana.
Finger. 1. To point out a victim to a gunman, or a criminal to the police. 2. A fingerman. 3. To inform theives as to the location, values, etc., of potential loot.
Fingerman. Slang: An associate of a criminal gang or operation who obtains information on prospective victims of robbery or places to be burglarized and furnishes the information to others who perform the criminal acts.
Finger on, Put the. To point out or mark a person who will be the victim of a killing or other violence.
Fingerprint, Latent (*lay* tent). A chance fingerprint left accidentally or otherwise on a surface (other than inked prints taken by someone on paper or similar material.
Fingerprint Classification. A system of classifying fingerprints according to the patterns of the friction ridges on the fingertips. This is done by the use of a definite formula.
Fingerprint Patterns. The configuration of the friction ridges on the fingers is called a pattern. There are basically three patterns: arches, loops, and whorls. These basic patterns are subdivided as follows: Arch—plain arch; tented arch. Loop—radial loop; ulnar loop; central pocket loop; lateral loop; twin loop. Whorl—plain whorl. In addition to the three basic types of fingerprints, there is a catchall or nondescript pattern called accidentals. For descriptions of the various patterns see listings.
Fingerprints. Also referred to as dactyloscopy. The prints or impressions produced by the friction ridges of the inner surface of the fingertips. The impressions may be left accidentally or otherwise on surfaces touched by the fingers, or they may

be taken by two methods: 1. Rolled—the fingertips are rolled on a freshly inked surface and then rolled on a white paper; 2. Plain—the fingertip is pressed on an inked surface without rolling and the print made on a light-colored surface. See **Fingerprint Patterns; Fingerprint Terms.**

Fingerprint Terms. The following terms are used in the study, classification, and identification of fingerprints: **Core; Bifurcation; Bridge; Delta; Dot; Enclosure; Ending Ridge; Ridge Count; Ridge Ending; Ridge Line; Short Ridge; Spur; Trifurcation; Type Lines.**

Fink. Slang: 1. A strikebreaker; a person hired by an employer to help break a strike. 2. To inform to the police; an informer.

Fire. 1. The command to shoot a gun; the shooting or discharging of a firearm. 2. To terminate or discharge an employee.

Firearms (*fire* arms). Guns, pistols, revolvers, "automatic" weapons, shotguns, machine guns, and other guns that may be carried by a person.

Firearms Examination. Crime laboratory examination of a firearm and/or projectiles, cartridge cases, and shotgun shells. The usual object of such examination is to determine whether such bullets, cartridges, or shells were fired in a certain gun.

Firearms Range. A place or area suited for use to fire weapons in practice and to teach the use of firearms.

Fireball. Slang: One with much energy and enthusiasm.

Fire Brigade (bre *gaid*). The fire service organization of an industrial plant or private institution, as distinguished from the public fire department.

Firebug. Slang: Uncomplimentary term for a person suspected or known to have set fires; arsonist.

Fire Detection System. A thermostatic or photoelectric system for detecting the presence of abnormal fire or heat.

Firepower. The ability to deliver firearm projectiles (bullets or shot) on a target. "Where shooting may occur, the officers should have superior firepower."

Firetrap (fire trap). A structure that, due to interior arrangement, contents, lack of private protective equipment, and/or inadequate exits, is considered likely to contribute to a major loss of life in the event of fire.

Fire Wall. A wall or partition built or provided to prevent the spread of fire.

Fire-Water Complex. Sex deviation term: Part of the symptom complex occurring in sexually psychopathic incendiarists. After lighting a fire, there is a period of exhibitionism followed by a desire to urinate.

Firing Pin (*Fye* ring). Firearms term: An elongated, slender piece of metal in a firearm, which is activated by the hammer or other mechanism and which strikes the detonator in the ammunition, thus causing the latter to fire.

Firing Pin Impression. The impression left on the base of a cartridge case or shotgun shell by the firing pin striking it. "The crime laboratory made an identification of the weapon by the firing pin impression."

Firing Range. A firearms practice field or area; a specially designated and/or equipped area for teaching marksmanship and proper handling of firearms. Also called firearms range, pistol range, police range.

Firsthand (furst hand). Obtained

directly from the original source; "from the horse's mouth." "It was firsthand information."

First Instance. A court of original jurisdiction; for example, a trial court.

First Offender. One who is prosecuted as a law violator for the first time; one who violates the criminal law the first (known) time.

First-Rate. First-class; satisfactory; OK; worthwhile. "It was a first-rate show."

Fish. Slang: 1. A prisoner recently arrested; first offender arrestee. 2. One dollar.

Fishtail. Slang: To swing from side to side; said of a car or truck where the rear end swings from side to side. Spinning of the rear wheels while accelerating will often cause the rear end to fishtail.

Fishy. Questionable; probably untrue; unbelievable; truthfulness in doubt. "He told a fishy story."

Fisticuffs (*fis* ti kufs). Fistfight; hand-to-hand combat; a blow with the fist.

Fit. Medical term: A spasm of muscular convulsions usually ending in unconsciousness.

Fit, A. Drug user's slang: The equipment (outfit) for administering drugs directly into the vein (usually an eyedropper with a needle attached).

Five. Slang: A penitentiary sentence of five years.

Five-Fingers. Slang: 1. A prison sentence of five years. 2. One who steals.

Fix (fiks). 1. A dose or shot of narcotics. 2. To arrange for or take care of a violation of the law so as to avoid prosecution or payment of penalty. "He said he would fix the traffic ticket." 3. A predicament. "He is in a fix." 4. To arrange (bribe, etc.) for a person (such as a jockey) to lose a race or contest.

Fixation (fik *say* shen). An unhealthy mental attachment to something; an obsession; formation of a habit.

Fixed-Focus Camera. A type of camera in which the lens is fixed in a given position, which allows for taking photographs of distant and moderately close objects.

Fixed Sentence. A sentence for a specified amount of time that is to be served by a convicted person; also called determined sentence.

Fixed Surveillance. A surveillance operated from a fixed or semifixed location, such as a building or a parked vehicle.

Fixer. Slang: A person with political connections to protect his gambling operation.

Fix is in. Slang: Being in a state of receiving protection from someone after paying a bribe.

Flagellation (flaj el *ay* shun). Sex deviation term: The condition whereby sexual excitement is obtained from the act of whipping or being whipped. It is a form of masochism.

Flagrante Delicto. Latin: In the act of committing a crime.

Flake. Slang: Cocaine.

Flame. Slang: Sweetheart, or the object of one's affection or infatuation.

Flame Zone. Ballistics term: Burned area on clothes, skin, etc., caused by a weapon fired close to the body.

Flammable (*flam* a bull). Capable of burning or producing flame at moderate temperature; easily ignited; inflammable.

Flammable Liquid. Any liquid that has a flash point of 70 degrees F or less, as determined by a tagliabue or equivalent closed-cup test device.

Flap. Confrontation with the police; a fracas between rival gangs.

Flash. 1. Slang: The initial feeling after injection of drugs or narcotics. 2. To show or display.

Flashback. A recurrence of the effects of LSD that occurs in some persons long after LSD was last used.

Flash Gun. The attachment for a camera, containing the flashbulb, reflector, and energy source (batteries or electric current), that furnishes the light for taking photographs.

Flash Paper. Paper that, because of its composition, will burn quickly. Used by "bookies" and others for record keeping. In case of a raid or search by the police, it can be quickly destroyed. The paper leaves no residue.

Flash Point. The lowest temperature at which the vapors of a flammable liquid will ignite.

Flashy. Noticeable; showy. "He is a flashy dresser."

Flask. A leather or other animal skin container for holding liquor.

Flatfoot. Derogatory slang: A police officer, especially a patrolman who walks a beat.

Flat Passers. Gambler's term: Dice on which certain sides have been altered in order to increase the chances of certain sides or numbers appearing more often than usual.

Flattie. Slang: Any uniformed officer.

Flea Powder. Slang: Poor quality narcotics.

Flea Trap. Slang: A cheap, usually dilapidated hotel or rooming house.

Flee. Run; escape; get away from; depart hurriedly. Flee from justice: to become a fugitive; to hurriedly leave the place where one is wanted for investigation of a crime or where he is being sought for arrest.

Fleshpot. Slang: A house of prostitution or place of entertainment where girls strip or partially strip. A place catering to the weaknesses of the flesh, such as gambling, or drinking.

Flighty (*fly* tee). Unstable emotionally or mentally.

Flimflam (*flim* flam). Slang: To trick, swindle, or deceive; a fraud, swindle, or trick.

Flip. Slang: Become psychotic; to change one's ways—reform.

Fliver (*fliv* er). Slang: An old automobile, especially an old Ford car.

Floater (*flow* ter). One not steadily employed at the same place; one who works at different jobs periodically.

Floating Casino. A gambling casino that moves its location frequently to avoid police detection. A casino that operates aboard a converted ship or barge. Several were known to operate in this manner off the California coast in the early 1940s.

Floating Crap Game. Slang: A dice game that moves from place to place at frequent intervals to avoid detection by the police.

Flog. To whip or beat someone with a lash, whip, or switch.

Floorboard (*flor* bord). Slang: To accelerate a motor vehicle to the limit.

Floor Leader. A member of the United States Congress chosen by his party to lead and direct the party members in their actions on the floor of either the House or the Senate (one is chosen for each house). A person acting in such capacity in the state legislature.

Floor Show. A show put on informally in a place such as a night club.

VOCABULARY

The performance is usually among or near the patrons.

Floozie. Slang: An attractive woman.

Flop. Slang: A bed or motel room.

Flophouse. Slang: A cheap motel or place of lodging.

Florid (*flor* id). Ruddy colored; reddish flush. "The subject has a florid complexion."

Flower Child. Slang: Hippie; beatnik.

Fluoresce (*flor* css). The emission of visible light from a surface after it is exposed to light of a short wavelength, i.e. ultraviolet light.

Fluorine (*flor* een). A chemical sometimes added to drinking water in very small quantities, where it acts to prevent tooth decay.

Fluoroscope(*flor* es kope). A machine for seeing shadows projected upon a fluorescent screen by objects placed between a beam of x-rays and the screen.

Fluoroscopy. Examination made with a fluoroscope.

Flush. 1. To cause to move from a hiding place or place of concealment. "The plan was to flush them out of the woods." 2. In the game of poker, where all cards are of the same suit. Straight flush, where all cards are in sequence in the same suit; royal flush is the same as straight flush, from ten to ace. 3. The initial feeling one gets when injecting a drug like methamphetamine.

Flute (Fluter). Slang: A male homosexual.

Fly a Kite. To illegally smuggle a letter in or out of a penitentiary.

Fly-by-Night. A financial operation that is questionable; not responsible. "It seems to be a fly-by-night operation."

Flymug. Slang: Any uniformed officer.

FM. Abbreviation for **Frequency Modulation.**

F-number. Photographic term: A number used in a system to show the size of the opening of the shutter; lens opening; diaphragm opening.

Focus (*foe* kus). To bring the lens of a camera to such a position that the object to be photographed will be clearly defined. To adjust a camera or microscope so as to clearly see the object. "The camera was out of focus, which resulted in a poor picture."

Foeticide (*feet* eh side). The act that produces a criminal abortion.

Foetus. See **Fetus.**

Fog. Slang: Confused state of mind. "He was in a fog."

Folie Brightique (*foh* lee bree *teek*). French for an excess of insanity, resulting from Bright's disease.

Folie Circulaire (sir q *lair*). French for manic-depressive insanity.

Folklore (*foke* lor). Historical facts, traditions, or sayings that are preserved and passed on through descendants of certain groups of people.

Folktale (*foke* tale). A story or song originating among common people and handed down to subsequent generations.

Following Too Close. In highway traffic one vehicle follows another at such short intervening distance that the driver of the vehicle following is unable to stop quickly enough to avoid colliding with the vehicle in front when it stops suddenly.

Food and Drug Administration. An agency of the United States Department of Health, Education, and Welfare. It protects the purity, proper strength, and truthfulness of advertising of foods, drugs, cosmetics, and milk.

Footage (*fut* ij) (fut as in put). 1. Length in linear feet. 2. The number of feet of exposed film in a movie camera.

Footballs. Narcotics slang: Amphetamine sulfate in oval-shaped tablets of various colors.

Foot Line. One of the elements of the walking picture. It shows the angle at which each foot is put down.

Foot Patrol. Patrol duties done on foot by an officer, usually confined to a designated area.

Footprint (*fut* print) (fut as in put). The imprint or impression of a foot or the shoe a person is wearing. Such an imprint may be made on a solid surface by dirt, grease, blood, etc., adhering to the foot or shoe, thus creating visible tracks, or as impressions in a soft surface such as the ground.

Footstep. The noise made by walking; footfall. "I recognized his footsteps."

Foray (*for* ay). A raid or excursion to plunder.

Forbearance (for *bare* ens). Act of forbearing; act by which a creditor is waiting for payment from a debtor after payment is due; refraining from action.

Force (fors). 1. The degree and power of effective action. 2. An organization or group equipped for action, e.g. a police force.

Force, Reasonable. Law: The amount or degree of force that can be reasonably used by persons in protecting themselves or others. The force that can be used by law enforcement officers in the conduct of their duties, as authorized by law. The general rule is that an officer can use force no greater than that which is necessary for the purpose. To effect an arrest, an officer may use reasonable force to overcome resistance.

Force Majeure (meh *jyou* ree). Natural, unavoidable, irrestible force, e.g. a flood.

Forcible Entry (*for* sih bul). Criminal law: To enter on the lands or other property of another by the use of force or fear and without the free consent of the owner or possessor of such property. A law enforcement officer is legally given the right to forcibly enter the property of another after announcing his identity and purpose to make an arrest if his entry has been refused or obstructed.

Foreclosure (for *klo* zher). Act of barring a mortgager's right to redeem mortgaged property; act of foreclosing a mortgage.

Forehead (*for* hed). The part of the face between the hairline and the eyes. Used in the descriptions of persons as receding, bulging, etc. It is a good descriptive feature, as it is not readily subject to change.

Foreman. Spokesman of a grand or petit jury.

Forensic (for *en* zik). Relating to the courts or the judiciary. "He studied forensic medicine."

Forensic Medicine. The study or application of the field of medicine as used in judicial or court matters.

Forensic Pathologist (path *ol* oh jist). A medical doctor, specialized in pathology, who conducts examinations to determine the cause of death in suspected homicide cases and who is in a position to testify to his findings in a court of law. He also makes pathological examinations on persons who have been injured or are suffering from disease, and the

VOCABULARY

findings are useable in legal proceedings. "The work of a forensic pathologist is most important in homicide cases."
Forensic Science. Science as applicable and useable in judicial matters.
Foreseeability (for see eh *bil* eh tee). To see or know in advance. Knowing that harm or injury is a result of acts or omissions.
Foreskin. The skin that loosely covers the glans (head) of the penis. Synonym, prepuce.
Forewarn. To warn in advance of an event; to prewarn.
Forfeit (*for* fit). Lost by reason of fault, default, or neglect. "If he does not appear in court at the designated time, he will forfeit his bail."
Forfeiture (*for* fih cher). A punishment for the illegal use or possession of specific property, by which one loses to the government his rights and interest in that property. The loss of goods or other property as punishment for the commission of a crime.
Forgery (*for* jer ee). Law: The false making or material altering, with intent to defraud, of any writing which, if not genuine, might apparently be of legal efficacy or the foundation of a legal liability (*Black's Law Dictionary*). See **Traced Forgery; Simulated Forgery.**
Fork. 1. Fingerprint term: A bifurcation of a ridge line in a fingerprint pattern. 2. A line branching into two lines. 3. Slang: A pickpocket; to pick someone's pocket.
Fork Over. Slang: Hand over something; give it to me.
Formal Structure. An organizational pattern that includes established rules, procedures, and hierarchies of power and authority.
Format. The layout or physical arrangement of writings. "The format of the written report is good."
Formed Design. The intention to commit a crime; premeditation.
Fornication (for ni *kay* shun). Illegal sexual intercourse between unmarried persons. If one of the persons is married, it becomes adultery.
Forswear. To falsely swear; an untrue oath; differs from perjury in that perjury deals only with oath taken before a competent court officer. Forswear is a much broader term than perjury.
Forthwith (forth *with*). As soon as possible; immediately; promptly. "The court ordered the accused to be discharged forthwith."
Fortuitous (for *tue* i tus). Occurring without design, but by chance; accidental.
Fortune Teller. One who ostensibly tells of events to occur in the future. "Swindlers have used the technique of fortune telling to cheat the victims out of money and property."
Forty-Eight. Slang: The ability of the police to hold a person for forty-eight hours without actually arresting him.
Forty-Five. Slang: A 45 caliber pistol.
Forty-Five Minute Psychosis. Slang: DMT.
Forty-Four. Slang: A gun of that caliber.
Forum. 1. A law court; tribunal. 2. An assembly, place, radio program, etc., for the discussion of public matters or current questions.
Forwards. Slang: Pep pills, especially amphetamines.
Foundling (*found* ling). A baby found after abandonment by the parents.
Four Bits. Slang: Fifty cents.
Four Corners. The face of a docu-

ment without additional information.

Four-Flusher. Slang: A bluffer; one who is not truthful or sincere in work or actions.

Four Freedoms. President Franklin D. Roosevelt used the expression in 1941 to enumerate the four necessary freedoms of humans. They are freedom from want, freedom from fear, freedom of worship, and freedom of speech.

Fourth-Cent Line. Gambler slang: A price line of a bookmaker that has a difference of two points between the take and lay odds.

Fox. Slang: A good looking man or woman.

Foxy. Slang: Cunning; sly; devious. "He's a foxy person."

Fracas (*fray* kas). A melee; fight; brawl; noisy disturbance; altercation. "He was involved in the fracas."

Fractious (*frak* chus). Displaying temper; irritable; unruly.

Fracture (*frak* shur). Break or crack something. "A study was made in the laboratory of the glass fracture to determine the direction of the blow that broke it."

Fracture, Compound. A bone fracture where the broken end or ends of the bone protrude through the skin.

Fracture, Simple. A bone fracture where the ends of the broken bone do not penetrate the skin.

Fragging (*frag* ing). An attack by a "GI" using a fragmentation grenade or other explosive against another American, usually his sergeant or an officer.

Frame (fraim). 1. The physical makeup of structure of a person, especially in reference to the bone structure. In descriptions of persons the terms large, medium, or small frame are used. 2. Slang: Frame-up—to conspire against one who is innocent in an effort to show he is guilty of wrongdoing; to use false evidence against a person.

Frame-Up (*fraim* up). The act, plan, or scheme to use false evidence or indicate or prove an innocent person is guilty of criminal violations or other questionable activities; the "framing" of a person. "It was a frame-up." Peace officers should carefully avoid such acts. It is a technique used at times by criminals and hoodlums against an honest peace officer.

Franchise (*fran* chize). 1. The voting right; suffrage. 2. A government grant of a privilege or right to a person or persons (real or corporate). "He was granted the franchise to operate the ferry." 3. Right given to a person or company to sell products of the manufacturer.

Frank. The right to send communications (letters, packages, etc.) without charge. "The United States government agencies have the right to frank their mail."

Frantic. Slang: Nervous, jittery drug user.

FRAT. Free Radical Assay Technique. A proprietary device for detecting the presence of drugs of abuse. Manufactured by Syva Corporation, 3221 Porter Drive, Palo Alto, California 94304.

Fraternize (*frat* er nize). Associate together; to keep company with. "The suspect is fraternizing with a known burglar."

Fratricide (*frat* ri side). The act of killing or murdering one's brother.

Fraud (frawd). Law: To obtain some right or property from another by deceit, trickery, or subterfuge; the intentional cheating or deceiving of

VOCABULARY

another in order to obtain something of value.
Fraudulent Cheating. Act of deliberate deception to secure something by taking unfair advantage of another; committing a fraud; cheating.
F.R.B. (FRB). Federal Reserve Board.
Freak. Slang: A male homosexual.
Freakout. Slang: A bad experience with psychedelics; also a chemical high.
Freak Trip. Slang: Adverse drug reaction, especially with LSD.
Freeboard. That part of a ship or boat between the water line and the deck; usually pertains to the side of the ship or boat.
Freedom Marches. A term used for some of the demonstrations staged by activist groups in the South in the 1960s. The demonstrations ostensibly were for the purpose of calling attention to the needs of minority groups, especially black people.
Freehand (*free* hand). Done by hand, without the use of scales or instruments. "He made the drawing freehand."
Free-Lance. One who does his work independently of being regularly employed. Used to describe writers, artists, actors, etc.
Free on Board. See **F.O.B.**
Freeway. Expressway. A limited-access multilane road or highway.
Free Will. Something done without force, compulsion, or coercion. "The accused made the statement of his own free will."
Freeze. 1. Slang: Stand still; do not move; stay where you are. 2. Narcotics slang: Turn down a sale.
Freeze Out. Slang: Force or defraud out of a business undertaking or group. "A and B tried to freeze out C."

Freight-Carrying Vehicle. Every motor vehicle designed for and used primarily as a carrier of freight transported for commercial purposes, which vehicle is licensed for six thousand pounds or more. This shall not include pickup or panel trucks unless they are so heavily loaded with such freight as to exceed six thousand pounds gross weight and shall never include any passenger-carrying vehicle.
French Way. Slang; Taboo: Sexual act done orally by fellatio or cunnilingus. Also known as "French."
Frequency (*freek* wen see). The number of complete oscillations per second of an electromagnetic wave.
Frequency Modulation. See **FM; AM.**
Fresh. Slang: Impudent, brazen. Improper advances toward the opposite sex.
Fresh and Sweet. Slang: Out of jail.
Fresh One. Prison slang: A person who was recently incarcerated.
Friction. The result of rubbing two bodies together.
Friction, Coefficient of. The amount of friction on a (roadway) surface as determined in calculating the speed of a vehicle as shown by skid marks. Speed and weight of the vehicle are factors as well as the surface that the vehicle was travelling upon. The coefficient of friction is also referred to as the drag factor.
Friction Ridges. The ridges of the skin on the palms and palmar side of the fingers. Similar ridges are found on the sole of the feet and the lower side of the toes. The prime function of the ridges is to afford friction with surfaces and objects touched by these parts of the body. These ridges are the means by which fingerprints are formed.

Friend of the Court. Law: *Amicus curiae* (Latin). 1. Someone, usually an attorney, not officially involved in the case, who gives advice or information to the court on a point of law. 2. A person who has no right to appear in a lawsuit who is allowed to be heard so as to protect his interest.

Frigidity. Slowness in or inability of a female to reach a sexual orgasm during sexual intercourse.

Frisk. Slang: A quick search of a person's garments; the patting or feeling of the garments worn by a person. See **Stop and Frisk.**

Frisk Room. Slang: 1. Room where players are searched prior to entering a gambling room. 2. Room used to search prisoners.

Frog-Sticker. Slang: A long-bladed knife.

Front. Slang: 1. Physical appearance or activity (by one person or a group), purporting to be a legitimate undertaking but which is used as a cover for illegal or condemned practices. A person, group, or business establishment operating legally for the purpose of concealing illegal activities. "The grocery store was a front for bootleg operations." 2. One who wears fine clothing or jewelry without being able financially to afford same. 3. Juvenile slang: A suit of clothing.

Front Breech. Slang: Front pants pocket.

Front Group. A group of people operating for the stated purpose of a popular goal but actually operating for the purpose of achieving sinister or subversive objectives. The Communist Party, in countries where it has not attained control, frequently operates through "front groups."

Front Man. Slang: A person, who is apparently reputable, acting for others who are not reputable.

Frotteur (fro tur). Sex deviation term: A person, usually a male, who receives sexual pleasure by rubbing or pressing against the buttocks of a female (sometimes a male) while in a crowded place. This is a form of masturbation and is closely associated with buttock fetishism.

Frozen Area. A term used to demote the area around radioactive material that has been involved in an incident. The police should clear people out of this danger area and not let any unauthorized person enter the area. The diameter of such an area should not be less than two hundred feet, with the radioactive material at the center. Consult radioactive experts for the appropriate distances for specific amounts of radioactive material.

Fruit. 1. Result or outcome; in law of evidence, material objects obtained from commission of crime itself. 2. A degenerate or a person not well liked. 3. A homosexual.

Fruit of the Poisonous Tree. Law: A term used by the courts to denote evidence tainted as the result of it being derived from evidence (based upon evidence or information) obtained illegally or in such fashion that it (the basic evidence) was inadmissible. If certain evidence was obtained as the result of an illegal search and, based upon information secured by the search, other (derivative) evidence was located elsewhere, the latter evidence is also inadmissible, even though properly obtained, and as the courts say it was tainted or was the "fruit of the poisonous tree."

Fruits of the Crime. Things taken or acquired by means of and as the

VOCABULARY

result of the commission of a crime. They may be the objects for which the crime was committed.

Frustration-Aggression Theory. A theory of deviance that asserts that frustration leads to aggression and thus to deviant behavior.

Fry. Slang: Execution in the electric chair.

F-stop. The number or symbol on a scale indicating the size of the opening of the shutter of a camera (when the camera has an adjustable shutter). The size of the opening is a factor in the exposure of the film. The larger the opening, the smaller is the F-stop number.

F.T.C. (FTC). Federal Trade Commission.

Fugitive (*few* je tiv). 1. One who flees, or cannot be located by law enforcement officers, to avoid arrest, incarceration, or questioning concerning an alleged violation of the law. 2. One wanted for crime who goes outside the state or the territorial jurisdiction of the court. Also called a "fugitive from justice."

Fugitive Felon Act. A federal law that makes it a federal criminal violation for a person to flee from one state to another to avoid prosecution or detention for a felony under the state law.

Fugitive from Justice. See **Fugitive**.

Fugitive Interception Network Design (F.I.N.D.). A plan established by the Philadelphia, Pennsylvania, Police Department to prevent the escape of felons from the scene of major crimes. Reference: O'Neill, Joseph F.: Operation F.I.N.D. *FBI Law Enforcement Bulletin.* November 1971, p. 3.

Fugitive Warrant. An arrest warrant issued for a person wanted for a violation of the criminal law in another state or jurisdiction; a warrant for a fugitive from justice.

Full. Slang: Intoxicated.

Full Faith and Credit. The recognition of one state's laws and proceedings by all other states.

Full House. In the game of poker, a hand having three of a kind and two of a kind.

Fume. Slang: To fuss; to show anger; to be emotionally upset.

Fundamental Fairness. The belief that crime control efforts must be fair, even if it means an impairment of enforcement efficiency.

Fundamental Law. Law that determines government in a state; the constitution; foundation or basis.

Fungible (*fun* ji bull). Designating movable goods, as grain, any unit or part of which can replace another unit, as in discharging a debt.

Funky. Juvenile slang: Progressive. Also, bad smelling or having a bad odor.

Funny. Slang: Queer; sex deviate; homosexual.

Funny Business. Slang: Something that is not on the "up and up"; questionable; crooked operation.

Funny House. Slang: A mental hospital or sanitarium; a facility where drug addicts or alcoholics are treated.

Furiosos (fyou ree *oh* so). An insane person.

Furor. Tumult; loud group activity; fracas; melee.

Furtherance (*fur* ther enss). Anything that aids or assists the commission of a criminal offense.

Fuse. A cord or tube containing combustible material which will burn at a predetermined rate. Used for detonating explosives. Note: Detonating fuses are explosives. Unless the officer knows the types of fuses encountered he should treat them with care.

Fusee. A flare, used principally by railroads, which burns with a bright red flame. They are cylinder shaped with a metal spike on one end by which they are stuck into the ground or wood and held into position.

Fusillade (*fue* ze laid). Numerous and rapidly firing gunfire.

Fuzz. Slang: Derogatory term for police officer.

Fuzzbuster®. An electronic device, placed in a civilian's automobile, designed to detect the radar used by the police in speed traps.

G

G. Slang: One thousand dollars; a grand.
Gabby. Slang: Talkative.
Gaffed. Gambling term: Altered, doctored, or crooked gambling equipment.
Gaffer. Slang: A boss or supervisor.
Gag. Something placed over or in a person's mouth to prevent talking or making noise.
Gal-Boy. 1. Slang: Homosexual. A male who assumes the passive role in an act of oral sodomy or pederasty. 2. Prison slang: A young inmate who has "turned out" and adapted to the environment.
Gallery Load. Firearms term: A cartridge loaded lightly for use inside a building.
Gallivant (*gal* e vant). To move about looking for pleasure.
Gallon. A United States gallon consists of 231 cubic inches of water weighing 8.336 pounds. An imperial gallon is 1.201 U.S. gallons.
Galloping Dominoes. Slang: Dice.
Galvanometer (*gal* ve *nom* e ter). An instrument for measuring small amounts of electricity.
Gamble. To play at a game for money or anything of value; to bet or wager.
Gambling. Playing for stakes or money; the intentional conducting, or directly assisting in the conducting, of any game, contest, lottery, or contrivance as a business, whereby a person risks the loss of anything of value in order to realize a profit. The definition varies according to the states.

Gambling, Legalized. Gambling that has been made legal by law. Nevada has such legislation. Many states allow legal betting on horse races, at the tracks.
Gambling Device. A machine or contrivance for playing a game that may result in the winning or losing of money. There are three groups: 1. Gambling devices in themselves, such as slot machines, roulette wheels, poker tables, dice, etc. 2. Those devices that become gambling equipment when used for that purpose, such as pinball machines, card tables, etc. 3. Those objects generally not considered gambling devices but may be so classified if used as such. An example is money used in a gambling organization.
Gambling Devices, Crooked. Gambling machines, devices, paraphernalia, or items that have been so rigged, built, or altered that they operate very much in the favor of the person knowingly using them as such. They decrease the chances of the "sucker" winning.
Game. A plan or scheme.
Game of Chance. A game that requires no skill; a game entirely dependent on luck.
Game Warden. One who enforces the game (wildlife) laws in a certain area; a wildlife agent.
Gamma Rays. Electromagnetic radiations given off by radioactive substances. Deadly gamma rays are emitted in atomic explosions.
Gams. Slang: A woman's legs.
Gander. Slang: One who is a lookout

for persons engaged in illegal activities.
Gang. A group of people travelling or operating together, usually for a common purpose; more than two persons engaged in a common criminal activity.
Gangbusting. Juvenile slang: Gang fighting.
Gangland. The underworld racketeers.
Gangster. Slang: A member of a criminal organization or a member of the underworld.
Gang War. Hostility usually accompanied by violence and killings between groups of gangsters or hoodlums, common in the underworld as between competing or rival groups.
Gaol (jale). A place for confinement; jail; prison.
Garbage. Slang: 1. Poor quality drugs. 2. Bad food. 3. Worthless goods or trinkets; talk that has no foundation or value. 4. Worthless or invalid information fed into a computer.
"Garbage-In-Garbage-Out." An expression in the computer field to indicate if you put worthless information into the computer you will get the same kind of information out.
Garnish. Law: To use legal action brought by a creditor, whereby the debtor's money (or property) is impounded or attached, while in the hands of a third party (the garnishee). The garnishee is warned not to deliver the money or property to the defendant debtor until the lawsuit is concluded. This is a civil action.
Garnishee (*gar* nish ee). 1. To legally attach property or debt in the hands of a third person that belongs to the debtor with orders that same be held pending a court order. 2. The party who has been served the notice of garnishment.
Garnishment. A legal notice or warning to a person, who holds property of another, not to deliver it to such person but to hold it and appear to answer the plaintiff's suit.
Garrote. To strangle by a device or instrument around the neck; to strangle and rob.
Garroting (*gare* ret ing). The act of strangling another person.
Gas. 1. The least dense state of matter in which each molecule moves independent of the others and the number of molecules per unit volume is very small. 2. Slang: Idle talk; boasting talk. 3. Slang: Whiskey. 4. Juvenile slang: Intoxicant. 5. Slang: Process one's hair.
Gash. A long, deep cut or wound.
Gas House. Slang: A beer parlor or saloon.
Gas Mask. A mask fitted with a filter of chemicals to protect the wearer from obnoxious or poison gases. Officers wear gas masks as protection against tear gas or smoke.
Gassing. Slang: Sniffing gasoline fumes.
Gat. Slang: A hand gun-revolver or other type of pistol.
Gate-Keeper. Slang: One who initiates another into the use of LSD.
Gatekeeping. A process of simple tabulation or headcounting, such as the gatekeeping conducted by prison authorities who count the number of prisoners who enter and leave the institution.
Gate Money. Slang: Money given to a penitentiary releasee (one who is released from a penal institution) when he has completed his period of incarceration.
Gauge. 1. Slang: Marijuana. 2. Firearms term: Inside diameter of the

barrel of a gun, especially a shotgun. It is determined by the number of round lead balls, of the diameter of the gun barrel, that will weigh one pound.

Gault, *In re.* A landmark decision of the United States Supreme Court in the juvenile field. Its holding was that a juvenile is entitled to substantially the same rights under the due process clause of the Fourteenth Amendment as is given to adults in the adjudicatory stages.

Gay. Slang: A homosexual.

Gaycat. Slang: A thief who steals only when necessity compels him to raise the money.

Geed Up. Slang: Feeling "high" from drug use.

Gee-Gee. Gambling term: A race horse.

Gee-Head. Slang: Paregoric abuser.

Geepo. Slang: An informer.

Geetis. Slang: Money.

Geeze. Slang: Injection of drugs.

Geezo. Slang: An "old time" convict who has been incarcerated for many years; one who has served time for many years in a prison.

Gendarme (zhan *darm*). A member of an armed police organization such as in France.

Gene. A section of DNA on a chromosome that possesses genetic information.

General. Pertaining to a common class, group, or community; majority; the whole.

General Appearance File. A file maintained by law enforcement agencies wherein photographs and descriptions of persons known to have engaged in certain types of crime are maintained. Confidence game operators, jewel thieves, and fur thieves are maintained in such files.

General Court Martial. The highest level of court in the military in which the most serious offenses are tried.

General Creditor. A creditor at large or one who has no lien or security for the payment of his debtor claim.

General Damages. Damages such as the law itself implies or presumes to have accrued from the wrong complained of, for the reason that they are its immediate or direct result.

General Execution. Taking of personal property of the defendant to satisfy judgement.

General Fertility Rate. Total number of births per group of 1,000 women from fifteen to forty-four years of age.

General Intent. Conscious wrongdoing (*mens rea,* mind of the thing), which is inferred unless expressly denied, as a method of legal proof.

Generalization (jen er rul ih *zay* shun). A style of policing focusing on broader roles for the police agency rather than specific or specialized roles of the agency and its officers.

General Jurisdiction. The authority that permits the court to engage in the full range of trial activities in a wide variety of cases; as opposed to special or limited jurisdiction.

General Legacy (*leg* eh see). A pecuniary legacy, payable out of the general assets of a testator.

Genetics of Violence. See **Y Chromosomes**.

Genial. Friendly; agreeable; pleasant.

Genitals. The external sex organs.

Genocide (*ji* no side). The murder of a race, such as the Nazis and the Jews.

Genuineness (*jen* you in ness). The ability to be real, not be phony.

Georgia Scuffle. Carnival slang: The rough handling of swindle

victims who are unaware that they are being set up for a theft.
Germane (jer *main*). Pertinent; connected to; relevant.
Gestapo (ge *sto* po) (sto as in stop). Secret police in Germany during Hitler's regime.
Gesture (*jes* cher). Motion of the limbs or body. Some people have peculiar gestures that constitute a personal descriptive characteristic.
Get. Gangland slang: With the presence of malice to kill, injure, hurt, or cause trouble to another to repay for some injury or damage. "The gang decided to get Smith, who had arrested one of their members."
Get a Gift. Narcotics slang: Acquire narcotics.
Get a Head. Juvenile slang: To physically attack someone.
Getaway (*get* e way). Escape. "The criminal made a getaway." A means of escape. "The getaway car was found abandoned."
Getaway Day. Slang: Final day of racing season at a racetrack.
Get Away With (Something). Slang: To succeed in an illegal or unethical undertaking.
Get off the Gun. Slang: To achieve a sexual release through drugs or alcohol.
Get off the Nut. Underworld slang: To satisfy sexual desire; to achieve an emotional release.
Get to. Slang: To bribe a public official so as to receive favored treatment such as to be free from arrest for violations of the law.
Ghetto (*get* oh). Modern common usage: A poor, run-down section of a city (slums) where many poor people live. "Minority groups frequently live in the ghetto."
Ghost (The). Slang: LSD.

Gibbet (*gib* it). A place where people are hung; a gallows.
Gideon v. Wainwright, 372 U.S. 335 (1963). A landmark case wherein the U.S. Supreme Court held that an indigent defendant was entitled to be represented at trial on a felony charge by an attorney even though he could not hire one.
Gig. 1. Juvenile slang: A party. 2. Gambling term: A three number play. All Three numbers must be pulled at the drawing to win.
Gig and Saddle. Gambling term: A popular double play. The saddle is sometimes referred to as an insurance play. If the player misses the gig but two of the three numbers are pulled, the saddle would win.
Giggles Smoke. Narcotics slang: Marijuana.
Giggle Weed. Narcotics slang: Marijuana.
Gimmicks. Slang: The equipment for injecting drugs.
Gimp. Slang: A person who walks with a limp.
Ginhead. Slang: An alcoholic.
Gin Mill. Slang: A public drinking place; a saloon.
Ginned. Slang: Drunk or intoxicated.
Ginny (*gin* nee). Slang: An Italian person.
Girl-Boy. See **Gal-Boy**.
Girlie Show. Slang: Show having undressed females participating.
Gist (jist). The essential, important part without which a pleading or action would be legally deficient.
Give him the Ax. Slang: To fire or dismiss an employee.
Given a Pass. Slang: Excused from punishment for a violation after a light reprimand.
Given Name. Name of a person,

VOCABULARY

other than his family name (surname). "Frank Jones has the given name of Frank."
Glad Rag. Slang: A piece of cloth saturated with glue or gasoline, usually a sock. Also, "wad."
Glass Eyes. Narcotics slang: Narcotic addict.
Glassine (gla *seen*). A tough, thin semitransparent paper. Used as an envelope to dispense narcotics.
Glass Jaw. Slang: A weak or sensitive jawbone, easily injured or broken.
Glimmer (Cards). Slang: A mirror used by a cheat to look at the cards.
Glom. Slang: To seize or steal.
Gloomed. Slang: Arrested; snatched.
Glossary (*glos* a re). A list of words pertaining to certain works or fields, together with their definitions.
Glue Sniffer. Slang: One who inhales the fumes from glue, intentionally, to obtain the intoxicating or other sensations.
Gluey. Slang: Glue sniffer.
G-man. A name, originating in the 1930s, for a special agent of the Federal Bureau of Investigation.
Go. To participate freely in the drug scene.
Goal. Objective, course of action to complete.
Go-Along. Slang: A vehicle used by a law enforcement officer to haul prisoners.
Go-Between. Slang: An intermediary; a person who settles a dispute between two persons.
Go Down. 1. Juvenile slang: To declare war or attack on another gang. 2. Slang: The act of a homosexual in relation to the partner.
Go-Getter. Slang: A person who pursues objectives with energy, vigor, and determination.

Go High. Slang: Hands up.
Going Kicker. Slang: Opium or marijuana smoker.
Going on Blind. Burglary slang: A situation where a burglar does not have his place of burglary picked (selected) in advance. Also called "peddling a flat."
Going to Bat. Slang: Going to trial.
Going to Wear the Hair. Slang: Be sentenced.
Going Up. Slang: Taking drugs for their effects, said of smoking cannabis or injecting "speed," etc.
Go in Sewer. Narcotics slang: Inject in a vein.
Goldbrick. Slang: One who shirks work by using various excuses, such as pretending illness or other incapacity. Used generally in the armed services.
Gold Digger. Slang: A woman who uses various schemes to get money from men.
Gold Dust. Slang: Cocaine.
Goner. Slang: A person who is in deadly peril or is dead or past assistance.
Gong. Slang: An opium pipe.
Gong Beater. Slang: Smoker of opium.
Gonger. Underworld slang: An opium pipe.
Gonorrhea (gon e *rea*). A venereal disease involving the sex organs. Manifested in the male by the presence of pus discharge from the penis, together with pain and a burning sensation when urinating. It may become serious if not treated medically. Usually contracted through sexual intercourse but may result from exposure to contaminated articles. Synonyms: clap; claps.
Good Behavior. Proper behavior, behavior that allows some prisoners

to be released early from jail or prison.
Good Butt. Slang: A cigarette of marijuana.
Good Cause. Sufficient grounds; substantial reason; legally sufficient.
Good Faith. Fairness; honesty; trust.
Good Go. Narcotics slang: Fair amount of narcotics for money spent.
Good H. Slang: Good quality heroin, approximately 50% pure.
Good Head. Slang: A person who can be trusted.
Good Person. 1. A loyal member of the underworld. 2. A person who does business with the underworld but is not a member of the underworld.
Goods, The. 1. Slang: Evidence proving guilt of someone. "I have the goods on you." 2. Narcotics slang: Narcotics in general.
Good Time. Time of reduction of a prison sentence given for good conduct or work on the part of the prisoner.
Good Trip. Narcotics slang: Happy experience with psychedelics.
Goodwill. The favorable reputation of a business or company perceived by the public.
Goofballs. Narcotics slang: Depressant drugs—barbiturates; sleeping pills. See **Depressants**.
Goofed Up. Slang: Under the influence of barbiturates.
Goofer. Slang: One who drops pills.
Goon. Slang: A strong-arm man or thug (hoodlum) who uses force or threats to intimidate; a thug hired to harass people involved in a dispute.
Goon Squad. Slang: Tactical police squad for control of hoodlums.
Gopher. 1. Juvenile slang: One who is gullible; an easily fooled person. 2. Slang: A small safe.

Gorilla. 1. Slang: A strong-arm man; a "tough guy" hoodlum; a gangster. 2. Juvenile slang: Forcibly fake; pugnacious.
Go to Bat. Slang: To be sentenced to prison; to be tried for a criminal offense.
Go to Bed With (Someone). Slang: To have sexual relations with someone.
Gow. Narcotics slang: A cigarette of marijuana; narcotics; one who is an active narcotics addict.
Gow Head. Slang: An opium addict.
Graft. Obtain money dishonestly by reason of one's position as a public employee.
Grain Alcohol. An alcohol, C_2H_6OH, made from fermented starches and sugars. It is constitutent of alcoholic beverages. Same as ethanol and ethyl alcohol.
Gram. Slang: Gram of heroin, approximately ten capsules.
Grand. Slang: One thousand dollars.
Grand Jury. Jury whose task is to hear evidence concerning persons accused of crime and return indictments if they are satisfied a trial should be held. The number composing this jury varies among the states.
Grand Jury, Charging. The grand jury attached to a court whose purpose is to ratify or reject the prosecutor's request for a formal charge to be levied against a specific defendant.
Grand Jury, Investigatory. The grand jury attached to a court empowered to conduct investigations into possible crimes or corruption.
Grand Larceny. A theft of anything of value over a certain limit as set by the particular jurisdiction.

VOCABULARY

Grandma's. Slang: Gang headquarters.
Grand-Nephew. Son of one's niece or nephew.
Grand-Niece. Daughter of one's niece or nephew.
Grand Seal. The most important seal of a government stamped on documents to signify that they are official.
Grant. 1. To bestow; something granted to someone. 2. To admit as true.
Grantee. A person to whom rights are granted.
Grantor. The person by whom a grant is made.
Grapevine. Slang: A method of rumor passing; circulating information in an unofficial manner among members of an organization or group.
Graphology (gra *fol* a je). The study of handwriting for the purpose of determining the character of the writer.
Grapnel (*grap* nel). A device with one or more hooks for seizing things. Many times used for "dragging" in water to locate a drowned body or other objects.
Grass. Slang: Marijuana.
Grass Brownies. Slang: Cookies containing cannabis.
Grasshopper. Slang: Marijuana user.
Gratuitous Bailment (grat *too* it us). Bailment in which the bailee does not pay a fee to the bailiff for use of his money.
Gravitation (gra vi *ta* shun). Force drawing bodies together.
Gravy. Slang: A large, unearned amount of money that is easily acquired.
Gray. Slang: A white person.
Gray Market. Sale of goods or products at prices higher than ordinary value.

Grease. 1. Slang: Illicit or bribe money; protection money. 2. Juvenile slang: Inflict harm; eat. 3. Slang: Butter; nitroglycerin.
Grease Ball. Slang: An Italian.
Greaser. Slang: A Mexican.
Greasy Aces. Slang: A card or cards from a deck of playing cards that have been trimmed in order that they may be felt and read by cheats without being seen.
Greasy Spoon. Slang: Dining room for inmates assigned to farm detail at a prison.
Greek Bottom. Carnival term: Dealing the second card from the bottom while dealing from a deck of playing cards.
Greenies. Slang: Green, heart-shaped tablets of dextroamphetamine sulfate and amobarbital.
Grenade (gre *nade*). An object, small enough to be thrown by hand, that contains chemicals, which are liberated by a timing device or by physical fracture of the device. Explosive grenades are used as military weapons. A tear gas grenade is used to move people or as a protection device.
Grid Search. A technique for searching crime scenes, usually outdoors, whereby an area that has been previously searched by the strip method is again searched after dividing the area into lanes or zones running at right angles to such plots used in the strip search. See **Strip Search**.
Griefo. Slang: Marijuana.
Grievance. Complaint or resentment, or a statement expressing this, against a real or imagined wrong.
Grievance Procedure. An established method of settling worker-employer conflicts.
Griffo. Slang: Cannabis.

Grifter. Slang: A confidence man; a gambling promoter who plays with small amounts.

Grimace (gri *mase*). Twisting the face; a peculiar smile.

Grind. Gambling slang: A gambler or a gambling game involved in small bets.

Gripe. Slang: Complain.

Grogged. A drunk; being intoxicated; being hung over.

Grooves. Firearms term: The depressed portion of the inside of a rifled gun barrel, between the lands, usually spiralled. They, together with the lands, grip the bullet as it travels through the barrel, causing it to spin.

Groovy. Slang: Good; OK; acceptable; something that meets with approval.

Gross. Slang: Bad; shameful.

Gross Negligence. Apparent failure to exercise care demanded by circumstances.

Gross Reproduction Rate. Number of female children born per 1000 newly born females who will survive the childbearing years.

Gross Weight. The weight of a vehicle and/or the combination of the vehicle without the load on all axles, including the steering axle, and the weight of axles thereon.

Grouchy (*grou* chy). Unhappy, sullen, in bad humor; abrupt in search.

Ground Control. Slang: Caretaker in an LSD session.

Groundless. Baseless; without foundation.

Grounds. Sufficient cause; a base or foundation; good reason. To maintain an argument or purpose.

Group Therapy. A form of psychotherapy where several patients interact under the watch of a group leader or psychotherapist.

Grubby. Slang: Dirty; greasy; grimy.

Gruesome. Horrible; frightful. "The crime scene was gruesome."

Guardian. A person, usually designated by law, who takes care of someone who is physically, mentally, or legally unable to take care of himself; one who has charge of another.

Guerrilla (guh *ril* uh). Member of a group or band who carries on harassment activities against the enemy by raiding supply bases, etc., many times behind enemy lines. Not considered an official part of the military establishment. See **Urban Guerrilla**.

Guff. Slang: Disrespectful talk; idle or meaningless talk.

Guide. Slang: One who "babysits" with a novice when he goes up on a psychedelic substance.

Guidelines. 1. Directions, rules, or instructions that delineate methods or procedures of doing something. 2. Actual lines drawn on a surface (ground, floor, or racetrack) to guide the route of travel.

Guillotine (*gill* o teen). A beheading device developed in France and used for execution. A heavy blade slides down grooves in each of two supporting posts.

Guilt. Being wrong; having committed an offense in violation of a criminal law.

Guilty. Having done something wrong involving or showing guilt. "The jury found the accused guilty."

Gumball Machine. Slang: Revolving light on a police car.

Gun. 1. A weapon, usually portable, from which a missile is thrown by a force such as explosives, springs, or compressed air. 2. Slang: A pickpocket. 3. Slang: A hypodermic needle.

Gun Control Laws. Federal, state, and local laws that regulate the importation, manufacturing, distribution, sale, purchase, or possession of firearms. The Alcohol, Tobacco, and Firearms Division of the United States Treasury Department has jurisdiction over the federal laws.
Gunfire. The discharge (shooting) of a gun.
Gunman. A person who uses a gun to commit crimes of violence.
Gun Moll. Slang: A woman companion or accomplice of law violators; a woman who is a thief or other type of criminal.
Gunpowder Test. The testing of objects for the presence of gunpowder residues.
Gunsel. Slang: A latent or passive homosexual.
Gunshot. The firing of a gun. "The victim was killed by gunshot wounds."
Guru. Slang: Companion on a drug trip who has tripped before.
Gushy. Sentimental; overly friendly.
Gut-Box. Slang: Compartment on a safe containing the combination mechanism.
Guts. Slang: Determination; "grit"; courage.
Gutter Hype. A drug addict who uses a safety pin to puncture the skin and then lets the heated drug drip down the pin into the perforation.
Guzzle. Drink fast; drink large quantities swiftly.
Gyp Artist (jip). Slang: A proficient swindler or cheater.
Gyp Joint (jip). Slang: A place of business where the customers are cheated or overcharged on items purchased.
Gypsy (*jip* see). 1. A person belonging to a group of wanderers, having no permanent place of residence, usually having dark skin and hair. Origin unknown, probably India. 2. Gambling term: An unreliable carnival worker or operator.
Gyve (jive). Slang: Marijuana cigarette; marijuana.
Gyves (jives). Chains or shackles for the legs.

H

H. Slang: Heroin.

Habeas Corpus (*hay* be us *kor* pus). Latin: "You have the body." Law: A court order (writ) requiring that a prisoner be brought before the court to determine if he is being held legally.

Habit. 1. A behavior pattern of doing things in a certain way. 2. Slang: Narcotic addiction. "He has a big habit."

Habit, Off the. Slang: No longer a drug addict; cured of drug use.

Habitual (ha *bich* oo el). Doing something by habit; doing something frequently and from habit.

Habitual Criminal. One sentenced to prison for a long sentence because of a specified number of prior convictions. This may be two or more prior convictions.

Habitual Intemperance. The use of intoxicating drinks that causes a person not to attend to business or inflicts mental anguish upon an innocent party.

Habituation. A psychological dependence upon a substance such as marijuana or tobacco. Withdrawal from such is essentially psychological in nature.

Hack. Slang: Convict term to denote penitentiary guard or official.

Hacksaw. A device having a rigid frame suspending a sturdy hard steel saw blade capable of sawing metal. The blade alone will slowly penetrate metal. Frequently used to cut through prison bars.

Hag. Slang: A vicious or malicious ugly old woman.

Haggard (*hag* erd). Having an abnormal appearance resulting from fear, pain, or fatigue.

Hair. A threadlike filament that grows from the skin of humans and most other mammals. On humans it is described as head and body hair. In law enforcement, hair is used as a descriptive term or factor.

Hair of the Dog that Bit Me. Slang: A drink or intoxicant that had previously made the drinker sick or intoxicated; alcoholic beverage drunk in the hope of it relieving a hangover.

Hair Trigger. The trigger of firearm so adjusted that it operates at slight pressure.

Half a Yard. Fifty dollars.

Half Blood. Person related to another only through one parent; the relationship of persons having one parent in common.

Half-Breed. Son or daughter of parents of different races.

Half Brother. A male person related to a brother or sister through only one parent.

Half Sister. A female person related to a brother or sister through only one parent.

Halfway House. A facility to meet the needs of individuals who are in transition between residential institutions (such as mental hospitals, prisons, alcoholism centers, and addiction treatment centers) and life in the community. The halfway house provides a supportive, partly structured atmosphere that facilitates development of independence and social skills.

VOCABULARY

Halifax Law. A lynch law to hang people without a fair trial.

Hallucination (ha loose sigh *nay* shun). Unrealistic perception (seeing, hearing, feeling) of things. Such experiences usually occur from disorders of the nervous system and are not caused by external stimuli; a sense perception not founded in objective reality; an illusion.

Hallucinogenic (ha loose ana *jin* ick). Producing or causing hallucinations.

Hallucinogens (ha *loose* a na jins). Drugs or substances that may cause hallucinations. Hallucinogens make up one of the three general categories of dangerous drugs (stimulants and depressants are the others) and are so named because they may produce hallucinations or illusions of the various senses.

Haloperidol (hal o *pair* i dall). A new nonnarcotic, nonaddicting drug for treating and controlling withdrawal symptoms associated with both heroin and methadone addiction. This drug was reported on at the drug symposium at Xavier University held in New Orleans in the summer of 1971.

Ham. Slang: 1. An amateur radio operator. 2. An amateur; a poor or inexperienced performer.

Hammer. 1. The part of the firearm that strikes the firing pin, which in turn detonates the charge. 2. Juvenile slang: Girl (many of them carry their boyfriends' weapons.)

Hammerlock. The twisting and bending of an opponent's arm behind the back of the opponent.

Handbook. Slang: Place where horse race bets are handled, other than at the racetrack.

Handcuffs. Hinged bands, usually metal, joined by a short chain, which can be locked on the wrists of a person to restrain him.

Handicapper. Gambling term: A person who establishes the approximate odds on events—sporting events or horse races.

Handkerchief Switch. A con game where the victim is enticed to put some money in a handkerchief into which one of swindlers has placed some. The victim is to hold the handkerchief until a specified event happens. The handkerchief is switched before being given to the victim and the swindlers escape before the fraud is detected.

Handle. 1. Gambling term: The total amount of wagered money handled by the betting promoters. The amount of money bet in a day or in a certain period of time at the tracks or by bookies. 2. Slang: A name or nickname.

Hand Printing. Printing by hand the letters of the alphabet and arranging them into words. This may be done with a pen, pencil, or other writing instrument. It is contrasted with handwriting. The document examiner cannot make adequate comparisons of handwriting if the known specimens are in hand printing and vice versa.

Hand-to-Hand. 1. At close quarters; physical combat at close quarters. 2. Narcotics slang: Delivery at time of payment.

Hand-to-Mouth. Slang: Consuming what is available without providing for the future; improvident; not thrifty.

Handwriting. Writing by hand, usually with a pen or pencil; a style of writing different from hand printing.

Hanged, Drawn, and Quartered. A method of executing traitors in old

England. The person was hanged until half dead and then cut up into pieces and beheaded.

Hangfire. Slow or delayed detonation or firing of a cartridge or shotgun shell in a firearm.

Hanging. Suspension by the neck until dead. This was a method of legal execution used in England from ancient times and generally followed in the United States until comparatively recent years when other methods of capital punishment were adopted.

Hanging in Chains. A practice in old England of taking the executed body and hanging it near the place where the crime was committed.

Hangout. Slang: Place of rendezvous, used by criminals; place frequently visited.

Hangover. State of intoxication continued into the morning from the evening before after the subject has slept, often accompanied by headaches and nausea.

Hangup. Slang: A delaying problem, something that slows down or stops progress of a project.

Hansen's Disease. Leprosy.

Happy Dust. Slang: Cocaine.

Harass. To annoy, torment, aggravate, or generally trouble someone.

Harbor. A place of refuge; to serve as protection.

Hard Case. A difficult case to adjudicate fairly by existing legal principles.

Hard Core. The permanent or central part of something.

Hard Liquor. Alcoholic content of a substance of 80 proof or more; includes whiskey, rum, and vodka and excludes beer and wine.

Hard Stuff. Slang: Heroin; opiates.

Hardware. 1. Computer term: The computer equipment or machinery; electric data processing equipment. 2. Slang: Weapons, usually guns.

Harlot. A prostitute; a whore.

Harness Bull. Underworld slang: A law enforcement officer.

Harp. Slang: To beef or complain.

Harry. Slang: Heroin.

Hash. Slang: Hashish.

Hashbury. Slang: Haight-Ashbury, a district in San Francisco.

Hashish (*hahsh* eesh). 1. A powdered and sifted form of the resin from the flowering top of the female cannabis (hemp) plant. It is a potent, intoxicating drug. 2. Slang: Marijuana.

Hatch. Slang: To think of and plan a scheme.

Hatchet Man. Slang: One who carries out acts of violence for a lawless group.

Haul In. Slang: Arrest and bring the person to jail.

Haunt. A hangout; a place frequented.

Hawk. Slang: 1. One who seeks to settle international conflict or war principally by means of military force. Term used extensively during the Vietnam war of the late 1960s and the early 1970s for those advocating a strong military stand in Vietnam. 2. A swindler and a con man.

Hawk, The. Slang: LSD.

Hay. Slang: 1. Marijuana. 2. Money.

Hay Bag. Slang: A woman who is a vagrant.

Hay Burner. Racetrack slang: A horse.

Hazardous. Risky; dangerous; fraught with danger.

H.C.U.A. (HCUA). House Committee on un-American Activities. A committee of the House of Representatives, United States Congress, which investigated various un-American groups, especially the

Communist Party and its front groups, during the 1960s.
Head (hed). 1. Top part of the human body; a feature used in describing a person. 2. Slang: Latrine; bathroom; toilet. 3. Narcotics slang: Person dependent on drugs.
Headbeater. Slang: A law enforcement officer.
Head Money. Gambling term: Win price.
Head of Family. An individual who supports one or more individuals in a household and provides for them under some moral and legal obligation.
Head of Household. The person who is regarded as head by members of the household; most frequently, the principal breadwinner of the family is considered as head. Also, a category of federal taxpayers who meet several requirements and pay lower tax rates.
Head Shrinker. Slang: Psychiatrist.
Health, Education, and Welfare (HEW). The United States Department of Health, Education, and Welfare.
Hearing. Law: An examination of an accused person before a magistrate (preliminary hearing). It may also involve testimony by witnesses. The purpose is to establish probable cause for the magistrate to "hold" the accused for further prosecutive action or release him if probable cause of guilt is not established.
Hearing Examiner. In an administrative agency, an official with judicial powers within the agency.
Hearsay Evidence. See **Evidence, Hearsay.**
Hearsay Exception. Evidence admitted in court from a witness that is not his personal knowledge but knowledge he has heard from others.
Hearsay Rule. The rule of evidence that prohibits the use of hearsay evidence in the trial of a criminal case. There are exceptions.
Heart. Juvenile slang: Courage.
Hearts. Slang: Stimulant drugs—amphetamines. Dexedrine tablets (from the shape).
Heat. 1. Slang: An intense search by police for certain criminals; to strictly enforce gambling laws. 2. Narcotics user slang: The police.
Heat, Bring to. Prison slang: To attract the attention of the police or prison officials.
Heater. Slang: A pistol or other handgun.
Heat of Combustion. The amount of heat required to burn a substance in oxygen.
Heat of Passion. An abnormal mental state of rage produced by some highly inflammatory event.
Heat Stiffening. A rigidity found in dead bodies after exposure to excessive heat.
Heatstroke. Illness or disability resulting from exposure to too much heat.
Heaven Dust. Slang: Cocaine.
Heavenly Blue. Slang: LSD.
Heavy. Slang: 1. Highly intelligent. 2. Significant, weighty; highly emotional.
Heavy Man. 1. Slang: A safeblower; a violent type of person. 2. Narcotics slang: One who has narcotics.
Heavy Paint Work Passers. Dice slang: Crooked dice that have been weighted with a heavy paint in spots.
Heckle. To annoy someone, usually a speaker, by asking many bothersome questions or making statements or other noises; generally bothering a speaker.

Hedge. 1. Failure to give a direct answer or to take a clear or definite stand on a matter. 2. Gambling term: To protect a bet by placing bets against the thing originally bet on.
Heel. Slang: 1. A person held in contempt due to low character or traits. 2. To sneak; an undependable companion.
Heeled, Well. Slang: Well supplied with money.
Heifer (*hef* er). Slang: A girl or young woman.
Height. Measurement from head to foot. Factor used in describing a person.
Heinous (*hay* nus). Horrible; repulsive; hateful.
Heir. A person who inherits or is legally entitled to inherit, through the natural action of the law, another's property or title upon the other's death.
Heist. Slang: To rob or hijack, especially merchandise in transit.
Heist Man. Slang: A robber or "hold up" criminal.
Held. To stand as fact, rule, or reason; to express one's view.
Hellcat. Slang: A malicious person.
Helmet. Protective headgear. Recommended where head injury is probable, such as in motorcycle riding or in dealing with unruly groups.
Helpee. Any person who needs or seeks help.
Helper. The person who accepts the helper role and responsibilities.
Hematoporphyrin Test (he ma to *pour* frin). A chemical confirmation test for the presence of blood.
Hemoglobin (*hiem* oh *globe* in). A protein found in red blood cells that aids in transporting oxygen to living cells and gives the blood its red color.

Hemophilia (*he* ma *feel* ya). Hereditary bleeder. An inherited trait where the blood does not clot normally, thus causing excessive bleeding from a slight wound.
Hemorrhage (*him* er ij). Profuse discharge of blood; bleeding from a broken blood vessel.
Hemp. Slang: Marijuana.
Henceforth. From now on; the present to the future.
Henry. Narcotics slang: Heroin.
Hep. Slang: Knowledgeable; having inside information.
Hepcat. Slang: One who likes lively music.
Herder. Slang: A prison-assigned correction officer.
Hereafter. 1. At a future time; after the present; used in statutes and legal documents.
Heredity. Traits or characteristics transmitted from parents to child.
Herein. In this matter; into this.
Heretofore. Up to this time; before the present.
Hermaphrodite (her *maf* re dit). A person who possesses the apparent genitals of both sexes.
Heroin (*herr* oin). A white crystalline powder; addictive narcotic made by chemical process from morphine; an opium derivative. No known medical value. It is outlawed in the United States, and the laws do not allow it to be produced here. Government agents estimate that over three thousand pounds are smuggled into the United States annually. Much of it originates in Turkey, some from Mexico and the Far East. The resin from the opium poppy goes to France, where it is refined and is then smuggled into the United States, much of it through Canada and Mexico. Attorney General John

VOCABULARY

N. Mitchell in 1969 said that about 20 percent of the heroin in this country comes from Mexico.

Hesitation Marks. When a person commits (or attempts) suicide by cutting, usually several small cuts are found near the large wound. These cuts are called hesitation marks and are probably caused by nervousness or the person trying the cutting instrument for sharpness.

Heterosexuality. Sexual attraction to persons of the opposite sex.

Heuristic. Guiding or revealing but not capable of proof.

Hex. Slang: Put on a magic spell.

Hiatus (high *ay* tus). A break or gap in something. For example, if some part of a written or spoken message is omitted, there is a hiatus in the subject matter. The word is frequently used in legal terminology.

Hick. Slang: One who is ignorant of daily goings-on of society.

Hideout. A place of hiding; place of seclusion. "The gang fled to their hideout."

Hierarchy (*hire* ar kee). A structural organization of persons, things, ideas, etc., in order of importance or rank, with fewer at the top than at the bottom of the order.

High. Slang: Heavily intoxicated. "He was high as a kite." Under the influence of stimulating narcotics or drugs. Intoxicated on drugs or narcotics.

High Energy Explosive. An explosive whose velocity of detonation exceeds 1,000 meters per second.

High-Hat. Slang: To treat people as being inferior.

High Roller. Slang: A big-time gambler.

High Seas. The ocean or sea that is outside (beyond) the territorial jurisdiction of a nation. "Crimes on the high seas come under federal jurisdiction."

High Treason. Treason against the sovereign or state.

Highway. A principal or main road, usually of considerable length, which is used by the public.

Highwayman. One who robs and commits crimes of violence on people travelling the public highways.

Highway Patrol or Police. A state law enforcement agency the functions of which vary among the states. "Patrol" generally involves power only to enforce traffic laws on the highways; "police" infers that the agency has jurisdiction over crimes on the highways of the state. The officer should become familiar with the authority and jurisdiction of the agency in his state. It may be synonymous with the state police in some states.

Highway Robbery. Robbery committed on or near a highway.

Hijack (*high* jack). To take by force goods or merchandise being transported. "The robbers hijacked the liquor truck." Many passenger-carrying airplanes have been "hijacked" and forced to fly to a foreign country that was not the original destination. This is a serious federal violation.

Hijack Alert System. A system worked out by trucking concerns, trucking associations, and law enforcement agencies whereby a theft or hijack is immediately reported to designated law enforcement agencies and to a designated trucking association. The latter, per a prearranged schedule, notifies certain strategically located trucking companies, who in turn notify others until all truckers in a given area are notified. The drivers and other employees search for and report the stolen equipment. It is called the "Domino Alert Theory."

Hillbilly. A somewhat disparaging term: One who is from the hill or mountain country—a country or backwoods locale.

Hip (Hep). Slang: To understand; opposite of square.

Hippies. Beatniks.

Hipster. Slang: One who is up to date on cheating and the gambling odds.

His Honor. A term of respect used to describe a member of the judiciary.

Hit. Slang: 1. One dose of a particular drug. 2. The killing or execution of a person designated for elimination by a gangster or other criminal. 3. To win at gambling. 4. To be dealt another card in the game of blackjack.

Hitherto (*hith* er *tu*). Thus far; up to the present; period of time already passed.

Hit Man. Prison slang: A killer; a robber.

Hit Slip. Gambling term: A slip prepared at the bank on a winning number.

Hit the Pipe. Slang: 1. To smoke marijuana or opium. 2. To furnish a fanciful story to the police.

Hit the Street. Slang: Discharged from a criminal charge without conviction.

Hoax. A false incident; a fictitious story.

Hock. Slang: To put something in a pawnshop.

Hockey Do. Juvenile slang: Uninteresting talk; a lie.

Hock Shop. Pawnshop.

Hocus. A narcotic solution ready for injection.

Hog. Slang: 1. A Cadillac automobile. 2. A motorcycle. 3. Prison slang: An inmate power figure who controls a number of other inmates to the extent that he may rent some of them as male prostitutes.

Hogwash. Slang: Nonsense.

Hoist. Slang: A holdup; armed robbery.

Hold. To prevent from getting away; a request to detain; a detainer; a request by one official to another to hold a person, who is in custody, for him.

Holder. A person who is legally entitled payment of a bill, note, or check.

Holding. Slang: Having drugs in one's possession.

Holdout. Gambling term: An apparatus used to cheat at cards.

Holdout Man. A card shark who cheats by palming a card and using it later in the game.

Hole. 1. Gambling term: Location of a telephone where bets are called in. 2. Slang: Solitary confinement.

Hole, In the. 1. In debt. 2. Prison slang: Imprisoned or confined in an isolated cell for special disciplinary purposes.

Hole, The. Slang: Isolated prison cell for solitary confinement.

Hole Up. Slang: To hide from the police; to secrete one's self.

Holocaust (*hole* o kost). A large, uncontrollable, very destructive fire.

Home Brew. Homemade beer or liquor.

Home Rule. Administration of county, city, or local governments by local citizens.

Homicide (*hahm* i side). The killing of a human being by the act, procurement, or culpable omission of another. Criminal homicide is the illegal (unjustified) killing of a human by a human.

Homicide, Felonious. See **Felonious Homicide.**

Homicide, Justifiable. The killing of a human by another who is justified by the law in doing so. Such is the case where one kills in self-defense or in the defense of another, or where the executioner carries out the death penalty imposed by law.

Homicide by Misadventure. An accidental killing, where the killer is doing a lawful act but is careless or reckless.

Homicide by Necessity. A form of justifiable homicide.

Homicide *per Infortunium.* Homicide by misfortune or accident. See **Homicide by Misadventure.**

Homicide Stab Wounds. Multiple stab wounds, generally found in a definite place on the body. Defensive wounds are sometimes found on the arms and hands.

Homo. 1. Slang: Homosexual—either man or woman. 2. A human being.

Homosexual. One who is attracted sexually to persons of the same sex.

Honky. Slang: Police officer disliked by activists.

Honky Tonk. Slang: A cheap tavern where gambling, dancing, and women of questionable reputation are found.

Hooch. Slang: Illegally made whiskey or related drink.

Hood. Slang: A ruffian, hoodlum, gangster, or person engaged in gang activities of violence.

Hoodlum. Slang: Same as **Hood.**

Hoodwink. Use of trickery to mislead.

Hook. 1. A fingerprint term, also called a "spur"—a hooklike ridge or small branch emanating from a single ridge line. 2. Slang: A thief. 3. Slang: To flee; to escape.

Hooked. Narcotics slang: To be addicted to narcotics.

Hooker. Slang: A whore or prostitute.

Hook Up. Slang: To become associated with a gambling organization.

Hooligan. Slang: A tough guy; hoodlum.

Hoosier-Up. Slang: Playing innocent; inexperienced.

Hophead. Slang: One addicted to narcotics.

Hopped-Up. Slang: Under the effects of narcotics or alcohol.

Horizontal Mobility. Changing occupations without any change in status.

Horning. Slang: Sniffing narcotics through the nasal passages.

Hornswoggle. Slang: To deceive, misrepresent, cheat, or swindle.

Horny. Slang: Lewd; desiring sex.

Horse. Slang: Heroin.

Horse Degenerate. Slang: One who has a compulsion to bet on horses.

Horse Room. A bookie's place of operations that is operated fairly openly.

Horses. Race horses that run in the races.

Horsey. Slang: To be contrary or disagreeable.

Hosticide. A person or persons who kill others who are their enemies.

Hostile (*hos* tel). Unfriendly; opposed to; uncooperative. Law: Where a witness is uncooperative with the party who calls him, with court approval he may be questioned as a hostile witness.

Hot. Slang: 1. Angry. 2. Passionate. 3. On a lucky streak; winning regularly. 4. Wanted by the police.

Hot Balling. Slang: To fix a game of bolita by heating the ball.

Hot Blooded. Easy to anger; hot tempered; passionate.

Hot Chair. Slang: The electric chair.

Hotel Game. Slang: A gambling game operated in a convenient location in a populous area that caters to travelling people.

Hot Horse. Racetrack gambler term: A horse that has been held back in races so as not to win, thus building up the odds, which will be taken advantage of when he runs in a race where he is expected to win.

Hot Seat. Slang: The electric chair.

Hot Shot. Prison slang: A fatal dose of heroin or other drug, usually to get rid of an addict who is "too hot," or about to be arrested, or one who is already in jail.

Hot Stuff. Slang: Goods that have been stolen.

Hot Tempered. Becomes angry quickly.

Hot-Water Ordeal. Old England practice of having the accused put his arms up to the elbows into seething hot water and the guilt was determined by the reaction.

House. Gambling term: The operators of a gambling business, either private or commercial.

Housebreaking. Breaking and entering a house for the purpose of commiting a felony.

House Committee On un-American Activities. See **HCUA**.

Household. A household consists of (1) all persons, whether present or temporarily absent, whose usual place of residence at the time of interview is the housing unit and (2) all persons staying in the housing unit who have no usual place of residence elsewhere.

Household Incident. See **Incident**. Crimes of burglary, attempted burglary, household larceny, attempted household larceny, and motor vehicle theft are considered household incidents.

Household Larceny. Theft or attempted theft of property or cash from the home or its immediate vicinity. Involves neither forcible entry nor unlawful entry.

House Mob. Two or three house burglars working together to burglarize flats, apartments, or houses. They coordinate their activities so that one acts as a lookout while the others ransack the premises.

House Percentage. The odds in favor of the operator; the percentage of profit calculated for the one owning the gambling operation.

House Trailer. A trailer used as a permanent dwelling.

Housing Unit. A group of rooms or a single room occupied as separate living quarters; that is, (1) when the occupants do not live and eat with any other persons in the structure and (2) when there is either direct access from the outside or through a common hall or complete kitchen facilities for the unit.

HP. Highway patrol; high police. The letters are usually preceded by the first letter in the name of the state, i.e. MHP for the state of Mississippi.

Hue. Sound alarm by shouting. In olden times a criminal was pursued by "hue and cry." The citizens would chase the criminal with shouts and cries.

Hull. The metal portion of a cartridge (ammunition).

Human Relations. An understanding of why people act in a certain manner, how they get along together in a group setting, and the characteristics of persons and groups. The officer in the field is concerned with

VOCABULARY 131

linking the larger view of human relations to the tasks and functions of the law enforcement agency, particularly as to how organization changes occur, and the resulting interaction of individuals in a day-to-day situation. A fuller understanding of community organizations and their human elements.

Humidity (hue *mid* ity). The moisture content of the atmosphere.

Hummer. Juvenile slang: False charge.

Hump. Slang: To have sexual intercourse.

Humpback. A person having a hump or raised area on the back.

Hung. Slang: Involved in a love affair.

Hunger Strikes. Prisoners going without food to bring attention to their cause.

Hung Jury. A jury that is unable to agree on a verdict.

Hunky. Slang: A derogatory term referring to a European-born laborer.

Hush Money. Money paid to someone as payment for keeping quiet or not telling what he knows about a matter; a bribe.

Husky. A strongly built person, one who is robust.

Hussy. Slang: A woman of low repute or character.

Hustle. Slang: 1. To solicit as a prostitute. 2. Activities involved in obtaining money to buy heroin. 3. Criminal subculture slang: To "get by" without working; working at one's chosen racket or profession.

Hustler. Slang: 1. A prostitute. 2. One who gets by without working; member of the underworld in general.

Hydrocarbon (*high* dro *car* bon). A simple compound that consists only of carbon and hydrogen.

Hydrocyanic Acid (high dro sigh *an* ick). A water solution of hydrogen cyanide. It is a colorless, extremely poisonous liquid. The odor is bitter. It is also known as muriatic acid.

Hydrodynamics of Blood Drops and Splashes. The patterns, shapes, and sizes of blood drops and splashes produced by factors such as height of fall, direction, and speed of body from which they emanated.

Hydrostatic Test (high dro *stat* ick). A test to determine if an infant was born alive or not. It involves placing the lungs in water to check for air.

Hymen. A thin membrane across part of the vagina, usually found in a virgin.

Hype. Slang: 1. Narcotics addict. 2. A short-change artist.

Hype Outfit. Equipment for injecting drugs.

Hypertension. 1. High blood pressure. 2. Maximum blood pressure in the arteries when the heart is pumping.

Hype Stick. A hypodermic needle.

Hypnosis (hip *no* sis). A condition resembling normal sleep brought about by a hypnotist whose suggestions the subject accepts readily.

Hypnotic Drug. A drug that induces sleep similar to that of hypnosis.

Hypo. 1. Slang: A narcotic addict who administers the drug by hypodermic needle; a hypodermic needle; a narcotics user. 2. Medical slang: The giving of a prescribed injection by a hypodermic.

Hypomania (hi po *ma* ne a). A mild form of mania.

Hypostasis (hi *pas* te sas). Medical term: 1. The deposit of sediment in the body. 2. A congestion or flushing of the blood vessels.

Hypothesis (high *poth* e sis). Something assumed to be true; a guess that something is correct; something likely to be true; supposition or thesis.

Hypothetical Question. In the law of evidence, a question asked an expert witness that asks him to assume that certain facts are true and then formulate an opinion based on these assumed facts.

Hysteria (hiss *tier* e uh). A psychoneurologic condition characterized by loss of memory, loss of motor functions, or disassociations. A wild state of excitement.

I

I.A.A.I. (IAAI). International Association of Arson Investigators.

I.A.C.P. (IACP). International Association of Chiefs of Police, Inc.

I.B.P.O. (IBPO). International Brotherhood of Police Officers.

I.C.C. (ICC). Interstate Commerce Commission.

Ice. Slang: Pure diamonds.

Ice Cream Habit. Sporadic use of drugs.

Ideal Sadism. Fancied, imaginary sadism; in this condition sadistic acts exist solely in the imagination of the subject. It may precede actual sadistic acts.

Identi-Code® Index. A letter-number symbol appearing on each capsule and tablet and on each label of suppositories and of powders for oral suspension on Lilly products. The Identi-Code Index shows the specific product name and its formula.

Identification. Imagining ourselves in other's roles.

Identification Number. The number assigned to a person whose fingerprints are on file in an identification bureau of a police agency. The record of this person showing all arrests, convictions, and dispositions, is shown under this number for that department.

Identification Order (IO). The official wanted notice of the FBI, issued for persons wanted by the FBI for crime violation. Each is numbered (in sequence), is dated, and has the following information: the criminal charge, name and aliases of the subject, subject's fingerprints, description and photograph, criminal record, information of caution concerning the subject, and request that the FBI be notified of any information concerning the subject. These are widely distributed to law enforcement agencies, post offices, and government agencies having frequent contact with the public.

Identification Record. Criminal record. The record of an individual as maintained in the identification bureau of a law enforcement agency. The identification of the person should be made on fingerprints. The record shows the arrests, convictions, and dispositions of the individual.

Identify. To recognize a person or thing as being the same as a particular person or thing. In the area of physical evidence, to place markings on evidence or place it in marked containers so it can be positively recognized at a later time.

Identi-Kit®. A trade name for a commercial product utilizing many transparent overlays, by which one may prepare a sketch of a person based on descriptions. A state appellate court in New Jersey in 1970 upheld the use of such sketches upon which the accused was apprehended.

Idiopathic Insanity (id e o *path* ik). A result of a brain disease, lesions of the cortex, etc.

Idiot (*id* e it). A person having such a severe degree of mental deficiency as to require someone to care for him constantly.

Ignite (ig *night*). To catch fire; to burn; to set fire to.
Ignition (ig *nish* in). The beginning of flame propagation or burning. The starting of a fire.
Ignition Temperature. The lowest temperature that will cause spontaneous ignition of a given fuel.
Il Capo. Synonymous with the "Boss" in the Cosa Nostra.
Illegal. Not legal; against the law; something prohibited by law.
Illegal Arrest. An arrest made without a warrant or probable cause.
Illegal Detention. The unlawful detention of a person where there is not sufficient cause to believe the person has committed a crime for which he could be arrested. Under such conditions a court has ruled that a confession, even though given voluntarily, is not admissible in evidence.
Illegible (ill *lege* i ble). Difficult or impossible to read.
Illegitimate (ill le *jit* i mitt). Born of parents not married to each other; born out of wedlock.
Ill Fame. Bad reputation.
Illicit (il *lis* it). Unlawful; contrary to criminal law; illegal.
Illusion (i *lue* zhun). Something that is different from the way it appears; a mistaken or false belief or idea.
Image (*em* ij). The mind's picture of something or someone; concept. Idea of things or people.
I'm Beat. Narcotic slang: I need a marijuana lift.
Imbecile (*im* be sill). One whose mental age is between that of a moron and that of an idiot; one who is stupid.
I'm Down With You. Juvenile slang: I'll fight on your side.
I'm Holding. Narcotics slang: I have drugs. Immaterial. Not pertinent; not material; not importantly related to the case.
Immediacy. Ability to understand what is going on between a helper and helpee, also used to describe immediate or short-term goals.
Imminent. Just about to happen; threatening.
Immoral (i *mar* el). Having bad morals; not compatible with good conscience or public morality; contrary to the rules and principles of morality.
Immovable. 1. That which is not movable. 2. Law: Houses, land, structures, etc.
Immunity (i *mu* ne ty). Law: 1. Freedom or exemption from certain duties and/or offices that the ordinary citizen is required to do. 2. The legal right to force a person to testify concerning his knowledge or involvement in a matter with the agreement that he cannot be prosecuted for offenses about which he testified.
Immunity, Diplomatic. Immunity from arrests and other legal involvement that an official diplomat of another country has while in this country.
Impact. Firearms term: The force on an object by the projectile, i.e. the force of the bullet on what it strikes.
Impact Cities. A set of eight central cities in which LEAA funded various anticrime programs. Victimization surveys also were sponsored by LEAA in these cities in 1972 and in 1975. The term impact cities has been used as a convenient descriptor of this set of victimization surveys.
Impair. Weaken, make worse, lessen, or otherwise hurt.
Impalement (im *pail* ment). An ancient method of punishment consisting of thrusting a sharp pale through the body.

VOCABULARY

Impanel. Select, from a list a group of persons and bring them together to serve as a jury; enter on a list for jury duty.

Impeach. 1. To accuse, to discredit, or to censure. 2. To remove a public official from office for reasons of misconduct or illegal activity, by prescribed methods. 3. In the Congress of the United States proceedings are started in the House of Representatives by a written accusation called the articles of impeachment, which is directed to the Senate where the case is tried.

Impeachment. 1. Questioning the ability or integrity of a person or a thing with the intention of discrediting them. 2. The impliance of defective performance or fault, particularly that of a public officer. 3. Seeking the removal of a public officer upon formal charges of official misconduct, neglect, or the commission of a crime. 4. To impeach a person is to blame, censure, or accuse him.

Impeachment of Witness. Offering proof that a witness who has testified in a judicial proceeding is not worthy of belief; attacking the credibility of a witness.

Impediment. Legal inability to make a contract; for example, an impediment to marriage might be a prior marriage that is still valid.

Impersonate. Pretend to be someone else.

Impertinence. Irrelevance in the sense that the proof offered may be relevant to an issue but the issue is irrelevant to the trial.

Implications Role. Possible results of playing a role in given ways.

Implied. Known indirectly; known by analyzing surrounding circumstances or the actions of the persons involved; the opposite of express.

Implied Consent. See **Consent, Implied.**

Implied Contract. Contract where the intention is not manifested by explicit or direct words but is deduced or implied from the circumstances, the general language, or the conduct of the parties.

Implied Remedies. The right to file suit in order to protect your constitutional rights, even though the lawsuit itself might not be provided for by law.

Imply. Means to suggest or infer; to deduce, as in implication and inference.

Impotence. Medical term: Inability of the male to have sexual intercourse.

Impound. To secure; to make safe; to confine.

Imprimatur (im pre *mat* er). Let it be printed.

Imprison. To incarcerate; to lock up a person; to put someone in jail or prison.

Impulse. Irresistible or uncontrollable desire.

Imputed. Charged or attributed to a person, not as the one who personally created the situation or perpetrated the wrong from which injury has resulted, but as one who, due to his relationship to another person, is deemed responsible for that person's acts and omissions. Also, to be implicated or held responsible for the acts or ommissions of another person due to your relationship with that person.

Imputed Knowledge. Concerning facts that a person has the means of knowing, and that which it is one's duty to know.

Imputed Negligence. Holding a person responsible for the negligence of another person by reason of his relation to that person.

Inadmissible. Facts or things that cannot be admitted into evidence in a trial.

Inadvertent. Not done intentionally; done through carelessness; negligent.

Inalienable (in *alien* able). Something that cannot be given away, waived, or taken away.

INC. Incorporated.

In Camera. In privacy or in chambers. A hearing in private with the judge, either in his chambers or in court with the spectators excluded, is said to be heard *in camera*.

Incapable. Legally unable to do something. By law, certain persons, or persons with defects, are considered incapable of violating the criminal law. Among these are children under certain ages, mental incompetents, and those who act through mistake of fact or in ignorance.

Incapacitation (in ka *pas* i *tay* shun). An objective of sentencing, the aim of which is to restrain a potential offender from committing new and/or different crimes, usually by holding him in a maximum security prison.

Incapacity. 1. Lack of legal ability or power to do something; for example, a child has a legal incapacity to vote or make contracts. 2. An injury serious enough to prevent working.

Incarcerate (in *kar* see rate). To confine in jail or prison; to imprison; to hold in a place of confinement such as jail or prison.

Incendiary (in *send* e ery). Involving a deliberate, illegal burning of property.

Incest (*in* sest). Criminal law: The act of sexual intercourse between persons closely related by blood, the relationship being prescribed by law.

Incestuous Adultery. (in *ses* chew us). A married person having sexual intercourse with a relative.

Incestuous Bastard. A person who is the offspring of parents who produced him by illicit intercourse and who were related to the degree as is prohibited by law for marriage.

Inchoate (in *ko* et). Partially existent; just begun; not completely formed; incomplete.

Incident. A specific criminal act involving one or more victims and offenders.

Incidental. Chance, accidental; appertaining to or depending upon something else as primary; a less important characteristic or quality found in association with a principal or more important quality.

Incidental Authority. Such authority as is directly and immediately appropriate to the execution of the authority expressly granted.

Incise (in *size*). To cut into with a sharp instrument.

Incite (in *sight*). To instigate some action; stir up trouble.

Inciting a Felony. The acts by one person to incite or procure another person to commit a felony.

Incognito (in cog *neat* o). In disguise; unrecognized.

Incompatibility. Disagreement; unable to be used together or live in harmony together.

Incompetent Evidence. Restricted evidence in a legal proceeding; inadmissible.

Incompetent Persons. Persons who by law have been declared not competent and therefore not responsible for their criminal acts. Such are young children and insane people. This type of person is also dealt with in the laws of evidence,

where testimony from such persons is declared incompetent.
Iconolagy. Sexual gratification by looking at lewd pictures or interpreting works of art in a pornographic manner.
Inconsistent. Contradictory, so that if one thing is valid, another thing cannot be valid or that if one thing is allowed to happen, another thing cannot be.
Inconvenience. A broad word meaning anywhere from trivial to serious hardship or injustice.
Incorporeal. Without body; the opposite of corporeal.
Incorrigible (in *car* ridge able). So fixed in one's ways that one cannot be changed; a law violator who cannot be rehabilitated; a hardened criminal; one who repeatedly violates the law.
Incriminate (in *krim* i nate). To reflect guilt; to impute guilt or violation of the law; to imply illegal activity or guilt; to tend to show guilt; to charge with a crime or fault.
Incriminatory. To appear guilty of; to incriminate.
Inculpate (in *kul* pate). To imply guilt or wrongdoing; to accuse of crime; to involve in illegal or wrongful activity.
Inculpatory (in *kul* pa tory). Law of evidence; showing involvement in criminal activity; tending to establish guilt; indicating guilt; reflecting guilt; incriminating.
Incumbent (in *kum* bent). 1. A person who is serving in public office or position. 2. Obligatory, imperative.
Incumbent Role. Person occupying a given role.
Incur. Get; get something bad, such as a debt or liability, because the law places it on you; for example, you incur a liability when a court gives a money judgement against you.
Indecent. Repugnant; in bad taste; not proper.
Indefensible. That which cannot be made void or defeated; not to be avoided or defeated.
Indefinite Sentence. A system, not used in the United States, where a person is sentenced without minimum or maximum limitations and the length of time in prison is determined by his behavior and other factors.
Indemnify. To reimburse; protect against damage or loss.
Indemnity. A contract to compensate or reimburse a person for possible losses of a particular type; a type of insurance.
Indenture. Old word for a formal paper, such as a deed, with identical copies for each person signing it.
Indeterminate Sentence. A sentence of imprisonment that is not definite in extent or period. Technically such a sentence would not have a minimum or a maximum, and a judicial body would determine the length of the sentence based upon certain circumstances. As it is used in a practical sense in the system of justice in the United States, the law fixes the maximum sentence (at times the minimum and the maximum). The court pronounces the sentence within the guidelines, and the correctional system may reduce the time served if certain criteria are met by the prisoner leading toward his rehabilitation.
Indictment (in *dite* ment). A formal written accusation returned by a grand jury. The grand jury returns an indictment or "true bill" when it finds adequate cause to suspect that the accused committed a crime.

Indigent (*in* dee gent). Without financial means. Poor (financially); in poverty. Law: "Free counsel must be provided the indigent defendant in a serious criminal case."
Indigent Insane Person. An insane person who cannot pay for his stay in a hospital.
Indirect Evidence. Evidence that is not directly shown by documents or witnesses but is derived by inference from other proof offered; evidence of weight and value because of the inferences and presumptions arising therefrom; evidence based on and consisting of both presumptions and inferences.
Indorse (Endorse). To sign a paper or document.
Inducement. Statement leading on to some action; anything that induces, persuades, or provokes.
Industrial Espionage. A spy system whereby industrial trade secrets and information are obtained from other persons or industries. This practice is allegedly prevalent in industry.
Industrial Security. Security and protection of industry and businesses.
Industrial Security Organization. American Society for Industrial Security, 404 NADA Building, 2000 K Street, N.W., Washington, D.C. 20006. Phone (202) 338-7676.
Inebriate (in *e* bre ate). To make one drunk; to intoxicate.
Inequity (in *ek* wi ty). Unfairness; injustice.
In Extremis (in x *treme* iss). At the point of death.
Infamous (*in* fi mus). Disgraceful; heinous.
Infamous Crime. Generally a crime punishable by imprisonment in a penitentiary, with or without hard labor. Such crimes include a felony, treason, or perjury.
Infamy. Loss of good reputation because of conviction of a major crime.
Infancy. A general word for being a very young child. In some states, this means the same as minority.
Infant. 1. A person under the age of adulthood. 2. A very young child.
Infanticide (in *fan* ti side). The killing of an infant or a young child.
Inference. A fact or proposition that is shown to be probably true because it is the logical result of another fact or proposition that has already been proved or admitted to be true; for example, if the first four books in a set of five have green covers, it is the logical inference that the fifth book has a green cover.
Inferior Court. A court of limited, statutory, or special jurisdiction, whose record must show the attaching existence of jurisdiction in order to give its judgement presumptive validity.
Infernal Machine. A homemade bomb; an explosive device made to illegally destroy property or life.
Infinity (in *fin* e tee). The state or situation of having no limits; the state of boundlessness. The setting of an adjustable-focus camera that brings the camera into focus at a point at a given distance and beyond.
Inflammable (in *flam* e bul). Burnable; flammable.
Inflammatory Evidence. See **Evidence, Inflammatory.**
Influence, Political. The control, influence, or effect that a politician has in the operations of a law enforcement of other organization; the influence of a politician.
Informal Social Control. As by social rejection, ostracism by.

VOCABULARY

Informant. One who discreetly furnishes information to the police; an informer.

In Forma Pauperis. Latin: In the character or form of a poor person; upon appropriate application the courts may absolve a poor person of certain legal costs.

Information. A formal written charge against a person for committing an offense—a criminal violation of the law. It is presented or brought by a competent legal officer, such as the District Attorney or prosecuting official. It differs from an indictment in that it is not a charge brought by a grand jury. In some states an information may be used in lieu of an indictment in all cases except where the penalty is death.

Information, Direct Value. Important, pertinent information to a case; physical evidence, eyewitness accounts.

Information, Indirect Value. Information that is secondary to direct information, such as a criminal's background history.

Information, No Value. Information that has no pertinence to a case.

Informed Consent. A personal agreement for the allowal of something to occur, based upon the full factual disclosure that would be deemed necessary in order to make an intelligent decision.

Infraction. 1. Violation of a minor law. 2. A violation or breach of a contract or duty.

Infractions (in *frack* shens). Class of lesser offenses coming into criminal code.

Infrared Light. A light having a wavelength greater than the visible red. It is in the region of 8,000 to 9,000 angstroms. Used in the police laboratory to read writings that have been erased or obliterated and those that are not visible to the naked eye because of a dark background. It is at the opposite end of the spectrum from ultraviolet light.

Infringement. 1. A breach or violation of a right. 2. The unauthorized making, using, selling, or distributing of something by a patent, copyright, or trademark.

Inherent. Derived from and inseparable from the thing itself; for example, "inherent danger" is the danger some objects have by merely existing.

Initiation. An initial step or beginning; first step; also used to describe the additive or second phrase of the helping model (helpers phase 2).

In Judgement. In a court, for example, "the judge sits in judgement on the accused."

Injunction. Judicial order or decree requiring a party to do or not do certain acts. Most often the person is ordered not to do certain things—he is enjoined.

Injure. 1. Hurt or harm. 2. Violate the legal rights of another person.

Injurious Falsehood. To cause someone intentional harm or damage by making an untrue or fraudulent statement, even if it is not defamatory. (To make an untrue or fraudulent statement or accusation with the purpose of causing someone intentional harm or damage, even though it is not defamation.)

Inked Fingerprints. Fingerprint impressions taken after the fingertips have been inked, i.e. ink has been applied to the fingertips.

Ink Eradicator. A chemical solution used for making writings invisible to the eye. By the use of certain laboratory methods such writings can be seen.

In Kind. Same, but not identical; similar.
In Lieu of. In place of or in substitution for.
In-Line Machine. Slang: Pinball machine of the bingo type used for gambling.
In Loco Parentis. Latin: Discharging someone from parental duties and assuming the parental role oneself, although not the real parent.
Inmate. A person who is confined in a jail, prison, or asylum.
Innocent. Not guilty of the charge; having done no wrong.
Innovate (*in* i vate). To do something new; to introduce a new way of doing things.
Inorganic Compound (*in* or *gan* ick). A chemical compound that does not contain carbon.
In Personam (in per *so* nim). Latin Law: A legal action against a particular person.
Input. Something that is put in; in electronic data processing information put into the computer; information that a person receives from someone orally or in writing.
Inquest (*in* kwest). An inquiry by a coroner or a court into the cause of death where such occured under unusual or questionable circumstances; a legal inquiry into the cause of death under suspicious circumstances, to determine if crime was involved.
Inquiry Processing. Relates to electronic data processing computers. Incoming messages trigger a file search to retrieve information.
Inquisition (in que *zish* shun). A detailed and intensive investigation or inquiry.
Inquisitorial System. A system in which the burden of proof is upon the defendant to prove his innocence, not upon the prosecution to prove his guilt; it is the complete opposite of the adversary system used in trials in the U.S.
In re. Latin Law: In the matter of; in the case of; concerning.
In Rem. Latin Law: A legal action against property.
I.N.S. (INS) Immigration and Naturalization Service, under the United States Department of Justice.
Insane. Demented; mad; crazy; mentally unbalanced to the extent that the legal standards set forth by law are not met. In some states the legal test in criminal matters is whether the person was so demented that he did not know right from wrong.
Insanity (in *san* i tee). Mental illness; mental derangement.
Insanity, Partial. Mental unsoundness always existing, although only occasionally manifest.
In-service Training. Continuous training provided for law enforcement officers after the completion of their service, academy, and field training.
Inside Men. Gambling term: Bookkeepers who use computing equipment and other modern machinery for listing all bets and payoffs.
Inside Work. Gambler slang: The altering of dice by placing something inside them, i.e. loading dice.
Insolvency. The condition of inability to pay debts as they become due; bankruptcy.
Insolvent. Having more debts than one is able to pay; bankrupt.
Inspection. The right to see and copy documents, enter land, or do other things in order to gather evidence through the discovery process.
Inspector. A high ranking law en-

forcement officer, who is usually immediately below the head of the agency.

Instance. 1. Forceful request. 2. Situation or occurrence.

Instanter. Immediately; forthwith; without delay. Courts issue subpoenas or other orders specifying they are returnable "instanter," meaning the person upon whom served should perform, as ordered, immediately.

Instant Zen. Slang: LSD.

In Status Quo. Latin: In the same or former state or condition.

Instigate (*in* ste gate). Start; stir up; cause to happen.

Institute. Create; set up; bring into being; establish.

Institution. An establishment having a specific purpose to reform, educate, etc.

Institutional Racism (in sty *two* she nul *ray* sism). Policies of institutions that indirectly discriminate against minorities and ethnic groups.

Instrument. A tool; a device used to accomplish a given task.

Instrumentalities. The tools or means, such as guns and burglar tools, by which a crime is committed.

Instrumentality. 1. A means of accomplishment. 2. An agency that is under the total control of another agency.

Insubordination (in se *bor* di *nay* shen). Defiance; resistance to authority; disobedience; willful failure to obey orders; open refusal to obey orders. Insubordination is a basis of disciplinary action in a law enforcement agency.

Insulation (in se *lay* shen). The condition of being so far removed and so well concealed in the organizational structure of a criminal operation that proof of guilt is made difficult. This is a term used to describe the position of the leaders in organized crime.

Insulation, Safe. Fireproof material used between the outer and inner walls of a vault or safe so as to protect the contents against the effects of heat or fire originating on the outside of the container.

Insurance. Gambling term: A ten percent addition to a horse race bet that will assure the bettor of being paid track odds if he wins.

Insurrection (in sir *rek* shun). A rebellion, revolt, or uprising against established authority.

Intake Interview. The initial interview of a juvenile entering the juvenile justice system, where facts relative to the juvenile are examined by a representative of the court.

Integrate (*in* te grate). To bring parts together and make a whole. In recent years it has been referred to intermixing people of different races, especially the whites and non-whites.

Integration (in te *gray* shun). The fitting together of parts or units to make a whole. The mixing of races in public facilities. Desegregation; unification; amalgamation.

Intelligence (in *tel* i jens). Information about people, things, and events, which has been procured, evaluated, and stored for probable use at a later time in relation to criminal investigations.

Intelligence Files. Files in which intelligence information is stored in a systematic manner.

Intelligence Quotient (*kwo* shent). Designation of a person's mental development by a number arrived at by multiplying his mental age by 100 and then dividing this by his age in chronological years.

Intelligence Test. A standardized test designed to determine the mental capacity of an individual as compared with criteria that have been developed from testing many people.

Intelligence Unit. A unit of a law enforcement agency charged with the duty of obtaining, filing and disseminating intelligence information.

Intemperance. See **Habitual Intemperance.**

Intensify. To make more acute, sharpen, aggravate, heighten, or enhance; to describe levels of feelings.

Intent. Design, resolve, or determination with which a person acts; being a state of mind, it is rarely susceptible of direct proof, but must be ordinarily inferred from the facts (*Black's Law Dictionary*). Mere intent to commit a crime is not a criminal violation. An overt act must accompany or follow the intent. The law in some states declares that a person intends to do what he does. Most crimes require intent as an essential element; however, some do not have this requirement, particularly those that are less serious and do not involve moral turpitude. Some crimes, such as theft, require specific intent, others require only general intent, and others may find that constructive intent is sufficient. In cases of culpable negligence and in minor offenses, such as traffic violations, no intent is required.

Intention (in *ten* shun). Determination to do something a certain way.

Inter Alia (*in* ter *ail* ya). Latin: Among other things. A term used by legal writers and judges.

Interchangeable. Equal in feeling and meaning, content and intensity.

Intercourse (*in* tur korse). Dealings or communications between people; sexual intercourse is sex act between people.

Interdict (in tur *dikt*). To prevent or forbid someone from doing something.

Interface (*in* ter fais). Electronic data processing term: Ability of two or more computer machines to work together, i.e. to receive and transmit material to and from the other. "The computer of my department, although of a different make than that of the State Department, is interfaced with it."

Interim (*in* ter im). Gap in time between events; meanwhile. "An interim officer is appointed to fill a temporary vacancy."

Interior (in *teer* ee ur). The inside; the part of a country away from the border. "The interior of the house was dark."

Interlocutory (in tur *lock* you tory). Temporary; not final. Law: An interlocutory degree is a temporary court order pending the final determination of the case or matter.

Interlocutory Decision. A temporary judgement pending the resolution of the facts at issue.

Intermediary (in tur *meed* ee air ee). A person who is the connecting link or message carrier between other people; go-between. "John acted as intermediary for Henry and Tom during their dispute."

Intermediate Appellate Courts. The third level of state courts; appellate courts between trial courts and courts of last resort.

Intern; (Interne) (*in* tern). A student in a field who works with an organization engaged in that type of work. "The young man working toward his degree in Police Science worked as

VOCABULARY

an intern in the Police Department."
Internal (in *tur* nal). Inside of a body or thing.
Internal Affairs. The branch of a law enforcement agency that investigates possible wrongdoing within the organization.
Internalization. Interpreting others' responses to us.
International Association of Arson Investigators (IAAI). Address: 20 North Wacker Drive, Chicago, Illinois 60606. Publishes *The Fire and Arson Investigator.*
International Brotherhood of Police Officers (IBPO). First nationwide union of policemen formed at Denver, Colorado, May 25, 1970. Its first President was John Cassese, ten-year head of New York City's Patrolmen's Benevolent Association. Its headquarters, temporarily in New York City, were moved to Washington, D.C., in 1970. The Constitution contains a "no strike" clause.
International Criminal Police Commission (ICPC). An international organization of police administrators of different countries working in cooperation through a central international office. First organized in 1923 with headquarters in Vienna, Austria, it operated until World War II. It was reestablished in 1946 and its headquarters moved to Paris, France, located in the Police Nationale. Among its branches is the International Bureau, which works directly with the national bureaus of the participating nations. All participating nations except West Germany use the telegraphic address "INTERPOL." Reference: Soderman, Harry: *Modern Criminal Investigation*, 5th ed. New York, Funk and Wagnalls, 1962, p. 24. As of 1970 there were 107 nations, representing every continent, which were members. It is commonly referred to as INTERPOL. It is a cooperative agency, a clearinghouse for international exchange of information, doing no investigation itself. The United States joined the group, pursuant to federal legislation, in 1958. The United States Treasury Department is designated as the agency in this country responsible for liason with INTERPOL. References: Nepote, Jean: International Police Cooperation, *The Police Yearbook.* Washington, D.C., IACP, 1970, p. 135.
International Law. The principles and rules that regulate (govern) the dealings and relations of nations with each other.
International Police Academy. See **Academy.**
Internships. The training of employees of several agencies by temporarily exchanging these employees in order to learn more about the other agencies.
Interpleader. A legal proceeding by which a person sued by two or more persons having the same claim against him may compel them to go to trial with each other to arrive at a settlement.
INTERPOL. See **International Criminal Police Commission.**
Interpose (in ter *poze*). Come between; interject; intercede; place something between two or more things.
Interrogation (in tair o *gay* shun). An interview in great detail; to probe with questions persons believed involved in crime; to question in detail with the purpose of obtaining information relative to the involvement in crime of the person being ques-

tioned. The officer should know the requirements of the Miranda decision before interrogating.

Inter Se. Latin: Between (or among) themselves.

Intersection (*in* tur *sex* shun). Point where one thing crosses another; where lines, which are not parallel, cross; where streets cross.

Interstate. Between states. Many of the federal criminal laws are based on interstate commerce, i.e. movement from one state to another.

Interstate Commerce Commission (ICC). An independent United States government agency whose responsibility is to regulate and enforce regulations of common carriers engaged in interstate transportation.

Interstate Compact. An agreement between or among states that has been passed as law by the states and has been approved by Congress.

Interstate Gambling. Gambling transacted between states. Usually involves a wire service.

Interstate Highway. A road or highway located in more than one state. It usually means a highway extending across the nation.

Interstate Transportation. Transportation or movement between states; travel or transportation from one state to another or the District of Columbia.

Interstate Transportation of Stolen Motor Vehicle (ITSMV). The federal law forbidding the interstate transportation of a stolen motor vehicle (including aircraft), U.S.C. Title 18; Sections 2311-13.

Interview (*in* ter vyou). A conversation with a purpose; talking to a person about something.

Interview, Clientele Aspect. A subject being interviewed.

Interview, Language Aspect. Proper utilization of words and expressions in order to result in accurate and clear communication between the interviewer and the person being interviewed.

Interview, Method Aspect. Technique used by the interviewer during an interview.

Interview, Setting Aspect. The place where the interview is held.

Interview, Situation Aspect. The aspect of an interview that pertains to the crime itself under investigation.

Inter Vivos. Latin: Between living persons; from one person to another or others before their deaths.

Intestate (in *tes* tate). Law: Having no will; at the time of death not having disposed of property by will. "He died intestate."

In the Pocket. Gambling term: Controlled or being controlled.

Intimidate (in *tim* i date). To put one in fear; to frighten; to use threats or coercion to influence one to act or not to act.

In Toto. Latin: Entirely or completely.

Intoxicate. To get drunk; to saturate the bloodstream with alcohol, thereby causing damage to the brain and nerve tissue.

Intoximeter® (in *toks* i mee tur). Trade name of a device to test the breath to determine the amount (percentage) of alcohol in the blood.

Intrastate (*in* tra state). Occurring within a single state. "Travel is intrastate when it is done between points within a state."

Intrigue (*in* treeg). Crafty conspiracy; secret planning or scheme.

Intrinsic Evidence (in *trin* zik). Facts or information derived directly

VOCABULARY

from a document itself, without any outside explanation.

Introduction of Evidence. The presentation of evidence to be considered for use in a trial.

Introvert. One who thinks more about himself than he does about things going on around him.

Inure. To take effect; habituate.

Invalid. Without foundation; not correct; not valid; with no effect.

Inventory. Itemized list of articles, property, etc.

Invert. Sex deviation term: An individual with erotic inclination toward his own sex (homosexual).

Investigation (in *ves* ti *gay* shun). A careful search for facts. Synonyms; Examination, inquiry, search. "Facts are determined by a thorough investigation."

Investigation, External Function. Personnel, equipment, and other resources used in conducting an investigation.

Investigation, Internal Function. The experience, knowledge, intuition, and expertise of the investigator important to an investigation.

Investigation, Presentence. An official investigation, ordered by a judge or court, subsequent to conviction or a plea of guilty, for the use of the judge or court in arriving at the sentence to be given to the offender.

Involuntary Manslaughter. The unlawful, though unintentional, killing of a human being by a person engaging in an illegal act that is not a felony, not usually endangering to life, or engaging in a legal act in an illegal manner.

Iodine (*eye* oh dine). A chemical element (inorganic), which, among other things, is used in a crime laboratory to develop fingerprints on paper. The fumes of iodine are used for this purpose.

Ion (*eye* on). An atom or molecule that has gained or lost an electron, giving it a positive or negative charge.

Ipso Facto (*ip* so *fak* toe). Latin; Law: By the fact itself; by the mere fact; by that very fact.

I.Q. Test. See **Intelligence Quotient.**

Irrefutable (ear *ref* u ta ble). Impossible to disprove; undeniable; conclusive.

Irrefutable Presumption. Presumptions that the law will not suffer to be refuted by any counterevidence.

Irrelevant (ih *rel* e vant). Not related to; not applicable; off the point. "Irrelevant evidence is not admissible in court."

Irreparable (ih *rep* ur abul). That which cannot be repaired or restored. "The fire caused irreparable damage."

Irreparable Injury. An injury that ought not be submitted to or inflicted upon a person, and that cannot receive reasonable redress in a court of law.

Irresistible Impulse (ir i *zis* ti bel). As used in criminal law it refers to a situation where a person, due to a mental condition, is driven by impulse to do certain acts and his willpower or reasoning is insufficient to prevent it.

Irrevocable (ih *rev* o ka bul). Cannot be revoked or withdrawn; cannot be annulled. "He made an irrevocable commitment to the cause."

Irrumation. Obtaining an orgasm by the mouth, as in fellatio.

Isomorphism Role (eye sow *morph* ism). A condition in which the content of expectation, self-identity, and a cultural value is identical.

Isotope (*eye* so *toap*). A different form of an element in that the number of neutrons in the nucleus is different.

Issue. To put out; to put forth; to publish. "The court issued an order on the matter."

Italian Policy. Gambling term: Italian National Lottery. Lotto, Keno, and Binco resemble Italian Policy.

Itemize. List by separate articles or items; break down something by listing its separate parts.

I.T.S.M.V. (ITSMV). Interstate Transportation of Stolen Motor Vehicle.

I Wanna Thank You. Juvenile slang: I agree.

J

J (Jay). "Joint" or marijuana cigarette.
Jab and Burn. Juvenile slang: Double-cross.
Jabber. Slang: 1. Talk fast; chatter; talk with such speed as to be unintelligible. 2. A narcotic addict who takes drugs by injection.
Jack. Slang: Money.
Jacked Up. To be interrogated or arrested.
Jacket. Firearms term: Bullet covering.
Jackpot. Gambling term: Winning at long odds; hitting a combination on a slot machine that wins the money stored in the jackpot compartment of the machine.
Jackroll. Slang: To rob a drunk person; to steal or rob.
Jackroller. Slang: A robber who steals in dark alleys, whose main victims are intoxicated.
Jag. Slang: A drunken spree; an episode of intoxication or drug use.
Jail. A prison; building where persons are confined while awaiting trial or serving a sentence for minor offenses.
Jail Bait. Slang: Young seductive girls, especially below the age of seventeen. So called because of criminal penalties involved for sexual relations with them.
Jailbird. A person incarcerated in jail or one who has a substantial jail record—one who has been in jail several times.
Jailhouse Lawyer. A slang term for a prisoner who is well versed in legal matters and procedures and who gives his fellow inmates advice on their legal problems.
Jake. Slang: Good enough; pleasing to heart; correct.
Jam. Colloquialism: A tight spot; in trouble.
Jammed. Juvenile slang: Caught unaware and beaten by a group.
Jams. Juvenile slang: Jazz and "rock and roll" recordings.
Jam Session. Juvenile slang: Meeting of juveniles where "rock and roll" music is played.
Jam-Shot. Slang: A method of safe blowing.
Jane. Slang: A woman or a girl.
Jap. Juvenile slang: To ambush and attack.
Jar Dealer. A person who sells drugs in 1000 tablet or capsule bottles.
Jaywalk. To walk across the street without regard to regulations or traffic law requirements.
Jazz. Slang: Talk, usually talk about which there is some doubt.
J.D. Juris Doctor; Doctor of Laws.
Jedburgh Justice. Similar to a lynch law, where a person is hanged without a fair trial or any trial.
Jeopardy (*jep* are dee). Danger; peril; hazard. Law: The danger of conviction and punishment that the defendant in a criminal action incurs when he is lawfully charged with a crime before a tribunal properly organized and competent to try him. When jeopardy begins may differ slightly among the states; often it is when the petit jury has been impaneled and sworn or, if trial is before a judge without a jury, when the first

witness is sworn. See **Double Jeopardy.**

Jerk. Slang: A person who is not well liked.

Jerry House. Slang: Railroad section house.

Jesus House. Hippie term: A religious commune, where youths who have no regular home or job may stay if they embrace Christianity.

Jimmy. A tool, such as a screwdriver, crowbar, tire tool, or other similar instrument, used to pry open doors, windows, etc. To pry open a door, window, drawer, etc, with a jimmy.

Jive. Juvenile slang: 1. Not reliable; insincere. 2. Marijuana.

Jive Sticks. Narcotics slang: Marijuana.

Job. Slang: 1. A criminal act or accomplishment. "He pulled a safe job last night." 2. To inject drugs.

Jockey-Boxing. Slang: "Prowling" glove compartments of autos.

John. 1. Gambling term: A sucker. 2. Slang: A toilet or bathroom. 3. Prostitution: A customer.

John Doe. A made-up name used in some types of lawsuits where there is no real defendant, in a legal proceeding against a person whose name is not yet known, or as a person in an example used to teach law.

John Law. Slang: A law enforcement officer.

Joinder (*join* dur). Law: The joining of two or more persons or elements in a legal action.

Joint. Slang: 1. A place of questionable reputation where often illegal activities are carried on, such as sale of illegal alcoholic beverages. "He went to the beer joint." 2. Prison slang: A penitentiary. 3. Narcotics slang: A marijuana cigarette; syringe and needle; opium smokers' den.

Joint and Several. A liability where the creditor may sue one or more of the parties for a liability separately or all of them together, at his option.

Joint Sticks. Slang: Marijuana.

Joint Trial. A trial where two or more defendants, charged with the same crime, are tried simultaneously or together.

Jolly-Beans. Slang: Stimulant drugs—amphetamines; pep pills.

Jolt. Slang: 1. Narcotics injection or shot; first reaction from a shot of narcotics. 2. A penitentiary sentence.

Journal. A daily record; record of the transactions of a legislature.

Joy-Pop. Narcotics slang: A shot in the muscle of the arm rather than in the vein; to inject narcotics regularly.

Joy Powder. Heroin.

Joy Riding. Slang: Riding in a motor vehicle, for pleasure, without the consent of the owner. Law: Unauthorized use of a motor vehicle.

Joy-Smoke. Slang: Marijuana.

Judge. An officer, so named in his commission, who presides in some court; a public officer, appointed to preside and to administer the law in a court of justice (*Black's Law Dictionary*).

Judge Advocate. Prosecutor at a court-martial. His duties are to swear in the other members of the court, to advise the court, as well as to act as prosecutor.

Judgement. The final, official, and authentic order of a court of law concerning the issues that have been presented to it.

Judicial. Set by order of a judge; law courts, judges, or their functions.

Judicial Branch. That segment of government charged with the interpretation of law and the administration of justice; for example, United

States Supreme Court, state supreme, superior, and appellate courts, county courts, and magistrates' courts. The court subsystem falls under this branch of government.

Judicial Notice. An act whereby a court, in conducting a trial or framing its decision, will of its own motion and without the production of evidence recognize the existence and truth of certain facts, having a bearing on the controversy at bar, which are matters of general or common knowledge of every person of ordinary understanding and intelligence. Among such matters are the laws of the state, historical facts, the Constitution, and principal geographical features.

Judicial Question. A question that may only be properly determined by a court of justice, as distinguished from questions that may only be properly determined by the legislative or executive branches of government.

Judicial Review. The power of the courts to review and determine the constitutionality of statutes or administrative acts.

Judicial Sale. A sale made under the process of a court having competent authority to order it, by an officer duly appointed and commissioned to sell, as distinguished from a sale by an owner in virtue of his right or property.

Judiciary. The branch of government that interprets the law; the branch that judges.

Judo (*jew* dough). Special ability or technique to physically control or cope with another person; jujitsu.

Jug. Slang: 1. Jail or prison; a bank. 2. Juvenile slang: Horseplay; to antagonize; to provoke.

Jugs. Narcotics slang: Injectable amphetamine.

Juice. 1. Slang: Whiskey; the electric chair; a very high rate of interest on a debt. 2. A gambling game controlled by electromagnets. 3. Gambling term: An amount that is deducted from winnings on a sporting event; payment for protection. 4. Slang: Nitroglycerine.

Jujitsu (jew *git* su). Method of wrestling or physical combat with no weapons that uses the weight and strength of an opponent to his disadvantage. Originated in Japan; judo.

Jukebox. Slang: A coin-operated phonograph; usually taking a nickel or more to play one record.

Juke House. Slang: A house of prostitution.

Juke Joint. Slang: A roadhouse or tavern where music consists of a jukebox.

Jump. Slang: To assault and rob.

Junk. Slang: Heroin; morphine.

Junked-Up. Slang: Under the influence of drugs.

Junkie. Slang: A heroin user; a narcotics user.

Jurisdiction (jure iss *dik* shun). Area or extent of official legal authority of a government agency to deal with a matter. The jurisdiction of a police agency may apply to specific laws or to the geographical area in which it operates. The jurisdiction of a court may apply to the person of the offender or to the subject matter of the offense. "The state has jurisdiction over the matter."

Jurisdiction, Federal. Matters over which the federal government courts or agencies have control, supervision, or the right to investigate because of being a violation of federal criminal law or because of federal regulations.

Jurisdictional. The power to hear and decide cases; dealing with jurisdiction; the execution of justice.

Jurisprudence (jur is *prude* ence). The science or philosophy of the law and its applications; the body of the law as interpreted by the judiciary. "Before I give you an answer I need to check the jurisprudence."

Juror (*jew* ror). One who is sworn for or serves on a jury.

Jury. (*jew* ry). An officially authorized body of people whose funtion and duty is to find facts and report on their findings. There are two principal kinds: grand jury and petit jury (trial jury). The first is involved with bringing formal charges against a person, and the latter is to determine guilt after hearing the facts brought out in a trial. The number of jurors is set forth by law and varies among the states. At common law the number was not more than twenty-three and not less than twelve for the grand jury.

Jury Box. The enclosed area containing seats where the jury is seated during a trial.

Jury List. A list of names of all persons in a city, district, county, or other venue subject to be called in to serve on a jury.

Just Got Up. Slang: Just out of jail.

Justice (*jus* tis). 1. The quality of being fair; the dispensation of earned reward or punishment. 2. The title of the members of the Supreme Court of the United States and of some states.

Justice Court. A court presided over by a justice of the peace rather than a judge.

Justice of the Peace. A judicial officer (magistrate) of a lower court (inferior court) first appointed in England in the fourteenth century for the purpose of keeping the peace in a specified district. He had jurisdiction in minor cases, civil and criminal. In the United States he has limited civil jurisdiction and is limited to minor prosecutions and the commitment of offenders. His duties are fixed by law.

Justinian Code. The modernized Draconian code of laws, forming the basis for most modern European laws.

Juvenile. A person under legal age; generally under eighteen, but the age limit varies from state to state.

Juvenile Court. A court set up to handle cases of either delinquent or neglected children.

Juvenile Delinquent. One who is a criminal offender or whose conduct is antisocial, but because of his tender age he is not punished as an adult criminal.

Juvenile Hearing. The juvenile trial, equivalent to the adult trial.

Juveniling. Prison slang: Horseplay.

K

Kangaroo Court. Slang: An unofficial "court" organized by criminals in a jail or prison. Every new inmate goes before the court, where it is decided what money and other things, such as tobacco, he must turn in to the common pool. He is also assigned certain tasks of housekeeping.

Katatonia. (Catatonia). Medical term: A type of insanity with periods of acute mania and melancholia.

Kee. Kilo (2.2 pounds).

Keester. Slang: A safe; locked compartment inside a safe.

Keg. 25,000 amphetamine capsules or tablets, or more.

Kelly. Juvenile slang: Knock someone down with a punch.

Key. 1. A term used in fingerprint classification. It is obtained by counting the ridges in the first loop appearing in the set of fingerprints. The loop may be either ulnar or radial, and in any finger except the little finger (it is reserved for the final). The thumb may be used. 2. Narcotics slang: Kilo.

Key, The. Slang: The person in a jail or penitentiary who has the key or keys for locking or unlocking the cell doors.

Keyhole. Firearms term: An elongated hole made by a bullet that is travelling partially or entirely sideways in its flight.

Keystone Cop. A small-town, comical, or curiously uniformed private policeman.

K.G.B. In the Soviet Union (Russia), the Commission of State Security, an intelligence system for detecting and accumulating information from abroad.

Kick. Narcotics slang: Get rid of the habit; withdraw from the use of narcotics.

Kickback. Slang: 1. Rebate—return part or all of stolen property to the original owner. 2. Pay a commission on the purchase of goods or services to someone who has arranged for the sale.

Kickbook. Slang: Police complaint sheet.

Kicking the Gong. Narcotics slang: To spend time around a place where narcotics are sold.

Kick-In Job. Operation of a gang of burglars who drive up to the victim's premises, quickly force entry to the place of business, load the stolen goods into a getaway vehicle, and hurriedly depart from the scene.

Kick It. Slang: To break a habit, such as narcotics.

Kicks. A drug experience.

Kicksheet. Slang: Police complaint sheet.

Kick the Gong Around. Slang: To smoke marijuana or opium.

Kick the Habit. Slang: To stop using narcotics; break the habit; take the cure.

Kid. Slang: A passive homosexual.

Kidnapping. Federal law enacted in June, 1936, referred to as the Lindbergh Act, as it was passed following the Lindbergh kidnapping case. The law makes it a crime to carry away a person against his will, transport him interstate, and hold him for ransom,

reward, or otherwise. The law was later amended to create a presumption of interstate transportation after the victim had been kidnapped for twenty-four hours and not released. Many of the states have kidnapping laws. This is considered a major crime, and many laws carry the death penalty, especially if the victim is not released unharmed.
Kike. Slang: A Jewish person; a cheap merchant.
Kilo (*key* low). Two and two-tenths pounds (usually refers to heroin.)
Kilowatt. A unit of electrical power.
Kin. Family relationship.
Kinds-of-People Theories. Social theory attributing deviant behavior to pyschological or biological characteristics of certain kinds of people.
Kinky. Slang: Crooked or dishonest.
Kisser. Slang: A lawyer.
Kissing Cousins. Slang: A close friend; a likeable person who is distantly related; a female friend.
Kit. Same as outfit—narcotic paraphernalia.
Kite. Prison slang: Smuggling of letters or contraband in or out of a prison; may be used to transport drugs; a letter.
Kiting, Check. A system of building up deposit balances in a number of banks by drawing (writing checks) on a series of banks where small accounts have been opened. The "kiter" endeavors to gradually increase the amounts in the various checking accounts and pass checks for the amounts of the deposits (or more). It is a scheme or procedure to defraud and is illegal in many states.
KKK. Ku Klux Klan.
Kleptomania (*Klep* tow *mane* e ah). A desire to steal or appropriate articles. In many cases psychopathic personalities manifesting the impulsive desire to steal come under the heading of fetish-thieves and during the act of stealing receive sexual gratification, sometimes to the point of orgasm.
Kleptomaniac (*klep* tow *mane* e ack). A person who steals uncontrollably or by mental compulsion. It is believed to be a mental or emotional disorder that results in compulsive acts of theft; one afflicted with kleptomania.
K-nine (K-9). Trained dogs used in police work; the unit of a law enforcement agency that utilizes trained dogs.
Knocking on Door. Narcotics slang: Addict attempting to stay away from other addicts; attempting to break the habit.
Knock Off. Slang: To kill a person or to have him killed.
Knock-Off Device. A part of the gambling-type pinball machine that registers (records) the payoffs to winners. This device on a pinball machine is there for the purpose of making it a gambling device and not one played for skill or fun.
Knockout Drops. Slang: Drugs, such as chloral hydrate, administered usually in a person's drink to cause him to lose consciousness.
Knock Over. Slang: 1. To rob a place of business. 2. To arrest someone or raid a place.
Knock Up. Slang: To cause a woman to become pregnant.
Knowingly. Having knowledge of something; aware of.
Known Specimens. Items of physical evidence that are obtained from known sources. Handwriting specimens taken from, or known to be the writings of, a person are such. A pistol taken from a person is a known specimen.

VOCABULARY

Kokomo. Slang: A cocaine or drug addict.

Koprolagnia (*cope* ro lag ne ah). The condition in which a person is sexually aroused by the sense of smell or taste of filthy substances, such as fecal matter or urine.

Ku Klux Klan (KKK). A post-Civil War organization formed and operative in the South to maintain the position of the white race. It was active in the 1920s and again in the late 1950s and 1960s.

L

L. LSD.
Lab. Equipment used to manufacture drugs illegally.
Labeling Theory. A theory of deviance that attempts to explain deviant behavior as a reaction to a group's expectation of someone who has been labeled as a deviant.
Labile (*lay* bile). Changeable, adaptable.
Laboratory, Crime. A laboratory staffed with personnel and equipped with technical devices so as to conduct scientific examinations and/or analysis of evidence obtained in criminal investigation.
Laboratory, FBI. The crime laboratory of the Federal Bureau of Investigation was established in 1932, and its facilities are available without cost to all duly constituted law enforcement agencies in the conduct of criminal investigations. It is located at the FBI headquarters in Washington, D.C.
Laboratory, Law Enforcement Standards. The National Bureau of Standards operates a laboratory, located at Gaithersburg, Maryland, funded by the National Institute of Law Enforcement and Criminal Justice, to test equipment used in the field of law enforcement. The standards and information are available to law enforcement.
Laboratory Report. The report prepared and furnished to the contributor of specimens that were submitted to the laboratory for examination. The report contains, among other things, the name or title of the case, the name and address of the contributor (the agency that submitted the evidence), a listing of the known and questioned specimens, and the results of the examinations made in the laboratory. The FBI Laboratory suggests the use of a standard form for submitting evidence to the laboratory. A copy of this may be obtained from the FBI.
Labor Racketeering. Racketeer activity in, or by persons involved in, labor groups.
Lacerate (*lass* e rate). To wound by tearing roughly.
Laches. Failure to do the required thing at the proper time, e.g. inexcusable delay in enforcing a claim.
Lachrymator (*lack* re may ter). A substance that causes severe weeping or tear production in the eyes. Such chemicals are used in tear gas.
Lacing. Slang: A beating or thrashing.
La Cosa Nostra. The name of an organized crime group in the United States.
Lacrimator (*lack* re may ter). See **Lachrymator.**
Lady, Old. Prison slang: Passive homosexual who is "married" to another inmate. He assumes the female role to the extent of doing laundry, etc.
Lady-Lover. Slang: A female sex deviate or homosexual—a lesbian.
Lagging. Slang: A term of penal servitude.
Laid Out. Being informed on.
Lam. Slang: To "take off"; to run away.

154

Lam, On the. Hiding out or running away from law enforcement; to be a fugitive from justice.

Lam-Beam. A leg shackle that permitted slow and limited movements to road gang prisoners.

Lame. Not very smart; dumb; green; not streetwise.

Lamster. Slang: A fugitive; a member of a pickpocket gang who leaves with the loot.

Landlord. A person who leases owned property to others.

Lands. Firearms term: The raised spiral surfaces between the grooves on the inside of a rifled gun barrel. The grooves are cut in the inside surface of the barrel, thus leaving the lands. The purpose of the lands and grooves is to grip the bullet and cause it to rotate as it travels down the barrel.

Laned Highway. Any marked roadway or passage for vehicular movement or traffic consisting of at least two lanes.

Lanky. Slang: Slim, slender and awkward; tall.

Lapse. Moral slip; error or fault; termination of a right through failure to meet certain obligations.

Larceny. Theft; the taking and carrying away of the personal property of another with the intent to deprive the owner of its use permanently. In some states there are various grades or kinds of larceny according to the nature of the things stolen and the differences in prescribed punishments.

Larceny-Theft. The unlawful taking or stealing of property or articles of value without the use of violence or fraud.

Lascivious (la *siv* e us). Tending to incite lust; lewd; indecent; obscene; relating to sexual impurity.

Lascivious Carriage (las *cive* i us). Connecticut law: A term including those wanton acts between persons of different sexes that flow from the exercise of lustful passions and that are not otherwise punished as crimes against chastity and public decency.

Lascivious Cohabitation. The offense committed by two persons (not married to each other) who live together in one habitation as man and wife and practice sexual intercourse.

Last Clear Chance. The doctrine that a party who has the last clear chance to avoid damage or injury is liable.

Late. Having died recently or having formerly held public office.

Latent. Concealed; lying hidden away.

Latent Fingerprint. See **Fingerprint, Latent.**

Lateral Entry. The entry of a person into an organization on a level other than the lowest level, based on his abilities to handle a specific job.

Lateral Pocket Loop. A fingerprint pattern.

L.A. Turnabouts. Narcotics slang: Long-lasting amphetamine sulfate capsules, found in many colors.

Laughing Grass. Slang: Marijuana.

Laundry Marks. Identification marks or numbers put on clothing or other washable materials processed by a public laundry doing business with many people. These may be visible (seen by the eye) or invisible (visible only with the aid of something such as an ultraviolet light). Such marks may be helpful in a criminal investigation.

Law. Any rule or procedure expected to be followed; rules of conduct established and enforced by legislation.

Law, Common. See **Common Law.**

Law Abiding. Law obeying; not disorderly or violating the law.

Law and Order. Phrase suggesting hard-line enforcement with little regard for human factors.

Law, John. Slang: The law enforcement officers; the law.

Law, The. Slang: Law enforcement officers.

Law Enforcement. The field of crime prevention, enforcement of the criminal laws by investigation and apprehension of the offenders, and preservation of the peace; persons and/or agencies involved in law enforcement activities. Some include prosecuting officials, criminal courts, and corrections.

Law Enforcement Assistance Administration (LEAA). An agency created by federal legislation, the Omnibus Crime and Safe Streets Act of 1968. It is a part of the United States Department of Justice. Its function is to work with and assist all phases of persons and agencies involved in criminal justice. It administers funds appropriated by Congress to implement the program. The majority of the funds go to states by block grants.

Law Enforcement Intelligence Units. An association of law enforcement intelligence officers and units, participated in by officers from some 150 communities, cooperatively exchanging information concerning criminal activities and criminals.

Law Enforcement Officer. One who is employed (usually by a public agency) to prevent crime, arrest violators of the criminal law, and preserve the peace.

Lawful Done according to provisions of the law; not unlawful.

Lawless Without laws; lawbreaking.

Law of the Case. The decision, judgement, opinion, or rulings on former appeal or writ of error become "law of the case."

Law of the Land. General public laws and customs that are held to be applicable to all people in certain states, countries, or geographical areas.

Laws. Enacted statutes and ordinances, with sanctions.

Lawsuit. Cases presented for decision before a civil court.

Lawyer. A person who has a valid legal license to practice law and give counsel on matters of law and legislation.

Lay. 1. Ordinary people, not belonging to a specific profession. 2. Slang: Woman of loose morals; a prostitute; sexual intercourse. 3. Place to be robbed.

Lay Dead. Juvenile slang: Stay away; inactive.

Laying the Hypo. Narcotics slang: Taking a shot of narcotics.

Lay-In Job. Operation of a loft burglary group where they conceal themselves in the building of the victim, or in the premises of an adjoining business, during business hours and commit their burglary at night.

Lay Odds. The betting odds (line) offered to the bettor by the tracks or bookie. Used as an inducement by the track or bookie to interest the bettor in the transaction. The risk (in theory) is proportionate to the odds given.

Lay Off. 1. Slang: Stop doing something. 2. Gambling term: A hedging bet made by one bookie with another to protect the first, who has taken more bets on one contestant than he wants to carry by himself.

VOCABULARY

Lay of the Land. Slang: The existing situation or facts.

Layout. Slang: 1. Equipment for injecting drugs. 2. Gambling term: The arrangement of the tabletop used for various kinds of gambling games.

L.C.N. (LCN). La Cosa Nostra.

L.E.A.A. (LEAA). Law Enforcement Assistance Administration.

Lead. 1. The distance a firearm is aimed ahead of a moving object in order for the projectile to hit it. 2. Abbreviation for Undeveloped Lead.

Leading. Firearms term: The depositing of lead on the surface of the inside of the gun barrel.

Leading Case. A decision or case that has been often followed and cited as authoritative and generally regarded as settling and determining the point of law in question.

Leading Question. A question asked a witness during a trial or court proceeding that suggests an answer and thus may elicit an answer that otherwise might not be recalled by the witness. Leading questions are not ordinarily allowed; however, under certain conditions, leading questions are permissable.

Lead Poisoning. 1. Slang: Death resulting from being shot. 2. Poisoning by lead compounds, frequently used in medieval times.

Leaf, The. Slang: Cocaine.

Leak. To unofficially pass out information.

Lean. A non-drug user.

Lean on, To. Prison slang: To apply pressure on someone; to assault someone or otherwise inflict punishment or injury upon the person of another.

Leaper. Narcotics slang: Cocaine user.

Learning. Learning may be cognitive—essentially an intellectual process based on knowledge or judgement. Or it may be affective—facilitated or impeded by emotions such as desire, joy, fear, or prejudice.

Leary. Slang: Doubtful; skeptical.

Lease. A contract by which one party gives to another the use and possession of lands, property, etc., for a specified time and for fixed payments.

Lease System of Convict Labor. Leasing the prisoners to contractors who pay the institution.

Leather. Slang: Pocketbook.

Leather, Dropping the. A swindle or con game, the same as pigeon dropping. See **Pigeon Dropping.**

Leeward (*lee* ward). The direction in which the wind is blowing; downwind; the downwind side or direction.

Left. The radical part of a lawmaking body or other group. This is heard frequently in current times; some refer to Communist sympathizers or fellow travellers as belonging to the left. Some place so-called liberals in this category. It is a relative term, and some who are categorized on the left by one group are considered conservative or on the right by others. Has the same general meaning as left wing. See **Left Wing.**

Left, New. A designation used by certain activist groups in the United States active in the late 1960s and early 1970s. They allegedly have as their goals the changing of structure and operations of the government, especially as concerns certain policies relative to war and related activities.

Leftist. Slang: A member of or

sympathizer of a radical or left wing group.

Left Wing. Slang: The liberal or radical segment of the nation, state, or other group. This is a relative matter. Those who are so characterized by some might be described as conservatives by others. Its origin was in the French Parliament where conservatives sit on the right in the chamber and the liberal and radical members sit on the left.

Legal. In terms of or required by law. Enforced in a court of law.

Legal Age. 1. The age at which a person is deemed to have the lawful capacity to do particular things. 2. The age, usually fixed by statute, at which a minor acquires the capacity to conduct business as an adult, make conveyances and transfers of property, and bind himself by contract.

Legal Aid. A community organization that exists for the purpose of aiding indigent people who need assistance in enforcing their rights or are in need of legal advice.

Legal Assistant. A paralegal; a non-lawyer who does "legally related" work and is legally skilled to a certain degree.

Legal Counsel for Police. Attorneys who work with and are employed by law enforcement agencies as legal counsellors, advisors, or "house counsel." Reference: The IACP police legal center: *The Police Chief.* December 1970.

Legal Ethics. The customs and usages among lawyers involving moral and professional duties toward their clients, the courts, and each other.

Legality. Lawfulness. "We must determine the legality of the action."

Legal Moralism. The idea of making laws to control morals (as regards drugs, alcohol, homosexuality).

Legal Points. A monthly publication by the IACP Police Legal Center, Research Division, Washington, D.C. 20036. Contains valuable information on points of value in the legal field for law enforcement.

Legal Proceeding. Any special proceeding or action in court, or "at law" rather than in equity.

Legal Realism. A legal philosophy that explains how many legal decisions that are made are often influenced by such things as politics, psychology, sociology, economics, and many other things.

Legal Right. A recognizable and enforceable claim at law.

Legation (lee *gay* shun). The official establishment (offices, residence) of the diplomatic personnel of a nation in a foreign country. It is lower in rank than an embassy. Problems of diplomatic immunity exist in regard to both, and the officer should act with care.

Legible (*leg* i bul). Can be clearly read; readable.

Leg Irons. Shackles; apparatus consisting of anklets that are secured (fastened or locked) around each leg of a person and that are connected with a chain. They impede the speed of walking or running by restricting the length of the step and by their cumbersomeness.

Legislate. To adopt laws; to enact statutes; to pass laws.

Legislation. Laws that are made or adopted.

Legislative Act. A law or statute adopted or passed by the legislature.

Legislative Branch. That segment of the government responsible for the consideration, drafting, and enactment of the law.

VOCABULARY

Legislator. A member of a legislature for a country or a state.
Legit. Slang: On the square; not a crooked game.
Legitimate. Born of married parents.
Leitmotiv. A recurring theme.
Lemonade. Slang: Poor heroin.
Lemon Game. Gambling term: A scheme to swindle whereby a pool shark entices a victim into playing the game for money, indicating he is a novice.
Lemon Man. Con game slang: A pool shark confidence man. See **Lemon Game.**
Lenient (*lean* yent). Soft-hearted; compassionate; indulgent; merciful.
Lent. Slang: Morphine.
Leprosy (*lep* re see). A disease that affects the skin, the nerve ends, and muscles of the arms and legs. It may also affect the lining of the nose, throat, and larynx. It is caused by a bacterium. It is not highly contagious and can be successfully arrested. The United States Public Health Service Hospital, Carville, Louisiana, is maintained for the care of leprosy patients. All patients are admitted on a voluntary basis. The hospital is not equipped to imprison persons convicted of crime. For information, contact Officer in Charge, U.S.P.H.S. Hospital, Carville, Louisiana. Telephone: Baton Rouge, Louisiana, (504) 642-5421.
Les. Slang: A lesbian.
Lesbian (*les* be in). Female homosexual; one woman who has sexual love for another woman. This may be manifested by kissing, breast fondling, cunnilingus, or mutual masturbation.
Lesion (*lee* zhun). A change to, or in, tissue or an organ of the body due to damage, injury, or disease.

Lessee (less *ee*). One who leases from another. The lessor is the one who does the leasing. "A, the lessee, leases the house from B."
Lesser Included Offense. A criminal offense included in an indictment for a more serious offense, for which the accused may be convicted if he is not convicted on the more serious offense.
Lessor. The person who leases something to someone else.
Lethal (*lee* thel). Producing death; deadly; fatal.
L.E.T.S. (LETS). National Law Enforcement Teletype System, a cooperative interstate system of information exchange between law enforcement agencies, started in the mid-1960s.
Leuco-Malachite Test (*lu* ko *mal* i kite). A preliminary test for the presence of blood. A positive test is not conclusive, but a negative reaction eliminates blood as being the substance tested.
Levy. To seize property in order to satisfy a judgement.
Lewd (leud). Obscene; indecent; filthy; smutty.
Lewd and Lascivious Cohabitation. A couple not married living together as husband and wife.
Lex Loci. Latin: The law of the place.
Lex Talionis Latin: An ancient code of punishment—a life for a life, an eye for an eye, a tooth for a tooth.
Liability. The state of being liable; being held responsible for one's acts. As for police officers, see **Sovereign Immunity; Nineteen Eighty-Three.**
Liable. Responsible by law to pay; chargeable; answerable; legally responsible.
Liaison (*lee* a zon). Contact or connection between groups or indi-

viduals. "He was liaison between his agency and the police department."
Libel (*lye* bul). Statement made in writing that damages a person's reputation; written defamatory statement; a non-oral defamatory communication made with malice to persons other than to the person injured.
Liberal. One who is not narrow minded; a liberal thinker; one who espouses the cause of change; tolerant.
Liberal Arts. College courses that are not the exact sciences or professions. Subjects included in liberal arts are history, languages, literature, and philosophy.
Liberate. To set free; to release from captivity or confinement.
Liberty. Freedom to do, speak, etc., as opposed to license—excessive use of liberty.
Libido (le *bee* dough). The sex drive or desire; instincts of sex manifested in energy, behind all human activities (Freud).
License. Legal permission to do something, a document granting permission for something.
Licentious (lie *cent* shus). Lustful; debauched; immoral; lewd; lacking moral restraints.
Licentiousness. Morally unrestrained; disregard for accepted rules and standards.
Lid. One ounce of marijuana in a plastic container (plastic bag).
Lidford Law. A type of lynch law where a person was hung with little or no trial.
Lid Proppers. Slang: Stimulant drugs—amphetamines.
Lie Detector. See **Polygraph.**
Lie in Wait. To conceal one's self so as to commit an act (usually illegal) upon a person who is expected to appear at or near the place of concealment.
Lie Low. Slang: To hide out, as from the law.
Lien (lean). A legal claim or right of a creditor to sell the property of another for the payment of a debt.
Lieu, In (lu). In the place of; instead of; to take the place of.
Lieutenant. 1. A rank of an officer in a law enforcement agency, lower than a captain and higher than a sergeant. 2. Similar rank of a commissioned officer in the army. 3. The title given to a person in an organized crime family, below the underboss and above the soldiers. It is also called Caporegima.
Life on the Installment Plan. Prison slang: Successive parole violations where the person keeps returning to prison.
Lifer (*lie* fur). Slang: One serving a life sentence.
Light, Out like a. Slang: Passed out; unconscious.
Light Artillery. Slang: A hypodermic needle.
Light a Shuck. Slang: To run away fast; depart with speed.
Light Fingered. Slang: Accomplished at picking pockets.
Light Meter. See **Exposure Meter.**
Light Time. 1. A short prison sentence. 2. Any nonviolent crime.
Light Trailer. Every vehicle of the trailer or semitrailer type having a loaded gross weight of not more than five hundred pounds.
Light Work. Gambling slang: Cards that have been altered by marking them with thin, barely visible lines.
Likeness. Resemblance; copy.
Lily. Slang: A male homosexual or an effeminate male.
Limited Jurisdiction. Authority by which the court is limited in the

VOCABULARY

activity it can engage in when trying a case—for example, it may not be able to call a jury; also called special jurisdiction.

Limp Wrist. Slang: A man who is effeminate; one suspected of being a homosexual.

Lindberg Act. A federal statute, enacted in 1932, which makes the transportation of a kidnapped person across state lines for the purpose of reward, ransom, or otherwise a federal offense that may be punishable by life imprisonment.

Line. 1. Gambling term: The odds to be paid by the bookie; point spread in some sports gambling. 2. Slang: A statement the truthfulness of which is doubtful; untruthful statements. "He is feeding her a line."

Lineage. Ancestry.

Linear. Relating to a line; straight.

Line Beat. The dispatching of patrol officers to those areas heavily traveled to control traffic violations.

Line Functions. Those things that constitute the main objectives of the department or police agency. Among these are criminal investigations, traffic control, vice suppression, etc. Contrasted with Staff Function.

Line Officer. An officer assigned to perform work that is the main objective of the department—such as traffic control, crime investigating etc. Contrasted with the Staff Officer.

Line Spectrum. An emmission spectrum consisting of bright, thin lines separated by black areas.

Lineup, Police. A procedure of placing crime suspects with others, not believed implicated in the crime, in a line or other position so that witnesses can view them for the purpose of making possible identifications. Since 1967, in the case of U.S. v. Wade, 388 U.S. 218, the court requires that an attorney for the accused be present during the line-up.

Line Work. Gambler slang: The altering of the design on the backs of cards so the crooked player can distinguish the cards from the backs.

Lipton Tea. Poor quality narcotics.

Liquidate. Slang: To kill someone.

Liquidated Damages. Applicable when the amount of the damages has been ascertained by the judgement in the action, or when a specific sum of money has been expressly stipulated by the parties to a bond or other contract as the amount of damages to be recovered by either party for a breach of the agreement by the other.

Litigation. Carrying on of a lawsuit.

Little Bird. Juvenile slang: An informer.

Little Button. Slang: The badge of a federal officer.

Little People. Slang: Members of a gang who are young.

Lit Up. Slang: Under the influence of drugs.

Live Helpee. The use of real helpees in helper-helpee exercises.

Lividity, Postmortem (li *vid* e te). A condition caused by the draining of the blood in a dead body. The blood flows by gravity to the lower parts of the body and causes a peculiar discoloration—usually bluish red. The condition appears in about three hours after death. Due to pressure on the part of the body touching the surface upon which the body rests, that part does not assume the discoloration. If the body is moved after lividity has developed and is placed in a different position, this will be indicated by lividity. A

dead body should be examined with this point in mind.
Living with the Folks. Slang: At liberty on bail.
Load. Slang: He is carrying a load—he is drunk; he is loaded—he is drunk.
Loaded. High on drugs; under the influence of drugs.
Loaded Dice. Gambling term: Altered or crooked dice, which are out of balance due to extra weight being added to one side.
Loads. Gambler slang: Dice that have been loaded.
Loan Shark. One who loans money at a very high interest rate—usually an unlawful rate.
Loan Sharking. Loaning money at exorbitant rates of interest. Engaged in by unscrupulous, unethical, and law-violating persons. Although not restricted to organized crime, it is one of the most lucrative sources of income for organized crime.
Lobby. A group representing special interests that endeavors to influence legislation; to endeavor to influence legislation.
Lobbyist. One engaged in lobbying; one who seeks to influence legislation.
Lobo. Slang: A criminal; thug; hoodlum.
Local Control. The idea that schools, police, etc., should be organized to maximize neighborhood control of policy but without bearing the appropriate share of financial cost. Decentralization is another term used, stressing delegation of functional power to neighborhoods.
Local Municipal Authority. Every council, commission, or other board given authority by the constitution and laws of the state to govern the affairs of a municipality.

Local Parish Authority. Every police jury, commission, council, or other board given authority by the constitution and laws of the state to govern the affairs of a parish of the state.
Location Finders. Slang: One who locates business places into which juke boxes can be placed.
Locking In. The procedure used by the telephone company whereby a "tone set" will make it possible for a "nuisance" caller to disconnect his line until his phone has been identified as the source of the call.
Lock Oneself Up. To request being removed from other prisoners for protection.
Lockup. 1. A jail or place of detention. 2. To put someone in jail; incarcerate.
Loco Weed. Slang: Marijuana.
Locus Criminis. Latin: The location of a crime.
Loft Burglars. Burglars who steal merchandise from storage rooms of business houses.
Log. A written chronological record of events as they occur, showing times and dates. Especially in major cases, the keeping of a log, giving details of dealings with suspects, is considered good practice.
Logistics (low *jis* ticks). The area of activity in a police operation pertaining to supplies, equipment and facilities, and the maintenance and support of personnel.
Loiter (*loi* ter). To "hang around" doing nothing; to be idle.
Lombrosian Positivism (lom *bro* shin). A theory of deviance that attempts to explain criminal behavior as resulting from a genetic defect.
Loner. 1. One who stays to himself; one who has few close associates. 2. Juvenile slang: Member of an estab-

lished gang with no responsibility assigned; does not have to go out on gang fights.

Long Haired. Slang: Highly educated; intellectual; description of a college teacher.

Look Bad. Juvenile slang: Give a "dirty look."

Lookout. 1. A person who is carefully watching for an event to occur or persons to appear. 2. The act of looking for certain persons or events. 3. Gambling term: A gambling house employee who sees that everything runs smoothly and is on alert for crookedness by players or house personnel.

Loop (lup). A fingerprint pattern. It has ridge lines that enter from either side, recurve, touch or pass an imaginary line between delta and core, and pass out or tend to pass out on the side from which the ridge or ridges entered. Central pocket loops and double loops are classified as whorls.

Loose. 1. To break away; free oneself. 2. Slang: Having questionable morals or conduct.

Loot. Slang: Stolen money or merchandise taken by robbery; term now used by young persons in referring to wedding presents.

Lop Eared. Slang: Having loose hanging ears.

Loquacious (low *kway* shus). Talking excessively; talkative.

Lose Out. Prison slang: To lose a certain job assignment because of violation of rules.

Loser. Slang: One who has been convicted more than once.

Lose Time. Prison slang: Reduction or suspension of good time credit due to violations of rules; to reduce time earned toward parole.

Lottery. A form of gambling. A plan or system for distribution of winners by chance or lot. A large number of chances (tickets) are sold, and the number of winners is relatively small. A wager on a number that it will be the number drawn in a raffle. Bingo and Keno are other games played with numbers.

Lottery, Puerto Rican. Gambling game. See **Bolita**.

Lottery, Spanish. Gambling game. See **Bolita**.

Lounge. A place to relax, drink, smoke, and usually listen to music. Many bars and short-order eating places are called lounges.

Love Weed. Slang: Marijuana.

Low Belly Strippers. Gambler slang: Cards in a deck on which the edges have been altered on the high ones, facilitating the drawing of cards of certain size.

Low Down. 1. Slang: Confidential information. 2. Being of low repute; mean, disreputable, disgraceful, contemptible.

Low Energy Explosive. An explosive with a velocity of detonation less than 1,000 meters per second.

LP Gas. Liquified petroleum gas. Petroleum products such as butane and propane.

LSD. Lysergic acid diethylamide, a hallucinogenic drug.

Lubricated. Slang: Intoxicated.

Lucid (*lu* sid). Clear to the understanding; plain; sane.

Lucid Interval. Period of life of the insane person when the person is rational and sane and has the ability to perform legal acts that are not disqualified because of his usual mental condition.

Lucre (*lu* ker). Money that may not be used for the best purposes.

Lugger. Slang: An accomplice in an

unlawful game who steers players to the game; a beggar.

Luminol. A chemical that is used to detect the presence of blood.

Luminous Readers. Gambler slang: Cards that have had the designs on the backs marked with material that can be seen through tinted glasses.

Lunatic (*lune* a tick). A mentally deranged person.

Lush. Slang: A heavy drinker.

Lush Roller. Slang: One who steals from drunks.

Lust. Sexual appetite; excessive sex desire or craving; especially that which is satisfied immediately by brutal acts of violence.

Lust Murder. Sadistically brutal murder. The victim's body generally has been mutilated, especially the sex organs. The lust murderer is obsessed with a "mutilation madness" wherein he is driven by his cruelty and bloodthirsty propensities to horrifying acts of violence, cannibalism, and vampirism.

Lying in Wait. A phrase, used in the definition of murder, that connotes concealment for the express purpose of committing murder.

Lynch. To execute or kill a person by other than legal methods.

M

Mace®. Trade name for an aerosol irritant projector.

Machinegun. A gun that fires automatically or semiautomatically. The type of weapon encountered in law enforcement in this category is usually the shoulder weapon, which is more accurately called the submachinegun.

Machine Rest. Firearms term: The attaching or fixing of a rifle to a support when firing it for accuracy testing.

Machinery. Equipment for injecting drugs.

Macroscopic. Large enough to be seen with the naked eye, as contrasted with microscopic, which means invisible without the aid of a microscope.

Mad. Crazy; demented; mentally deranged; insane.

Madam. Slang: The female operator (manager) of a house of prostitution.

Made a Score. Slang: Committed a successful robbery, burglary, confidence game, or other offense.

Made. Slang: Identified.

Made Fag, Gunzel, or Punk. Someone made to perform as a homosexual through the use of threats or use of force.

Mafia. A well-organized confederation, secret in nature and operation, whose members are largely of Sicilian or Italian descent, which carries on criminal and some legal activities. It originated in Sicily but allegedly exists in many nations, including the United States. It is called by many names including the confederation, the Syndicate, La Cosa Nostra, Cosa Nostra.

Magazine. Firearms term: The holder of cartridges from which the cartridges are automatically chambered.

Magdalene, Mary. Underworld slang: A prostitute who has been reformed.

Maggie's Drawers. Slang: A red flag used on a firing range to show that the target has been missed.

Magic Mushroom. A Mexican species of mushroom, containing psilocybin, a psychedelic.

Magic Paper. Paper that dissolves quickly in water. Used by "bookies" and others for record keeping. In case of raid or search by the police, violators can quickly destroy the paper by submerging it in water.

Magistrate (maj is *trate*). A judicial officer as provided for by the law; a judge; justice of the peace; mayor of a mayor's court; city judge.

Magistrate, Police. A judicial officer who has jurisdiction of minor criminal offenses.

Magna Carta (*mag* ne *kar* ta). The great charter. A charter given by King John of England at Runnymede on June 15, 1215. It was the result of pressure brought by the barons, who had the backing of the common people. It is considered the basis of the English constitutional liberties and contains some rights that are contained in the United States Constitution. Among the rights guaranteed people were local control in the communities and the right of an accused to be tried by his peers.

Magnetism. Power of attraction.

Maidenhead. Membrane in the vagina; denotes virginity if intact.

Maiden Name. Woman's family name (surname) prior to her marriage.

Mail Buzzer. Slang: Woman pickpocket.

Mail Drop. A place where, by arrangement, communications (written or recorded) can be deposited or left to be picked up by an accomplice.

Main Drag. Slang: The largest or most important street in a town or city.

Mainline Bang. Slang: Narcotic injection by hypodermic in the large vein of the forearm.

Mainliner. Slang: A narcotic user (usually an addict) who takes the drug by injection into a vein.

Maintaining. Slang: Keeping at a certain level of drug effect.

Majonda. Underworld slang: Narcotics.

Major. The rank of an officer in the army; also used in state police, municipal police, and some other law enforcement agencies. It is above the rank of captain and below that of lieutenant colonel. It also denotes great importance or a serious condition.

Major Classification. A part of the system of recording fingerprint classifications.

Major Division. A fingerprint classification term. Sometimes called Major Classification. Applies to classification patterns in the thumbs. The symbols are written in capital letters, such as I/O.

Majority. 1. Greater than half of the total in number. 2. The age when a person is legally responsible. In most states it is twenty-one.

Make. Slang: 1. To steal a thing. 2. To recognize or identify a person.

Make a Croaker. Narcotics slang: Deceive a doctor into giving narcotics.

Make a Meet. To purchase drugs.

Make a Reader. Narcotics slang: Have a doctor write a prescription.

Make Book. To operate a book where bets are accepted, usually on the horse races.

Make Citizens. Slang: Extorting aliens by making them believe they will get citizenship quicker or else face deportation.

Make It. 1. To buy narcotics; to leave the scene, area. 2. To succeed.

Make the Bughouse. Slang: Getting out of prison by pretending insanity.

Make the Net. Juvenile slang: Arrested by the police.

Mal. Prefix meaning bad; wrongly; evil; ill.

Mala Fides. Latin: In bad faith.

Mala In Se. Latin; Law: Acts that are wrong or immoral in themselves, such as murder, rape, arson, burglary, etc.

Mala Prohibita (*mal* a pro *hib* i *tah*). Latin: Those acts prohibited by statute inasmuch as they infringe on the rights of others but are not necessarily immoral or seriously wrong.

Malarkey. Slang: Idle talk, nonsense, untruths.

Malcontent (*mal* kon tent). Dissatisfied, especially with the system of government; discontented.

Malefactor (*mal* e fak ter). A criminal; a wrongdoer; a convict; an outlaw; a hoodlum.

Malevolent (ma *lev* o lent). Desiring evil for others; evil-minded; ill-intentioned; treacherous.

Malfeasance (mal *fee* zens). Misconduct by an official in relation to his duties of office; violation of an official position; evildoing; wrongful conduct; doing something one is not to do.

Malice. Spite; ill will; desire to injure others; ill feeling; hatred; evil intent.

Malice Aforethought. Premeditation to commit an illegal act; predetermination to commit an illegal act. Malice prior to and at the time of the commission of an offense.

Malicious (ma *lish* us). Spiteful; evil-minded; malevolent; ill-willed.

Malicious Abandonment. Deserting a husband or a wife for no reason.

Malicious Mischief. A crime consisting of willful damage to or destruction of personal property of another motivated by ill will or resentment toward its owner or possessor.

Malign (ma *line*). To speak evil of someone; besmirch; depreciate; slander; libel; defame.

Malinger (me *ling* er). To use the pretense of illness to avoid work or duty; pretend to be ill as as excuse for not working.

Malpractice. Improper medical treatment.

Malum in Prohibitum. Latin: An act designated criminal and legally prohibited but not inherently evil.

Man, Old (Ole Man). Prison slang: The "husband" partner to a passive homosexual.

Man, The. Slang: 1. A police officer or private detective, especially used by drug addicts. 2. The head man—leader. 3. Prison slang: An authority figure—the warden or the captain 4. A connection (drug supplier).

Manacles (*man* a kuls). Restraining devices such as handcuffs or leg irons.

Management. Regulating, governing, or directing groups of persons; the process of directing, regulating, or governing. The thought is prevalent that "management is management," i.e. the same principles of management apply to any organization or organized group activity. An understanding of the principles of management is highly desirable in law enforcement operations.

Mandamus (man *day* mus). A writ issued by a court of competent jurisdiction ordering a person, legal entity, or a lower court to do something.

Mandate (*man* date). An order or command. A directive or order of a superior court, or its judge, to a lower one.

Mandatory. Obligatory; required to carry out or execute in obedience to an order.

Mandatory Release (*man* da *tow* ry). The release of an inmate prior to the full expiration of his sentence, usually under supervision.

Manhandle. To "rough up" a person; treat a person roughly.

Manhattan Bail Project. Developed by the Vera Foundation (agency of the Vera Institute of Justice) in cooperation with the New York University Law School and the Institute of Judicial Administration. Its function is to arrange for the release of offenders awaiting trial, after arraignment, on their own recognizance after an investigation reveals they are "rooted in the community" and otherwise meet criteria indicating they will appear in court at the proper time. It was started in the 1960s, and the results have been good. Its operation has been in New York City.

Manhattan Summons Project. A

procedure developed in New York as an outgrowth of the Manhattan Bail Project. After arrest for minor crimes, the defendant is brought to the local precinct station, where he is searched and questioned by the arresting officer. He is then interviewed by law students, and if he meets the standards of having local "roots in the community," a summons is issued for him and he is released until the time of arraignment.

Mania (*main* ee ya). Type of insanity wherein great excitement and sometimes violence is exhibited; manifestations of various psychoses displayed in the form of elation and excitement.

Maniac (*main* ee ak). A crazy person; one who is mentally deranged; one who is insane.

Manic-Depressive (*may* nik dee *pres* iv). One afflicted with mania and depressions that alternate.

Manicure. Slang: Remove the dirt, seeds, and stems from marijuana.

Manicured Marijuana. Marijuana that has been cleaned by removal of the dirt, stems, and seeds.

Mann Act, The. A federal law making it a crime for a person to transport a woman or girl from one state to another for immoral purposes, or to cause such transportation. It is also referred to as the White Slave Traffic Act. U.S. Code, Title 18, Sec. 2421. See **White Slave Traffic Act**.

Mannequins In Court. The Los Angeles Sheriff's Department used mannequins in lieu of color photographs of murder victims' bodies in the trial of cases. These were more illustrative than descriptions and less objectionable than photographs. Reference: Pitchess, Peter J.: Mannequins in court. *FBI Law Enforcement Bulletin,* December 1970, p. 14.

Manslaughter (*man* slaw ter). Illegal killing of a human being without malice or premeditation; the killing of a person illegally but with some element of the crime of murder lacking.

Mapp v. Ohio, 367 U.S. 643, 81 S.Ct. 1618 (1961). The case that extended the rule to the states that illegally obtained evidence could not be used in state courts. This is a landmark case pertaining to evidence, and every officer should be familiar with its holdings.

Marathon House. See **Therapeutic Community**.

Marbles, Doesn't Have All His. Slang: Mentally defective.

Marijuana (mare i *wahn* a). Comes from the leaves and flowering top of the hemp plant, *Cannabis sativa*. When the leaves and flowering top of the female plant are smoked or ingested, a hallucinogenic effect is produced in some persons. The drug is considered a poison. At the federal level marijuana is rigidly controlled by the Marijuana Control Act of 1937 and subsequent legislation. There has been much controversy about marijuana. Some indications are that it is harmful. It has been shown to be an effective treatment for glaucoma; research is continuing. The leaves of the cannabis plants are deeply serrated and grow in clusters of odd numbers—three, five, seven—at the end of the leaf stem. Among the many names used for marijuana are pot, grass, joint sticks, hashish, tea, Mary Jane, Mary Warner, reefers, loco weed, giggles smoke, love weed, griefo, Texas tea, ea-tay, joy-smoke, laughing grass, eed-way, eed-waggles.

Marijuanaholics. Slang: A use of marijuana and alcohol.

Marital. Related to or of marriage; matrimonial.

Maritime (*mare* i time). Of or pertaining to the sea or activities on or about the seas.

Maritime Law. Law pertaining to the seas, navigable waters, ships, seamen, and other related matters.

Mark. Slang: The victim in a confidence game; one easily victimized, a sucker.

Marked Cards. Gambling term: Playing cards that have been marked so they can be read from the back.

Marked Paper. Same as **Marked Cards**.

Marker. Slang: 1. An IOU or written document obligating the maker to pay a certain amount. 2. Gambling term: A written wager; the paper or other thing on which the bet or action is recorded; see **ABC Sheet**.

Marking Evidence. Placing identifying marks or writings on physical evidence so it can later be positively identified as that obtained at a specific place, date, and time. It is most important that physical (real) evidence be handled in such fashion so that it can later be identified when it is introduced as evidence during a trial.

Marks. A term used in described persons, denoting blemishes on the individuals that are not scars. It is usually listed under the heading "scars and marks."

Marshal (*mar* shel). An officer of the law who has duties similar to a sheriff or constable in a limited jurisdiction and pertaining to the lower courts, such as city or municipality. In old England there were several kinds of marshals, each of whom had specific duties (*Black's Law Dictionary*).

Marshal, United States. An official of the federal judicial system whose functions are the following: make arrests of persons charged with federal criminal violations, transport federal prisoners and insure their incarceration pending trial; maintain order in the federal courts; carry out orders of the federal courts; serve processes in the federal judicial district for which he is appointed. His duties correspond to those of a sheriff of a county in many respects.

Martial Law (*mar* shel). Under special circumstances civil authority and law are replaced by rule of the military, and its law is administered by military courts. "The Governor called out the National Guard and declared martial law."

Marx, Karl (1818–1883). A German philosopher who brought forth the theory of socialism, which is the foundation of modern socialism and communism.

Marxism. The body of socialist theory as developed by Karl Marx and Friedrich Engels, which involves class struggle based on the theory of dialectical materialism and which puts certain values on labor.

Marxism-Leninism. The theories of Karl Marx on socialism as altered by Vladmir Ilyich (Nikolai) Lenin.

Mary Jane. Slang: Marijuana.

Mary Warner. Slang: Marijuana.

Masher. Slang: A male who seeks to force his attention (infatuation or lovemaking) on a woman against her desires or consent.

Masochism (*mas* o kizm). A condition where sexual pleasure is obtained from the infliction of pain or suffering (physical or mental) on one's self; sexual gratification derived from suffering.

Mason-Dixon Line. Commonly refers to the physical division between the North and the South. It actually was the boundary between Pennsylvania and Maryland surveyed in 1763 by Charles Mason and Jeremiah Dixon, Englishmen. There is no such line.

Mass. A property of matter, consistent throughout the universe, which measures the amount of matter present.

Massacre (*mas* a ker). Intentional and malicious killing of many people or animals. The killing of a large number of people without necessity and without mercy.

Mass Hysteria. A compulsive and irrational state, which may exist among a large number of people or may be expressed in scattered instances.

Mass Suggestion. The phenomenon of many people in a group being affected in their thinking and actions by mutual suggestion. This has a powerful influence on people and develops thinking and ideas that are often entirely foreign to a particular individual and that he regrets very much after he has the opportunity to think about them calmly. This enters into mob activity.

Masturbation (mas ter *bay* shun). Sexual excitement produced by self-manipulation of the sex organs.

Mat. Underworld slang: A prostitute.

Matchbox. A small amount of cannabis sufficient to make between five and eight cigarettes; about a fifth of a lid.

Matching Points. See **Point of Identification.**

Material Evidence (ma *teer* ee el). See **Evidence, Material.**

Material Witness. One who possesses information of value in the trial of a criminal case. Proper magistrates may force a witness of this nature to post bond to insure his appearance in the proceedings, or in lieu of bond being posted the witness may be detained. The defense also has rights to insure the testimony of material witnesses if circumstances reflect they may be unavailable at the time of the hearing or trial.

Materiel (ma tear e *ell*). Supplies and equipment used by an army or other organization.

Matinee-Prowl. Slang: Ransacking homes while the owners are away.

Matriarchy Family. A family where authority and inheritance are vested in females.

Matrons, Jury of. If a pregnant woman is tried for a capital offense, then a jury of matrons is selected.

Matter. Material substance that occupies space and has weight and constitutes the observable universe.

Matter of Law. Issues or questions of law that are to be determined by the court.

Max. Slang: Receiving the maximum sentence allowed by law.

Maxim. A concisely expressed principle or rule of conduct, or a statement of general truth; precept.

Max X. Slang: Short for Maximum "X." Means the maximum prison sentence for a particular crime.

Mayhem (*may* him). Law: Unlawfully and violently depriving a person of the use of any of his limbs by maiming or injuring him to the extent that he is unable to defend himself. This definition may vary among the states.

McNaughton Case. An important English case that considered insanity as a defense.

MDA. A hallucinogen, methyl-3,4-

VOCABULARY

methylenedioxyphenethydamine.
Mealymouthed. Speaking insincerely; telling untruths in a jumbled or mixed-up manner.
Meatball Hotel. Slang: State penitentiary.
Mechanic. 1. Prison slang: A safe man—a peeler. 2. Gambling term: A gambler who uses devices to win in a crooked manner; a person adept at betting the cards.
Medicolegal (*med* e ko *lee* gul). Law relative to medical matters.
Medulla of Hair. The inner portion of a strand of hair. Some hairs have no medulla. The medulla can be continuous or interrupted. It is an important item in the identification of hair.
Meet. 1. Juvenile slang: A meeting, usually of gang chiefs. 2. Gambling term: To make a contact, usually secretly. 3. To buy drugs.
Megalomania (*meg* e low *may* nee uh). A mental derangement in which the person has delusions of grandeur, i.e. he believes he is someone of great importance or repute, he believes himself to be exalted.
Melancholia. Medical term: Insanity characterized by extreme mental depression with delusions and hallucinations.
Mellow Yellow. Refers to someone smoking banana skins, a hoax, as they contain no mind-altering drugs.
Melter. Slang: Morphine.
Menace (*men* iss). A threat; a dangerous situation; to threaten; to have a dangerous situation.
Mens. The mind.
Mens Rea. Law: The intent to commit a proscribed harm, or recklessness regarding its commission; a guilty mind; intent to commit crime.
Mental Alienation. Medical term: A phrase sometimes used to describe insanity.
Mentally Deranged. Mentally ill; insane; See **Abnormal Behavior**.
Mentally Ill. A condition of mental derangement; insanity.
Mercenary (*mer* see naery). Person doing something only for a monetary purpose.
Merchandise. Narcotics slang: Narcotics in general.
Mere Evidence. Law: Evidence that will aid in the proof of the commission of a crime but that does not fall in the evidential categories of contraband or the fruits or instrumentalities of a crime.
Mere Evidence Rule. Law: A rule of evidence that forbade the legal search for and use in testimony of mere evidence obtained as a result of a search. This rule was abrogated in Warden v. Hayden, 387 U.S. 294, 87 S.Ct. 1642 (1967), and the use of such evidence obtained by a search was allowed.
Meretricious. Of the nature of unlawful sexual connection. Often used to describe a void marriage by reason of legal incapacity.
Merger. Combination of businesses or things; a joining together.
Merit. The good or value of something.
Merits. The substance or fundamentals of a case.
Mesc. Slang: Mescaline.
Mescaline. A hallucinogenic narcotic extracted from mescal buttons (buttons of the Peyote cactus).
Message Switching. Computer term: Incoming messages are sent to the computer for rerouting to other terminals.
Metal Bullet Point. A metal-tipped bullet that has a lead bearing.
Metallic Ear. Slang: An unwelcome

listener; a dictograph or other mechanical device.

Metal Tire. Every tire, whose surface that is in contact with the highway, is made wholly or partly of metal or other hard, nonresilient material.

Metaphysical (*met* a *fiz* i kel). Supernatural.

Mete (meet). Pass out or distribute.

Meth. Narcotics slang: Methamphetamine, a stimulant drug.

Methadon. Another name for methadone.

Methadone. A fine white powder, methadone is a synthetic drug with opiate effects. Although it is addictive, its withdrawal is milder than that of opiates. It is used to detoxify heroin addicts so that they can withdraw from heroin without the painful reactions. Dr. Lewis Yablonsky, a sociologist at San Fernando State College in California, stated methadone is addictive and is leading many of its users to alcohol. Methadone is under federal regulation. It is also known as amidone, Dolophine, adanon, methadon, dollies, dolls.

Methamphetamine (*meth* am *fet* a mean). A chemical that is related to amphetamine but has more central nervous system activity and correspondingly less effect on blood pressure and heart rate than amphetamines; a drug stimulant.

Methodology (meth e *doll* e jee). The practices and procedures used in a branch of learning to achieve given goals.

Methyl Alcohol. Methanol; wood alcohol. A poison—not used for drinking.

Metric System. A system of measurement, used by many nations, wherein the meter (39.37 inches) is used for measuring length, the gram for weight, and the liter as the unit for volume.

Metroplexity (*met* tro *plex* i tee). The aggregate of problems resulting from urbanization—the trend of U.S. people to gravitate to cities and suburbs: Standard Metropolitan Statistical Areas (SMSA). In roughly 80 years, the population has shifted from 80% rural to 80% urban. The problems include providing for, financing, and controlling utilities and sanitary, fire, and police services, whether by decentralization—operating from local jurisdictions, or under the metropolitan approach—pooling some police and other services while maintaining separate central city and suburban autonomies, or by politically merging government units to provide a broad financial and administrative base to avoid duplication of services. See **Local Control**.

Metropolis. The chief city of a nation, state, or county; a populous city.

Metropolitan. Pertaining to or being a part of a big city or metropolis.

Mexican-American. An American of Mexican ancestry; also known as Chicano.

Mexican Horse. Narcotics slang: Mexican (brown) heroin.

Mezz. Marijuana.

Mickey Finn. Slang: A strong narcotic or drug, usually mixed with an alcoholic drink, which causes the drinker to become unconscious; a drink containing such a drug.

Microchemistry. The field of chemistry in which minute quantities of substances are involved. In the crime laboratory this branch is essential in analyzing small amounts of material that may be found at the crime scene or elsewhere.

Microscope. An optical device having lenses, used for magnifying objects that are so small as to be invisible to the naked eye; used to magnify the surface of visible objects to create a more discernable image. The microscope is important in a crime laboratory. The comparison microscope is used to compare questioned and known specimens in the firearms and tool mark types of examinations as well as in other types.

Microscope, Comparison. A microscope that has two objectives or lens systems converging into a single field of vision. Two separate objects can be seen simultaneously and thus compared. Among other uses, the crime laboratory examines bullets to determine if the markings on them match, thus reflecting that they were fired in the same weapon.

Microscopic. So small as to be seen only by the use of a microscope.

Microscopic Dot. A photograph so reduced in size that it approximates the size of the dot over a typed or printed "i." A photograph of a document or other object can be so reduced. The "dot" photograph can be read by use of a microscope or enlarged photographically. This technique was used in World War II by secret agents for transmitting intelligence information.

Microscopy. Investigation by the use of the microscope.

Middle Stages. The stages of the criminal justice system where formal charges are brought and innocence or guilt determined, and where convicted offenders are sentenced.

Midwife. Woman who assists in childbirth.

Migration (my *gray* shun). Movement into or out of a specific area.

Mike. Slang: Microphone.

Mikes. Narcotics slang: Microgram (millionth of a gram).

Mile. Unit of linear measurement (5280 feet or 1760 yards).

Milepost. A marker alongside a road or highway to mark each mile in distance or to indicate the miles from a given point.

Militant. Aggressively warlike; participating in violence.

Military Police. Police of the army; soldier police.

Military Training Programs. See **Operation Police Manpower; Transition Program**.

Militia (me *lish* a). Citizen's army trained for emergency situations or war; the National Guard.

Millbank Prison. A prison where convicts are placed while awaiting sentencing or the order to be executed.

Mind Blower. Pure, unadulterated drugs.

Mineral. A crystalline solid that occurs in nature.

Minor. One who has not reached the legal age of maturity; one who is not of legal age.

Minority Group. A group kept from attaining a high status on the basis of race, religion, sex, or culture.

Miranda Warnings. The information that the court in Miranda v. Arizona, 384 U.S. 436, said must be used in warning a person in custody of his rights prior to interrogation about a crime. They are in substance—(1) You have the right to remain silent. (2) Anything you say can be used against you in a court of law. (3) You have the right to have an attorney with you during the interrogation. (4) If you are unable to hire an attorney, one will be provided for you without cost. (5) If you waive these rights and furnish information, you have the right to stop talking at any time.

Misappropriate (miss a *pro* pre ate). To wrongfully appropriate; to use wrongfully; to misapply.

Misbegotten. Illegally begotten; illegitimate.

Miscarriage (miss *kar* ige). 1. Mismanagement. 2. Premature birth of a child who is unable to live.

Miscarriage of Justice. Failure to accomplish or deliver due process or fairness in a legal proceeding or other official action.

Miscegenation (miss edge e *na* shen). Racial mixture, particularly cohabitation or marriage of a Caucasian and one of another race. This has been legally forbidden and made a crime in some states. The United States Supreme Court in Loving v. Commonwealth of Virginia held such a law unconstitutional.

Miscellaneous Services. Duties performed by the police that are not within the traditional scope of their duties, such as rendering first aid and helping persons locked out of their house.

Miscreant (*miss* kre ant). A villain; a rascal; a culprit; a criminal; a jailbird.

Misdemeanor. Law: A criminal offense less serious than a felony. The definition varies among the states and in the federal law. It is usually based on the length of possible period of incarceration and/or whether hard labor can be imposed in the sentence.

Misdemeanor Summons. A summons issued for a misdemeanor offense.

Misdirection. An error committed by a judge in his charge or instructions to the jury.

Misfeasance (miss *fee* zuns). The wrongfully doing of some act that ordinarily it is lawful to do.

Misprison. Neglect of duty, specifically of a public official.

Misprison of Felony. Concealment of information relative to the commission of a felony by another; the failure of one who knows of the commission of a felony by another to report it to proper authorities.

Misrepresentation (miss rep ree zen *tay* shun). Statement of something as a fact when it is knowingly untrue; a deceiving or misleading statement; a statement made with the intention that another rely on it as truth when it is not true.

Miss Emma. Slang: Morphine.

Misses. Gambler slang: Dice that have been altered so they make more of certain combinations than others, i.e. some are gaffed to make more sevens.

Missing Persons. Persons who have disappeared. Law enforcement is frequently called upon to locate persons who have run away or just dropped out of sight. This constitutes an appreciable part of police work. Under certain conditions the FBI will place a "missing person" stop in its files when requested to do so by a law enforcement agency or by the family of the missing person. The person must not have been gone for as long as seven years. For further details contact the field office or a Special Agent of the FBI.

Missouri Plan. A plan used in the state of Missouri for the selection of judges (State Supreme Court, Appellate Courts, the courts of Jackson County–Kansas City, and in the city of St. Louis). A commission, composed of a judicial officer serving ex officio and lawyers selected by the governor, nominates three candidates for the position. The governor appoints one. At the end of a year, this judge goes before the people at a general election, where the people vote on the question, "Shall Judge X be retained in office?" If he receives a majority in his favor, he serves the remainder of his term, at which time he may become a candidate for reelection merely by certifying his wish to have his name placed on the ballot. He is not allowed to contribute financially to or participate in any political campaign.

Mistrial (*miss* try el). A trial officially terminated by the judge before completion because of some error in the proceedings, such as lack of jurisdiction or some other factor provided by law as the basis for such action.

Mitigate (*mit* i gate). Make less severe, or painful; mollify; lighten; diminish. "The sentence was mitigated."

Mitigating Circumstances. Facts that, while they do not excuse or justify an action, may be considered extenuating enough to reduce the extent of moral culpability, and possibly lower the extent of criminal or civil punishment or loss.

Mittimus (*mit* i mus). Law: A court order to a peace officer directing him to take a person to jail.

M'Naughten Rule. A legal rule or test for holding a mentally ill person responsible for his criminal acts. If the accused knew the difference between right and wrong, he is deemed responsible for his acts.

Mob. 1. An assemblage of many people, acting in a violent and disorderly manner, defying the law, and committing, or threatening to commit, depredations upon property or violence to persons (*Black's Law Dictionary*). 2. Slang: A gang of criminals.

Mob's Stoolie. Slang: Used by criminal gang members to denote a crooked law enforcement officer.

Model. Helping guide or road map used in the formal correctional counseling program.

Model Penal Code. The final draft in 1962 by the American Law Institute contains suggested revision of the substantive law of crime and proposes a model sentencing structure.

Model Sentencing Act. Drafted in 1963 by the Advisory Council of Judges of the National Council of Crime and Delinquency (NCCD), this thirty-five page document proposed model sentencing structures.

Modi-Pac®. Proprietary name for a seminonlethal weapon.

Modus Operandi (*moe* dus op er *an* dee) (M.O.). Method of operation; a way of doing something; a pattern of action.

Mojo. Narcotics.

Mold. In field of moulage: The reproduction of an impression made or left by an object.

Molding. In field of moulage: The process of reproducing the impression of the object.

Molecule (*moll* e kyule). Two or more atoms chemically bound.

Molester, Woman (mo *les* ter). One who annoys or attacks a woman, usually for sexual purposes or robbery.

Moll. Slang: 1. A criminal's girlfriend or sweetheart; female companion; many times an accomplice in the crime; may be a prostitute. 2. A woman.

Moll Buzzer. Slang: Pickpockets

who choose women for victims; a female pickpocket.

Molly Maguires. A secret crime syndicate operating in the coal region of Pennsylvania in 1861 to 1871.

Molotov Cocktail (*moe* le tof). A fire bomb or hand grenade, usually made from a breakable bottle containing a flammable liquid (such as gasoline) with a rag wick protruding from the mouth of the bottle. It is used by lighting the wick and throwing the container against an object, causing the bottle to break, thus igniting the fuel.

Money Bets. Gambling term: In the game of craps or dice, money is used instead of chips.

Money-Making Machine. A fake money-printing machine that is used by con men to swindle victims, who are enticed to buy the machine for a substantial amount of money.

Money Mover, The. A person in the Cosa Nostra who finds channels for the use of money for the organization, i.e. enterprises where the money can be used for the profit of the organization, with the money mover getting a percentage of the profits.

Mongoloid (*mon* go loyd). A standard descriptive term for Orientals or American Indians.

Monitor (*mon* i tur). A device for receiving radio or television transmissions by signals. Used to check on such transmissions by listening or viewing.

Monkey. A drug habit where physical dependence is present.

Monkey Business. Slang: Fooling around; questionable or criminal activity; sexual overtures toward one of the opposite sex.

Monkey Cage. Slang: A jail or prison cell.

Monkey off, Get the. Slang: To break a narcotic addiction.

Monkey on my Back. Slang: Having a narcotic addiction; being hooked with a drug habit.

Mooch. 1. Slang: To ask for handouts; to steal, particularly small items. 2. To wander about; to leave or walk away from.

Moonlight. Slang: To work at one or more jobs in addition to one's main job or position.

Moonshine. Slang: Illegally made and sold whiskey, generally distilled in rural areas. Gets its name from the fact that the moonlight was used as a means of light to avoid detection.

Moot (moot as in boot). A discussion or argument, especially of a hypothetical law case, as in a law school.

Moot Court. A simulated or practice court, conducted for training of students. Law enforcement training and education programs use this method to acquaint students with the procedures and practices of the courts.

Mor A Grifa. Marijuana.

Moral (*mor* el). According to the standards of society, ethical, good, honest, upright, virtuous.

Morale (mor *al*). A state of mind where people have confidence, pride, and conviction regarding an undertaking or organization so that they will put forth extreme effort to achieve progress and objectives. It is something that means a great deal to an organization. It is a driving force necessary for outstanding accomplishments.

Morals Cases. Investigations or cases involving the morals of individuals and the public in such matters as prostitution, gambling, organized crime, etc. Large departments frequently have special units to conduct such investigations. The officers must have high moral stamina, as many of the people succumb to bribery or in other ways become obligated to persons engaged in such unlawful activities.

Moral Turpitude. A criminal act of baseness or depravity, contrary to the social standards and beliefs concerning morals, ethics, and duty between men.

Moratorium. Delay of payment of a legal authorization.

Mores (*mor* ayz). Sociology term: Traditions, customs, myths, or conventions that influence people greatly, having the effect of law.

Morgue (morg). Place where unidentified dead bodies, or those killed by violence, are kept pending identification.

Morgue, Newspaper. Place where copies of past issues of publications are kept. Many publishers index names and occurrences that are written about in the publications. A newspaper morgue can be a useful source of information for an officer.

Morning Line. The first odds quoted on the races for that day, together with information concerning the racing situation for that day. As of 1971, the nationwide morning line for sporting events originated in Las Vegas, Nevada. It came out on Sunday nights or Monday mornings for football games.

Moron (*mor* on). A person who is somewhat feeble-minded; one who is mentally retarded. One who has the intelligence of a child between the age of eight and twelve years old when his age is twenty or more.

Morph. Slang: 1. Morphine. 2. Hermaphrodite.

Morphie. Slang: Morphine.

Morphine (mor *feen*). A narcotic drug prepared from opium, legally and illegally. It is used in the medical field, principally as morphine sulfate, to reduce pain. Morphine may be taken orally or by injection, the latter method used chiefly by addicts. It is addictive and is regulated by law. Slang names for it are morph, junk, lent, cotics, unky, fix, shot, etc.

Morpho. Slang: Morphine.

Morphodite (*mor* fo dite). A pederast or oral sodomist.

Mortgage (*mor* gij). Law: A pledge, or placing as security, of property to act as security for a debt or other obligation. At common law the property was actually conveyed with the agreement that the conveyance was void if the terms of the contract were fulfilled (the debt paid as agreed). In some states in modern times the mortgage is akin to a lien against the property. See *Black's Law Dictionary*.

Mortgage, Chattel (*chat* el). A mortgage on movable property, such as automobiles.

Mortgagee (mor gi *jee*). The person in whose favor the mortgage is given; the one to whom property is mortgaged; the first mortgage holder.

Mortgagor (*mor* gi *jor*). The one who mortgages the property; the one against whose property the mortgage is issued; the debtor who signs a mortgage.

Mortis Causa (*mor* tis *cause* ah). Latin: A term used in legal phraseology meaning "in contemplation of death" *(Black's Law Dictionary).*

Mortuary (*mor* choo air ee). A funeral home; an undertaker's establishment; a place where the body is received and kept temporarily before interment.

Moslem Law. A system of customary law found by the English in India.

Mota. Spanish: Marijuana.

Mother. Helper characteristics that illustrate the responsive conditions in a helping relationship.

Motion (*moe* shen). Law: A formal application or request to the court for some action, such as an order or rule. "Your honor, I hereby submit a motion in arrest of judgement." See **Move.**

Motion for a Bill of Particulars. An action before a court asking that the details of the state's case against the defendant be made known to the defense.

Motion for Continuance. An action before a court asking that the trial or hearing be postponed.

Motion to Dismiss. An action before a court asking that the court dismiss the case against the defendant for a specified reason.

Motivate (*moe* ti vait). To induce or provide an incentive for one to do something.

Motive (*moe* tiv). The incentive, inducement, cause, or purpose that makes a person act. In criminal investigations determining the motive is important. Proof of motive is not an essential element of a crime but is an important aid to the prosecutor in presenting the case.

Motor Carrier. Any person, owning, controlling, managing, operating, or causing to be used or operated any motor-propelled vehicle used in the business of transportation of persons or property for hire, over the public highways of a state, whether as common carrier contract, or charter carrier, or as a transportation agency, or howsoever utilizing said public facilities.

Motorcycle. A two-wheeled automotive vehicle.

Motorized Bicycle. A pedal cycle that may be propelled by human power or helper motor, or by both, with a motor rated no more than one and one-half brake horsepower, a cylinder capacity not exceeding fifty cubic centimeters, an automatic transmission, and producing a maximum design speed of no more than twenty-five miles per hour on a flat surface.

Motor Vehicles. A vehicle that is propelled by a motor contained in the vehicle; a self-propelled vehicle.

Motor Vehicles, Interstate Transportation of Stolen. Motor vehicles that are stolen and transported, or caused to be transported, from one state to another or to the District of Columbia. It is a federal violation provided for in 18 USC 2311-13.

Motor Vehicle, Stolen. A self-propelled vehicle that has been stolen. This term is used in federal law concerning stolen vehicles that are transported interstate. The Act is entitled Interstate Transportation of Stolen Motor Vehicles, U.S. Code, Title 18, Sec. 2311-13.

Motrous Civiliter. A French law where the convicted person was sentenced to civil death (all the property went to the heirs).

Moulage (*moo* lahje). A term synonymous to molding and casting in criminal investigative work but which is used in the field of criminal justice to designate certain materials used in molding and casting, sold under trade names. Moulage is cast materials manufactured commercially, consisting of two kinds: (1) for making a negative mold and (2) for making the positive cast. It will record fine detail. It can be obtained from law enforcement supply companies.

Mounties, The. Canadian colloquialism: Royal Canadian Mounted Police.

Mouthpiece. Slang: A lawyer; an attorney who defends those accused of crime or those involved in crime.

Mouth-To-Mouth Resuscitation (re sus i *tay* shun). A procedure whereby a person places his mouth over the mouth (and nose, in the case of a child) of one who has stopped breathing and forces breath into the victim's lungs to bring about a restoration of breathing in the victim.

Movables (*moo* va bulz). Law: Personal property that can be carried or moved from place to place, such as radios, refrigerators, automobiles, etc. They are contrasted with immovables, such as houses, land, etc.

Movant (*moo* vent). One who makes a motion before a court.

Move. Law: To formally ask for something; to apply to a court for an order or rule.

Moving Surveillance. A surveillance that is mobile or moving in order to follow a mobile person or vehicle. A moving surveillance may be on foot, by motor vehicle, by common carrier, or by a combination of these methods.

Mud. Slang: Opium prior to its refinement to the stage where it can be smoked.

Mudder. Slang: A horse that runs well on a muddy track.

Mug. Slang: 1. A law enforcement picture of a person—a mug shot. 2. A form of robbery where the criminal uses physical force on the victim, usually by choking from the rear by partially strangling the victim with the arm. Other methods of force or violence may also be used. 3. Gambling term: The sucker.

Muggles. Slang: Marijuana.

Mulatto (mu *lat* o). One who has ancestors both Negro and Caucasian; having one Negro and one Caucasian parent.

Mule. Slang: A person who, for a steady income, will assume the risk of arrest for illegal activity.

Muled. Gambling term: The failure of a bookie to pay off a winner of a wager made with a bookie.

Multiple Cause Theory. A theory of deviance holding that criminal behavior is caused by the interplay of physical and emotional aspects of a person's life-style.

Multiple-Lane Highway. Any highway with two or more clearly marked lanes for traffic in each direction.

Multiple Offender. A person who has violated the criminal law more than once; repeater; recidivist. "He is a multiple offender."

Multiple Victimization. If a person has been victimized on more than one occasion in a specified time period, he is considered to have experienced multiple victimization for that time frame. (Note that it is a broader concept than series victimization.)

Municipal Court. A court presided over by a judge hearing misdemeanor and preliminary felony cases.

Municipality (myou nis i *pal* i tee). A place, usually a city or town, that has its own government.

Murder (*mer* der). Law: The killing of a human being with malice aforethought, or with premeditation, or when the offender has the specific intent to kill or do great bodily harm, or when the offender is engaged in the commission of a crime inherently dangerous to human life (armed robbery, etc.) and the death of a human being is caused, even though there was no intention to kill (statutory). The definitions of murder vary among the states.

Murder, Inc. A group of individuals operating in New York City area in the 1930s and early 1940s who killed many people. Some of them were tried for killings, and the news media referred to them as "Murder, Incorporated." Ralph Salerno, in *The Crime Confederation,* states this group was the "hit squad" of the syndicate or crime confederation of that area.

Murder, Vicarious. If accomplices engage in a crime inherently dangerous to human life (such as armed robbery), and the actions of one or more are sufficiently provocative of lethal resistance, and one or more of the accomplices are killed, the surviving offenders may be guilty of murder.

Muscle. Slang: To use force or the threat of force to get one's way, as in trying to break into a gang or a graft racket.

Muscle In. Slang: To move in on another's territory, business, or racket. To force one's way into a place.

Muscleman. Slang: The bouncer in a gambling establishment.

Muscular (*mus* kyou lar). Strongly built; muscles evident.

Mushroom. Firearms term: The flattening or expansion of a bullet when it strikes an object.

Mutatis Mutandis. Latin: The necessary changes have been made.

Mute. Silent; not able to speak or make sound; dumb. Usually expressed deaf-mute—one who is deaf and never learned to speak.

Mutilate (*myou* te late). To dismember a person or animal of limbs or parts of limbs; to damage severely a person's body or parts of the body.

Mutilation (myou ti *lay* shen). Destruction of written documents by making them imperfect because of an essential part being removed.

"Mutt and Jeff" Questioning. A technique of interrogation where two investigators are involved; one is friendly to the suspect, the other unfriendly.

Mutual Aid. An arrangement between law enforcement agencies in given areas, which work out and accept an agreement to render assistance to one another on request of the agencies involved.

Mutual Transfer. When two or more objects come in contact with one another, trace evidence from each may be left on the other. This is called mutual transfer. Such is often the case when one vehicle (such as a bicycle) is struck by a car. Each usually leaves some evidence on the other, such as an exchange of paint traces.

Muzzle (*muz* el). The front end of a firearm barrel from which the projectile exits; the open end of a firearm barrel.

Muzzle Blast. The sound produced by the bullet and powder gases forceably pushing the air away from the front of the barrel when a shot is fired.

Muzzle Distance. The distance the front of the injuring firearm was away from the victim when the shot was fired, i.e. the distance between the muzzle and the object shot. See **Powder Pattern**.

Muzzle Velocity. Firearms term:

The speed of the bullet as it leaves the muzzle of the weapon.

Myth, Society, and Culture. The concepts can be conceived as meshed gear wheels. Myths are the central beliefs around which society organizes the culture—the total characteristics of the people. If the myths change (direction) gradually, society may adjust, thus changing the culture. But if the myths change (direction) abruptly or totally, the gears of society are stripped and the culture becomes dysfunctional.

N

Nab. Slang: To arrest, apprehend, or catch someone.
Nag. Slang: A horse, usually a horse of little value; a race horse.
Nail. Slang: To catch or arrest a criminal.
Nailed. Slang: Caught in the act of cheating or stealing.
Nalline Test. A test used to determine if a person is using narcotics. It is administered by a physician.
Nance. A man who is effeminate or who is a passive pederast or oral sodomist.
Narc. Addict slang: Narcotics detective.
Narcolepsy (*nar* ko lep se). Sleep that cannot be controlled. Principal symptoms are frequent and uncontrollable "catnaps" not caused by fatigue. The cause is unknown, but physicians can medicate to relieve the symptoms. It is thought to be the cause of many major traffic accidents.
Narcotic. A drug, which in medicinal amounts relieves pain, causes sleep, and diminishes sensibilities but in large doses is a poison. Opium and morphine are two of a large number of narcotics.
Nark. Slang: Stool pigeon; law enforcement informant.
Narrative. Events related as a story; story told in sequence of events. In law enforcement the term is used to describe a recorded statement by an accused or a potential witness as compared to a question-and-answer type of statement.
N.A.T.B. (NATB). National Automobile Theft Bureau.

National Automobile Theft Bureau. A national organization, funded by insurance companies, that is concerned with investigating theft and arson of motor vehicles.
National Bank. In the United States, a bank that is a member of the Federal Reserve System.
National Bomb Data Center. Established in 1970 to provide technical data and services to law enforcement agencies relative to bombs and explosives. Data is published that is available to law enforcement agencies. Details of the service may be obtained from the International Association of Chiefs of Police, 11 Firstfield Road, Gaithersburg, Maryland 20760.
National Clearinghouse for Drug Abuse Information, The. An organization operated by the National Institute of Health. It is the focal point agency for federal information on drugs and their abuse. It provides information on request through publications, has a computerized information service, and refers technical matters to the proper agencies. Its address is 5454 Wisconsin Avenue, Chevy Chase, Maryland 20015.
National Commission on Law Observance and Enforcement. A commission created by President Hoover in 1929, composed of ten attorneys and a woman college president. Its purpose was to study crime as a national problem. It was called the Wickersham Commission, after its chairman, George W. Wickersham, former United States Attorney Gen-

eral. It completed its last report, in a total of twelve, in 1931.

National Commission on the Causes and Prevention of Violence. Created by Executive Order #11412 (by President Johnson) June 10, 1968. Its function was to investigate and make recommendations pertaining to the causes and prevention of violence, with the cooperation of other executive departments and agencies, and to report its findings and recommendations not later than one year from June 10, 1968. The term was extended by President Nixon on May 23, 1969, to completion of the report or December 10, 1969, whichever was earlier.

National Computerized Criminal History System. Inaugurated by and through the National Crime Information Center (NCIC), United States Department of Justice, in 1971. As of November, 1971, approximately fifteen states participated. The goal is to have all fifty states participate. To participate, each state must have the following: (1) A computer capable of interfacing with the NCIC computer for the interstate exchange of criminal history information under the management control of a criminal justice agency authorized to function as a control terminal agency. (2) A communication network serving all criminal justice agencies throughout the state. (3) A central state agency capable of processing all fingerprint cards generated in that state and updating the NCIC files. (4) A computerized state criminal history capability certified by the NCIC as meeting national standards.

National Council on Crime and Delinquency (NCCD). A national organization concerned with studying the causes, extent, and means for correcting crime and delinquency in the United States. Its address is 44 East 23rd Street, New York, New York 10010.

National Council on Organized Crime. An organization created by President Nixon on June 4, 1970, for the purpose of controlling organized crime by coordinated efforts of the various pertinent federal agencies. Attorney General John N. Mitchell was named chairman. Membership is composed of the Postmaster General, Secretaries of Labor and Treasury, and heads of all federal investigative agencies.

National Crime Commission. Synonym: President's Commission on Law Enforcement and Administration of Justice. Established by President Johnson on July 23, 1965, to study the whole field of criminal justice, bring comments on its findings, and make recommendations for its betterment. The study was divided into five task forces: Assessment of the Crime Problem; Police and Public Safety; Administration of Justice; Corrections; and Science and Technology. Its first report, "The Challenge of Crime in a Free Society," was released February 18, 1967. Other reports followed.

National Crime Information Center. Computer center at the headquarters of the Federal Bureau of Investigation, Washington, D.C., which serves terminals in the states of the United States and in Canada. It provides data regarding wanted fugitives, stolen automobiles, and other stolen items, such as stolen automobile license plates, securities, guns, office equipment, television sets, appliances, etc. It started operating January 27, 1967. The use of such equipment is a great asset to law enforcement.

National Criminal Offender Data File and Statistics System. See **National Data Center.**

National Data Bank. See **National Data Center.**

National Data Center. Synonym: National Data Bank. A proposed national center for storage and utilization of information on people (offenders) and statistics involved in the operation of the criminal justice system in the United States.

National Fire Protection Association. A nonprofit and technical association formed in 1896, with headquarters at 60 Batterymarch Street, Boston, Massachusetts, devoted to the protection of life and property from fire loss through the development of fire protection standards and public education.

National Fraudulent Check File. Maintained by the FBI Laboratory, this file serves as a clearinghouse for information on worthless checks. Worthless checks sent in by law enforcement agencies are compared against reproductions of checks already in file to determine if the writing, printing, check protector, etc., can be identified with that on other checks on file. If an identification is made, all interested agencies are notified. If no identification is made, a copy of the check is placed in the file for future reference. This file is of tremendous value in worthless check cases.

National Guard. The state militia. A military organization in each state, provided for in the Second Amendment to the Constitution, which says, "A well-regulated militia, being necessary to the security of a free state, the right of the people to keep and bear arms, shall not be infringed." The National Guard is under the control of the governor of the state and can be called to duty by him.

National Institute of Law Enforcement and Criminal Justice. The research branch of the Law Enforcement Assistance Administration. It is federally funded through Omnibus Crime Bill and Safe Streets Act monies. Research projects through the institute are evaluated, approved, and financed through its national headquarters in Washington, D.C.

Nationality. The fact or state of belonging to a nation, as by birth, citizenship, or allegiance.

National Safety Council. An organization concerned with improving safety for the American people. Its address is 425 N. Michigan Ave., Chicago, Illinois 60611.

Naturalization (*nach* er ru li *za* shun). The conferring upon an alien of the rights and privileges of citizenship. This is achieved through federal laws administered by the Bureau of Immigration and Naturalization and the federal courts.

Natural Law. Common and prevailing views concerning standards of moral and ethical human behavior.

Nautch Joint. Underworld slang: House of prostitution.

Nautical Mile. A unit of linear measurement equalling approximately 6082 feet.

Navigable Waters. Those waters that afford a channel for useful commerce.

Navigable Waters of the United States. Waters are navigable waters of the United States when they form, in their ordinary condition by themselves, or by uniting with other waters, a continued highway over which commerce is or may be carried on with other states or foreign countries in the customary modes in which such commerce is conducted by water.

NAZI (*not* see). One who is a member (or supporter) of the National Socialist Workers' Party. It originated in Germany under the direction of Adolf Hitler.

N.C.C.D. (NCCD). National Council on Crime and Delinquency.

N.C.I.C. (NCIC). National Crime Information Center.

NCJISS. National Criminal Justice Information and Statistics Service, a component of the Law Enforcement Assistance Administration of the U.S. Department of Justice.

NCP. National Crime Panel. A term sometimes used to designate the national component of the National Crime Survey, as contrasted with the city-level component.

NCS. National Crime Surveys. The NCS includes the National Household Survey, the National Commercial Survey, and the set of City Commercial Surveys—all concerned with criminal victimization. When the context is clear, NCS refers to the National Household Survey only.

Necessary. Those things essential to maintaining a dependent or incompetent in comfort and well-being.

Necktie Party. Slang: Unofficial hanging by a person or persons such as a lynching party.

Necrofetishism (nek row *fet*ish izm). A fetish for dead bodies.

Necrophilia (nek row *feel* e ah). Sex deviation term: An erotic attraction to dead bodies, which may involve sexual relations.

Necropsy. A postmortem examination.

Nee (nay). Family name of a woman prior to her present marriage. When placed after the name of a married woman, it denotes her maiden name. "Mrs. Grace Jones, nee Edwards." The use of this word is a time saver in report writing. It is a good procedure to record the maiden name of a married woman.

Needle. 1. That part of a syringe (hypodermic) for injections under the skin. Slang: In narcotic language, the taking of drugs by injection. 2. Slang: To do or say things that will aggravate or disturb another.

Needle-Man. Underworld slang: A person addicted to drugs who uses a hypodermic needle.

Need-to-Know Principle. One is supplied with full information in the particular field in which he is employed, but information of a confidential nature in other fields is made known to him when he needs to know it. This principle is used in intelligence work in government and is also used as a means of insulating the leaders in organized crime.

Nefarious (nee *fair* e us). Sinful; corrupt; villianous.

Negate (nee *gate*). Cancel; deny; revoke.

Negative. 1. In the field of moulage: The impression left by or a mold made from an object. 2. In photography: The processed film after exposure in the camera.

Neglect. To leave undone; disregard.

Negligence (*neg* lee jense). Lack of care; heedlessness; carelessness.

Negligent (*neg* lee jent). Prone to neglect; careless; disregarding standards of care.

Negotiable Instrument. 1. Transferrable and negotiable written securities or documents. 2. A signed, written document that is legally transferrable from one person to another, either by delivery or by endorsement and delivery.

Negroid (*nee* grawid). Evidencing racial physical characteristics of the Negro or African branch of the Black race. A standard descriptive term in law enforcement for persons of the Negro race.

Nephew. Slang: A youth who is supported by homosexuals.

Nepotism (*nep* o tizm). The hiring of relatives to fill public positions by one who holds a public office resulting from appointment or election. It infers the appointment of relatives to such positions without regard to merit.

Neurosis (new *row* sis). An abnormal nervous condition or sickness.

Neurotic (new *rot* ik). Suffering from an abnormal nervous condition; one who is afflicted with neurosis.

Neutron (*new* tron). A particle in the nucleus of the atom that has no charge and is equal in weight to a proton.

Neutron Activation Analysis. A procedure for detecting the presence and amounts of chemical elements in a substance even when present in extremely small quantities (trace elements). Radioactive materials are used in the test. It is useful in crime laboratories for analyzing such substances as poisons, traces of contaminants, and residues on the hands of homicide suspects to determine if a handgun has been recently fired by them.

Nevada Bank. Gambling game. See **Razzle Dazzle**.

New Fish. Prison or jail slang: A newly arrived convict.

Newgate. A prison in London that had a horrible reputation for conditions.

New Hampshire Rule. A test of criminal responsibility to see if the defendant had a mental disease.

New Left Movement. Organizations active in the late 1960s, aggressive in their tactics, leaning toward or embracing the Marxist-Leninist ideology. In 1969 leading proponents of the movement in the United States more clearly established themselves as Marxist-Leninist revolutionaries dedicated to the violent destruction of our society and the principles of free government. Principal organizations of the New Left Movement in 1969 were Students for a Democratic Society (SDS); Young Socialist Alliance (YSA); Student Mobilization Committee (SMC) (Nationally controlled by communist SWP/YSA members); Socialist Workers Party (SWP), and the New Mobilization Committee to end the war in Vietnam (NMC).

News Media. Means of disseminating news; newspapers, magazines, radio, television, and others.

NFPA. National Fire Protection Association.

Nibbler. Underworld slang: A male homosexual.

Nickel. Gambling term: Bet of five dollars.

Nickel Bag. Slang: Five-dollar packet of drugs.

Nickname. The use of a name for a person other than his real name. Nicknames are important in law enforcement, as many persons are better known by a nickname than they are by their real name.

Nigger. A contemptuous or derogatory name for a Negro or black person.

VOCABULARY

Nigger Lover. A derogatory term; one who fraternizes with or is sympathetic to Negroes or black people.

Night House. Gambling term: Bolita played daily in the nighttime.

Night on the Rainbow. Near-west slang: Use of narcotics for a short period of time.

Night Watchman. A person who guards or watches during the night. Many private businesses use such persons to safeguard their property.

Nihilism (*nigh* a lizm). 1. Total rejection of belief in laws. 2. Use of force and violence against authority or those representing such authority.

Nimby. Slang: Depressant drugs—barbiturates.

Nineteen Eighty-Three. Contraction of the title of a civil rights law found in U.S. Code, Title 42, Section 1983, which reads as follows: "Every person who, under color of any statute, ordinance, regulation or usage, of any State or Territory, subjects, or causes to be subjected, any citizen of the United States or other person within the jurisdiction thereof to the deprivation of any rights, privileges, or immunities secured by the Constitution and laws, shall be liable to the party injured in an action at law, suit in equity, or other proper proceedings for redress."

Nisei (*nee* say). American-born citizen whose father and mother were natives of Japan.

Nitro. Slang: Home preparation of nitroglycerin, usually cooked or steeped from commercial dynamite by the criminal.

Nitroglycerin. A chemical $C_3H_5(ONO_2)_3$, which is an explosive. It is the explosive substance in dynamite. It is an oily, amber-colored liquid, which is sensitive to shock (can be detonated by shock). It is dangerous and should be handled with great care. It is known in the safe burglary vernacular as "soup."

Nix. Slang: A negative response, meaning no; do not proceed; be careful.

N.K.V.D. (NKVD). Abbreviation for the former secret police of Russia. Has been replaced by the MVD.

N.L.R.B. (NLRB). National Labor Relations Board.

No Bebop. Juvenile slang: No tough guy.

No Exeat. Latin: A court document or order forbidding a person to leave, depart, or abscond from a certain area.

No Furniture in her Parlor. Juvenile slang: Toothless female.

"No Knock" Law. A law that empowers an officer to enter a home or other place, with a suitable court order, without knocking or announcing his identity when to do so would imperil the safety of the officer or when evidence might be easily and quickly disposed of or destroyed.

Nolle Prosequi. Latin; Law: An official entry of record by the prosecutor reflecting he will not pursue the prosecution any longer. This usually has the effect of ending the prosecution in a criminal case.

Nolo Contendere. Latin: Law: No contest; a plea by the defendant in a criminal prosecution in which the defendant does not plead guilty or not guilty. It has the effect of a guilty plea, and the defendant may then be sentenced just as if he had pleaded guilty.

Nomenclature (*no* men *clay* cher). A naming system.

Non-Age. Under full legal age.

Nonbailable. An offense not subject to bail.

Noncombustible (non kom *bus* ti bul). Not subject to combustion under ordinary conditions of temperature and normal oxygen content of the atmosphere.

Non Compos Mentis (non *kompus men* tis). Latin; Law: Unsound mentally.

Nondescript. Not subject to easy descriptions; not fitting the description of any particular type or kind.

Nonfault Automobile Insurance. As enacted in Massachusetts, each person's insurance company pays that person for damages suffered by him, regardless of fault. The amount coming under this provision is limited by law.

Nonfeasance. Failure of a public official to carry out a required duty of his office.

Nonflammable. Will not burn under conditions normally found in fires.

Nonjuror. A person who declines to take an oath required in a proceeding.

Non Obstant Verdicto. Latin: Notwithstanding despite the verdict.

Nonresident. 1. Not residing in the community where employed or in school. 2. Law: One who lives in another state.

Nonsecretor (non see *kree* tor). A person whose saliva and other body fluids (except blood) do not contain blood group antigens. It is not possible to type the saliva and other body fluids of such a person (blood not included) into blood type groups.

Nonsuit. A judgement against a plaintiff because of his failure to proceed to trial, to establish that he has a valid case, or to produce adequate evidence.

Nonsupport. Failure to provide legal dependency.

Non Vult Contendere. Latin: A variation of *nolo contendere,* where a person will not contest the charge.

Norm. Required or acceptable behavior.

Normal Mind. A person of average strength and capacity as the rest of society as a whole.

Normative Behavior. Approaching the standard for the group or culture.

Northerner. One who is a resident of or is a native of the northern part of the United States.

Notary Public. A notary; official authorized to certify documents.

Not Sufficient Funds (NSF). Banking term: The amount of a check or draft that exceeds the amount the maker or drawer has on deposit at the bank. The bank returns the check marked "NSF" or "Not Sufficient Funds."

Nuclear Family. The family consisting of a couple and their unmarried children.

Nucleus (*newck* le us). The center of an atom, which consists of protons and neutrons.

Nuisance (*new* sens). Something that is obnoxious, annoying, or bothersome. Public nuisance: Something declared by law to be a nuisance, such as a house of prostitution or gambling house.

Null. Without effect; having no legal effect. Null and void: Used in legal language to denote something that is worthless or has no legal effect; void.

Nullify. To legally make null.

Number. Slang: A joint; marijuana cigarette.

Numbers. A gambling game, also called the policy numbers game, in which the bettors buy a number or numbers and the winner is determined by such things as the parimutuel racetrack reports, the reports from the stock exchange, clearinghouse balances, or the United States Mint daily totals.

Numbers, Obliterated. Serial or identification numbers on objects that have been removed (ground off) or made unreadable by being hammered or punched. Thieves use this technique on such things as guns, motor vehicles, and other items of value that have an identification number, thus making it difficult or impossible to identify the item. The crime laboratories can restore and read such numbers in many instances by use of acid etching or the application of heat.

Nut. 1. Slang: Crank; screwball; lunatic; unpredictable. 2. Gambling term: The cost of any operation; the amount a casino must realize before profit starts.

Nymphomaniac (nim fo *may* ne ack). A woman with strong sexual urges that are not satisfied.

O

Oath. Law: The formal swearing by God that what one says, or is about to say (orally or in writing), is true and correct.

Obiter Dictum. Latin: An incidental opinion expressed by a judge, having no bearing upon the case in question, hence not binding.

Objection. During a trial, the expression of disapproval or dislike of a statement or method of proceeding, done by counsel for plaintiff or defendant.

Obligation (ob li *gay* shun). Specific enforceable duty.

Obligee. One to whom duty is owed.

Obligor. Person responsible for owing duty to another.

Obliteration. To do away with; leave without a trace.

Obscene. Indecent; dirty; immoral; foul; offensive to chastity or decency. Obscene material may consist of printed matter, photographs, drawings, or motion pictures. "Material is 'obscene' if to the average person applying community standards, the dominant theme of material taken as a whole appeals to the prurient interests, if it is utterly without redeeming social importance, if it goes substantially beyond customary limits of candor in description or representation, if it is characterized by patent offensiveness, and if it is hard-core pornography." Roth v. U.S., 354 U.S. 476; Jacobellis v. Ohio, 378 U.S. 184; Manual Enterprises, Inc. v. Day, 370 U.S. 478; U.S. v. Klaw, C.A.N.Y. 350 F. 2d 155, 164.

Obsolete (ob so *leet*). Old-fashioned; no longer being used; outmoded.

Obstructing Justice. Interfering with the functions and acts of those who have the authority and power of administering justice or enforcing the law.

Occupation. 1. Physical possession. 2. Business or profession.

Occupational Behavior. As modified by one's vocation.

O'Clock. Firearms term: The position of points on a target when compared to the face of a clock or watch. As the target is viewed from the front, it is compared with a clock face held in front of the viewer with the face toward the viewer. Three o'clock position is the right side of the horizontal line drawn through the center of the target and in line with a vertical line drawn through the center of the target.

O.C.R. (OCR). Organized Crime and Racketeering Section of the United States Department of Justice.

Ocular (*ock* u lar). The eyepiece of an optical device, such as a microscope.

O.D. (OD). Overdose of narcotics.

Oddball. Slang: Peculiar person.

Odds. The proportion existing between two bets; the amount paid a winner in a parimutuel bet.

Odds-On. Slang: Better than even chance of winning in gambling; the side of a bet that is favored.

Off. Withdrawn from drugs.

Offender. Person who is alleged by an NCS respondent to have committed crimes in one of seven major categories surveyed.

VOCABULARY

Offense (ah *fence*). A violation of the law; a crime; a misdemeanor; a felony.

Off his Rocker. Slang: Mentally unbalanced.

Office. Gambling term: Control center or location of the telephone where bets are centralized.

Officer Friendly. An educational program sponsored by Sears, Roebuck Foundation for elementary schools, using police officers and materials to help children see police as friendly protectors.

Officer of the Court. 1. One who is officially employed by the court in a position of trust or authority, such as a judge, sheriff, marshall, clerk, bailiff. 2. One who is employed by the court in an official capacity to fill a position of trust or authority, such as a judge, bailiff, etc.

Officers. Anyone holding office or holding a position of authority in an organization.

Off the Cuff. Slang: Confidentially; offhanded; aside from the main point.

Off the Pigs. Jargon for "kill the police." It is a slogan used by the Black Panther Party members at rallies of the Party.

Off Time. Gambling term: Actual starting time of the race.

Off-track Betting. Bets made at places other than the racetrack, usually where betting is legal at the track but not off the premises. Some states have legalized state-controlled off-track betting.

Oil. Slang: 1. Nitroglycerin, 2. To flatter.

Oiled. Slang: Drunk; intoxicated.

Okie. Slang: An itinerant worker from Oklahoma; anyone from Oklahoma.

Old Army Game, The. Slang: Crooked gambling game or swindle.

Old Head. Slang: Member of a gang who is older than a juvenile; over eighteen years of age.

Old Man. 1. The "Boss" of the Cosa Nostra family. 2. Slang: A long-handled tool used in safecracking.

Ombudsman. One who heads an independent government office that represents the people and investigates citizens' complaints against alleged abuse by government officials in all departments. First started in Sweden in 1809 and later spread to other Scandanavian countries.

Ominous. Foreboding; portentuous.

Omnibus Crime Bill. The Omnibus Crime Control and Safe Streets Act of 1968, Public Law 90-351, approved June 19, 1968. Also referred to as the Safe Streets Act.

Omnibus Crime Control and Safe Streets Act of 1968. Passed by Congress in 1968 and approved June 19, 1968. Also known as the Safe Streets Act and the Omnibus Crime Bill. It created the Law Enforcement Assistance Administration and provided for financial aid to the field of criminal justice in Title I. Title II deals with the admissibility of evidence and confessions; Title III with wiretapping and electronic surveillance; Title IV with disqualification of firearms; Title V with disqualification for engaging in riots and civil disorders; Title VI the confirmation of the Director of the Federal Bureau of Investigation; Title VII with the unlawful possession or receipt of firearms; Title VIII with providing for an appeal by the United States from decisions sustaining motions to suppress evidence; Title IX with additional grounds for issuing warrants; Title X with prohibiting extortion and threats in the District of Columbia.

On a Trip. Under the influence of LSD or other hallucinogens.

Once in Jeopardy. A statement or plea that the accused has already been placed in jeopardy for the offense. Therefore, he cannot be tried again for it.

One. Slang: A homosexual.

One-Armed Bandit. Slang: A slot machine operated by pulling a lever on the side of the cabinet; any slot machine.

One Dollar. Gambling term: Betting term for 100 dollars.

Onerous (*on* ur us). Oppressive or burdensome. In law, constituting a liability; a legal burden.

On juice. Gambling term: Person taking payment for providing protection.

On the Ball. Slang: Alert; capable; doing a job well; knowledgeable.

On the Beam. Narcotics slang: Feeling fine.

On the Boards. Slang: Police show-up.

On the Filtertips. Juvenile slang: Smoking.

On the Kick. Juvenile slang: Habitual.

On the Nod. Slang: Sleepy from narcotics.

On the Nose. Gambling term: An expression used in placing a racehorse wager. The amount wagered is bet to win only.

On the Scene. At or near the crime scene, contrasted with action taken at police headquarters or at a point distant from where the crime occurred. The courts draw a distinction between the two situations, and more freedom of action in questioning persons is allowed "on the scene."

On-the-Scene Questioning of Suspects. Questioning that occurs at or near the crime scene with the purpose of determining what occurred and who might be involved. If the questioning is truly exploratory or investigatory, the necessity to warn persons with the Miranda requirements is not as strict as when suspects are questioned in a more formal surrounding, especially if the person questioned is not detained or his freedom of movement substantially restricted.

On the Street. Out of jail.

On the Turf. Slang: Practicing prostitution.

Onus Probandi. Latin: Burden of responsibility of proof.

Ope. Opium.

Open. Slang: To allow gambling and vice to operate without police interference.

"Open Areas." Areas of the country (United States) into which any Cosa Nostra family can move and carry on operations.

Open Class System. A society in which maximum vertical mobility is assured.

Open Contract. Underworld: A given amount is offered by a gangster boss for the killing of a person. It can be claimed by any person who kills the designated individual. The arrangement is similar in design to law enforcement agencies offering a reward for the capture of a criminal.

Opening Statement. Statement that is first made by the prosecutor to the jury in which he outlines the case, pointing out the general proof that will be offered. The purpose is to give the jury a brief summary of the

VOCABULARY

case so they will be able to understand the evidence.

Open Shop. A business establishment that employs both nonunion and union workers.

Open Up. Gambling term: Increase the operation.

Operating Capital. Slang: Money with which a released convict can buy a gun.

"Operation Intercept." A program instituted on the United States-Mexico border September 21, 1969, to cut off the flow of narcotics, marijuana, and dangerous drugs into the United States. The program was jointly undertaken by the United States Treasury and Justice Departments, with the Bureau of Customs, Immigration, and Naturalization Service, Bureau of Narcotics and Dangerous Drugs, Coast Guard, Federal Aviation Administration, and General Services Administration participating.

"Operation Neighborhood." A neighborhood police team program, used in precincts in New York City.

Operation Police Manpower. A program offered to military personnel, prior to their release, as a part of the "transition program." It consists of 240 hours of police training, which meets the mandatory highest state standards required in the United States (1970). Except for learning local law, ordinances, and procedures, the trainee in this course is equipped for police work.

Operator. 1. Gambling term: One who runs or manages a numbers lottery. 2. Anyone who is in the habit of operating or driving a vehicle on the highway or roadway.

Opiate (*o* pee it). A substance that contains opium or its derivative; anything that calms, soothes, or quiets.

Opinion. Belief short of knowledge but greater than mere impression. Usually a person is not allowed to state his opinion in testimony in court unless he qualifies as an expert in a particular field.

Opinion Evidence. See **Evidence, Opinion.**

Opinion Leaders. High status person whose opinions are often influential on public issues.

Opium. A narcotic drug that diminishes pain and induces sleep. It comes from the dried juice of the opium poppy. Most of it is produced in Turkey and the Far East. Morphine and heroin are derivatives of it.

Opium Derivatives. Morphine, heroin, Dionin, Dilaudid®, apomorphine, metopon, codeine.

O.R. (OR). 1. Abbreviation for "owner's risk." 2. An abbreviation for "own recognizance," where a person is "released on his own recognizance" without bail upon the agreement that he will appear before the court at the time summoned.

Oral. Spoken, as compared with written.

Oral Evidence. Evidence given by the spoken word as opposed to documentary or real evidence. Sometimes referred to as Parol Evidence.

Oralism (*o* rel *izm*). Sex deviation term: Sexual satisfaction attained by the use of the mouth on the sexual organs.

Oranges. Narcotics slang: Dextroamphetamine sulfate in orange-colored, heart shaped tablets.

Order. 1. In accordance with rules. 2. To command or request. 3. An organized group of people united for specific purposes.

Order Horse. Racetrack gambler slang: A horse entered in a race without any expectation or design for him to win. He is the "order horse" in the process of building to the day when he will run as a "hot horse."

Order Maintenance Police. As through licensing, inspection, traffic control, crowd management, crisis intervention, etc.

Ordinance. A law of an authorized subdivision of the state, such as a city or county.

Oregon Boot. A device placed on the ankle and foot of a person to impede his walking or running. It has been used on convicts working outside of prison, such as on road gangs and also in transferring prisoners. It consists generally of heavy metal contrivances something like shoes or boots, which are joined by a chain of such a length that a person can only take a short step.

Organic Compound. A chemical compound that contains carbon and usually hydrogen.

Organization, The. When used in connection with organized crime, it refers to the Cosa Nostra, the Confederation, the Syndicate, or the Outfit.

Organized Crime. 1. "The product of self-perpetuating criminal conspiracy to wring exorbitant profits from our society by any means—fair or foul, legal and illegal. Despite personnel changes, the conspiratorial entity continues. It is a malignant parasite that fattens on human weakness. It survives on fear and corruption. By one or another means, it obtains a high degree of immunity from the law. It is totalitarian in its organization; a way of life, it imposes rigid discipline on underlings who do the dirty work while the top men of organized crime are generally insulated from the criminal act and the consequent danger of prosecution." The above definition was worked out by the Oyster Bay Conference on Combatting Organized Crime (1965). 2. A continuing, self-perpetuating criminal conspiracy, which operates for a profit motive and thrives on fear and corruption.

Organized Crime and Racketeering Unit. An agency, under the direct administration of the United States Attorney General, to coordinate the functions of federal agencies to cope with members of crime syndicates.

Organized Crime Control Act of 1970. Signed into law by President Nixon on October 15, 1970. The law broadens the fight against organized crime, charges the FBI with investigating bombings of, and bombing attempts on, any property of the federal government or that of any institution or organization receiving federal financial assistance.

Original Jurisdiction. In reference to a court, it means it has jurisdiction of a case or in a matter from the beginning. The court having original jurisdiction has the authority to hear the facts, apply the law, and render a decision, contrasted to an appellate court, which only has the authority to review the case when sent up from a lower court.

Orwellian (or *wel* ee en). Reference to George Orwell's novel *1984*, portraying the government as keeping an all-seeing and dominating eye on a thoroughly regimented citizenry (Big Brother is watching).

VOCABULARY

Oscar. Slang: Underworld term for a gun.

Osmium Tetroxide (*oz* mee um). Used in liquid or vapor to develop latent prints on paper. Silver nitrate is usually preferred.

Oust. To put out by the use of force; to remove one; dispossess; expel.

Ouster. Law: Ejection from real property.

Outcast. One who is rejected, put out from home and friends, friendless.

Outen. Juvenile slang: To punch one into unconsciousness.

Outfit (FIT). Equipment for injection by hypodermic method; a "hype" outfit—eyedropper and needle, spoon, pacifier, etc.

Outfit, The. Slang: Organization; gang; the Syndicate. With specific reference to organized crime: The Organization. See **Organization, The.**

Outlaw. 1. One who is generally known to be a lawbreaker; a lawless individual. 2. Juvenile slang: To take by force.

Outlawry (*out* law ree). In English law a process by which a defendant or a person in contempt on a civil or criminal process was declared an outlaw. If for treason or felony, it amounted to conviction and attainder (*Black's Law Dictionary*). As used in England it was a form of community retaliation against the criminal. The retaliation was of such severity that the criminal seldom escaped death.

Outlaw Strike. Slang: A labor strike not authorized by the high union officials. Synonym: Wildcat strike.

Out of Court. Law: Without a trial; settling a case without a trial.

Out of It. Not in contact, not part of the drug scene.

Out of Sight. Good; groovy; a positive descriptive term.

Outside. Slang: Freed from jail or prison; the world outside of jail or prison.

Outside Work. Gambler slang: Any alteration done to the outside of the dice.

Outskirts. The outer edge of a town, city, or community; border.

Over a Barrel. Slang: A position of disadvantage.

Overdraw (oh ver *draw*). To take out of an account more than the person is entitled to; to pass a check for a greater amount than the maker has in his account. "Due to his financial situation he will overdraw at the bank." When done by check the bank may not honor it and return it marked "NSF"—not sufficient funds.

Overlook. Gambling term: In the numbers game a hit that was made and not paid.

Overrule. 1. To reject or supercede 2. To reject an objection made during a trial.

Overshot (*oh* ver shot). A descriptive term for an individual whose upper jaw extends beyond the lower.

Overt (oh *vert*). Apparent; manifest; obvious; unconcealed; open. Contrasted with **Covert.**

Overt Act. Criminal law: An act done in furtherance of a plan, conspiracy, or intent. In a criminal conspiracy case mere planning is insufficient to constitute the crime, an overt act in furtherance of the plan must be done; the same rule applies in a criminal attempt case.

Over the Hump. Narcotics slang: Having completed withdrawal.

Owe Time. Slang: When a person is paroled from prison with time still remaining on the sentence, he is subject to return if parole is violated.

Owner. One who has or owns as property the legal title of any vehicle.

Owsley's Acid. LSD purportedly illegally manufactured by Augustus Owsley Stanley III; also infers that it is good quality LSD.

Ox. Abbreviation for ounce. Refers to an ounce of narcotics, usually heroin or methedrine.

Oxidation (ox i *day* shen). In chemistry, the loss of an electron in combination. Comes from the combination of a substance with oxygen, which causes the same reaction.

Oxidizing Agent. An agent that supplies oxygen necessary for a chemical reaction.

Oyer and Terminer. French: "Hear and decide;" some higher state criminal courts are called by this name.

P

Pacify (*pass* a figh). To calm down; to quiet someone; to satisfy the demands of a person.
Pack. Slang: To carry a weapon, especially a gun.
Package Store. Establishment that sells alcohol in package form, not to be consumed in the store.
Pad. Slang: 1. A bed or cot in a cheap hotel or rooming house. 2. Hippie term: One's own living quarters.
Padding the Payroll. Slang: Placing the names of people on the payroll for whom checks are issued when such persons are actually not employed or working.
Paddy. Slang: Caucasion.
Paint Examination. The examination of paint specimens by a crime laboratory. In cases where a vehicle has struck another object, this type of examination may be most helpful. If there has been a mutual transfer of evidence, it is well to get specimens of paint near the points of mutual transfer.
Pallid (*pal* id). Colorless; pale. Descriptive term to denote the appearance of the skin, usually the face.
Palmistry (*pah* mis tree). The procedure of telling fortunes from the interpretation of the lines in the hands.
Palmprints. The ridge impressions, inked or latent, of the palms of the hands.
Pan. Slang: To criticize strongly.
Panama Red. A potent type of South American cannabis.
Pander (*pan* dur). To pimp; to cater to the gratification of the lust of others; to entice or procure a female (females) by promises, threats, fraud, or artifice; to enter any place in which prostitution is practiced, for the purpose of prostitution.
Panel. 1. List of persons summoned to jury duty. 2. The persons summoned or the jury itself.
Panhandle (*pan* han dull). To approach people and beg, especially in a public place.
Panic (*pan* ik). 1. Fear affecting a large number of people so that they lose control of themselves; an overpowering fear. 2. Slang: Shortage of narcotics on the market.
Panic Man. Narcotics slang: Addict whose source of supply has been terminated.
Pansy (*pan* zee). Slang: Homosexual male who usually takes the female role.
Panther, The Black. An extremist group, militant in its goals, made up largely of black members. Active in the United States in the late 1960s and early 1970s.
Pants-Pocket Worker. A highly skilled pickpocket who specializes in picking pants pockets.
Paper. Slang: 1. Worthless checks. 2. Gambling term: Slips or sheets on which bets are placed. 3. Counterfeit money. 4. A container of drugs.
Paper-Hanger. Slang: A person who makes or passes counterfeit money or bad checks.
Paper-Pusher. Slang: Counterfeit money passer or operator.
Paraffin Test (*pair* eh fin). A tech-

nique of coating the hands of a person with melted paraffin (cooled to the degree that it will not burn). After the paraffin cools and hardens, the "glove" is removed by cutting with scissors, and the inside surface is treated with a diphenylamine solution. If nitrates or nitrites are present, a distinctive color is produced, thus indicating the presence of gunpowder residue. This test is not considered reliable due to the prevalence of nitrates and nitrites.

Parajudge (*pair* eh juj). A term used by President Nixon in March, 1971, to describe a trained administrator, working under the supervision of attorneys and judges, whose role is to relieve judges of some of their administrative burdens.

Parallel (*pair* a lel). Running or extending side by side and of equal distance from one another at all points. "The rails on the railroad track are parallel."

Paramour (*pair* a moor) An illegal or illicit lover. May be man or woman, i.e. a person of either sex may assume the role of husband or wife in having an "affair" with one of the opposite sex.

Paranoia (pair a *noi* a) Abnormal mental condition, which is usually attended by delusions.

Pardon (*par* den) Forgiving one of his crime on which he has been found guilty and releasing him from punishment. This can be granted only by the highest executive of government—the governor of a state for a state crime or the President of the United States for a federal crime. Pardons may be recommended to the executive officer by Pardon Boards.

Paregoric (pair e *gar* ick). A drug containing camphor and a small amount of opium, which has a soothing effect. The distribution of this drug is restricted by law.

Parens Patriae (*pay* renz *pay* tri e). Latin: The state with its sovereign power of guardianship over disabled persons. This term is frequently used to describe the role of the state (through its courts) in dealing with juvenile delinquents. The United States Supreme Court in *in re* Gault, prescribed the formalities to which the court must adhere in dealing with juveniles.

Parenticide. The act of a child who murders one of his parents.

Paresis. Medical term: A progressive paralysis leading to insanity.

Parfocal (*par* fo cal). A property of microscopes in which if one focuses on an image with one objective, the image will remain in focus if another objective is moved into position.

Pari Delicto. Latin: In equal fault; equal in guilt or in legal fault.

Pari-Mutuels (*pair* i *mew* chew els). A race betting system where the odds and winnings are determined by the total amount wagered in a particular race.

Parish. 1. A church district that has its own clergyman. 2. Louisiana has parishes, which are equivalent to counties in other states.

Park (Parking). 1. To keep (as an automobile) standing for a time at the edge of a public way or in a place reserved for the purpose. 2. Slang: To kiss in a parked car.

Parlance (*par* lens). Manner of speaking; speech; language. "In legal parlance these words mean . . ."

Parlay (*parr* lay). Slang: The betting of a given amount with the agreement that it and the winnings will be

VOCABULARY

bet on the ensuing event or events. Used in horse racing, to build a small investment or outlay into a large amount. The amount is bet on one horse to win, and if he wins, the winnings are wagered on the second designated horse.

Parliamentary Law. Rules of a type of government or public assembly; rules of parliament.

Parol (*pe* roll). Expressed by word or speech (contrasted to expressing something in writing). "Parol evidence is that which is furnished by word of mouth or speech."

Parole (pe *roll*). Conditional pardon; the conditional release of a prisoner prior to completion of his sentence in jail or prison. The parolee (person released on parole) is placed under the supervision of a parole officer.

Parolee (pa *roll ee*). A prisoner who has been released on parole.

Parole Officer. A person, appointed by the court or some other official agency, who supervises persons placed on parole.

Parole Revocation. The decision of a paroling authority to return the parolee to serve his sentence in an institution because he did not live up to the conditions of parole.

Parolitis. Prison slang: An acute anxiety experienced by convicts just prior to parole release.

Parry (*pair* ree). Act to ward off or evade a weapon, such as a knife or sword, or a question.

Partial Fingerprint. A latent fingerprint that is composed of only part of the total finger impression.

Particeps Criminis. Latin: A participant in crime; an accomplice.

Party. 1. A person or group of persons constituting one side of an issue, undertaking, or dispute. 2. Law: The person or persons involved in different sides of a legal action. 3. Contracts: A person or persons constituting one or more sides of a contractual agreement.

Pass. There are many uses for this word. 1. Succeed or accomplish something. "I passed the examination." 2. Pronounce. "The court passed sentence on the man." 3. Become unconscious. "He passed out." 4. Cause to circulate or negotiate an instrument or commerce. "He passed three worthless checks." 5. Slang: Advances to one of the opposite sex.

Passers. Gambling term: Dice that due to their alteration, will make more passes than regular dice.

Passion. Emotion; excitement; fury; lust; strong feeling. "Fear and hate are passions." "Manslaughter is legally defined in many states as unpremeditated homicide, committed while under the influence of sudden passion."

Passport. An official government document issued to a person, certifying his citizenship and authorizing him to travel to other countries with the full protection of the country issuing it.

Paste. Slang: Simulated precious stones, such as diamonds, which are made to resemble the real thing but are imitations.

Past-Post. In racehorse gambling: To bet after the bettor knows the horse has won in the race on which he is betting. The one betting has received information about the outcome of the race prior to the bookie knowing about it, thus the latter has not closed his book for the race.

Pat. A light touch or strike, as with the fingers. "The officer patted down the suspect to determine if he had a weapon."

Patch Pocket Worker. A pickpocket who specializes in stealing pocketbooks from women's coat pockets.

Pat Down. A physical search of the suspect's outer clothing (not inside pockets), which is conducted to protect the officer from a possible weapon. It is distinguished from a search in the respect that the officer is not searching for contraband or physical evidence of a crime on the person.

Patently (*payt* ent ly). Manifestly; obviously; without doubt. "The allegations are patently incorrect."

Paternity (pe *ter* ni ty). Fatherhood; being the father of a child.

Pathogenic (path o *jen* ick). Something that caused disease.

Pathologist (pe *thol* e jist). A person who is highly educated and trained in pathology, which is the area of medicine dealing with the nature and causes of illness or injury of people. A competent pathologist is a great asset to law enforcement, especially in determining the cause of injury or death.

Pathology (pe *thol* e je). The study of diseases, their causes, and characteristics.

Patriarchy Family (*pay* tree ark ky). Patristic; a family where the authority and inheritance is vested in males.

Patricide (*pat* re side). The act of a person who kills his own father.

Patrol. 1. To make the rounds or travel over certain areas; to watch and protect. 2. Men or women who patrol.

Patrolman. 1. The law enforcement officer who walks a beat or patrols areas by motor vehicle. 2. An official rank of a police officer, generally the beginning rank.

Patronage, Political. The giving of jobs in public offices by politicians; the distribution of public office jobs.

Patsy. Slang: One without guilt, who is blamed with crime by others who are guilty; one commonly referred to as a "fall guy."

Pattern. 1. Fingerprints term: The ridge formation on a person's fingers, palms, or feet. 2. Firearms term: The manner of distribution of the shot of a shotgun after they leave the gun barrel.

Patterned Wounds. A mark on a body that clearly shows the impression of the object by which it was struck.

Pauper. One who lives on charity; a poor person.

Pavor Nocturnus. Latin; Medical term: Nightmare; one of the main causes of anxiety.

Pawn. Turn over possession of something to another as security that money borrowed from such person will be repaid in a specified time.

Pawnbroker. Person who takes articles as security on loans with interest.

Payable. 1. Owing and to be paid in the future. 2. Owing and due for payment now.

Pay Line. The middle line on the payoff line on a slot machine.

Payoff. Slang: 1. Graft money payment. 2. To pay for illegal or unethical services. 3. The final outcome of a problem or situation. 4. Gambling term: Money received for picking the winning number.

Payoff Man. Gambling term: The person who delivers the money on a win bet.

Payoff Odds. Gambling term: Bets paid off at odds lower than the actual or correct odds, thus giving the house more profits.

Payola. Slang: Payoff, especially for graft, blackmail, or extortion; the

VOCABULARY

payments for police protection or other questionable advantages.

P.C. (PC). Gambling slang: A percentage of the profits.

P.C.P. (PCP). Refers to the drug phencyclidine, originally an anesthetic for dogs.

P.C.R.O. (PCRO). Police Community Relations Officer.

P.D. (PD). Police Department.

Peace Bond. A bond or bail fixed by a magistrate to insure that the person bonded will keep the peace and not molest or injure someone against whom he has made threats or endeavored to do harm. In 1970 the peace bond was declared unconstitutional by a Hawaiian court.

Peace Cross. A sign or symbol displayed frequently by various "peace groups" in the late 1960s and early 1970s. It is in the form of a circle enclosing a cross with the cross bars broken down. The type of cross is sometimes called the "broken cross" or "crucified cross." It has been said by some that this type of cross signifies Satan's contempt for Christian principles and is an ancient sign of evil.

Peace Officer. Law enforcement officer, such as the sheriff, deputy sheriff, police officer, constable, or marshall. It is defined differently by various states, by statute.

Peace Pill. Refers to the drug phencyclidine, originally an anesthetic for dogs.

Peaches. Narcotics slang: Amphetamine sulfate in rose-colored, heart-shaped tablets.

Peanuts. 1. Depressant drugs—barbiturates. 2. A small amount of money.

Pearls. Slang: Teeth.

Pearly Gates. Slang: LSD.

Pecking Order. In a poultry yard, each hen picks at the next smaller below it in their "social" order without fear of retaliation. Hence, a social hierarchy of ranks.

Peculation. The wrongful conversion of property in one's custody or control to one's own use; embezzlement.

Pecuniary. Monetary; related to money.

Peddle. To move from one place to another selling products; used frequently in the narcotic field.

Peddler. Narcotics slang: One who sells narcotics to users.

"Peddling a Flat." See **"Going on Blind."**

Pederasty (*ped* e *ras* te). Sex deviation term: Sodomy; sexual intercourse by inserting the penis in the anus of the sex partner.

Pedestrian (pe *des* tree en). Person who travels by walking.

Pedigree (*ped* e gree). Law enforcement term: The criminal history of a person.

Pedometer (pe *dom* e ter). Device for recording the number of steps taken, which can then be used to compute distance traveled.

Pedophilia (Paedophilia) (ped o *feel* ya). Sex deviation term: Situation where a child is selected as the sexual object. The person afflicted with this sex deviation is called a pedophile.

Peek. Racetrack gambler term: An arrangement whereby one who is situated outside the track can read the race results from the totalizer board and pass this information to his confederates.

Peek Store. A gambling establishment that cheats by peeking a number and miscalling it or changing it subtly.

Peel, Sir Robert. English official and statesman. He initiated the Police

Act of 1829, which created the Metropolitan Police Force (London area), the first police system.

Peeler. Slang: Nickname given to policemen, after Sir Robert Peel.

Peeling. A system used by safe burglars, whereby the outer surface of the safe door is peeled off, thus making access to the locking device available.

Peepers. Slang: Eyes.

Peephole. A hole in something, such as a wall or door, through which a person might look.

Peer. Equal; same rank; to match.

Peer Group. A group of persons who share the same or similar social, economic, or other social status.

Peg. Slang: To recognize.

Pellagrous Insanity. Medical term: Insanity caused by an endemic disease of Southern Europe.

Pelvis. The cavity in the skeleton of many vertebrates (man included) formed by the hip bones and adjoining bones.

Pen. Slang: Penitentiary.

Penal. Pertaining to punishment.

Penal Code. Laws covering crimes against the state.

Penalty. Punishment for a crime; loss due to an action committed.

Pencil. The right or power of signing payoff checks at a casino.

Pending. Imminent; not yet decided.

Penetration. A term used in criminal law and denoting (in case of alleged rape) the insertion of the male part into the female part, to however slight an extent, and by which insertion the offense is complete without proof of omission.

Penis (*pea* nis). Male organ of copulation.

Penitentiary (pen e *ten* shure ree). A place of incarceration for convicted criminals; a prison. May be a state or federal institution.

Penny. Slang: Derogatory term for a law enforcement officer.

Pennyweighter. A jewelry thief who has a simulated copy made of an expensive piece of jewelry and substitutes it for the real jewelry while examining it in the jewelry store.

Penology (pea *noll* o gee). The study of crime, punishment, and administration of prisons.

Pen Register. A device placed on the telephone line of a person suspected of making nuisance phone calls. It records the time and date of each call and the number called. This is then compared with the information recorded by the person called and is used to prove that the suspect made such calls.

Peonage (*pea* en ij). Act of holding individuals to work off debts. It is a federal criminal violation.

"Pepperbox." An obsolete type of revolver (pistol), which had a group of barrels that revolved.

Pep Pills. Slang: Stimulant drugs—amphetamines.

Per. A prescription.

Per Annum. Latin: By the year.

Per Capita (pur *kap* e te). Latin: By heads; per person; by or for each person.

Percentage Dice. Gambler slang: Dice that, due to their structure, are in favor of the operator over the "long haul." One of the pair of dice is misspotted by having one of the numbers, usually the two or the five, appearing twice.

Percentage of Pattern. Number of pellet marks in a 30 inch circle, over a 40 yard range, divided by the number of pellets in the load.

Per Curiam. Latin: Literally, "by the court"; an opinion of the full court,

VOCABULARY

as opposed to one with some judges affirming and others dissenting. Usually a brief decision, without detailed argument.

Percussion Cap. That part of a "round" of ammunition (the cartridge) consisting of a cap enclosed in thin metal containing a detonator, such as fulminate of mercury, which when struck by the hammer or firing pin, explodes and ignites the propelling charge.

Per Diem (per *dee* em). Latin: Per day.

Peremptory (pur *emp* to re). Positive; decisive; absolute; final.

Peremptory Challenge. Law: The right given each side (prosecution and defense) in a jury trial to object to the acceptance on the jury of prospective jurors without giving any reason for such objection (challenge).

Peremptory Ruling. A judge's ruling that takes the final decision away from the jury.

Performance Rating. An evaluation of the work of a worker or employee.

Peripheral Vision (pur *rif* e ral). Side vision; the ability to see things other than through direct vision; to see objects to the side of where vision is focused.

Periphery (pur *rif* e ry). Outer boundary; external limit.

Perjure (*purr* jer). To commit perjury.

Perjury. Law: The intentional making of a false statement, oral or written, in or for use in a judicial proceeding, or any proceeding before a board or official wherein such board or official is authorized to take testimony. The false statement must be made under oath or affirmation and must relate to matters material to the issue or question in controversy. The false statement must be made knowingly; however, an unqualified statement of that which one does not know or definitely believe to be true is equivalent to a statement of that which he knows to be false; violation of an oath.

Perpendicular (purr pin *dick* ye ler). At right angles to the horizontal; straight up.

Perpetrate (*purr* pea trait). To violate a law or do something bad; to commit a wrongful act.

Perpetuation of Evidence. Insuring the availability of evidence for a later trial.

Per Se (pur *say*). Latin: Through or by itself.

Perse. A new drug developed by Dr. Emanuel Revici, a New York biochemist. It is a nonaddictive drug to cure addicts of heroin, barbiturates, and methadone, and it has no apparent bad side-effects. To relieve physical addiction, decreasing doses of perse are given; however, the patient still needs pyschotherapy. As of May, 1971, the Food and Drug Administration had not certified the drug as safe.

Persecute. To harass; to annoy; to torment.

Person. A human being, or a corporate entity.

Personal Identification. The means by which a person can be identified. This may be such things as an official card (commission card), letter, or driver's license. There is in use a personal identification fingerprint card. Many citizens have their fingerprints taken on such cards and placed on file with government agencies so as to have a personal identification on record.

Personal Incident. See **Incident**. Crimes of rape, robbery, assault, personal theft, and corresponding attempts are considered personal incidents.

Personality. The syndrome of habits, attitudes, and other characteristics of an individual.

Personal Larceny with Contact. Theft or attempted theft of purse, wallet, or other property by stealth directly from the person of the victim but without force or the threat of force.

Personal Larceny without Contact. Theft, without direct contact between victim and offender, of property or cash from any place other than the victim's home or its immediate vicinity; also includes attempted theft.

Personate (*purr* so nate). Law: With fraudulent intent, to assume character and/or identity of another, without the latter's consent, and to gain some advantage or obtain something of value as the result of such impersonation. To pretend to be or assume the identity of another.

Personnel Security. A program or procedure whereby an organization seeks to protect its technology, materials, or equipment from loss or embezzlement by its own employees and nonemployees who have contact with personnel of the organization. Employees who are considered "not good risks" are precluded from access to certain types of information and materials.

Persuader. Slang: A weapon; a gun; a club; a knife; a policeman's nightstick.

Persuasion. Criminal's slang: Pressure put on someone to coerce him to do something.

Persuasive Authority. All sources of law that a judge might use (but is not required to use) in making up his mind about a case.

Perversion (purr *vur* shun). Abnormal sexual desires and activities; the obtaining of sexual satisfaction by abnormal methods.

Pervert (*purr* vert). One who has turned away from what is normal, natural, or right. Sex pervert: One who engages in some form of sexual deviation or perversion.

Pete. Slang: Safe.

Pete Brother. Slang: A safe blower.

Pete Man. Slang: A safe burglar who opens safes with explosives.

Peter. Slang: A safe.

Peterman. Slang: A dynamiter; safe burglar using explosives.

Petition. Law: A formal (written) request submitted to a court requesting action.

Petition. Request or plea to one in authority; court action sought by a specific plea; a request; to solicit.

Petitioner. One who brings action in a court; presents a petition to court, officer, or legislative body.

Petit Jury. A trial jury; a trial jury of twelve jurors, to hear testimony in a case being tried in court and reach a verdict. It is not a grand jury. See **Jury.**

Petrography (pe *trog* ray fe). The study and identification of rocks and their derivatives, such as soil.

Pettifogger. A disreputable lawyer who operates in violation of his code of legal ethics.

Petting Party. Slang: Shooting scrape.

Petty. Of little value or significance.

Petty Jury. Same as **Petit Jury.**

Peyote Cactus Buttons. A cactus of the southwestern United States and Mexico that has mescal buttons, from which mescaline is derived. See **Mescaline; Hallucinogens.**

VOCABULARY

Pez. Pez® candies impregnated with LSD.
P.G. Head. Narcotics slang: User of paregoric.
pH. System of the measurement of acidity and baseness of substances. A pH of 7 is neutral; the lower pH is acidic, higher pH is basic.
Phase. A homogeneous, physically distinct, and mechanically separate portion of matter.
Ph.D. Doctor of Philosophy.
Phennies. Slang: Depressant drugs—barbiturates.
Phenobarbital (fee no *bar* bi tall). A barbiturate, white powder, which has hypnotic and sedative properties.
Phenol (*fee* nol). A poison or antiseptic—carbolic acid.
Phenolphthalein Test (fee nol *thay* lean). A preliminary test to determine if a stain is blood. If a positive reaction is obtained, then further confirmation tests are conducted.
Phenomenologism (fee *nom* e *nol* oge ism). Biosocial man responds to perceived phenomena.
Phobia (*foh* bi a). An unnatural, abnormal, illogical fear.
Phoenix House. A narcotic addict rehabilitation establishment.
Phoney. Slang: 1. Not true; not genuine; of no value. 2. A loaded die.
Photoelectric Intoximeter. A technical device for testing alcohol content of the breath.
Photoflash Bulb. A specially made lightbulb or lamp, fired electrically, which gives a brilliant light flash for taking photographs where there is not enough natural light. The flash and the camera shutter must be synchronized.
Photoflood Light. A sustained light bulb activated electrically, for taking photographs. This type is used for taking motion pictures where there is not enough natural light.
Photomacrograph (*fow* tow *mack* ro graf). A photograph through a microscope of an object large enough to be seen by the naked eye but where the lens of the microscope enlarges the size and detail of the object. Such is used in the examination of the cut surfaces of metal wire, etc., i.e. in tool mark examinations or firearms examinations.
Photomicrograph (*fow* two *mike* ro graf). A photograph taken through a microscope of objects so small as to be invisible to the naked eye.
Phrenology (free *nol* o gee). A criminology concept that crime is caused by lower pyschological characteristics of individuals.
Physical Dependence. A physiological addiction to a drug due to regular use, which is characterized by withdrawal sickness when usage is discontinued.
Physical Description. A description of the physical features of a person, including such things as age, height, weight, race, hair, eyes, complexion, build, etc.
Physical Evidence. Real evidence; evidence that, by its nature, "speaks for itself"; nontestimonial evidence. Contrasted with oral evidence.
Physical Fact. Irrefutable law of nature or science.
Physiognomy. Medical term: Judging criminological character by facial features.
Physique (fee *zeek*). Build or structure of the body.
P.I. 1. A pimp. 2. One who loafs at street corners or dance halls.
Pica. A type size (typewriter or printing), 12 point. This is the larger of the two types of type commonly

used on typewriters. The other is called elite.

Piccolo Player. Slang: 1. Male homosexual who takes the active role in oral sex relations. 2. A female (many times a prostitute) who favors fellatio.

Pick. Gambling term: A choice of bets.

Picket (*pick* it). Worker who stations himself in such position as to discourage other employees from working or customers from doing business with certain establishments.

Pickpocket. A thief who steals money or things from a person's pockets.

Pickup. 1. The act of or request for arresting someone. 2. Slang: An arrest by police. 3. Juvenile slant: Listen carefully.

Pickup Man. Gambling term: One who picks up the work from a numbers writer and deposits it at a drop designated by the controller. Bankers may also use pickup men.

Piece. 1. Narcotics slang: One ounce of heroin or cocaine. 2. Gambling term: A share or portion of the action. 3. Underworld slang: Gun.

Pie Wagon. Slang: Paddy wagon; black Maria; vehicle used by police to haul arrested persons to jail.

Pig. 1. Slang: A derogatory name for law enforcement officers used in recent years by members of some extremist groups. 2. Juvenile slang: A woman. 3. A drug user who takes all of a drug he can get his hands on.

Pigeon. An informant; a stool pigeon; an easy victim for a con game.

Pigeon Dropping. An old and commonly used confidence game where two con men work together to defraud a victim of money or property. One form is where one operator drops a pocketbook, which is picked up by the second, who is in company with the victim. It contains some money, usually counterfeit. Arrangements are made to split the money later, and the victim is to hold it until then. The victim gives the operator some money or property for security and never sees him again. There are many variations of the game.

Pigiron Joint. Slang: Hardware Store.

Pig-Sticker. Slang: A long-bladed knife.

Pike. Slang: 1. Street, 2. To look.

Pill. 1. Slang: A person who is disagreeable or obnoxious. 2. The birth control pill; oral contraceptive. 3. Certain forms of narcotics or dangerous drugs.

Pillhead. Slang: Heavy user of pills—barbiturates, or amphetamines, or both.

Pill Pad. Slang: Gathering place for drug addicts.

Pimp. 1. A panderer or procurer for prostitutes. 2. Slang: One who informs on another; an informer. 3. Slang: Male sex deviate who acts as a prostitute to homosexuals.

Pin. Slang: To seize or steal.

Pinball. The game of playing a pinball machine.

Pinball Machine. A device in which a ball (or balls) is activated by a driving mechanism, after which it rolls down an incline having obstructions (pins) and comes to a rest in numbered holes. It can be used as a gambling device if payoffs are made for certain scores. The operator deposits coins in the machine in order to play.

Pinch. Slang: To apprehend or take into custody.

Pink. Slang: One who is associated

VOCABULARY

with or inclined toward communism.

Pinkerton Detective Agency. A nationwide private investigative agency, founded by Allan Pinkerton in 1850. It established the reputation of conducting efficient investigations and of having honest investigators. It is still in operation.

Pinks. Slang: Depressant drugs—barbiturates.

Pin-Shot. Narcotic slang: Drug injection made with an instrument (safety pin or eye dropper) other than a hypodermic.

Piquers (*pee* kwers). Sex deviation term: Persons who use sharp instruments by which they stab their victims, usually female.

Pistol. A handgun; a firearm characterized by being short enough to be fired while held in one hand.

Pitcher and Catcher. Racetrack gambler term: A procedure whereby one inside the track signals to an associate outside the track, who in turn relays the information on the outcome of the races to gamblers who are interested in getting the information quickly.

Pit Man. Gambling term: An employee of a gambling establishment who supervises a gaming table. He watches for cheating and corrects errors.

Place. Gambling term: 1. In a horse race, the racer who comes in second. 2. A right or wrong point bet in a dice game.

Plain Arch. A fingerprint pattern in which the ridges come in from one side and go out the other without recurve or turning back and in which there is a smooth upward thrust of the lines at or near the center of the pattern.

Plainclothesman. Law enforcement officer, usually a detective, who works while dressed in civilian clothes, rather than in uniform.

Plaintiff. The complaining party in any litigation, such as the state in a criminal case.

Plain Whorl. A fingerprint pattern. See **Whorl**.

Plane-Polarized Light. A light ray confined to a specific plane of vibration.

Plant. 1. A person placed in a situation where he can play a role in a scheme or plan. 2. Slang: To secretly hide evidence or stolen goods on the person or property of another. 3. Slang: A hospital. 4. Narcotics slang: Hiding place for drugs.

Plants. Physical arrangements made by arsonists to facilitate the burning of a structure. These may include use of flammable liquids, laying of "trailers" of combustible materials, opening of containers, blocking open of fire doors, and various devices to cause ignition by remote control or when the "fire bug" is not on the premises.

Plant Security. The protection of a business or industrial plant from fire, burglary, sabotage, theft, or liability.

Plasma, Blood. That part of the blood that is a liquid. The other part is composed of the blood cells. Blood plasma is used as a transfusion.

Plaster of Paris. A powdery substance used in police work for making casts of impressions in the earth and other soft surfaces. Such impressions are usually caused by shoe or tire imprints. Plaster of Paris is composed of gypsum and can be obtained from a druggist.

Plastic Prints. Fingerprint impressions made in a plastic material, such as melted candle wax, putty, tar, soap, etc.

Plastic Surgery. Surgery where changes or restoration of parts of the body is accomplished. Some notorious criminals allegedly have used plastic surgery in efforts to change their appearance.

Play. Gambling term: The amount of action.

Play Football. Gambling game. See **Razzle Dazzle.**

Play the Dozens. Juvenile slang: Speak ill of someone's parents. Also, to swear at one another.

Play the Numbers. Slang: To bet on policy numbers, which are usually pari-mutuel racetrack figures.

Play the Stuff. Juvenile slang: Do as one pleases; participate.

Plea. The response by an accused to an official criminal charge presented against him in court, usually at the time of arraignment. The plea is usually "not guilty" or "guilty." Some courts will accept a plea of "nolo contendere."

Plea Bargaining. Agreements worked out between the prosecutor and the accused (with the defense attorney) whereby the accused will be allowed to plead guilty to a less serious crime rather than to go on trial for the crime with which he is charged. Arrangements may also be worked out whereby the defendant will plead guilty to the crime with which charged on condition that the prosecutor will recommend to the court that the accused get a reduced sentence. No threats or coercion should be used by the prosecutor. Plea bargaining was allowed by the United States Supreme Court in Brady v. U.S., 397 U.S. 742, and by the California Supreme Court in People v. West (1970).

Plead (pleed). Past tense: Pleaded or plead. Law: To respond to a charge in a criminal court.

Pleading. Claims of the plaintiff set forth to the court; answer of the defendant.

Pleasure Smoker. A person who smokes an opium pipe only occasionally.

Pledge, Legal. Law: A debtor puts up or turns over to a creditor certain property to be held until the debt is satisfied, with title to the property remaining with the debtor. The creditor must have a lien on the property.

Plenary (*ple* na ree). Complete; all requisites fulfilled; fully attended.

Plot. 1. A secret scheme or plan. 2. To draw, map, or diagram.

Plow. Slang: To rape; to have pederastic relations.

Pluralism. A group retaining its own cultural heritage while coexisting in peace and harmony with the dominant group and with other groups.

Plurality. The greatest number.

P.M. Medical term: Postmortem.

Pneumatic Tire. Any tire that is filled with compressed air for the purpose of supporting a heavy load.

Point. Hypodermic needle. Also, 1 percent of an enterprise or a contract.

Point Blank. Direct; directly at; straight at a point or spot.

Points. Gambling term: On handicapped bets, the player gives or takes points.

Points of Identification. In fingerprints, identical or matching ridge formations on more than one set or copy of fingerprints, as when comparing a latent print with known prints of a person. Eight to twelve matching points were made by the

same person; some courts require a minimum of twelve points.
Point Spread. Gambling term: The number of points given or taken by a bookie or betting establishment.
Point System. The method used by authorities for the adding or subtracting of points in the process of evaluating one's driving record, usually because of a violation.
Poison. Something (drug, chemical) that is injurious to the body or to life.
Poison Pen Letter. Slang: A written communication, usually anonymous, containing damaging information concerning someone. Many times the statements are not true.
Poke. A puff on a "joint."
Poker. A card gambling game.
Poker Flat. Gambling term: An apartment used for gambling card games.
Polar Method. Also called radial method. A method of sketching an area where it is necessary to record the outline of a broken or irregular line of objects, such as a forest.
Polecat. Prison slang: An inmate guard as referred to by other inmates.
Pole Trailer. The device used to transport things such as logs, pipes, etc. Consists of a flat bed supported by axles and wheels with supporting beams on the sides, yet it is not motor driven. Usually attached to a large moving vehicle for transportation.
Police. A law enforcement officer; usually of a city or state.
Police Advisory Board. A citizen's group organized to react to general police policy matters; sometimes organized on neighborhood basis.
Police Agent. Patrolmen who are specially trained in crime scene investigation and evidence collection.

Police Auxiliaries. Volunteer or paid citizen's groups who help with traffic, parades, PCR programs, etc.
Police Benevolent Associations. Police personnel organizations by rank, speciality, ethnic, or racial nature. Often serve as bargaining units.
Police Brutality. Physical, verbal, or attitudinal discriminatory treatment.
Police-Community Relations Officer. A law enforcement officer working in the field of police-community relations.
Police Court. In some states, an inferior court with jurisdiction over minor offenses and misdemeanors and the power to hold for trial those charged with felonies.
Police Decentralization. Theory that control of police should be on a neighborhood basis. See **Metroplexity**.
Police Force, National. One police agency for the entire nation, administered and directed by one person or one organizational structure. This is doubtless more efficient than a multiplicity of individual law enforcement agencies but is dangerous from the political standpoint.
Police Laboratory. A crime laboratory operated for the benefit of law enforcement. See **Laboratory, Crime**.
Police Ministerial Duties. Routinized; not requiring more than technical skills (as in much of traffic enforcement).
Police Officer. A member of the department that keeps public order and safety, enforces the laws, and detects and prosecutes lawbreakers.
Police Power. 1. The broad power of the state to act for the welfare of the people. This empowers the state

to restrict the actions of individuals if such acts are a detriment to the general public. 2. Authority delegated to the police by the people.

Police Professionalism. Elevating police philosophy, purposes, and procedures to the level of medicine, law, etc., through training, education, research, and association discipline.

Police Review Boards. Internal or external (civilian) bodies to exert discipline and/or process complaints.

Police State. A nation under control of a central police system.

Police Training. Training of and for law enforcement personnel.

Policy Bank. Gambling term: The headquarters office of a group conducting a policy-numbers lottery.

Policy Game. Gambling term: The numbers gambling game, where winners are determined by lottery.

Policy Shops. Slang: An illegal lottery in the 1800s where players selected their own numbers, betting as little as a penny.

Polish Off. Slang: To kill or eliminate a person.

Political Crime. A crime committed for some political purpose, such as assassination or kidnapping of a public official.

Politician (pol e *tish* en). One who is involved with politics; a person who runs for public office or who is engaged in politics.

Politics. 1. The discipline of government or of the operation of government. 2. The actions of those who seek power through public office.

Poll. The process by which more than one person is encouraged to communicate to a given situation.

Polling Jury. A practice whereby the jurors are asked individually whether they assented, and still assent, to the verdict.

Poll the Jury. A procedure in court whereby each juror is asked to state what his verdict was and is required to make it known.

Polly. Short for politician.

Polygamy (pe *lig* e me). Situation of having multiple wives simultaneously.

Polygraph (*pol* ly graf). Most modern polygraphs have three capacities for recording anatomical responses: the pneumograph—for recording respiration; the galvanograph—for recording skin electrical resistance changes; the cardiograph— for recording changes in blood pressure and pulse rate.

Polyneuritic Insanity. Medical term: An insanity arising from an inflammation of the nerves.

Pompous (*pom* pus). Acting the "big shot"; self-important.

Pool Selling. Gambling term: Selling tickets on the outcome of an event on which bets are made, such as a football game or horse race.

Poop. Slang: Information.

Poopbutt. Slang: A square; one who is not a member of a gang.

Pop. Slang: Inject drugs.

Pop Joint. Criminal underworld slang: A hop joint; an opium den.

Popper. Amyl nitrate in ampule form, inhaled.

Poppy. A flowering plant. Opium is obtained from one type of poppy, usually referred to as the opium poppy.

Popular Front. The combination of or grouping together of leftist groups, such as Communist, Socialist, and other similar political parties.

VOCABULARY

Population (pop u *lay* shen). The general body of prison inmates.
Population Mobility. A real movement of people: geographical, rural-urban, etc.
Pornography. Written or pictorial material that is obscene. See **Obscene Material.**
Pornography, Hard-Core. Pornographic material that is more obscene than picturing or describing nude persons.
Poroscopy (poe *ros* ko pea). The study of the arrangement and individual characteristics of sweat pores as seen in fingerprint impressions as a means of fingerprint identification. These sweat pore characteristics are especially important when there is only a fragment of the fingerprint impression available.
Port. A side of a ship. Facing the front or bow, it is the left side once aboard.
Portrait Parle (*pour* trayt par *lay*). French: A speaking likeness. A means of recording the descriptions of persons used in France.
Positive (*pos* i tiv). In the field of moulage, the reproduction of the original object.
Positive Law. Law enacted for government by the proper authority.
Posse (*poss* ee). A group of citizens called into service by a law enforcement official (sheriff) to aid in the apprehension of a criminal offender or in keeping the peace.
Posse Comitatus (*poss* ee kom e *tah* tus). The power or force of a county. The entire population of the county, above the age of fifteen, which a sheriff may summon to his assistance in certain cases; as to aid him in keeping the peace, arresting felons, etc.
Posse Comitatus Act of 1978. Prohibits the use of army personnel for the purpose of assisting civil authorities in the execution of civil (non-military) law enforcement.
Possession. Having possession of certain articles prohibited by law constitutes the criminal offense of possession. Possession of narcotics by persons not legally entitled to have them is such a case.
Possible. In firearms target shooting, the making of a perfect score. All the shots are placed in the part of the target having the highest value.
Possum Cop. Slang: A Wildlife and Fisheries agent, i.e. an officer of the wild game organization of the government.
Post. 1. A position (employment). 2. A place of assignment for an officer. 3. To record or make a record of. 4. Afterward in time; following. 5. Postmortem. 6. Abbreviation for Commission on Peace Officers Standards and Training, such as in California.
Postconviction Remedies. The various means a convicted person has of seeking redress for his incarceration or conviction.
Posterior. The rear end or hind end.
Posthumous (pos *chue* mus). Occurrence after death; a birth after the death of the male parent.
Postmortem (post *mor* tim). 1. Subsequent to death. 2. An autopsy. 3. Slang: Post.
Postmortem Lividity. See **Lividity, Postmortem.**
Post Time. Racing and gambling term: The time the race is scheduled to start.
Pot. 1. Slang: Marijuana. 2. Gambling term: the total amount bet in a single round of a betting game.
Potassium Chloride. A deadly poisonous chemical (KCN), white pow-

der. Referred to at times as cyanide.
Pothead. Narcotics slang: Heavy marijuana user.
Pot Likker. Cannabais tea, usually made with regular tea boiled with cannabis leaves.
Pot Party. Slang: A marijuana party, where participants smoke marijuana.
Pound the Bricks. Slang: To walk the streets; for a policeman to walk his beat.
Poverty Programs. Programs operated or sponsored by government or private agencies to aid the economically deprived people.
Powder. Gunpowder. The propellant charge for ordinary firearms ammunition. The three types are smokeless, semismokeless, and black powder.
Powder, Black. A propellant for firearms ammunition, composed of charcoal, sulphur, and nitrate of potassium. Was used in years past in firearms ammunition of that period. Has been largely replaced by smokeless powder.
Powder, Residue Analysis of. The chemical analysis of the residue of powder particles found on the object fired into or in the gun barrel of the suspected weapon.
Powder, Smokeless. A modern gunpowder consisting primarily of nitrocellulose or a combination of nitroglycerin and nitrocellulose.
Powder, Take a. Slang: To run away; to escape and hide.
Powder, Tatooing by. A pattern around a wound caused by gunpowder particles striking the surface of the object fired into.
Powder Charge. Firearms term: The weight of powder used in ammunition.

Powdered. Juvenile slang: Searched by police; frisked.
Powder Pattern. The pattern of powder residue deposited on an object when fired into by a firearm. At contact range there is little or no powder deposited, and what there is is in a small circle. As the distance between the gun muzzle and the object increases, the size of the powder pattern increases until a distance is reached where the discharge of powder particles does not reach the object. See **Powder Pattern Test**.
Powder Pattern Test. A crime laboratory test of garments to determine the pattern of powder residue and thus determine the distance between the muzzle of the weapon and the person shot. It is a useful test in homicide cases, especially where suicide is falsely claimed. Among others, the FBI Laboratory is equipped to conduct this test.
Power of Attorney. The giving of legal authority for one person to act for another. It must be in writing.
Practicum (*prak* ti kum). That part of a course of study involving practical field experience.
Pratt. Slang: One who bumps into the victim while a pickpocket makes the touch.
Prayer. A request or petition to a court for certain desired relief.
Precedent (*press* a dent). Law: A judicial decision used as a guide or example for later decisions.
Precept (*pree* sept). To teach; a rule of conduct.
Precinct (*pree* sinkt). An area or district, so defined that its jurisdiction or boundaries are known, for government or administrative purposes; for example, police precinct, voting precinct, school precinct.

VOCABULARY

Precipitan Reaction Test (pree *sip* i tan). A crime laboratory test to determine if blood is of human origin.

Preempt (pree *empt*). Law: Move into a field or area and take possession or jurisdiction with priority ahead of others. "The federal government preempted the field of national security, and the states cannot legislate on it."

Pregnancy, Plea of. A plea made by a pregnant woman convicted of a capital offense, the result of which causes the woman to be given a stay of execution until the child is born.

Pregnant. The condition of a female who has conceived; carrying an unborn child or fetus.

Prejudice (*prej* ewe dis). An opinion or judgement (prejudge) formed concerning something or someone, prior to having or considering all the available facts; usually refers to an unfavorable opinion. A frame of mind based on emotions rather than rationality. It is something we learn from those around us or from some experience and is not an inherited trait.

Prejudicial Evidence (prej you *dish* el). See **Evidence, Prejudicial**.

Preliminary Examination. See **Preliminary Hearing**.

Preliminary Hearing (pree *lim* in air ee). A hearing held before a magistrate for a person arrested for a felony, at which time the prosecution must show probable cause that the accused committed the crime for which he was arrested. If such showing is made by the prosecution, the accused is ordered held (or released on bond, if it is a bondable offense). If the prosecution does not show sufficient evidence to constitute probable cause, the accused is released from custody. This is also known as **Preliminary Examination**.

Premeditation (pree med i *tay* shun). Prior planning of an act, which shows intent to do the action.

Prenatal (pree *nay* tel). Before birth; prior to birth.

Preponderance (pree *pon* dur ens). Surpassing in amount, weight, power, influence, importance; predominance.

Preponderance of Evidence. That evidence that is most convincing or most important.

Prerogative. 1. A special privilege. 2. Special official power.

Prescribe (pree *skribe*). To become invalid because of lapse of time. Sometimes called "statute of limitations." If prosecution is not started within a certain time (as set forth by law), the right to prosecute is lost. Usually in capital offenses prescription does not apply or it is a long period of time.

Prescribed Role. A role as it is expected to be played. **Prescription** (pre *skrip* shen). 1. Civil law: Acquiring some advantage or title to property by the possession for specified periods of time. 2. Time limitations, provided by law (statute), within which prosecutions must be commenced after the commission of a crime and within which the trial must be started in criminal matters. See **Statute of Limitations**.

Presentence Investigation. An investigation of an accused, who generally has pleaded guilty or has been convicted of crime. It is ordered by the judge or court and is usually done by the probation and/or parole officers. The purpose is to aid the judge in fixing sentence of the accused.

Presentment (pree *zent* ment). A written accusation prepared or presented by a grand jury, based on its own investigations and findings, without having a bill of indictment laid before it.

Preservative (pre *zer* vah tiv). Something, usually a chemical, added to a substance to prevent it from spoiling or deteriorating.

Preservice Training. The training of law enforcement officers before they enter into the criminal justice system.

Presiding Judge. Chairman of a court; judge having control or authority.

Presumption, Conclusive (pree *zump* shun). A conclusive presumption, created by law, is one against which no evidence is permitted, such as that which attaches to *res adjudicata* and recitals contained in acts of the legislature. See **Presumption, Legal**.

Presumption, Legal. The law that provides that the judiciary shall assume certain facts exist from a set of circumstances. These assumptions or inferred facts persist until disproven. See **Presumption, Rebuttable**.

Presumption, Rebuttable. A legal presumption that relieves one in whose favor it exists from the necessity of offering proof; however, it can be disproven or rebutted. Such is the presumption of innocence of an accused.

Presumption of Fact. An inference of a fact based on other facts and circumstances. It can be rebutted (disproven). "A presumption of fact exists that a person stole property found in his possession when same had been recently stolen."

Pretermit (pree tur *mit*). To pass by, disregard, or take no action concerning. In relation to a grand jury, it means that the jury passes a matter before it without finding a "true bill" or a "no true bill." This is brought about by lack of agreement among the grand jurors or by the intentional act of the grand jury. The next grand jury may consider the case.

Pretrial Detention. The procedure of not releasing on bond or bail, between arrest and trial, certain dangerous persons. This procedure has been considered by legislative bodies. Congress considered such in H.R. 12806 in 1969. See **Preventive Detention**.

Pretrial Publicity. Publicity about an accused, a criminal case, or the details of an investigation prior to the trial of persons accused of the crime. This may prevent the accused from obtaining a fair trial and thus creates a real problem.

Pretrial Screens. Stages in the criminal justice process that are designed to exert quality control over police arrests and prosecutor's charging decisions in order to reduce the chances of unwarranted and also unnecessary trials.

Prevaricate (pree *vear* e kate) (vear as in bear). To depart from the truth; not follow the truth; to lie.

Preventive Detention. Laws that allow the magistrate or judge to hold an accused in jail and not release him on bail where evidence is produced that if released he probably would commit other crimes while awaiting trial for the first offense.

Price Line. Gambling term: Odds by which a bookie will bet either way on certain events at specified odds; for example, 4 to 3 on A to win over B or even money on B to win over A.

Prima Facie (*prime* ah *fay* she). Latin: At first sight; on the first appearance; on the face of it; so far as can be judged from first disclosure; presumably; a fact presumed to be true unless disproved by some evidence to the contrary.

Prima Facie Case. A case that "at first glance" seems to be well established, but which can still be rebutted by the adversary in the case.

Primary Classification. A term used in classifying fingerprints. A numerical value is given to each of the ten fingers. This is written in the classification formula after the Major Division as 1/1 or whatever the count requires.

Primary Evidence. Key evidence; most essential evidence.

Primary Groups. Gemeinschaft (intimate) relations (family, peers).

Primer (*prime* ur). 1. A device, usually a cap, used to fire a charge of explosives. 2. Firearms term: The device used to ignite the powder propellant.

Principal (*prin* si pul). Law: A person held accountable for a crime. The person who actually commits the crime is a principal. In some states persons who aid or assist in the commission of the crime are considered principals even though they did not actively participate in the commission of it.

Principal Registration. A system of classifying and identifying fingerprints based on all ten fingers of the hands. It is necessary to have fingerprints of all ten fingers of the hands in order to classify one's prints. It is also necessary to have the same kind of fingerprints (all ten fingers) in order to search for and locate a duplicate set of fingerprints on file in this type of registration. Provisions are made for amputations in the classifying system. See **Single-Fingerprint Registration**.

Principle. A rule or law; an established truth.

Print. Short for fingerprint.

Prison (*priz* en). A penitentiary, where convicted persons are detained, usually to serve sentences imposed by the courts.

Prisonation. A process by which the prison inmate comes to strongly identify with and gain status within the inmate structure.

Prison Bounds. The limits of the territory surrounding a prison, within which an imprisoned debtor, out on bond, may go at will.

Prisoner. One who is deprived of liberty or freedom of action.

Prisoner at the Bar. An accused person, while on trial before the court, is so called. One accused of a crime who is actually on trial is in legal effect a "prisoner at the bar," not withstanding that he has given bond for his appearance at the trial. He is a " prisoner" if held in custody either under bond or other process of law, or when physically held under arrest, and when actually on trial he is a "prisoner at the bar." The term is as applicable to one on trial for a misdemeanor as to one on trial for a felony.

Prisoner Control. The process by which prisoners of an agency are booked, arrested, convicted, and transported. All agencies have some sort of prisoner control, whether it be simple or complex.

Prisoner's Rights. The legal rights of a prisoner.

Prison Reform. The whole concept of bettering prisons to meet the needs of the prisoners and still meet the needs of the community.

Privacy, Right of. The right to be left alone; to not be interfered with as to conversations or the possession of and use of property.

Private Eye. Slang: Private detective; a detective who is not regularly employed by a law enforcement agency.

Private Game. A game between private individuals, not in a casino or other gambling house and without a house fee.

Private Law. 1. That law which is administered between private citizens. 2. A law that only affects certain individuals or groups.

Private Police. Licensed property or personal protection service.

Private Road or Driveway. Any area or strip of land used for a thoroughfare that is privately owned and is restricted to outsiders except by special permission.

Private School. Not supported by public funds. Parochial (church supported) or preparatory (supported by tuition and/or endowment). Term currently being used also for those schools created to avoid integration.

Privilege (*priv* e lij). Law: A right or advantage granted by law.

Privileged Communication. Law: A right or advantage granted by law to certain types of communications, whereby the person to whom information is made known is not in the position to divulge it without the specific authority of the person making the statements. Such privileges exist in private conversations between husband and wife, attorney and client, priest and pentinent, and doctor and patient.

Privileges and Immunities. Law stating that a person from out-of-state may not be mistreated in another state.

Pro. Slang: A professional.

Probable Cause. Facts, not mere suspicions, that will warrant the belief that a person is guilty or that certain facts exist. In obtaining an arrest warrant the magistrate must be presented with enough facts to warrant him having probable cause to believe that the person to be arrested committed the crime. The same amount of information must be present for the officer to arrest without a warrant. In obtaining a search warrant, the facts in the affidavit must cause the magistrate to believe that the place to be searched contains evidence of the crime. The courts put emphasis on this in the areas of arrest and searches.

Probate (*pro* bait). The proof of a will according to law.

Probate Court. A court that has jurisdiction to handle matters pertaining to wills: estate settlements, appointment of guardians, etc.

Probation (pro *bay* shun). Letting a person go free, by the court, to test him. After a first offender has pleaded guilty or has been convicted, the judge may suspend his sentence and place him on probation for a certain period and set up rules or conditions by which the probationer must abide. If he violates the rules or commits another crime, the judge may revoke his probation and cause him to serve the original sentence. Ideally the probationer is under the supervision of a probation officer while he is free.

Probationer. One who is on trial; one who is allowed to remain out of prison as long as he maintains his good behavior.

Probation Officer. A person, appointed by the court or some other official agency, who supervises persons placed on probation by the courts.

Probation Subsidy. A correctional program that compensates probation agencies for supervising the probationee.

Probative Value (*pro* be tiv). Having value as proof; value of absolute proof.

Probe (prob). An intensive and thorough investigation into a situation of crime or misconduct.

Pro Bono Publico. Latin: For the good of the commonwealth.

Procedural Law. That part of the law which pertains to how to enforce rights in a court or how to take legal action, rather than the substance of the rights themselves.

Procedure. The established way of carrying on the business of a legislature, law court, etc.

Procedure, Criminal. The law pertaining to procedure in the field of criminal law.

Proceeding. Action in conducting judicial business in a court or before a judicial officer.

Process. Any order or writ issued by the judiciary at the beginning or during a court action. Subpoenas, citations, and summonses are examples.

Proclivity (pro *kliv* e ti). A strong inclination toward something.

Procurer (pro kur er). A pimp; one who obtains women to satisfy the sexual desires of men.

Profanity (pro *fan* e ti). Cursing or swearing; profane language.

Professional Criminal. A person who makes a living through criminal activity.

Proffer (*prof* fur). To offer or present for acceptance.

Profile. A side view photograph or sketch of a person.

Prognosis (prog *no* sis). A prediction of how things will develop.

Prohibition Act. The Eighteenth Amendment to the United States Constitution prohibited the manufacture, sale, or transportation of alcoholic beverages. This became effective in 1920 and was repealed in 1933. Based upon the adoption of the Eighteenth Amendment, Congress passed the Volstead Act, which made the violation of the provisions of the Eighteenth Amendment a criminal offense. This is known as the "Prohibition Act."

Prohibition Agents, United States Treasury Department. Federal officers who investigated violations of the Volstead Act while it was effective from 1920 to 1933. The Alcohol and Tobacco Tax Division of the Internal Revenue Service, a branch of the United States Treasury Department, still has jurisdiction over violations of alcohol, particularly as to the enforcement of tax provisions concerning it.

Pro Hoc Vice. Latin: For this occasion.

Projectile (pro *jek* tel). Something that can be shot or thrown; usually refers to such things as bullets.

Projection. Expecting others to act or feel as we do.

Project Search. System for Electronical Analysis and Retrieval of Criminal Histories. LEAA awarded an initial grant of $600,000 to finance the project, and grantee states matched with more than $400,000. Grantee states include Arizona, California, Maryland, Michigan, Minnesota, and New York, with participating observer states. The project ran from July 1, 1969, to August 31, 1970, as a pilot project. There were two principle objectives: (1) computerized data from all segments of criminal justice on a standardized basis, furnishing same to participants, and (2) develop statistical records and meaningful research data from the files.

Proletariat (pro lee *tare* it). Working class of people. The Communist theorists use this term in their philosophies, saying that the government is ruled by the proletariat. In practice, the Communist governments are ruled by strong men or a man (dictator).

Promise. A statement that legally binds one person to do something or give something to another person.

Promotion (pro *mow* shen). 1. An advance in rank or position. 2. The act of furthering a project or undertaking.

Promulgate (*pro* mul gate). To formally announce or make known something; to officially make known such things as laws.

Proof. Method of establighing the truth of an allegation; establishment of the facts; evidence when used to establish a fact.

Proof, Burden of. See **Burden of Proof**.

Propaganda (*prop* a *gan* de). An attempt to convince a person to unquestioningly accept a particular belief or to make a certain choice.

Propensity (pro *pen* si tee). A tendency toward; a natural inclination; a leaning in the direction of. Pertaining to crimes committed by the accused, other than that for which he is being tried is not admissible for the purpose of showing mere propensity; such evidence is admissible if related to or is part of a plan or scheme involving the crime for which the accused is being tried.

Proponent. One to propose; one to put forth for consideration.

Proposition Bet. 1. A side bet in a betting game. 2. A bet made between two persons over a difference of opinion.

Proposition Cheat. A gambler who induces wagers with people in which they have no chance to win.

Proposition Hustler. A person who makes a seemingly fair bet that is actually very favored to his advantage.

Proprietary Name (pro *prye* e ter i). Trade name of a product.

Propriety (pro *pry* it ee). Principle that holds that law enforcement must conduct itself in the proper fashion in obtaining confessions, guilty pleas, and so on that are trustworthy and accurate, and in providing humane treatment to all suspects or defendants.

Pro Rata (pro *ray* ta). Latin: In proportion.

Prosecute (*pros* e cute). To bring a matter or person into a court of law with a view of obtaining justice according to the law.

Prosecuting Attorney. The name of the public officer (in several states) who is appointed or elected in each judicial district or other subdivision of the state to prosecute accused criminal offenders on behalf of the government.

Prostitute. A female who indiscriminately has sexual intercourse with males for compensation. Prostitution is unlawful in most states.

Protection. Slang: Something paid or given to a policeman or politician in insure that illegal activities on the part of the payer will not be stopped or interfered with.

Protective Custody. Holding without criminal charge.

VOCABULARY

Proteins (*pro* teens). Long chains of amino acids that play important roles in structure and function of living systems.
Proton (*pro* ton). One of the particles in the nucleus of an atom.
Provocation (prah ve *ka* shun). Something that provokes, causes one to become agitated or disturbed.
Prowl. Slang: To investigate the scene of a planned crime or the scene of a potential crime.
Prowl Car. A car used by the police to patrol, usually equipped with two-way radio whereby communication is maintained with headquarters.
Prowler. Slang: A thief who comes in at night so as not to be seen; any sneak thief.
Proximate (*prok* se mit). Close; nearby; side by side.
Proximate Cause. The obvious or nearest cause attributed to injury.
Proxy (*prox* ee). Person appointed to represent another.
Prudent (*pruu* dent). Wise; considering all aspects; level-headed; not erratic in thinking.
Prudery (*prud* e re). Sex deviation-term: Aversion to sex; an abnormal modesty pertaining to sex.
Prurient (*prur* ee ent). Having lustful desires or cravings. This word is used in the legal definition of obscene or pornographic material
Prussian. Hobo term: An active pederast.
Pry Bar. A metal bar used by burglars to pry open doors, windows, or other enclosures.
Pseudocyesis. Medical term: A type of hysteria in women in which the abdomen is inflated, simulating pregnancy.
Pseudolalia Fantastica. Medical term: Self-accusation of a crime that the individual did not commit.
P.S.I. Pounds per square inch.
Psilocybin. Derived from the *Psilocybe* mushroom. A hallucinogenic narcotic.
Psychedelic (si ke *del* ik). Pertaining to unusual or abnormal stimulation of perception or mental alertness. Psychedelic drugs—drugs that tend to produce these effects.
Psychiatrist (sigh *ki* e trist). A physician who specializes in psychiatry.
Psychiatry (sigh *ki* a tree). The field of study (medicine) pertaining to the diagnosis and treatment of mental disorders.
Psychoanalism (sigh ko *ann* al ism). Theory stating that behavior results from conflicts between the id (biological desires), the ego (perceived realities), and the superego (irrational desires).
Psychoanalysis (sigh ko a *nal* e sis). A study of the mind, with special emphasis on the subconscious.
Psychodiagnosis (sigh ko di ag *no* sis). In medical jurisprudence, a method of investigating the origin and cause of any given disease or morbid condition by examination of the mental condition of the patient, the application of various psychological tests, and an inquiry into the past history of the patient, with a view to its bearing on his present psychic state (*Black's Law Dictionary*).
Psychological Criminal. A person who commits crimes because of some psychological imbalance in his personality.
Psychological Dependence. A mental dependency on a drug due to underlying emotional needs.
Psychological Fact. Evidence: A

fact that can only be perceived mentally.

Psychology (sigh *kol* e gee). The science of the mind of humans in all of its aspects.

Psychoneurosis (sigh ko new *roe* sis). Mental disease without recognizable anatomical lesion and without evidence and history of preceding chronic mental degeneration. Under this head come melancholia, mania, primary acute dementia, and mania hallucinitoria. (*Black's Law Dictionary*).

Psychopath (*sigh* ko path). Antisocial personality; one who has no feeling of guilt for misdeeds and no love for others; one who is irresponsible for acts; a person with character disorders bordering on insanity.

Psychopathic (sigh ko *path* ik). Relative to mental disorders, diseases. Bordering on insanity; pertaining to a character disorder.

Psychosis (sigh *ko* sis). Refers to a group of more than one mental disorder, drastic in nature, which interferes with organization of the personality and social relationships. It prevents adequate self-control and manifests itself in behavior that is not appropriate or reasonable. It may or may not be connected with organic diseases.

Psychosomatic (sigh ko so *mat* ik). Pertaining to mind and body and their interreactions, in reference to diseases.

Psychotherapy (sigh ko *ther* a pee). Treatment of mental disorders by means of psychological principles and methods.

Psychotic (sigh *kot* ik). A mentally ill person; one out of touch with reality; one who may be hallucinating (seeing things that really are not there) and/or delusional (has ideas that are not really true). The psychotic is overwhelmed with fear (unrealistic fear but frightening).

Puberty. The first stages of physical maturity of male or female, at which time they are capable of reproducing. This stage is approximately age fourteen in boys and twelve in girls.

Public(s). All of the people, or specific interest groups with possibly different reactions to a common stimulus, as to a policy statement.

Public Defender. An attorney attached to a court jurisdiction, whose job involves the defense of indigents.

Public Defender System. A system whereby defense attorneys are provided at public expense to defend accused who are not in position to obtain or employ legal defense attorneys.

Public Domain. Free from patent; public grounds.

Public Interest. Something in which the public has interest in that it may affect their liabilities or legal rights.

Publicity. Release of information to the news media relative to investigations, individuals, the department, or other things pertaining to law enforcement; information intended to further the cause of one's self, one's department, or law enforcement generally. Care must be exercised in releasing publicity, or allowing it to be obtained and printed, pertaining to persons accused or charged with crime, as it may prevent the accused from obtaining a fair and impartial trial.

Public Law. 1. Study of the branch of law concerning the relationship of government to constituents. 2. Common law.

Public Police. Federal, state, county (sheriff), city, or local law enforcement agencies.

Public Relations, Police. Doing a good job and selling one's self, one's department, and law enforcement and its meaning to the public.

Public Service Police. Public education, emergency service, crisis intervention, family crisis intervention, PCR programs, etc.

Puerperal Insanity. Medical term: A mental derangement common to women during or immediately after childbirth.

Pull. Slang: Status, situation or influence with people in authority so that special favors may be obtained; influence.

Pull a Bit. Prison slang: To serve a sentence in a place of incarceration.

Pull a Tough Bit. Slang: To serve a difficult time in prison due to such things as ill health, harsh treatment, or family difficulties.

Pull Books. Gambling term: A type of Bolita betting slip.

Pull In. Slang: To place under arrest.

Pulling Method. A screw-type device with a long handle used by safe burglars to pull the combination wheel and its attached spindle from the safe.

Pull Tec. Juvenile slang: To become technical.

Pull Through. A fake cut; the player seems to cut the deck but actually replaces the cards in their original order.

Pull Time. Prison slang: To serve time in a penitentiary.

Pulmonary (*pul* mo ner i). Involving the lungs. "T.B. is a pulmonary disease."

Pumpkin Ball. Slang: A slug or ball of lead or other metal used for firing in a shotgun or large-calibered rifle.

Punch Drunk. Slang: Confused; slow-witted. A condition of grogginess with slow speech and movements caused by repeated blows on the head, such as are received by some boxers (prize fighters).

Punching Tool. A tool used by safe burglars to batter away the safe lock and spindle so that the locking bars can be released and the safe opened.

Punch Job (Safe). A method of gaining entry to safes by safe burglars by means of a punch.

Punishment. Sanctions for unacceptable behavior.

Punishment, Cruel and Unusual. The Eighth Amendment to the United States Constitution says, "Excessive bail shall not be required, nor excessive fines imposed, nor cruel and unusual punishment inflicted." Such punishment has been defined by the courts as those things that are cruel and inhuman, especially if such forms of punishment have not been specifically provided for by law. However, this is no guarantee that they will not be held to come within this category. The court held that the use of convict guards in a penitentiary came within this classification.

Punitive Damages. The awarding of damages in a tort action to punish the one at fault. This may be in the form of monetary award or in some other form. Not all states allow such damages.

Punk. Slang: 1. Small-time criminal; one just beginning a criminal life. 2. Prison slang: One of low order; an oral sodomist or passive pederast. 3. A man with repressed homosexual tendencies.

Punk Out. Slang: Cowardly action.

Purchase, Make a. Slang: "To make a buy." To buy something the possession of which is illegal or which can be used as evidence against the seller.

Pure (The). Pure heroin, prior to adulteration. "This is the pure—you can cut it five or six times at least."

Purge. To cleanse; to rid individuals from a nation, organization, etc. Known to be undesirable. To remove a person from a will without nullifying or rewriting the rest of the will.

Purloin (purr *loin*). To steal.

Purple Hearts. Slang: Dexamyl®, a combination of Dexedrine® and Amytal®.

Purport. To claim as meaning; intending—sometimes falsely.

Purse Snatching. The illegal taking by force of a purse belonging to another. This crime is usually committed by the criminal snatching the purse of a woman, when she is not expecting such action, and running away with it. The purse is usually discarded after its contents have been removed.

Pursuant. To carry out; to follow up on.

Pursuit Driving. The technique of driving a vehicle by an officer in pursuit of one fleeing in another vehicle. This requires thought and training.

Purview. The body of a bill or act.

Push a Kite. Slang: 1. To smuggle an uncensored letter out of prison. 2. To pass a forged check.

Pusher. Slang: One who sells or distributes drugs or narcotics.

Pushover. Slang: An easy mark; a victim who can be easily taken; a woman who is lax in sexual moral standards.

Push Schmeck. Underworld slang: To steal drugs.

Push Shorts. Narcotics slang: Cheating; selling "short" amounts.

Putative. Accepted, assumed, or alleged; commonly known as.

Put Down, To. 1. Prison slang: To criticize or to express displeasure toward someone or to cease associating with someone. 2. Juvenile slang: To reveal actions or secrets of another; let alone. 3. To stop taking drugs.

Put on Airs. Slang: To act aloof, snobbish.

Putter-Down. Slang: Party who passes forged checks for the real forger.

Put the Arm on. Slang: Ask a favor.

Put the Pressure on. To force someone to do something by threatening violence.

Put the Snap on. Slang: Make an arrest.

Put-Up Job. Slang: Something especially arranged to reflect a desired result; a faked affair.

Pygmalianism. (pig *male* yun izm). Sex deviation term: Erotic reaction obtained from statues of women.

Pyro. Contraction of Pyromaniac.

Pyrolysis (pie *rol* i sis). Burning of organic matter.

Pyromania (pie row *mane* e uh). An unnatural desire to set fires. A mental disorder is involved; sexual reaction is involved in some cases.

Pyromaniac (pie row *mane* e ack). A pathological firesetter; one who sets fire due to a mental condition that causes him to have a compulsion to do so.

Q

"Q" Cards. Credit cards issued to a company; may be used by any employee of the recipient company without showing any other identification. These cards are in demand by credit card thieves.

Quack. Slang: 1. A doctor who works in a prison. 2. A fake doctor who does not have medical skills.

Quad. Slang: A prison.

Quantum Meruit. Latin: As much as he deserved.

Quarter. Quarter of an ounce of either heroin or Methedrine, usually 4 to 8 grams.

Quash. To annul or set aside.

Quasi (*kway* zi). Similar to; resembling but not the real thing; not genuine. A word frequently used in legal phraseology. "It was determined to be a quasi-contract."

Quasi-Caste System. A society in which cultural traditions make vertical mobility extremely difficult for certain people.

Quasi Contract. An obligation to do something imposed upon someone by law but bearing the force of a contract and subject to legal action as a contract; now imposed chiefly to prevent unfair gain at the expense of another.

Quasi-Judicial. Having certain powers similar to that of a court or judiciary; for example, as in an administrative agency having the function to decide certain cases.

Quasi-Legislative. Having certain limited legislative powers, such as an administrative agency having the function to be able to make certain rules.

Queen. Slang: A male (sex deviate) who plays the female role in an affair of homosexuals; a homosexual in a certain area who acts as the contact among homosexuals in that vicinity.

Queer. Slang: A sex pervert of either sex; a homosexual.

Queer Pusher. Slang: A person passing counterfeit money.

Query. Inquiry; a doubt; a question.

Question. To interrogate or interview. "I will question the suspect."

Questioned Specimens. Physical evidence specimens, the origin or ownership of which is unknown, as contrasted with known specimens, the origin of which is known. For example, a bullet found in the body of a deceased is a questioned specimen, whereas one fired from a gun by an officer or a laboratory technician is a known specimen. The FBI Laboratory and some others number the specimens and assign each a Q number, for questioned items, or a K number, for known items.

Quill. Slang: A matchbook cover for sniffing Methedrine, cocaine, or heroin.

Quinella. Racing term: Similar to the daily double except the player picks horses to win and place in the same race.

Quitclaim. A legal document showing that someone gives up a claim to ownership or right concerning property. "The heirs to the estate signed a quitclaim."

Quizzer. Slang: A public or private investigator.

R

Rabbit. 1. Juvenile slang: A baby. 2. A timid person. 3. A beginner gambler; A gambler who is easy to induce into foolish ways.
Rabbit Fever. Slang: The temptation to try to escape when placed on work detail outside the prison walls.
Rabble. A noisy, unruly crowd or group.
Rabble Rouser. One who works up emotional excitement with a group of people.
Rabid (*rab* id). Affected with rabies; overly zealous; violent.
Rabies (*ray* bees). Also called hydrophobia. A virus-caused disease that affects the brain and central nervous system and is usually fatal. It is common among dogs and is easily transmitted to humans by dog bite or physical contact with an infected animal, when the virus may enter through a break in the skin of the person. If one is bitten or otherwise exposed, he should have the animal impounded for observation and consult a physician immediately.
Racehorse Charlie. Narcotics slang: Old morphine user.
Racism (*ray* siz em). The opinion that people have different capabilities, intellect, etc., due to racial differences; the opinion that some races are superior to others; predjudice as to race.
Racist (*ray* cist). One who has racial predjudices; one who believes that one or more races are superior to others.
Racket (*rack* it). A crooked scheme; planned dishonest operation.

Racketeer (rack it *teer*). One who obtains money or goods by threats, violence, extortion, or injury to people or property.
Rack Up. Slang: To wreck.
Radar (*ray* dar). An instrument that measures the distance of objects by the projection of radio waves and the measuring of their reflection or return. It is extensively used by law enforcement in determining the speed of motor vehicles.
Radial Cracks in Glass. The cracks in broken glass running in spokelike fashion from the point of force that broke the glass.
Radial Loop. A fingerprint pattern. See **Loop**.
Radial Method. A sketching method. See **Polar Method**.
Radiation (*ray* de *a* shen). Diffusion of rays or waves into space.
Radical (*rad* i kel). An extremist; one who takes a positive stand on issues that are unusual.
Radioactive (*ray* de o *ack* tive). Emitting waves by the nuclear disintegration of atoms. The rays are gamma, beta, or alpha. For more details, consult information put out by the Civil Defense Agency.
Radioactive Materials. Substances that are radioactive, i.e. due to nuclear disintegration, which occurs spontaneously when certain emissions of nucleons or electromagnetic radiations take place. This can be a dangerous situation, and officers must operate within certain safety guidelines. Consult Civil Defense officials.

Radioactivity (*ray* de o ack *tiv* i tee). Radiation of gamma rays by an unstable nucleus of an isotope.

Radiograph (*ray* de o *graf*). A photograph made with x-ray or radioactive material. For a discussion of radiography in examinations of paintings, see Soderman: *Modern Criminal Investigation*, 5th ed. New York, Funk and Wagnalls, 1962.

Radio Telephone. A communication system that transmits vocal messages over long distances using radio waves.

Radium (*ray* de um). A chemical element (substance), metallic, which emits gamma, beta, and alpha rays. It is used to treat disease, especially cancer.

Rag. Scarf or handkerchief, usually tied around the top of the head.

Raid. Police raid—action by officers who enter and search a place to detect law violations, arrest law violators, or obtain evidence of criminality.

Railroad. A permanent road with rails fixed to ties and laid on a roadbed providing a track for cars.

Railroad Police. The largest private police group in the United States, numbering about 8,000 in the United States and Canada. Its function is to protect the property, cargo, and goodwill of the railroads.

Railroad Sign or Signal. Any safety device set up by officials for the protection of the public at any railroad crossing.

Railroad Train. A connected line of railroad cars hauled by a locomotive.

Rainbows. Slang: Tuinal®, a barbituate combination in a blue and red capsule.

Rainmakers. Slang: Lobbyists who claim they have more influence than they actually have.

Raise. To create; to suggest.

Rake-Off. Slang: A commission, percentage, or portion of money, usually an illegal profit.

Rampage. To act violently; rush about recklessly.

Rampant. Unrestrained; out of control; exceeding all bounds.

Range. 1. Rifle range; firearms range. Place equipped to practice the shooting of firearms. 2. The distance a firearm can shoot effectively.

Range, Firearms. See **Firearms Range.**

Range Finder. A device that will determine the distance between a fixed point and a distant object. Many cameras have a built-in range finder, which is used in focusing the camera as to distance. Also called a distance meter.

Rank. 1. The title or position of a police officer. 2. A strong, disagreeable odor. 3. Juvenile slang: To insult.

Ransack. To completely search a place, such as a house; to search with abandon, leaving things in disarray.

Ransom. Payment, demanded or made, for the release of a person or persons (or property). Usually the payment consists of a specified amount of money. This is a normal incident involved in kidnapping.

Rap. Slang: 1. Talk, 2. An arrest, 3. To take the punishment, especially on behalf of someone else.

Rape. The unlawful intercourse of a human male with a female, by force or threats and against the will of the woman.

Rape, Forcible. The carnal knowledge of a female through the use or the threat of force.

Rape, Statutory. The carnal knowledge of a female who has not yet reached a certain age, not requiring

the use of force or lack of consent.
Rap, Take the. Slang: To plead guilty to a crime; take responsibility for a crime, especially when not guilty.
Rap Partner. Slang: An accomplice or helper in a crime.
Rapper. Slang: Complainant.
Rapport (re pour). Sympathetic understanding between persons; harmonious relationship between persons; attentive interest among persons.
Rap Sheet. Slang: A written identification record; record of arrests; a written criminal record.
Rat. Slang: Untrustworthy person; a person who squeals or informs to the police.
Ratfink. Informer for the police.
Ratification (rat e fi ka shun). Act of confirming or approving.
Rat on. Slang: To furnish information concerning someone; to act as an informant for the police.
Rat-Shackle. Chains or shackles for the legs usually used in southern prisons at night in the sleeping quarters.
Rattlebrain. Slang: Unstable personality; "lamebrain"; a thoughtless person.
Ravage. To devastate; to destroy; to do damage to; to ruin; to rape.
Ravish. To commit rape.
Rawhide. Slang: To aggravate; to condemn or upbraid a person.
Razz. Slang: To make fun of, tease, or belittle a person.
Razzle. Gambling term: Gambling game. See **Razzle Dazzle**.
Razzle Dazzle. Carnival or casino-type gambling game consisting of a yardage chart, roll board, eight marbles, and a roll cup (may be played with dice instead of balls). The victim player, to win, must score 100 yards or more in a given number of plays. Due to the great odds in favor of the operator, the player usually loses. Also known as razzle, bolero, double-up, ten points, auto races, Nevada bank, and play football.
Reactionary (re ak shen ar i). One who opposes or reacts against something, especially a political ideology or form of government. Communists call everyone "reactionary" if they are opposed to communism.
Reader. 1. Slang: Circular notifying police officers to arrest the party described thereon. 2. Narcotics slang: Doctor's prescription.
Readers. Gambling term: Playing cards marked on the back.
Reader with Tail. Narcotics slang: Forged prescription.
Real Evidence. Law: Physical evidence; evidence furnished by things, without the necessity of being described orally; things that speak for themselves.
Real Image. An image that can be projected onto a screen.
Real Time. The time EDP (electronic data processing) equipment operates when random needs are processed in the equipment, i.e. unscheduled activity is processed as it arises; for example, message switching, data collection, and inquiry processing. Real time is the opposite of "batch processing," where the data is stored and later programmed into the equipment.
Ream. Slang: To reprimand someone severely.
Rear-End Collision. A collision where one vehicle strikes the rear end of another vehicle. Generally the one who collides with the rear end of another vehicle is at fault.
Reasonable. Sensible; logical; what

VOCABULARY

one should expect a person to do. The courts have put much stress on the reasonableness of officers' actions in searches. If the search was reasonable, the courts have upheld it on close questions of law.

Reasonable Clause. A condition for arrest, holding that the arresting officer must have enough evidence to believe that a certain crime has been committed and that the person being arrested committed the crime.

Reasonable Force. See **Force, Reasonable.**

Rebellion. Opposition or resistance to legally constituted government in an organized manner.

Rebut (re *butt*). Law: 1. Disprove; produce evidence to overcome a presumption. 2. Produce evidence on the other side or present arguments on the other side.

Rebuttable Presumption. See **Presumption, Rebuttable.**

Rebuttal. A contradiction, refutation, or opposition, especially in a formal manner by argument, proof, etc.

Recalcitrant (re *kal* se trent). Opposed to authority or direction; disobedient; uncooperative.

Recall. A legal procedure whereby a public official is removed from office by a vote of the people. The action is started by a designated number (or percentage) of citizens signing a petition requesting a recall of the named official.

Recant. Renounce or reverse a position previously taken on an issue, statement, opinion, or allegiance.

Recapitulate (*ree* ka *pitch* u late). Summarize the main points, usually after narrating the details.

Receiver. Law: One who is legally appointed to take custody of property belonging to others, pending judicial action concerning them.

Receiver, Criminal. One who receives stolen property, knowing, or having reason to know, it has been stolen or taken in an illegal manner; a fence.

Receivership (ree *see* ver ship). Condition or situation of a receiver having been placed in charge of the property of someone else, pending litigation.

Receiving Stolen Goods. The short name usually given to the offense of receiving any property with the knowledge that it has been feloniously or unlawfully stolen, taken, extorted, obtained, embezzled or disposed of.

Reception Center. Center where adjudicated delinquents are placed prior to the beginning of a rehabilitation program.

Recess. Time between work sessions.

Recidivist (ree *sid* e vist). A person who is a repeater in criminal activity; a habitual criminal; one who repeatedly violates the law; one who is convicted of crime repeatedly.

Reciprocal. On both sides; mutual; interchangeable.

Reckon. Colloquialism: Believe; estimate; suppose.

Recognizance (ree *kog* nee zens). 1. An obligation entered into before a magistrate or court whereby an accused agrees to appear in court at a certain time and place or perform other acts required of him by the court. This is given in lieu of bail involving money or property. This is in effect the accused pledging his word, instead of a cash or property bond or bail, to perform. 2. An amount of money deposited to insure fulfillment of the obligation or act and which will be forefeited for nonperformance.

Recoil. Firearms term: The "kick" of a gun; the backward motion of a gun when it is fired.

Recompense (*Rek* em pens). To pay or repay for a loss; to make amends for damage; compensate.

Reconcile (*rek* en sile). To restore friendly relationship after enstrangement; to patch a disagreement or anger and become friendly.

Reconciliation (*rek* en *sill* e *a* shun). To again become friends after a quarrel, misunderstanding, or separation through anger.

Record. An identification record, including arrests and dispositions.

Recorder of Deeds. An officer appointed to make record or enrollment of deeds and other legal instruments authorized by law to be recorded.

Recoup (*ree* kupe). To recover or make up for a loss; to regain that which has been lost, as a money transaction.

Recourse. The method by which a person gets payment on a negotiable instrument if the endorser fails to pay up.

Recovery. The gaining or regaining of possession of something that has been stolen.

Recross Examination. At a trial, the second cross examination made after initial examination and initial cross examination of a witness; the second time an attorney questions the witness immediately after the attorney for the opposing party examines the witness.

Recruit (ree *kroot*). A newly employed police officer; "rookie."

Recuse (ree *quz*). 1. To challenge or object to a judge or other person officially involved in the trial of a case on the grounds that he is prejudiced or has an interest in the case. 2. The nonparticipation of a judge or other official or person officially involved in the trial of a case because of personal interest, prejudice, or close relationship with the parties involved.

Red. Slang: 1. One who belongs to the Communist Party or is a communist sympathizer, 2. Seconal® (secobarbital sodium).

Red, In the. 1. To owe more money than you have. 2. Unable to earn a profit.

Redbirds. Slang: Depressant drugs—barbiturates.

Red Devils. Slang: Seconal®, a barbiturate.

Redeem. To repossess something by paying off the indebtedness on it, such as a mortgage or a pledge.

Redemption (re *dimp* shun). Recovery; restoration.

Red-Handed. In the process of committing a crime.

Red-Hot. Slang: Fresh, new, correct.

Redirect Examination. The questioning of a witness by the party offering him, after the witness has been cross examined. In a criminal trial the party offering a witness questions him first on direct examination. The opposing party questions him on cross examination, and the first party then questions him on redirect examination.

Red-Light District. Slang: An area containing houses of prostitution.

Redneck. Slang: In the South, a poor person, many times rural in origin, who is prejudiced in several things; one who comes from a rural environment.

Redress (ree *dress*). Compensation for a wrong; a remedy or reparation.

VOCABULARY

Reds. Slang: Depressant drugs—barbiturates. See **Depressants.**

Reds and Blues. Tuinal® (ambobarbital sodium and secobarbital sodium).

Red Tape. Slang: Unnecessary detail and record keeping. "The government is noted for its red tape."

Reef. Slang: To pick pockets.

Reefer. Slang: Marijuana cigarette.

Reentry. Drug user term: Return from a trip on psychedelics.

Reeve. The head law enforcement officer of a district or shire in England many years ago. It was from "shire reeve" that the term "sheriff" developed.

Reference Group Theory. A theory similar to the differential association theory, holding that deviant behavior is influenced by peer group association and social factors interaction.

Referendum (ref er *en* dum). Popular vote; direct vote on a matter by the people.

Reflect Back. Being empathetic or interchangeable.

Reformatory (ree *for* mah tor ee). A prison for first offenders or non-hardened criminals.

Refraction. The redirection or bending of a wave as it moves from one medium to another.

Refractive Index. The ratio of the speed of light in a vacuum to the speed of light in a particular matter.

Refreshing Memory. Witnesses may bring notes or other documents to reacquaint themselves with details of their testimony or to renew the details of their testimony by stimulating their memory by looking over their notes, reports, entries of evidence.

Refute (re *fewt*). Disprove a theory, claim, or statement. "The officer refuted the story of the accused."

Register. To wait until blood comes into the "hypodermic" before injecting a drug intravenously.

Registration, Principal and Single-Fingerprint. See **Principal Registration** and **Single-Fingerprint Registration.**

Regular. Slang: Capable of being trusted or relied upon.

Regulation (reg you *lay* shun). 1. A rule or instruction to be followed by members of an organization. "We studied the regulation of the department." 2. Approved, accepted, or specified by the employing agency. "He wore the regulation uniform."

Rehabilitation. An attempt to change an offender's values, perceptions, or personality so that he may become a responsible member of society.

Rehearing (ree *heer* ing). A new hearing; a second hearing.

Reich (rike). The German nation or its government.

Reimburse (ree em *berse*). To repay or pay back for what has been spent.

Reintegration (ree in teh *gray* shun). A correctional goal or style that stresses the merging of correctional agencies with community resources and the necessity of on-the-street adjustment of offenders.

Rejoinder (ree *join* dur). A statement in response to what someone else has said. A reply in response to a statement.

Relay Spot. Gambling term: A location where the employees receive bets by phone and pass the information on to the boss (superior) when he calls, thus concealing the phone number of the boss from the employees and the bettors.

Release (ree *leese*). Turn loose; free someone. "The accused was released on bond." Conditional release: the release of a prisoner from custody with the understanding he will not violate certain rules or the law for a specified period of time on penalty of being returned to custody.

Released on Recognizance (ROR). A person released from custody on a criminal charge without posting a bond (bail) secured by money or other property. The person is released on his promise that he will appear at the designated time and place.

Relevant (*rel* eh vent). Pertinent to; related to; connected with a certain matter. "For information or physical things to be legally admissible as evidence, they must be relevant." See **Evidence, Relevant.**

Relevant-Back. Being Facilitative, making appropriate responses, and demonstrating accurate discrimination.

Relevant Evidence. See **Evidence, Relevant.**

Reliable. Trustworthy; dependable; that in which confidence can be placed. "The informant had proven reliable in the past."

Relief. The assistance or redress sought by a complainant in a court, especially in a court of equity.

Remand (ree *mand*). To send a prisoner, offender, or accused back to jail or prison. "The prisoner, being unable to make bond, was remanded to jail by the judge after arraignment."

Remedial Statute. A law passed to afford a remedy or redress for an imperfection in a previous law.

Remedy. A means, as court action, by which violation of a right is prevented or compensated for; legal redress.

Remiss (ree *miss*). Careless; not careful; not doing something as it should be. "He was remiss in performing his duties."

Remit (ree *mit*). Pardon; forgive; relieve from punishment. "The judge remitted the fine of the offender."

Removal. The transfer of a suit from one court to another by a writ of error, certiorari, etc.

Removal Proceedings (ree *moo* vel). A procedure used by the federal judicial system for transferring an accused from one judicial district to another prior to his conviction for an offense. After a hearing on the matter, a federal judge signs a removal order, which authorizes the United States Marshal to transfer the accused to another district.

Remunerate (ree *mune* er ait). To pay for something; to compensate. "You will be remunerated for the work done."

Rendezvous (*ron* day voo). A meeting at a certain time and place in accordance with a prior agreement. "The robbers held a rendezvous at the warehouse just before the robbery."

Renege (ree *nig*). To refuse to pay when one loses a bet.

Renunciation. To give up a right.

Renvoi. 1. French: The doctrine that permits a court the application of the law of its own jurisdiction to a transaction, even though the law of another jurisdiction would apply under their rules of the "conflict of laws." 2. In public international law, a country's right to dismiss, expel, or send back foreigners, particularly diplomatic officers.

Rep. Juvenile slang: Reputation

VOCABULARY

(usually a fighting reputation).

Reparation. Repair of a wrong; pay for injury done. "The parents made reparation for the damage done by their children."

Reparation to Victim of Crime. A system where the victim of crime is afforded reparation by the government for loss or damage incurred by a criminal act or another.

Repeal (ree *peel*). To abolish; eliminate; rescind or to make law null and void. "The legislature repealed the law."

Repeater. Slang: A person who has been convicted for crimes more than once or has served time in prison more than once.

Repeaters. Slang: Crooked dice, so made that they repeatedly come up with the same number.

Replevin (ree *plev* in). Lawful recovery of property that had been wrongfully taken.

Reply. To answer a defendant's plea.

Report (ree *port*). The accurate recording of facts, usually in written form. The preparation of accurate and complete reports is one of the most important elements of law enforcement. An officer may be excellent as an investigator, but his total value is no better than his reports. They serve as a permanent record for the use of himself, his superiors, the prosecutor, court, correctional personnel, probation and parole officers, and for law enforcement in other parts of the world.

Reporting System, Court Case. A system of reporting, in pamphlet or book form, the case decisions of the courts, especially the appellate courts (courts of appeal and state and federal Supreme Courts).

Reprieve (ree *preev*). 1. To postpone or delay the execution of one scheduled to be put to death. 2. Temporary delay in executing a death sentence.

Reprobate (*rep* re bait). A sorry person; immoral; without principles; one with low morals and principles; corrupt.

Republic. The form of government of a state in which the supreme power is invested in a body of the people—the electorate. The power does not reside in the masses of the people but in the hands of an elite few.

Repudiate (re *pew* de ate). To reject; to disavow; to refuse to accept.

Reputable (*rep* ye te bul). Enjoying a good reputation; respectable.

Reputation (rep ye *tay* shun). What people think of one or of a thing.

Res. Latin: 1. A thing; object. 2. Matter; case; point; action.

Res Adjuticata (rez ad jew di *kah* ta). Latin: The thing is settled by a court of competent jurisdiction; a matter finally decided on its merits by a proper court.

Rescind. To cancel or annul a law or contract.

Research, Applied. As opposed to pure research, this kind of inquiry is directed toward the formulation or discovery of scientific principles that can be used to solve some practical problems, to the application of scientific theories.

Research, Pure. As opposed to applied research, this kind of inquiry is conducted for the purpose of formulating scientific principles and theories rather than for the purpose of solving a specific problem.

Reserve Officer's Training Corps (R.O.T.C.). A military training program conducted at institutions of learning—high schools and/or colleges.

Res Gestae (rez *jes* tee). Latin; Law: Events or utterances that speak for themselves under the immediate pressure of the occurrence, through the instructive, impulsive, and spontaneous words and acts of the participant and not the words of the participants when narrating the events; spontaneous words spoken during or immediately after an act of such nature that the speaker did not have time or opportunity to rationalize what was being said. What forms any part of the res gestae is admissible as an exception to the hearsay rule

Residence. Place where one resides or lives.

Resident. One living at a place, not just a visitor.

Res Ipsa Loquitor (rez *ip* sa *low* quer ture). Latin: The thing speaks for itself.

Res Judicata. Latin: A conclusive presumption attached to res adjudicata.

Resolution. An official statement of a legislative body.

Respect. To restrain from interfering with; to care.

Respondent. In appellate practice, the party against whom an appeal is taken by the appellant.

Response Time. Time between receipt of information about a crime and arrival of officers at the crime scene.

Rest. To voluntarily end the introduction of evidence in a case.

Restitution (res te *two* shen). A paying back of that which was taken wrongfully; the repaying for loss or injury.

Restrain. To limit or restrict.

Restraining Device. Things used to keep someone under control or in check.

Restraining Order. An order, issued by a court of competent jurisdiction, forbidding a named person or a class of persons from doing specified acts.

Resuscitate (re *sus* e tait). Revive; bring back to consciousness; to come or bring back to life. See **Mouth-to-Mouth Resuscitation**.

Retainer. 1. The act of employing or engaging the services of an attorney, lawyer, or counsel professionally. 2. A preliminary payment or fee given to a lawyer to engage his services or to prevent his employment by the opposing side.

Retch. To go through the motions of vomiting; to strain in the effort to vomit.

Retraction. Withdrawal; a statement taken back.

Retreat to the Wall. In the law relating to homicide in self-defense, this phrase means that the party must avail himself of any apparent and reasonable avenues of escape by which his danger might be averted and the necessity of slaying his assailant avoided.

Retribution (ret re *bew* shen). Revenge; requiting; equal infliction of justice; paying back in kind for an act done; "an eye for an eye."

Retroactive (ret ro *ack* tiv). Having effect at the time prior to a certain event or date.

Return. 1. To bring, send, or carry back. 2. The act of an officer to turn back to the court an official paper, such as a writ or warrant, with a brief description of his actions in executing the mandate, order, or warrant.

Reverse. To revoke or annul a decision.

Review. The reexamination of the

VOCABULARY 233

court of a matter that had been previously acted on by the court.

Revised Line. Gambler slang: The "late line"; a publishing of the latest betting odds on an event.

Revised Statutes (RS). The statutory law of the legislative body of a government printed to show the changes in the law as made by the legislature.

Revocation (rev o *kay* shun). Probation or parole may be revoked for commission of a new offense or for violation of any condition of the parole or probation; revocation is decided by the same agency that grants the conditional release.

Revoke (ree *voak*). To call back; annul; cancel; reverse; annul by taking back.

Revolution. A complete and radical change; act of throwing off or overthrowing an existing government or system.

Revolver. A handgun—pistol—that has a cylinder holding several cartridges. A mechanism turns the cylinder, which brings the cartridges successfully into firing position.

Reward. Money or other things of value offered for the identification or capture of persons responsible for unlawful acts.

Rh Factor. Characteristic or factor of blood that aids the laboratory technician in its analysis.

Rib. Slang: To "Kid", tease, or make fun of; to frame-up.

Ribmarks. Stress marks shown on the cross section ("edge") of a piece of broken glass, especially along a radial crack. From an examination of the rib marks it can be determined from which direction came the force that broke the glass.

Rice Paper. A water-soluble paper that dissolves quickly in water and leaves little residue. Used by bookies and others who need to destroy records fast.

Ricochet (*rick* o shay). A glancing, skipping, jumping, or deflection of a moving projectile (bullet) after striking something at an angle. This occurs when a bullet strikes a surface that does not halt its flight. An officer should keep this in mind in firing under conditions where a ricochet could be dangerous to life or property.

Ride. Slang: "Take someone for a ride"; to force a victim to accompany one to a secluded spot, where the victim is killed.

Rider. An addition to a document; a bill or amendment.

Ridge. 1. Fingerprint term: The marks or line shown when the fingerprints are taken. 2. Tops of hills or mountains.

Ridge Count. Fingerprinting term: The number of ridges intervening between the delta and the core. Ridges counted must cross or touch an imaginary line for the delta to the core.

Ridge Line. Fingerprint term: A line in a fingerprint pattern caused by a ridge in a pattern.

Riding the Wave. Narcotics slang: Under narcotic influence.

Rifle. 1. A firearm used primarily as a shoulder-fired weapon, having rifled lands and grooves in the barrel, which causes the bullet to spin as it travels through the barrel and in its flight. 2. To search out and steal; to plunder; to rob.

Rifling. Structure of the inside of a gun barrel containing spiral grooves and lands.

Rig. Devise, plan, or arrange by fraud or deceit with the purpose of gaining unfair advantage for one's self. To fix the outcome of an event, usually a sports contest.

Right. 1. Correct, lawful, true. 2. Something that is lawful, just, or correct. 3. Gambling term: In crap game, betting the player will make his point.

Right Dice. Gambling term: Dice made so that they can be controlled when thrown, thus they will roll certain winning numbers.

Righteous. Good quality drugs.

Right Guy. Slang: One who is OK; a person who will cooperate; a fair or honest dealer.

Rightist. One who is conservative in his political philosophy.

Right-Of-Way. 1. Land on which, and on either side of which, a road, highway, railroad, electric line, or pipeline is built. 2. Law: The right of passage over another's land—a servitude.

Rights. Something that a person is entitled to; privileges that exist in favor of persons. There are several kinds of rights existing in society and recognized in law. The ones most commonly encountered are "legal rights" and "civil rights." The former are those protected generally by law, and the latter usually refer to constitutional and/or those covered by the Constitution's Bill of Rights or legislation and court decisions in this area of law.

Rigor Mortis. Medical term: A rigidity or stiffening of the muscular tissue and joints of the body that progresses after death.

Rim-Fire. Firearms term: The type of ammunition cartridge that is detonated by the firing pin or other mechanism striking the rim of the cartridge at its head or base.

Ring. Slang: Criminals banded together for certain types of activities.

Ringer. 1. Slang: One who interferes in another's racket. 2. Gambling term: In horse racing, a horse that is a sure winner.

Ring In. 1. To secretly bring crooked gambling devices into a gambling game. 2. To coerce a person to go along with one's plans. 3. To force one's way into an operation.

Ringleader (*ring* lee der). 1. Leader of a group or a band of persons engaged in unlawful activities. 2. Slang: The leader of any group engaged in any sort of questionable activity.

Riot. A disturbance caused by the illegal assembly of persons. The definition varies among states; some specify the number of persons voluntarily assembled as three or more. Disturbing the peace or some other illegal public disturbance is usually part of the definition.

Riot Act. A celebrated English statute that provides that, if any twelve persons or more are unlawfully assembled and disturbing the peace, any sheriff, undersheriff, justice of the peace , or mayor may by proclamation command them to disperse (which is familiarly called "reading the riot act"), and that if they refuse to obey and remain together for the space of one hour after such proclamation, they are guilty of a felony.

Riotous (*rye* e tus). Riotlike conduct; involved in a riot; unruly, boisterous.

Ripe. Fully prepared or developed, especially for introduction or presentation to an appellate or Supreme Court.

Rip In. In craps, to change the dice in a game.

Rip-Off. Slang: Fraud or theft.

Rip-Off Artist. Drug user's slang: A "freak" who steals to support a drug habit.

Ripping Method. A method of opening safes by burglars. A can-opener-type tool is used to remove the metal from the top, bottom, back, or side of the safe.
Rip-Roaring. Slang: Uninhibited actions; noisy; having a "big time."
Rise. That part of the trajectory of a bullet in which it gains elevation.
Risque (riss *kay*). Bordering on indecency; close to being improper.
Roach. Slang: 1. A law enforcement officer. 2. The stub of a marijuana cigarette.
Roach Holder. A device to hold a marijuana cigarette stub so it can be smoked without burning the smoker's fingers.
Road Agent. A highway robber.
Roadblock. Obstruction to passage on a road or street placed in operation by law enforcement officers to slow or stop motor traffic, when endeavoring to apprehend criminals or perform other official functions.
Road Hog. Slang: An automobile driver who is inconsiderate in taking more of the road than he should.
Roadhouse. A restaurant or place of entertainment located near a public road, especially outside of a town or city.
Road Map. Operational model for helping and human relations.
Road Tractor. Any vehicle whose initial purpose is to draw or haul other vehicles carrying heavy loads, yet it alone cannot carry the loads.
Roadway. The travelled surface of a road.
Robber. A person who commits a robbery.
Robbery (*rob* er ee). By violence or intimidation and against the will of the person to take from a person or from his presence property that belongs to him or is in his possession; feloniously taking property by use of force or threats.
Robbery with Injury. Theft or attempted theft from a person, accompanied by an attack, either with or without a weapon, resulting in injury. An injury is classified as resulting from a serious assault if a weapon was used in the commission of the crime or, if not, when the extent of the injury was either serious (e.g. broken bones, loss of teeth, internal injuries, loss of consciousness) or undetermined but requiring two or more days of hospitalization. An injury is classified as resulting from a minor assault when the extent of the injury was minor (e.g. bruises, black eye, cuts, scratches, swelling) or undetermined but requiring less than two days of hospitalization.
Robbery without Injury. Theft or attempted theft from a person, accompanied by force or the threat of force, either with or without a weapon, but not resulting in injury.
Rock and Roll. Slang: Popular music of the 1960s and 1970s, with active performers, vocalists, and instrumentalists.
Rock Crusher. Slang: Presently an inmate in a prison or having served time in one.
Rocks. Slang: 1. Rare stones, especially diamonds. 2. Money.
Rocks, On the. Slang: Liquors served on ice cubes with no other liquid added.
Rod. 1. Slang: A handgun. 2. A ridge pattern in fingerprints.
Rod Man. Slang: A person armed with a gun.
Roger. Slang: OK; the message has been received satisfactorily.
Rogue (roag). A cheating, dishonest, unprincipled individual.

Rogue's Gallery. Photographs of criminals collected for use by the police.

Role-Self Theory. Social theory attributing deviance to a person's attempt to justify or validate his identification with a particular role.

Roll. 1. Slang: To rob drunks or persons while they sleep. 2. A wad of money. 3. A tinfoil-wrapped roll of tablets.

Roll Bar. A device consisting of a metal bar installed on an automobile to protect the driver in the event that the car turns over.

Roll Call. Formation of police officers, when going on tour of duty, for the purpose of verifying presence, inspection, and giving instructions or orders.

Roll Dealer. A person who sells tablets in rolls.

Roll Deck. A tinfoil-wrapped roll of tablets.

Roman Nose. Nose with a noticeable prominent bridge.

Rook (rook as in book). Slang: To obtain something by trickery, fraud, or deceit.

Rookie (rookie as in hooky). Slang: A newly employed police officer or an army recruit.

Roomer. One who rents a room in another person's home. By law a rented room has the same protection from searches as has a private home in which a person lives, except in certain situations, such as where a person has abandoned the premises (room) and/or has defaulted in rent payment. The landlord has no right to enter and search or to authorize anyone else to do so under ordinary conditions.

Rooter. Slang: A pickpocket.

Rooting. Slang: Stealing or "prowling" a car.

Rope. Slang: 1. Marijuana. 2. To cheat or swindle. 3. To induce an inexperienced or naive player into a crooked game.

Roped In. Slang: To become involved in some activity by trickery or deceit.

Ropes, Know the. Slang: To have knowledge about a business or enterprise. "He can help in the project because he knows the ropes."

Roping. Slang: The technique of gaining the confidence of a suspect.

Roscoe. Slang: A handgun or pistol.

Rosenberg Case, The. A case in which spies in an atom bomb case were sentenced to death. The case was exploited by the Communists.

Roses. Narcotics slang: Amphetamine sulfate in rose-colored, heart-shaped tablets.

Rotary Traffic Island. Any circular area on the ground, surrounded by a highway, which is designed to prevent the crossing of traffic on four or more otherwise intersecting highways, in order to require all traffic approaching it to proceed for some distance around a portion of the island before entering one of the intersecting highways and to prevent left turns onto such otherwise intersecting highways.

Rotgut. Slang: Poor quality liquor.

Roughhouse (*ruff* house). A game played roughly and noisily; disorderly actions.

Rough It Up. To bet high in order to liven up the game.

Roughneck. Slang: A coarse individual; rough person with little manners. "He is a roughneck on a drilling rig."

Roughshod (*ruff* shod). To act in an overbearing manner; to act without consideration for others. "He ran roughshod over his associates."

VOCABULARY

Roulette (roo *let*). A gambling device. A wheel or disc having some thirty-seven numbered and colored (red and black) spaces, each of which will accomodate a ball. The disc turns, and a ball is rolled until it drops into a space. Betting is on numbers and/or colors.

Round. A loaded cartridge (ammunition) for a firearm. "The officers, after taking positions on the firing line, were instructed to load their revolvers with six rounds."

Rounder. Slang: One who goes from one nightclub or disreputable place to another, i.e. he makes the rounds of such places; a drunkard or vagrant.

Round Robin. Gambling term: A bet with a bookie that involves the playing of all possible two or three race or sports parlays on three or more horses or teams.

Round-Shouldered. Having a rounded back or the shoulders bent toward the front. A feature used in describing a person.

Roundsmen. Early detectives in history, located in New York.

Round Up. Slang: To locate and apprehend a group or members of a gang and send them to jail.

Roust. An interrogation or arrest.

Rout. At common law, the taking of steps by persons in an unlawful assembly to carry out an unlawful plan. If they execute the plan, it becomes a riot.

Routeman. Gambling term: A trusted employee of a lottery. He takes care of the business on a route.

Row (row as in how). A noisy argument or quarrel. "The man and his wife got into a row over the money."

Rowdy (rowdy as in howdy). Disorderly; quarrelsome; noisy.

Rowdy Cart. Slang: Police van.

Rubber Ball. Slang: Description of the bouncing of a worthless check. "The check bounced like a rubber ball."

Rubber Check. Slang: A check that is returned unhonored from the bank on which drawn because of insufficient funds or because of having no account.

Rubber Stamp. 1. Slang: To approve something without careful study and consideration. 2. A person who does without question the bidding or instructions of another.

Rub Down. Slang: To search a prisoner by rubbing hands over his body.

Rube. Slang: An outsider to a certain circle or society; a farmer or rural dweller.

Rub it In. Slang: Irritate a person by continued criticism or teasing.

Rubric. A heading or title.

Ruckus. Slang: Loud disturbance or disorderly conduct. "We heard the ruckus and went to the scene of the fight."

Rude (rood; rewd). Not polite; inconsiderate; discourteous.

Ruffian (*ruf* ee en). A cruel, brutal, vicious person. "As we walked the dark street, a ruffian attacked us."

Rug Joint. A big-money well-designed gambling establishment.

Rule of Law. 1. A rule that guides the conduct of a community's citizens, supported by police or other executive body. 2. A system of law in which the law takes precedence over individuals or groups.

Ruler. A judge.

Ruling. A decision made by a court.

Rum. An alcoholic beverage made from fermented molasses or cane juice.

Rumanian Box. A swindle in which

people put money into a machine and it changes denominations.

Rumble. 1. Slang: A gang fight or fight between members of different gangs. "The Hell's Angels and the Breed motorcycle gangs had a rumble in Cleveland in March 1970." 2. Discover in the act of robbing; forewarning. 3. To catch a person cheating; to discover cheating devices in a game.

Rummy. Slang: An alcoholic.

Rumor (*roo* mer). A statement made or repeated without knowledge as to its truthfulness. "An officer should refrain from accepting rumors as fact and from repeating them."

Rumpus. Slang: A loud disturbance by people; a noisy argument.

Run. Slang: An amphetamine binge.

Run, On the. Slang: Being sought by the police; taking steps to avoid apprehension by the police.

Runaway (*run* a way). A person who runs away; a child who runs away from home or relatives.

Rundown. A sports bookie's odds and payoffs on the day's betting events.

Rundown Sheet. Gambling term: Itemized list of bets, games, teams, or numbers played in policy.

Run In. Slang: To place someone under arrest by a police officer.

Runner (*run* er). 1. A messenger. 2. One who delivers slips and collects bets in the numbers game—a gambling operation. 3. Juvenile slang: Gang leader. 4. A type of police officer in London in the Eighteenth century. They later became known as the "Bow Street Runners."

Runout Powder. To leave town quickly so as to avoid payment of gambling debts.

Run Strong. To run a crooked gambling establishment.

Rural (*rer* al). Pertaining to the country as distinguished from the city; not in a city or town.

Ruse (rooz). An action or acts to mislead or achieve something by trick or strategy.

Rush. The intense feeling the drug user has just after "fixing"; to throw up after "fixing."

Russian Roulette. Slang: A game of life and death where players put a single bullet into a revolver and spin the cylinder. The pistol is then placed against the head of each player and the trigger pulled once for each until it fires.

Rustle (*russ* el). Slang: To steal such things as cattle, sheep, etc. "He is a cattle rustler."

Ruthless (*Rooth* less). Cruel; displaying no mercy; without pity.

Rye (righ). Whiskey made from rye grain.

S

Sabotage (*sab* oh toj). Deliberate damage to property by persons who seek to intimidate or injure a person, corporation, or nation. "The enemy agents committed sabotage by destroying the munitions plant."
Saboteur (sab oh *tour*). One who commits sabotage.
Sacco-Vanzetti Case. A famous case in which two men were found guilty of murder in a prejudiced court by circumstantial evidence and sentenced to death despite public outcry.
Sack. Slang: Bed. "At 9 PM he was in the sack."
Sacred Mushrooms. Slang: Psilocybin, a hallucinogenic narcotic. See **Hallucinogens**.
Sadism (*say* dizm). Sex perversion manifested by acts of cruelty on another person.
Sadism, Symbolic. Acts of mutilation of an object or symbol that is a substitute for an actual sadistic act. By this method the person expresses his sadistic impulse.
Sadist. One who carries out acts of perverse cruelty against another person to satisfy sexual perversion.
Sadomasochism. A combination: Getting sexual pleasure from giving pain (sadism) and receiving pain (masochism).
Safe. A sturdy box for keeping money and other valuables safe.
Safe Cracker. A safe burglar.
Safe Streets Act. See **Omnibus Crime Control and Safe Streets Act of 1968**.
Safety Fuse. A cord of black powder used to carry a flame at a uniform rate to an explosive charge.
Said (sed). Law: Previously named or referred to. Used extensively in legal vocabulary. "The said document was signed by said witness."
Sake (*sok* ee). Japanese alcoholic beverage made from rice by a fermentation process.
Sale (sail). Narcotics slang: A sale of narcotics. "The narcotics pusher made a sale."
Salem Witchcraft Trials. Trials in Salem, Massachusetts, in 1692, in which nineteen young girls were hanged as witches before the townspeople altered their view of persecutions.
Salesmen. Juvenile slang: Police officers.
Saliva (sa *ligh* vah). The fluid in the mouth that keeps it moist and assists in digestion, secreted by the salivary glands. The crime laboratory can analyze it and determine its type, which has a correlation to the blood type of the individual.
Saliva Test. A test made on a horse's saliva to check for drugs.
Sallow (*sal* oh). Having a yellowish, unhealthy appearance (said of the skin). Used in describing a person's physical features.
Saloon. A bar; establishment for consumption of alcoholic beverages.
Salt. Slang: 1. To save, store up, or hoard. "He salted away half of his salary each month." 2. To enter ficticious entries into account books.
Salvation Army. A religious and "aid to the poor" organization start-

239

ed in England in 1865 by William Booth. The organization is located in many cities of the United States, furnishing lodging and meals, as well as clothing, to the needy.

Sam. Federal narcotic agents.

Same. Legal and business term: The identical thing or person previously referred to or mentioned. "I received your promissory note and have recorded same."

Sanction (*sangk* shen). 1. Official permission; approval. "It had the sanction of the officer." 2. A provision for obtaining evidence to the law, effected by legislation providing rewards and/or punishment. "The sanction in a criminal law is the penalty provided for violation of the law."

Sand. Slang: Courage; guts; "grit"; "intestinal fortitude."

Sandbag. Slang: To attack and injure a person from behind, usually from a position of ambush.

Sane. Mentally competent; not mentally deranged or crazy; having a normal mind; sound mentally.

Sanguinary (*sang* gwe nair ee). Bloody; accompanied by bloodshed; bloodthirsty.

Sanity (*san* i tee). Condition of being of stable, of sound mind.

Sanity Hearing. A procedure ordered by the court or other official for the purpose of determining whether a person is sane or insane.

San Quentin Quail. Slang: A good-looking girl who is under the age of consent.

Sap. Slang: 1. A stupid or silly individual. 2. A "blackjack" or weapon of similar nature.

Sapped. Slang: Beaten up.

Sapphist (*saf* fist). A woman homosexual who satisfies her desires not only through the common lesbian practices but also engages in cunnilingus.

Satch. Prison slang: Narcotics sent in a letter or clothing.

Satch Cotton. Slang: Cotton used to strain drugs before injection; may be used again if supplies are gone.

Satchel Man. Slang: One who collects payoff or bribery money; bag man.

Saturday Night Drinker. A person who drinks regularly, but usually only on weekends, and usually does not drink to excess during the week.

Satyriasis (sait eh *rye* eh sis). Sex deviation term: Abnormal sex craving on the part of the male.

Saunter (*sawn* ter). To walk slowly or leisurely.

Savvy. Slang: Intelligence; shrewdness; to comprehend; to understand.

Sawdust Joint. Gambling term: A cheap gambling operation.

Scab. 1. Slang: A nonunion worker who does not participate in a union strike; one who will work in the place of a striking union member. 2. Juvenile slang: A girl.

Scaffold (*skaf* fold). A platform upon which convicted criminals are executed by being hanged.

Scag. Slang: Heroin.

Scale. The ratio between the length of lines on a map or sketch and the distance between points. "One inch represents ten feet." This ratio is called the scale. Scaled drawings are useful in depicting a crime or accident scene. The scale should always be shown on the maps or sketches.

Scalper. Slang: 1. A person who sells tickets for an event (game or other entertainment) for a price greater than was paid for them (more than the regular price). 2. One who bets on two opposing teams in order to

minimize his losses through a mysterious mathematical system unknown to the bookies.
Scamp. A scoundrel; rascal; person of low repute.
Scan. Slang: Also called "bust out"; disposal of goods of a business by bankruptcy fraud.
Scandal (*skan* del). Acts of alleged wrongdoing that bring shame or disgrace on those who commit the acts.
Scapegoating (*skaip* go ting). Casting someone or something else the blame for one's own difficulties.
Scar (skar). Mark or blemish resulting from a break in the skin caused by an injury such as a cut, burn, or sore. Scars are important items of personal identification and should be described in detail.
Scat. Slang: Heroin.
Scatter. Slang: Meeting place of a gang after crime has been committed.
Scatterbrain. Slang: One who thinks illogically; one who speaks without proper thinking.
Scene (seen). 1. The place where something occurs, i.e. the scene of the crime or the scene of the accident. 2. Narcotics slang: Place where drugs are sold.
Scent (sent). 1. Odor or smell of something. "The bloodhounds followed the scent of the escapee." 2. The means of locating a person. "The officers are on the scent of the criminals."
Schizo (*skit* so). Slang: Schizophrenic; having a mental derangement.
Schmeck. A Yiddish-American term for powdered drugs.
Schmecker. Slang: A sniffer or user of powdered narcotic drugs.
School. Slang: Prison.
Schoolboy. Slang: Codeine.

Scienter (see *en* ter). Law: Guilty knowledge of the defendant.
S.C.LC. Southern Christian Leadership Conference.
Scmerber Case. The United States Supreme Court held that the prosecution could use as evidence in a drunken driving case the analysis of a blood specimen taken without the consent of the accused; this did not violate the Fifth, Sixth, or Fourteenth Amendments concerning self-incrimination, as such evidence was physical in nature and was not testimonial, i.e. spoken words of the accused.
Scoff. Slang: To eat.
Scoop. Slang: Getting and publishing or broadcasting a news item before other news media get it. It is usually good procedure for law enforcement agencies to release information to all news media at the same time, if it is such that all media would be interested.
Scooter Patrol. Special scooter-mounted police assigned to neighborhoods, having backup emergency support. Introduced by Detroit police as a means of restoring man-on-the-beat relationships.
Scope. The telescopic sight on a rifle.
Scopes Trial (1925). A trial as the result of a Tennessee state law making it illegal to teach the theory of evolution. Scopes was found guilty, but the sentence was revoked on a technicality.
Scopolamine (sko *pol* e men). A drug that produces drowsiness and stupor. It has been used in lie detection work where the suspect is administered the drug, which produces a "twilight" sleep. He is questioned while in this condition and allegedly will speak the truth as his inhibitions

are removed. The value of this procedure is questionable.

Score. 1. To count up the value of hits on a firearms target. 2. Slang: The successful conclusion of an episode of cheating, swindling, robbing, gambling, etc. 3. Slang: Make a purchase of drugs or narcotics. 4. Slang: Something owed; an obligation. 5. Juvenile slang: To accomplish. 6. Slang: The "fruits of the crime"; what the criminal has stolen.

Score a Big Touch. To cheat in a gambling game for a large sum of money.

Scot-Free. Slang: Free from punishment; unpunished.

Scotland Yard. The headquarters of London's Metropolitan Police.

Scottsboro Case (1931). Case in which two white girls were allegedly raped by nine black youths, who were sentenced to death. Even though one of the girls changed her story, the youths still had to serve life sentences.

Scoundrel. Unprincipled person; rascal; person of low repute.

Scram. Slang: Leave immediately; get out; go.

Scrap. 1. Pieces of metal the main value of which is to be melted for the recovery of the metals of which it is made. 2. Slang: To fight or struggle.

Scrape. A difficult position in which one finds one's self.

Scratch. Slang: 1. In horse racing, to remove a horse as an entry in a race because of certain conditions that arose after the horses in the race had been listed, usually after midnight on the night before the race. 2. Money, especially currency and banknotes.

Scratch Sheet. Racetrack gambler term: Printed sheets showing the scheduled events at the racetracks, including the names of the horses, their positions, etc. These are used extensively in off-track betting—bookie operations.

Screen Cell. A cell, whose door is made of a heavy screen, where mental patients are placed for observation.

Screening. The removal of selected persons from the criminal justice process.

Screen Out. To hide a cheating move in gambling.

Screw. 1. Prison slang: A penitentiary guard; a key. 2. Taboo: Sexual relations.

Screwball. Slang: An unusual person in that he does not think and act as a normal individual does; an eccentric person.

Screwed Up. Slang: Confused; mixed up; "fouled up."

Screws, Put on the. Slang: To put pressure on; to get someone under control by use of strong urging.

Script. 1. Racetrack gambler slang: The narration of the races, used primarily for the interest of bookie bettors. 2. Drug prescription. 3. Forged checks.

Script Writer. Underworld slang: A forger, especially of checks.

Scuffle. To struggle confusedly or in a disorderly manner; a confused fracas.

Scum of the Earth. Slang: Worthless, vile person or persons; persons of low repute.

Scuttlebutt. Slang: Rumors and unconfirmed statements of information.

S.D.S. (SDS). Students for a Democratic Society.

S.E.A.R.C.H. (SEARCH). System for Electronic Analysis and Retrieval of Criminal Histories. See **Project Search**.

VOCABULARY

Search. To explore or look thoroughly with the objective of finding something of value to the investigation.

Search, Crime Scene. A careful search of the area where a crime was committed. It may include adjacent areas and other areas where some evidence is found or action occured.

Search of Persons. A legal search made of a person or persons. It may be made upon authority of a search warrant, following arrest without a warrant, following an arrest made under authority of an arrest warrant, or made under the authority of a "stop and frisk" law, if such exists in a state.

Search Warrant. A written document, issued by a judge or magistrate in the name of the state, directed to a peace officer (sheriff, constable, police officer, etc.), commanding that the described structures, places, or persons be searched for things described in the warrant. The judicial officer issuing the warrant must have been furnished enough information in an affidavit to produce probable cause in his mind that the things to be searched for are in the place or on the person to be searched, and that they are pertinent to an offense.

Seat-Tipper. A thief who steals from handbags of female moviegoers by tipping the seat on which the bag is resting while the owner is watching the movie.

S.E.C. (SEC). Securities and Exchange Commission.

Seccy. Slang: Depressant drugs—barbiturates.

Seclude (see *klud*). To separate from others; to keep apart from others.

Secondary Classification. A term used in classifying fingerprints. In the classification formula it follows the primary classification and is written as capital letters, as T/W, or whatever the classification requires. It is based on the type of pattern in each of the index fingers.

Secondary Groups. Gesellschaft (impersonal) relations (officials).

Second Dealer. A gambling cheater who deals the second, not the top, card from the deck.

Second Story Job. Slang: A burglary of premises where the burglar operates above the first floor in the structure.

Secret. Well-kept information or knowledge concerning a particular thing. In government service, material or information that if disclosed without authority, could result in serious damage to the nation by endangering the international relations of the country, jeopardizing the effectiveness of a program or policy of great importance to the national defense, or exposing important military or defense plans, technological developments of importance to the national defense, or information relative to important intelligence operations.

Secrete (see *krete*). 1. To remove or keep from observation; to hide or conceal. 2. Biological: A function of certain glands of an animal that create and exude certain fluids.

Secretion Job. Operations of loft burglars where one or more conceals himself in the loft of the victim's store during working hours and makes a careful survey of the goods desired. He is later joined by confederates (after closing time), and they take the selected merchandise and quickly escape.

Secretor (see *krete* or). A person whose saliva contains blood group antigens. In such persons such antigens also appear in the blood and other body fluids. Contrast with nonsecretor.

Secret Service, U.S. Created in 1860 as the first federal general law enforcement agency. A branch of the United States Treasury Department. Jurisdiction: 1. Protection of the United States currency and certain valuable historical documents. 2. Protection of the following United States officials and persons: the President and his immediate family; widow and minor children of a former President; the President-elect; Vice-President.

Sector Search. Same as **Zone Search**.

Securities and Exchange Commission (S.E.C.). A federal agency involved with the registration of security issues, regulation of transactions in securities, and the investigation of fraudulent stock manipulations.

Security. 1. Freedom from danger or damage. 2. A thing deposited or put up as a guarantee for payment of money. Industrial security is a branch of an industrial organization that has the responsibility of safeguarding the physical plant, properties, and products of the organization.

Sedative. A drug that calms nerves and slows down reflexes and body functions.

Sedition. Beginning or contributing to a rebellion against a government.

Seduce (see *duece*). Cause one to be lead astray; to do wrong; to persuade one to engage in illicit sexual relations, especially for the first time.

Seduction (see *duck* shen). The offense of inducing a woman to surrender her chastity.

Seeds. Marijuana seeds.

Seedy. Ragged and poor; shabby.

Seggy. Slang: Depressant drugs—barbiturates.

Segregate (*seg* ree gate). To isolate or set apart from others.

Seizure (*see* zher). 1. Law: The seizing of something in accordance with law. A search carries with it the right of seizure if objects or materials are found that come within the scope of the search; under certain writs officers make a seizure. 2. A violent attack caused by such a disease as epilepsy.

Selective Enforcement. The deploying of police personnel in ways to effectively cope with existing or anticipated problems. If records reflect that traffic accidents occur most frequently in certain areas at certain times, greater numbers of officers are assigned to such areas at the critical times under the program of selective enforcement.

Selective Patrol. See **Selective Enforcement**.

Self-Confidence. Confidence in one's own ability to do things or in one's judgement.

Self-Control. Control of one's actions or faculties even under trying circumstances. It is important that an officer have and maintain self-control, as there are many situations encountered that tend to cause a loss of self-control. Some of these events are intentionally created by persons hoping to cause the officer to lose his self-control or "cool" and thus do something that will give the troublemakers a reason for complaint.

Self-Defense. The right to protect one's person or property against injury or destruction. It is used as a legal defense in criminal cases. Some states do not allow the taking of a life to prevent damage or destruction to property but do allow the taking of a

VOCABULARY

life of an assailant where (1) the victim is in danger of loss of life or great bodily harm and the killing is necessary to save himself from such danger, or (2) the killing was done by one who has reasonable cause to believe a violent and forcible felony, involving danger to life or great bodily harm, is about to be committed and that such action is necessary for its prevention. The law on self-defense varies among states.

Self-Discipline. Training one's self to do or not to do certain things—self control. The disciplining of one's self.

Self-Esteem Maintenance System. The hierarchical ordering of cultural values and role concepts within a personality system. Those on top are the most important to the self-esteem; those on the bottom, the least. It is a process of maintaining favorable images of the self.

Self-Evident. In itself proof or evidence of a point in question.

Self-Exploration. Process by which the helpee explores himself and attempts to understand himself.

Self-Incrimination (in krim i *nay* shen). Implication of one's self in crime or wrongdoing; incrimination of one's self. The Fifth Amendment of the United States Constitution provides that a person shall not be forced to incriminate himself. This has been interpreted to mean through the spoken word (testimonial), and the furnishing of physical evidence such as fingerprints and blood is not protected by the Constitution.

Self-Inflicted. Inflicted by one's self.

Self-Protection. Self-defense; protection of one's self.

Seller. Gambling term: One who sells bets on numbers; one who accepts bets in a numbers game.

Sell Out. Slang: To trick, cheat, or swindle; to do something unethical or illegal in an underhanded manner for money or other renumeration or advantage.

Semantics (see *man* ticks). The study of the meanings of words and phrases, especially the changes in the meanings of words.

Semen (*sea* men). The fluid of male animals that contain spermatazoa or the reproductive cells.

Semiannual. Occurring twice a year or every six months.

Semiconscious (*sem* i *kon* shus). Not fully conscious; partly conscious.

Seminal Fluid (*sem* i nel). See **Semen**.

Semispontaneous Combustion. See **Spontaneous Combustion, Semi–**.

Semitrailer. A freight trailer that, when attached, is supported at its forward end by the truck tractor; also, a semitrailer with an attached tractor.

Semiweekly. Occurring twice a week.

Send. Slang: To make one very joyful.

Senile (*see* nile). Exhibiting the slowing-down and mental malfunction of old age.

Sense. The means by which we gain knowledge of happenings in the world. The five senses are sight, taste, hearing, touch, and smell. We can testify on information acquired through these senses unless it is a violation of such rules of evidence as "hearsay."

Senseless. 1. Having no sense; stupid. 2. Unconscious.

Sensual. Lustful; having to do with the overinvolvement with appetite or sexual pleasure.

Sentence. The judgement of the

court in a criminal case; the formal pronouncement of a judge (or court) upon the person found guilty (either by trial or on a plea of guilty) in a court.

Sentence, Flat (Straight). A fixed sentence without a maximum or a minimum.

Sentence, Intermediate. A sentence to incarceration with a spread of time between a minimum date of parole of eligibility and a maximum discharge date.

Sentence, Maximum. A maximum sentence sets the outer limit beyond which a prisoner cannot be held in custody.

Sentence, Minimum. The time that an offender must spend in prison before becoming eligible for parole.

Sentence, Suspended. Technically a sentence, but involving unconditional, unsupervised release of the convicted felon.

Sentence Hearing. A hearing held shortly after conviction in which the judge reviews the circumstances surrounding a case and then renders the sentence.

Sentencing. The postconviction stage of the criminal justice process in which the defendant is brought before the court for imposition of sentence. Usually a trial judge imposes sentence, but in some jurisdictions sentencing is performed by jury or by sentencing councils.

Sentencing Alternatives. The range of possibilities the judge (or jury) has in sentencing an individual, e.g. probation, suspended sentence, prison, etc.

Sentencing Councils. A panel of three or more judges that confers to determine a criminal sentence.

Sentencing Juries. Trial juries attached to a court that impose sentence.

Separate but Equal. 1. A repudiated doctrine that sought to justify the segregation of races in facilities, particularly schools, where they provided accommodations and facilities that were of equal quality.

Separation of Powers. The doctrine of the separation of legislative, executive, and judicial powers where none of the powers may be jointly exercised by the same individual or group.

Sequester. To take possession of or remove.

Sergeant (*sar* jant). A police officer whose rank is higher than a patrolman and lower than a lieutenant. The sergeant is the first supervisory officer in ascending the chain of command. An efficient sergeant is an important and vital link in the administrative operation of the department. He is the line officer who is in closest contact with the field operations of a department.

Serology (see *rol* o gee). A science dealing with serums and especially their reactions and properties.

Serum. A clear, slightly amber-colored liquid that separates from blood when it clots.

Serve Time. To be incarcerated in a jail or penitentiary in connection with a criminal case.

Service. Law: The legal execution of a writ or process upon a designated person.

Set. An incendiary fire; point of origin of an incendiary fire; "touch off."

Set Aside. To make null or void a court's ruling or judgement.

Set Down. To put a case on the appropriate record or docket for argument or hearing in court.

VOCABULARY

Set-To. Slang: A squabble, dispute, or fight.
Set-Up. Slang: A sporting event that has been fixed.
Sewer. Narcotics slang: A vein.
Sex Crimes. Crimes committed by sex deviates; crimes committed as a result of abnormal sex manifestations.
Sex Deviate. One who performs sex acts in an unnatural or abnormal manner; one who manifests his sex drives abnormally.
Sex Maniac. One who is mentally deranged as to matters of sex; a sex pervert who is mentally ill; one who, because of mental illness, commits brutal sex crimes.
Sex Pervert. See **Sex Deviate**.
Sexy. Slang: Attractive sexually.
Shack Up. Slang: To cohabitate; to live together as man and wife; to have illicit sexual relations.
Shades. Slang: Colored or dark eyeglasses.
Shading. Marking cards by putting a light coat of ink on the back of a certain card.
Shadow. 1. To follow closely and secretly; to keep under observation; a physical surveillance. 2. Among loan sharks, the strong-arm collector of loans who uses physical force.
Shaft. Slang: To cheat someone; defraud; belittle; speak disparagingly about; tell lies about; to take advantage of someone.
Shakedown. Slang: 1. A search of the cells in a jail or prison for weapons, tools, or contraband. 2. To obtain property or money through extortion, blackmail, or threats.
Shakes, The. Slang: Nervous condition caused by the prior use of narcotics and alcohol; the need for a fix.
Shakeup. Slang: A rearranging or recognizing; a complete change made quickly.
Shall. Law: Denotes mandatory actions or requirements. If the law states something shall be done, it is a positive and definite requirement. If the word "may" is used, discretion is allowed. These words are important in criminal law and procedure.
Shamus. Jewish-American slang: Guard; any prison official.
Shanghai (*shang* high). To drug or intoxicate or render insensible and ship as a sailor, usually to secure advance money or a premium.
Shanty (*shan* ti). A small, crudely built house.
Shaped Dice. See **Shapes**.
Shapes. Gambler slang: Dice that are not perfect cubes, thus affecting their action.
Shark. Slang: Card shark; pool shark. One who is skillful in a certain field and capitalizes on this skill to win from unsuspecting opponents.
Sharpie. Slang: One who swindles, especially one who is a card shark or one who cheats at dice.
Sharpshooter. Gambling term: A gambler who is known to be dishonest.
Shavetail. Slang: A newly appointed second lieutenant in the armed services.
Shaving Points. Slang: The intentional making of fewer points in an athletic contest by a participant than could have been made, so that bets on the event will be affected by the score.
Shebang. Slang: The whole operation, incident, outfit, or affair.
Sheet. Slang: The police department's record of a criminal's charges, convictions, and sentences.
Shell Game. A swindling game in which the operator manipulates a

pea-sized object under three walnut shells. The victim bets he can tell which shell it is under. He fails because the object is concealed in the crook of the finger of the swindler.
Sheriff. An elected public official who is usually considered the most important law enforcement officer in the county. His principal duties are to aid in the conduct of the criminal and civil courts of record, to serve processes, make arrests, execute judgements, and conduct judicial sales. In some states he also collects taxes and operates the county jail. He is the conservator of the peace in the county. By agreement or otherwise, his criminal jurisdiction may cover only the area outside the municipalities in the county, or he may have joint jurisdiction with the police within the municipalities. The position in the United States is patterned after the English organization where the position evolved over a long period of history. It started as a "reeve" of a shire, thus shire-reeve, which developed into sheriff.
Sheriff's Office (S.O.). The department or office operated by the sheriff of a county or parish. Also called the Sheriff's Department.
Shift. Time of day during which a group of people work. In law enforcement the times of shifts vary, but many use a three-shift system: day shift—6 AM to 2 PM; night shift—2 PM to 10 PM; dog shift—10 PM to 6 AM.
Shifter. Gambling slang: A card player who secretly returns the parts of the cut deck of cards to their original position.
Shiftless. Ineffective; not ambitious; doing little or no work; lazy.
Shifty Eyes. Slang: Not looking another person in the eyes when talking to him; not looking at a person when addressing him.
Shill. Slang: A gambler's accomplice or assistant; also used by con men or auctioneers for the purpose of encouraging real customers to participate; one who hustles action for a gambler.
Shin Battle. Juvenile slang: Intragang practice or test-of-mettle fight among gang members.
Shine. Slang: A Negro.
Shiner. Gambling slang: A small reflective surface, such as a mirror, concealed in a ring or other object, which makes it possible to see the top card as it is dealt.
Shire-Reeve. In early England, the head of a geographical unit equivalent to a county. Today, in this country, this person is called a sheriff.
Shiv. Sharpened table knife smuggled from the dining hall of a prison or other institution.
Shocking Power. Firearms term: The force or energy created by a bullet upon striking an object. This is produced by momentum and penetration. Some small caliber weapons do not have enough shocking power to stop a person or an animal by their projectiles.
Shoe. Gambling term: A container from which cards are dealt.
Shooting Gallery. Slang: Place where addicts inject narcotics or a fix.
Shoot the Pin. Slang: Pricking the skin with a pin and dropping a liquid drug in the hole with an eye dropper.
Shoot Up. Slang: To give a shot of narcotics or a fix.
Short. 1. Prison slang: Approaching the end of a convict's prison term. 2. Narcotics slang: Heroin.

VOCABULARY

Shortchange. 1. To give less change than the amount that should be given. 2. Slang: To receive less of something than what should have been given or paid.

Shortchange Artist. Slang: The operator of a carnival booth or circus sideshow who is skilled in cheating customers by returning them less than their proper change.

Short Go. Narcotics slang: Take a small amount of narcotics.

Shortitis. Prison slang: The nervous anticipation of reaching the end of a prison term.

Short Ridge. Fingerprint term: A short broken ridge or line.

Short Sled. Vehicle.

Short-Tempered. Quick tempered; gets angry quickly; one whose temper flares with little provocation. This is something a law enforcement officer should work on and bring under control.

Shot. 1. Firing of a gun. 2. An injection of narcotics. 3. A drink of whiskey. 4. Slang: A high-ranking person.

Shotgun. A firearm, the barrel of which is not rifled (smoothbore) that fires a shell containing shot or slug. A shotgun is effective and an extremely deadly weapon at close range. The officer should remember that the shot pattern spreads, so others in the vicinity of the person fired at may also be hit.

Shot in the Arm. Slang: A hypodermic injection.

Shot Pattern. The dispersion pattern of shot fired from a shotgun. Shot separate from one another in flight. The shot pattern is determined by shooting at a target or other surface that will register the impact of the shots when they strike the surface.

Shover. Slang: A person who passes counterfeit money.

Show. Horse racing term: To come in third, i.e. the horse who finishes in the third position.

Showup. The same as lineup. In America it was started by Francis Turkey in 1851.

Shrewd (shrood). Intellectual; cunning; sharp; quick minded.

Shuckin. Juvenile slang: Kidding; joking; lying.

Shuffle. 1. A peculiar movement of the feet, involving dragging or scraping of the feet without lifting them while walking. Some authorities say that a homosexual has a characteristic shuffle when sexually aroused. 2. Juvenile slang: To engage in a fistfight.

Shutter. The mechanism in a camera that briefly allows light to pass from the lens to the film.

Shylock. Slang: To operate a loan sharking business.

Shyster (*shis* ter). A lawyer who uses unethical or improper methods in his legal business. A disreputable, dishonest attorney.

Sibling (*sib* ling). A sister or brother.

Sic (sick). A Latin word that, when used in brackets after a word or a phrase, denotes it is written or spelled incorrectly and it is being written as a direct quotation, regardless of its correctness.

Sick. In addition to its usual meaning denoting physical illness, it is often used to signify mental illness.

Sidearms. Weapons of such size and design as to be carried at the side, usually attached to a belt. In law enforcement such weapons are pistols, revolvers, or automatics (semiautomatic).

Side Bets. Gambling term: Bets made between individuals other than the house or the operator of the gambling establishment. This is common in crap games and at racetracks.

Side Games. Gambling term: Games of lesser attraction in a casino or gambling establishment.

Sidekick. Slang: A close associate or friend.

Sideswipe. A blow from the side; to strike with a blow from the side.

Sidewalk. A paved walk at the side of a road or street.

Siff (Siffs). Slang: Syphilis.

Sight Draft. An order for the payment of money drawn by one person for another, which is payable on presentation.

Signal (Sign). Private signal between gamblers, usually a cheating signal.

Signals, Ten-Dash. A system of signals used in law enforcement that consists of the numeral ten, followed by other numbers. Such signals have a prearranged meaning. They are used most frequently in radio communications but may be used in other types of oral communication.

Significant Others. People whose esteem we most treasure.

Silencer. 1. An apparatus attached to a gun that decreases the sound. 2. Underworld slang: A lethal weapon used to kill someone.

Silent Insolence. Silent disrespect toward a prison official; refusal to answer a direct question.

Silhouette (sil oo *et*). The outline of an image in a color darker than its background.

Silhouette Target. A firearms target composed of a dark outline of a man with a white background. This is used in the practical pistol course, in rifle practice, and for target practice with other types of weapons.

Silver Nitrate (*sil* ver *nigh* trate). A chemical, $AgNO_3$, used in photography and in a crime laboratory for the development of fingerprints on paper.

"Silver Platter" Doctrine. The doctrine long followed by the federal courts that evidence, although illegally obtained by state officers, could be used in federal cases if there was no collusion between state and federal officers. The evidence illegally obtained by state officers would be handed to the federal officers on a "silver platter." This doctrine was overturned in Elkins v. United States, 364 U.S. 206 (1960).

Silver Tongue. 1. A mob member of obvious upper-class background. 2. A lawyer or smooth talker.

Simple Assault. Attack without a weapon resulting in either minor injury, e.g. bruises, black eye, cuts, scratches, swelling, or in undetermined injury requiring less than two days of hospitalization. Also includes attempted assault without a weapon.

Simulated Forgery. Forgery of writing accomplished by the forger practicing imitating the writing until the forged writing is similar to the original.

Sine Die (*sigh* nee *dye*). Latin: Without a fixed date for further action; without setting a time.

Sine Qua Non (*sign* quay *nan*). Latin: Something one cannot do without.

Sing. 1. Slang: To confess one's participation in crime and to tell officers what one knows about certain activities. 2. Slang: To beef or complain.

Single Action. 1. Gambling term: To bet on one digit in a numbers game. 2. Firearms term: A revolver that does not cock the hammer when the trigger is pulled, or the operation of a double-action revolver by manual-

VOCABULARY

ly cocking the hammer and firing it from the cocked position.

Single-Base Powder. A powder in which the only explosive ingredient is nitrocellulose.

Single-Fingerprint Registration. A system of classifying single fingerprints so that single or multiple fingerprints (less than all ten fingers) left at the scene of a crime may be identified. Such a file is more effective if the number of fingerprints placed therein is kept small.

Single-O. To work single-O is to work alone.

Sinister (*sin* iss tur). Boding ill; evil; demonstrating evil will.

Siren (*sigh* ren). A device that makes a piercing sound by means of air, steam, etc., being forced through perforated revolving disks. It is used by official law enforcement vehicles as a warning and to make known the presence of an official or emergency vehicle. The use of the siren and warning lights does not relieve the officer from the exercise of care and caution in driving. It is not a license to violate the restrictions against stop lights and stop signs. It should be remembered that when the windows are closed and the radio is playing in another vehicle, the occupant may not hear the siren.

Sissy (*sis* ee). 1. An effeminate human male. A man or boy who acts like a girl. 2. Slang: One who demonstrates lack of courage in performing a dangerous task.

Sister-In-Law. Underworld slang: A woman who supports a man by prostitution.

Sit. To book bets by phone.

Sit-Down Demonstration. A situation wherein demonstrators sit or lie down, usually in a place where they will obstruct pedestrian or motor traffic. To remove them usually requires the use of physical force and results in the confrontation between police and demonstrators, which may result in the claim that excessive force and brutality were used by the police. Care should be taken not to use excessive force, and the demonstrators should not be injured if it is possible to remove them without physical injury.

Sit-Down Strike. A situation wherein striking workers stay in the place of employment, without working, for the duration of the strike. An officer should not take sides in a labor-management dispute but should maintain order and enforce the law.

Site Hardening. The making of an area, building, home, etc., harder for a criminal to successfully perpetrate.

Sitting Duck. Slang: A "setup"; an easy target.

Situational Drinker. A person who usually does not drink liquor but who does at certain events, parties, etc; a "social drinker."

Situation Theories. Theories attributing deviant behavior of normal persons to certain influential situations the persons are faced with.

Six-Shooter. Slang: A revolver holding six cartridges, all of which may be fired without reloading.

Sixty-Nine. Slang: Two people practicing oral sex simultaneously.

Skag. Narcotics slang: Heroin.

Skeleton Force. A part of the regular number of officers normally used to operate the department or shift; less than a full complement of officers who carry on an operation. Also called a skeleton crew.

Sketch, Measured Field. An accurate, detailed description of the crime scene.

Sketch, Rough. A general description of the scene of the crime.

Sketch, Scaled. An exact replication of the scene of the crime, drawn to scale by an expert.

Sketching. The drawing or charting of objects, places, or crime scenes to show details and/or the relative positions of objects and other evidence.

Skid. Narcotics slang: Heroin.

Skid Marks. The markings or imprints left on a travelled surface (road, street, or ground) by vehicle tires as a result of sliding or skidding. Skid marks are important in the investigation of traffic accidents. Calculations can be made of the direction and speed of a vehicle prior to the accident by examining the skid marks.

Skid Row. Slang: Section of a city where vagrants and derelicts are found. Cheap bars, sleeping quarters, and night spots are usually found there.

Skill or Science Game. 1. Any carnival game that requires some skill and/or practice to play. 2. Any game that the carnival operators call a skill game in order to mislead gambling authorities.

Skim. Gambling term: Money taken "off the top" in gambling operations and not reported or made known. This is a constant problem in gambling operations and is especially common in legalized gambling operations.

Skin. Slang: 1. To cheat or obtain something by fraud, deceit, or trickery. 2. One dollar bill.

Skin Game. Slang: A dishonest manipulation or trick; a game that operates through the use of trickery.

Skin Heist. Street slang: A rape or criminal assault.

Skin Popping. Slang: Injecting drugs under the skin.

Skulk. To move in a stealthy and concealed manner; to keep hidden.

Skyjacker. One who illegally hijacks an airplane. The United States government in 1970 started putting specially trained officers aboard passenger planes that were thought most vulnerable to such hijackers. The officers are called "sky marshals." See As the war against skyjacking steps up. *U.S. News and World Report,* December 28, 1970, p. 15.

Skylark. Prison slang: To engage in horseplay.

Sky Marshals. A group of officers who travel aboard passenger-carrying airplanes to protect against hijackers. They work in a federal program started in 1970 under the direction of Lt. Gen. Benjamin O. Davis, Director of Civil Aviation Security. As of December 23, 1970, a group of specially trained officers started replacing 1,200 marshals then in service.

Slab. The place of rest (table, carriage) upon which a dead body is placed in a morgue. "He was laid out on the slab at the morgue."

Slammed. In jail.

Slamming, It's. 1. "There is plenty of gambling action." 2. "Someone is cheating."

Slander (*slan* der). Statements made orally to persons other than the person being slandered, of a false, malicious, defamatory nature, which tend to injure the reputation, office, trade, business, or other means of making a living of the person to whom the statements pertain. "As a result of the statements made by Smith, I sued him for slander."

VOCABULARY

Slash. To cut or wound by a sweeping stroke or movement. "His wound was caused by a slash cut with a knife."

Sleeper. Slang: Something of value that has been overlooked.

Sleepers. A depressant-type drug, such as barbiturates.

Sleigh Ride. Narcotics slang: Under the influence of cocaine.

Sleuth (slooth). An undercover investigator; a detective (plainclothesman).

Slick. Slang: Smooth; sly; clever; tricky.

Slick Dice Missouts. Altered dice on which certain sides are made very smooth and other sides are made rough. This allows the dice to slide on the slick sides and roll when the rough sides are down, thus affecting the points on the sides opposite the slick sides.

Slip. 1. To move quietly and unobtrusively; to escape from; to get loose from. "He slipped away from the scene of the crime without being seen." 2. Gambling term: Record of a bet made with a bookie.

Slot Machine. A device for gambling into which the player drops a coin, in a slot; a "one-armed bandit." Slot machines are illegal in most states.

Slough (Slough Up). To close up. "We sloughed the game." "The police sloughed the town."

Sloven (*sluv* en). Dirty; not neat in dress, habits, or appearance.

Slow Pill. A depressant pill given to a race horse to slow its speed.

Slug. 1. A large piece of lead or other metal used as a projectile for firing in a shotgun. 2. Any bullet fired in a pistol or other sidearm or shoulder weapon. "He caught a slug in the shoulder."

Slums. A dirty, run-down, overcrowded part of a city or town.

Slut. An unkempt, dirty woman, usually with loose morals.

Sly. 1. Slick; cunning; crafty. 2. Doing things secretly. "He placed a bet on the sly."

Smack. Narcotics slang: Heroin.

Small Arms. Small firearms, such as pistols, rifles, shotguns.

Small Claims. Courts established and given jurisdiction over cases concerning very small amounts of money, usually fifty dollars or less. The fees are much less than other courts, but if the case is decided against the plaintiff, there is usually no right to appeal.

Smart Aleck. Slang: A conceited individual; a show-off.

Smart Bettor. One who knows winning odds in gambling.

Smart Money. Slang: Money bet by gamblers who, because of inside information, believe they have a bet that has little risk.

Smarty Pants. Slang: Smart aleck; one who overly demonstrates his knowledge.

Smashed. Intoxicated, "stoned," "high."

Smear. Slang: A malicious verbal or written attack made against a person, reflecting his character or reputation, usually by claiming that the attacked person did something that was wrong, unethical, or illegal.

Smog. Air polluted by smoke and fog.

Smoke. 1. Slang: Wood alcohol. 2. Denatured alcohol and water mixed to make a cheap smokey concoction.

Smoke Bomb. A grenade that emits smoke upon being triggered. Used to disperse crowds or to conceal someone so that protection against firearms attack will be increased.

Smokeless Powder. A gunpowder that gives off very little smoke when exploded.

Smoke Screen. A screen of smoke used for concealment. This may be useful in apprehending dangerous criminals where no suitable cover (protective objects) is near the location of the criminals. 2. Slang: A diversionary tactic that covers or distracts attention from the main point in question.

Smokey. Slang: A highway policeman.

Smoldering Fire. A fire that, because of insufficient oxygen, burns slowly and creeps along a wall or ceiling. Paints and resins in the wood are incompletely consumed, and the room is filled with nauseating black smoke. When fresh air is admitted to the room, it will immediately burst into flames.

Smoothbore. A gun that does not have a rifled barrel. "A shotgun is a smoothbore weapon."

Smother (*smuth* er). To kill by making breathing impossible; to suffocate.

Smudged Fingerprints. The imprint of finger ridges that is distorted—not clearly defined. This may be caused by lateral movement of the fingers while touching the surface on which the print is made, by having dirty or greasy fingers, or by having too much ink on the fingers.

Smudging. Ballistics term: Used to define smoke or soot that is deposited on the skin.

Smuggle (*smug* el). 1. To take goods (things of value) into or out of a country illegally. This is usually for the purpose of avoiding the payment of lawful duty on the items. 2. To clandestinely carry something in or out of a place, such as a jail or prison, without authority to do so. "The wife of the prisoner smuggled a hacksaw blade to him."

Smut. Dirty, obscene speech or written material, including obscene drawings and photographs; pornographic materials.

Snafu. Slang: Fouled up; disorganized; confused.

Snag. Slang: To attack an individual.

Snake. 1. Juvenile slang: Courier. 2. Slang: A crooked, dishonest person. 3. A habitual smoker of marijuana.

Snake Eyes. Slang: The "one" showing on both dice in a crap game.

Snatch, The. Slang: Stealing; kidnapping or abduction.

Snatch Man. A kidnapper.

Snatcher. A thief who grabs purses and other items believed to contain valuable things and quickly runs away with the stolen property.

Sneak. Gambling term: To operate gambling without the payment of hush money to anyone or to conduct a gambling operation without it being known to the police.

Sneak Thief. One who sneaks into unprotected property and steals miscellaneous articles. "While the door was open a sneak thief stole a typewriter."

Sneaky Pete. Slang: Inexpensive wine.

Sneeze. Slang: Arrest.

Snidebox. Slang: A safe that may be easily opened.

Sniffing (Horning). Using narcotics by sniffing through nasal passages, usually heroin or cocaine.

Sniper (*snigh* per). One who shoots at another from a place of hiding.

Snitch. Slang: 1. To steal or purloin. 2. An informer; to inform on someone.

Snob. One who looks down on those

beneath him in rank or position and caters to those above him; a "stuffed shirt."

Snooty (*snut* ee) (snut as in put). Slang: Conceited; "high-hatted"; thinking highly of one's self.

Snorting. Slang: Inhaling drugs.

Snow. Slang: Cocaine or heroin in crystalline form.

Snowbird. Narcotics slang: Heroin addict; cocaine user.

Snow Job. Slang: Flattery of someone to accomplish a purpose. "He did a snow job on me."

Sobriety (soe *bry* eh tee). Soberness; degree of soberness; degree of intoxication. Sobriety gauging device: See **Alcohol**.

Social. Concerning ways of behaving in or organizing a group.

Social Acceptance. Group approval of behavior.

Social Adjustment (Responses to). Making concessions to achieve greater goals.

Social Agencies. Political or social organizations.

Social Aggression. Overt hostility in word or action. In displaced aggression, A attacks B when he cannot attack C.

Social Alienation. Estrangement of a person from a group.

Social Anomie. Feeling of disorientation or social normlessness.

Social Attack. Assault on the object of one's frustrations.

Social Avoidance. Keeping away from the need to face realities.

Social Caste. An arbitrary social stratification system, with class-social ranking based on family, wealth, power, etc.

Social Change (Processes). Shift in existing relationships, status, beliefs, etc.

Social Clique (click). A small group of social intimates, exclusive in nature.

Social Compensation. Indulging in a substitute activity when the desired activity is impossible.

Social Competition. Vying of groups or interests for new positions.

Social Conflict. Frictions resulting from changed relationships.

Social Conformity. "Going along" when it is expedient to do so.

Social Constructs. Observable patterns of consistent behavior.

Social Control. Process of maintaining social organizational patterns.

Social Cooperation. Joining forces to achieve common goals.

Social Deviance. Behavior at variance with group norms.

Social Discrimination. 1. To distinguish between groups or individuals. 2. Unequal treatment.

Social Disorganization. Breakdown of normal patterns of behavior.

Social Displacement. Shifting viewpoints to rationalize behavior.

Social Distance. Degree of dissimilarity between groups.

Social Elite. Recognized superior group or individuals by power, birth, etc.

Social Function. What an aspect of society is supposed to do.

Social Gang. Group of like persons; connotes crudity.

Social Group. 1. Any aggregate of people. 2. Control (normal) versus experimental group.

Social Hierarchy (*high* er ar kee). Vertical social arrangement of classes, individuals.

Social Image. Impression an individual or group makes on self or others.

Social Inertia. State of social or cultural arrest.

Social Institutions. Organized ways of behaving; for example, family, school, church (getting married).
Social Integration. Fusing of groups to the extent of mutual interests, as contrasted to disintegration—the breakdown of former relationships.
Social Intervention. Introduction of new ideas, procedures, traits, etc.
Socialism (*soe* shel izm). A system of collective ownership of the means of production, distribution, and exchange with control being in the government, ostensibly operating for the benefit of all the people and not for profit. The slogan "from each according to his ability and to each according to his need" is a favorite of the socialists. Socialism is the early stages of communism. Russia still refers to itself as a socialist state. Under the socialism-communism governments the people have little voice in their affairs and their lives and activities are regulated by the government. See **Communism**.
Socialist Party (*soe* shel ist). A political party that works to establish and support socialism.
Socialization. Formal or informal learning processes by which individuals become committed to and accept the behavioral norms of a group. The process involves Self-concept—how we see ourselves as a result of forming perceptions of our social roles.
Social Justice. The fair distribution of important goods and services such as housing, education, and health care.
Social Marginality (mar jin *al* i tee). 1. Sense of identification with two or more groups. 2. Economics: Occupying the most precarious position.
Social Mobility. Movement up, down, or across social or geographical lines.
Social Model. Standard or norm. Possibly theoretical.
Social Ostracism. Rejection or isolation by or from a group.
Social Position. One's recognized place in the social hierarchy.
Social Problem. Tension resulting from change in relationships.
Social Sanction. 1. To approve certain conduct, programs, etc. 2. Legal, moral, or social pressures imposed on members of society in order to achieve conformity to group expectations.
Social Science. The discipline that pertains to man as a member of society; man and his society; the body of knowledge concerning man as a part of society.
Social Security. In the United States, a system organized and operated by the Social Security Administration, a government agency. It is a system of old-age and unemployment insurance. It also aids those who are blind and disabled. The funds supporting the program are paid by the worker and his employer.
Social Security Administration. A federal agency of the United States administering a legally constituted old-age and unemployment insurance program, as well as other programs. See **Social Security**.
Social Status. Achieved position earned by an incumbent; ascribed status position according to group consensus or wishes. See **Social Position**.
Social Stratification. The structural social inequality ranking of persons from high to low on the social ladder. It is the core of all fundamental conflicts between the powerful and

VOCABULARY

the powerless, the privileged and the deprived.

Social Structure. Organization of the elements of a society.

Social System. 1. A group in which each part is interdependent with the other parts and with the whole. The elements of social systems are individual group members interacting with one another. 2. Ordered arrangement of interrelated roles about which there is some degree of consensus.

Social Tolerance. Indulgence of ideas or people different from one's own.

Social Value Judgement. Emotional attachment to a norm, idea, or belief.

Social Values. The accepted beliefs of a group.

Society (so *sigh* eh tee). 1. A group of people who share a common culture in a relatively self-sufficient system of interaction. 2. The organizational aspects of a culture group. 3. Heterogeneous Society—Social group composed of multiple ethnic and/or racial elements. 4. Homogeneous Society—Social group of essentially similar traits.

Society for the Prevention of Cruelty to Animals (SPCA). A nongovernmental agency operating in the United States for the prevention of cruelty to animals. It has offices and functions in many principal cities.

Sociology (soe see *ol* o jee). The science that deals with the beginning and development of human society, and the development of civilization and its attendant laws, which control humanity.

Sociopath (*soe* see oh path). A person with a character disorder; an antisocial personality.

Sodium Amytal (*soe* dee um *am* i tal).

So-called truth serum. See **Truth Serum**.

Sodomite. A person who has committed sodomy.

Sodomy (*sod* oh mee). The unnatural carnal copulation of a human with another human, usually of the same sex; human sexual relations with an animal.

Soft Player. 1. A beginning gambler. 2. A gambler who bets small amounts.

Soft-Point Bullet. A lead tipped bullet encased in metal, which mushrooms on impact.

Software. Digital computer term: Programs prepared to accomplish desired objectives with the computer, including input, output, the operations of the equipment, control systems, assemblers, etc. Contrasted with hardware.

Soldier (*sol* jer). Member of the family organization in organized crime who is below the rank of lieutenant. It is the soldier who actually does the work of the organization, such as corrupting public officials, enforcing the edicts or orders, etc.

Sole Prints. The prints, impressions, or formations of patterns of friction ridges on the sole of the foot.

Solicitation. Inducing another to commit a crime; counselling or enticing another to commit a criminal offense.

Solicitor. 1. Gambling slang: The person who solicits and takes bets for a bookmaker in a gambling operation. 2. A practitioner of the law (attorney) who practices law in a court of chancery.

Solicitor, Stationary. Gambling slang: A person who solicits bets at a fixed location for a bookmaker.

Solicitor General. In states having

no attorney general, he is the ranking law officer. Where there is an attorney general, the solicitor general is the next ranking law officer under the attorney general.

Solid. 1. Slang: Firmly entrenched in one's regard, intimate. "I was in solid with the boss." 2. A state of matter more dense than liquid or gas with no independent movement of particles and a rigid shape.

Solitary. Slang: Solitary confinement; confinement of a prisoner under conditions where he has little or no contact with other people.

Songbird. Slang: One who talks about his and/or others' participation in crime or other matters of interest to the police; a "canary"; one who "sings."

Soothsayer (**suth** say er). A "fortune teller"; one who predicts things to come.

Sorcerer (*sor* ser er). A magician; conjurer; one who practices magic in conjunction with evil spirits.

Sordid (*sor* did). Dirty; unclean; filthy; degraded, vulgar. "It was a sordid affair."

Sore. Slang: Irritated; mad; angry; peeved; offended. "Smith is sore at me for some reason."

Sot. Drunkard; one whose wits are dulled because of drink.

Soul Music. Slang: Music that allegedly appeals to the deep emotions of a person.

Sound a Person. Juvenile slang: Talk loud; to agitate; to taunt or needle.

Sound Barrier. A condition or phenomenon that an aircraft encounters when passing from subsonic to supersonic speed. It is caused by the flow of air around the plane when it approximates the speed of sound. A shock wave is created, which is felt and heard on earth as a loud noise. It can cause physical damage to such things as glass.

Soup. Slang: Nitroglycerin, generally obtained by boiling it out of dynamite. See **Nitroglycerin**.

Source. Where narcotics are obtained; a supplier, such as a pusher, dealer, or connection.

Souse. Slang: To make intoxicated. "He was soused and unable to walk when arrested."

South. 1. That part of the United States located south of the "Mason-Dixon Line," especially that part east and south of the western and northern borders of Missouri. 2. The Confederacy.

Sovereign (*sov* er in). Supreme power; highest; higher in position than all others.

Sovereign Immunity. A doctrine under which the government and its subdivisions, in the conduct of governmental functions, is immuned from civil (tort) liability resulting from wrongful (tortious) acts of its agents (employees). This doctrine does not apply in a situation where the government is engaged in a proprietary function (such as owning and operating a public water system). In 1946 the Federal Tort Claims Act abolished this immunity as pertains to the federal government. Some states have also abolished the immunity. Courts in other states are striking it down. Reference: Walters, Douglas M.: Civil liability for improper police training. *The Police Chief,* Nov. 1971, p. 28.

Sovereignty (*sov* er in te). The possession of and right to supreme power.

Soviet. Council or legislative body. In the Soviet Union it is any of the

VOCABULARY

many assemblies, from the local level to the highest legislative body—the Supreme Soviet.

Soviet Union. Union of Soviet Socialist Republics. Composed of Soviet republics located in Europe and Asia.

S.P. (SP). State Police or Shore Patrol.

S.P.A. (SPA). State Planning Agency (under the LEAA program).

Space Out (Spaced). In a daze, particularly a daze resulting from a trip due to use of drugs.

Spadework. Slang: Fundamental and detailed work preparatory to accomplishing an objective.

Sparse (spars). Thinly distributed; scanty.

Spat. A small quarrel.

Spatz. Capsules.

S.P.C.A. (SPCA). Society for the Prevention of Cruelty to Animals.

Speakeasy. Slang: A place where alcoholic beverages are sold illegally.

Special Appearance. An appearance of a defendant in court for a particular purpose only, usually to challenge the court's jurisdiction.

Special Endorsement. An endorsement that can only be endorsed by the person so named on the instrument.

Special Verdict. A verdict in which the jury states the bare facts as they find them to be and asks the advice of the court thereon.

Special Police. Public or private security forces for parks, harbors, transit systems, buildings, personages, etc.

Specific Intent. The design or determination to do or not to do, or perform or not perform, a certain act. This specific intent is necessary in certain types of crime. See **Intent**.

Specimen. An item of physical evidence, or that which might be evidence, in a criminal case, especially as concerns items submitted to a crime laboratory. The laboratory may list or record the items as Questioned (Q) Specimens or as Known (K) Specimens, according to the nature of the evidence, i.e. whether it came from a known source. See **Questioned Specimens; Known Specimens**.

Spectrograph (*spek* tre graf). A device used for photographing elements of the light spectrum. It is used in the crime laboratory for making a spectrogram (the photograph), produced when various inorganic substances are examined to determine their composition. It is useful in detecting the presence of minute quantities of materials.

Speed. Narcotics slang: Methamphetamine and a variety of amphetamine drugs; a stimulant drug that can be fatal in overdoses.

Speedball. Slang: An injection of a stimulant and a depressant, originally heroin and cocaine.

Speed Detectors. Devices or systems used to measure the speed of moving vehicles. See **Radar; Vascar**.

Speed Freak. Slang: Habitual user of methamphetamines.

Speedy Trial. Law: The right to a trial at an early date as guaranteed by the Sixth Amendment of the United States Constitution. In 1970 the United States Supreme Court held that the state did not give the defendant a speedy trial where he was not tried for six years while he was serving a term in a federal prison during which time the state maintained a detainer against him and the defendant repeatedly asked for a trial by the state. (Dickey v. Florida, 90 S.Ct. 1564).

Sperm. Seminal fluid containing the male reproductive cells (spermatozoa); semen.

Spermatozoon (spur ma tow *so* on). Plural: Spermatozoa. Male animal reproductive cell contained in seminal fluid.

Spike. 1. To add alcohol beverage to a drink that did not contain alcohol. "Did he spike the punch?" 2. Narcotics slang: Hypodermic needle and syringe.

Spindle. A part of the combination lock mechanism on a safe. The combination dial fits on the outer end of the spindle, and its function is to turn the lock mechanism when the dial is rotated. On some types of safes, burglars gain entry by punching or pulling the spindle.

Spineless. Not strong willed; having little or no resistance to temptation; no "guts."

Spinster. An unmarried woman past the age when marriage normally occurs.

Spiral Cracks in Glass. The concentric cracks in glass that has been broken from a force applied against its flat surfaces. These cracks are comparable to the rim of a wheel and connect the radial cracks, which compare to the spokes of a wheel.

Spirits. Liquid containing ethyl alcohol and water that is distilled from an alcoholic liquid or mash.

Spitfire. Slang: A female who has a quick temper and "spunk."

Splash. Slang: Speed.

Splint. Support or brace, usually made of wood, steel, plastic or other rigid material. Used to hold a broken limb (arm, leg, etc.) in place. "If nothing else is available, a thick magazine or similar object can be folded around the limb and tied or strapped in place to act as a temporary splint."

Splinter Group. A minority group that breaks away from the main group. "The Communist Party and several of the major radical organizations have splinter groups."

Split. To leave, flee, break up with.

Spoils System. In American politics, "To the victor goes the spoils." The method of awarding public positions and jobs to the elected officials' friends and supporters without regard to public interest or welfare.

Spontaneous Combustion. A phenomenon of substances generating enough heat to ignite. Certain substances, such as coal dust, charcoal, flour, hay, fabric, or paper soaked in oil (especially linseed oil), retain and concentrate oxygen of the air on their surfaces. Heat is thus generated, and in the absence of sufficient circulation of air, fire will start.

Spontaneous Combustion, Semi–. A phenomenon of materials igniting when subjected to temperatures substantially lower than the normal ignition point. This is caused by the formation of a thin film of charcoal on the surface, which is oxidized by oxygen in the air, thus raising the temperature to the normal ignition point.

Spontaneous Declaration. An utterance made as a result of some sudden and/or shocking event, such as an accident or crime. See **Res Gestae.**

Spoon. A quantity of heroin, theoretically measured on a teaspoon (usually between 1 and 2 grams), 16 spoons per ounce.

Spooning. Inserting a spoon or similar device into the payout mechanism of a slot machine in order to cheat it.

VOCABULARY

Sport. 1. Form of amusement. 2. Game. 3. Slang: A flashy dresser or showy individual.

Sporting Games. Gambling term: Athletic events and races on which bets are placed; betting on such events.

Sports Line. Gambling term: See **Line.**

Sports Office. The formation of a working arrangement between two or more big (handling large volumes of bets) bookies so as to take care of a larger volume of betting business.

Spot. Gambling term: 1. A certain site used by a numbers writer in his part of the operation. 2. To allow an opponent a handicap. 3. To catch on to an irregularity in the game.

Spot Cash. Slang: Payment made immediately for merchandise bought or services rendered.

Spot Controller. Gambling term: A controller who usually makes large bets and who operates without pick-up men.

Spouse. The partner of a married person, i.e. the wife is the spouse of the husband and vice versa. "Mrs. Jones and her spouse were present."

Spreading the Play. Gambling term: Laying off of bets by the bookies.

Springer. Slang: One who can get by the bookies.

Spur. Fingerprint term: A ridge detail in a fingerprint, also called a "hook." A hooklike ridge or small branch emanating from a single ridge line.

Spurious (*spure* e es). Counterfeit; false; not genuine. "The document was spurious."

Squalor. Wretched poverty; dirt; filth.

Square. Slang: 1. One who does not know of or participate in the newest fads or styles. 2. "Hippie" term: One who does not engage in "hippie" activities or have the appearance in dress, hairstyle, etc. 3. Prison slang: One who is not a "dude" or a "character." 4. Narcotics slang: One who does not use narcotics or drugs. 5. A prostitute's term for a woman who does not engage in prostitution. 6. Gambling term: An honest police officer.

Square Deal. Slang: A fair and honest business transaction; to treat one fairly.

Square John. 1. Prison slang: Anyone who is not a "character." 2. A victim.

Square Up, To. Prison slang: To seek rehabilitation and be successful in getting a job and staying out of prison.

Squatter (*skwat* er). A person who occupies and lives on another person's real property without authority or title.

Squawk (skwok). To make a loud complaint or protest. "He squawked when arrested for the traffic violation."

Squeal. Slang: To inform on someone; to act as an informer.

Squealer. Slang: An informer to the police.

Squeeze. 1. The operating control on an electronic cheating apparatus. 2. Coersion.

Squib (Squib Load). A defective or weak load.

Stab in the Back. Slang: Injure or attempt to injure someone in an underhanded or treacherous manner.

Stacked Deck. A deck of cards secretly arranged to the dealer's advantage.

Staff. In the law enforcement agency organizational structure, staff is the person or group of persons who work with, advise, or do specialized work for the head or other line personnel of the agency. They do not do active law enforcement functions, such as patrolling or detective work. The latter are referred to as line officers.

Staff Functions. Doing things of an advisory, specialized, or technical nature that are not concerned directly with carrying out of the main objectives of the department. Such things involve fiscal matters for the department, personnel hiring and training, planning and research, etc. Contrasted with Line Functions.

Stake. Something put up or wagered in a bet; money or other things of value risked or bet on the outcome of some event or something. "Smith held the stakes of the bettors."

Stake Man. A financier of criminal venture.

Stake Out. Slang: To observe or watch a person or place.

Stall. 1. Delay by means of subterfuge or pretext. "He tried to stall the officer in making the arrest by claiming he was sick." 2. Slang: Member of a pickpocket gang; the partner or accomplice of a "pants-pocket" pickpocket.

Stamp. Gambling term: The fifty-dollar occupational stamp that federal law requires that gamblers (bookies) buy.

Stand. 1. Abbreviation for witness stand, chair, or seat in a court. 2. To stand firm or "pat" on some issue.

Stand (Standing). The halting of a vehicle, whether occupied or not, other than temporarily for the purpose of and while actually engaged in receiving or discharging passengers.

Standard Metropolitan Statistical Areas. Two hundred and twelve thickly populated areas in the United States as categorized by United States Census Bureau in its 1960 census. These metropolitan areas comprise 313 counties and 4,144 cities, each having its own police force. According to FBI reports, approximately 83 percent of Part I crimes (*Uniform Crime Reports*) occurred in these areas in 1965.

Stand-In. Gambler's term: An accommodation arrest.

Standing. A person's position in reference to his capacity to act in a particular situation, e.g. whether or not he has the right to bring suit against someone else.

Stand Mute. In the case of a felony charge, the refusal of a prisoner to plead, whether it be "guilty" or "not guilty."

Stand Pat. Unchanging on an issue; to stand firm on something.

Standup Guy. Slang: One who never confesses.

Stanley's Stuff. LSD purportedly manufactured by Augustus Owsley Stanley III. See **Owsley's Acid**.

Star, The Man who Wears the. Slang: A law enforcement officer. The star-shaped badge is widely used in law enforcement.

Starboard (*star* berd). The right side of a boat or ship when one is facing the front of the vessel when on board.

Star Chamber. A trial secretly held in early England where torture was used as a means to obtain a confession.

Stardust. Slang: Cocaine.

Stare Decisis (*stair* e dee *sise* is). Latin: The doctrine of precedent. Under this doctrine, judges are bound by previous court decisions.

Stash. 1. Slang: To hide something away for possible use in the future;

VOCABULARY

to put something away. 2. Drug user term: A supply of drugs in a secure place.

State Lawyer. A lawyer appointed by the court for indigent defendants.

State Police. The law enforcement agencies that operate at a state level rather than at a county or municipal level.

State's Evidence. Testimony by a codefendant, accomplice, or associate in crime, who admits his participation in the crime and testifies against the others involved in the crime; evidence offered by or on behalf of the prosecution in the trial of a criminal case.

State's Rights. The power and authority given to the states of the union by the United States Constitution. The rights of the states, under this doctrine, are based on the Tenth Amendment of the United States Constitution, which states, "The powers not delegated to the United States by the Constitution, nor prohibited by it to the states, are reserved to the States respectively or to the people."

Statistics, Crime. See **Crime Statistics**.

Status. A person's position in a social group, including ranking and rating.

Status Assignment System. The process of status ordering and giving within a social system. The hierarchy of cultural values and role concepts by the participants of a social system. Those on the top possess the most status and those on the bottom the least.

Status Inconsistency. The condition of having conflicting status position, such as a woman astronaut or a black doctor. A black doctor would be considered black before his status as a doctor would be considered.

Status Offense. An offense committed by a juvenile that would not be an offense if committed by an adult, e.g. truancy, running away from home, etc.

Status Quo. A thing or condition remaining as it has been.

Statute (*stach* ute). A law created and passed by a legislative body.

Statute of Frauds. The provision that no suit or action shall be maintained on certain classes of contracts or engagements unless there shall be a note or memorandum thereof in writing signed by the party to be charged or by his authorized agent.

Statute of Limitations. A statute (law) setting forth the time allowed the state for the beginning of prosecutive action against the accused and the time limitations between the date of institution of prosecution and the beginning of the trial in a criminal case.

Statutory (*stach* e tor e). Law: Pertaining to a law or statute, i.e. a law enacted by a legislative body.

Statutory Rape. Sexual intercourse between a man and a woman who is not his wife and is not yet of legal age; the offense may either be with or without the woman's consent. Legal age varies from state to state.

Stay. A postponement or delay in executing a court order; a court-ordered postponement of executing an act.

Steal (steel). To appropriate or take something of value that is in the ownership of another without the consent of the owner; to commit theft; purloin.

Stealth (stelth). The act of moving carefully without being seen; slyness; secretiveness.

Steam Horse. Gambler's slang: A sure thing; a certain winner.

Steerer (*steer* ur). The one, in certain types of confidence games, who guides the victim to do certain things. It is usually the steerer who arranges for the victim of the swindle to obtain the money and take other prescribed actions. He "steers" the victim.

Steer Joint. A gambling establishment that cheats its patrons.

Stench Bombs. Grenades or similar devices that contain foul-smelling chemicals; stink bombs.

Step Length. The distance between the centers of the two successive heelprints made by a person walking.

Step Out in Cuffs. To be released from prison to face another charge that is pending.

Stereotype. A mental construction of a typical member of a group or type of person.

Stern. The end of a boat or ship opposite to the bow. The back end of the vessel.

Stew. Slang: Worry or fret about a matter; a concerned state of mind.

Stick. Slang: 1. A marijuana cigarette. 2. Gambling slang: A house bettor under the guise of a regular player. 3. A carnival game bettor who does the same and adds to the buildup by winning prearranged games.

Stickers. Slang: Stamps.

Stickman. Gambling term: The person who operates a dice table.

Sticks. Slang: The suburbs of a city; rural country.

Stick-Up. Slang: An armed robbery; a "heist."

Stick-Up Man. Slang: A robber.

Stiff. 1. Slang: A dead body; a corpse. 2. Gambler's term: A horse to be held up, i.e. his speed reduced.

Stigma. A stain on one's reputation, a mark of disgrace or infamy.

Still. A distillery; a mechanism for distilling liquids; the distillery used by "moonshiners" for making illegal whiskey.

Stillborn. A baby born dead.

Stimulant. A drug or other substance that increases the physiological processes of the body.

Stink Weed. Marijuana.

Stipulate (*stip* ye late). To agree or covenant. An attorney representing one or more parties in a legal action may stipulate certain things as facts without a witness testifying to such.

Stipulation (stip ye *lay* shen). An agreement between attorneys representing different parties to perform or refrain from doing something in connection with a case in progress in court or pending court action.

Stir. Slang: A penitentiary.

Stir-Agent. Slang: A cheap lawyer who seeks clients in jails.

Stir-Crazy. Slang: Mentally lacking or deranged from a long period of imprisonment.

Stirwise. Slang: Knowing how to get by in prison.

Stock Joint. A carnival game that awards prizes to the winners.

Stocky. A descriptive term for the body; heavy-set; having a solid build; being wider than usual for one's height.

Stolen Property File. A file in which stolen property is listed by description and identification features (i.e. numbers) as a reference when suspected stolen property is recovered by law enforcement agencies. Much of this is now done with computers.

Stoned. Slang: Drunk or under the influence of narcotics (especially marijuana).

VOCABULARY

Stoned Smile. A fixed or constant grin sometimes caused by heavy use of marijuana.
Stool (Stoolie). Slang: An informant for the police.
Stool Pigeon. Slang: An informer, usually for law enforcement.
Stop. To cease to continue.
Stop and Frisk. A law operative in many states and upheld by the United States Supreme Court in Terry v. Ohio, authorizing a police officer to pat down a person who is suspected of having committed, is committing, or is about to commit a crime and the officer's life or limb is endangered.
Stop Sign. A sign placed at a road intersection or other appropriate place with the word "STOP" on it. The purpose is to cause moving traffic to stop before proceeding further.
Store. Any carnival game. See **Joint**.
Storefront. A rented facility used by police departments to promote PCR (Police-Community Relations). Used variously as a social service, complaint, or social center for citizens. The idea is to humanize police service in an unofficial setting.
Story. The relating of what purports to be facts by one who is being interviewed.
Stowaway. One who secrets or conceals himself aboard an airplane, bus, train, or ship, usually with the intent to avoid paying the fare.
STP. Popular designation for DOM: a hallucinogenic drug.
Straight. 1. Gambling term: A poker hand where five cards (not in the same suit) are in sequence. In roulette, a bet on one number. 2. Slang: An OK guy. 3. Living as a law-abiding citizen. 4. Not under the influence of narcotics. 5. Juvenile slang: Applied to a peddler—gives a good deal.
Straight Flush. Gambling term: In a poker hand, five cards of the same suit in sequence.
Straight Jacket. A strongly made garment (cloth) that restrains the use of the arms of a person on whom it is placed. Its purpose is to prevent a violent person (mentally deranged or one overly excited or disturbed from other causes) from injuring himself or others.
Strangers. Slang: Police.
Strangle. Choke; to prevent breathing by applying pressure to the neck; a frequent cause of death (strangulation).
Strategy. Design to strike at the heart of a problem. Compare with logistics—mobilizing resources to attack a problem.
Street, On the. Not in custody; not locked up; free either on bond or on recognizance or with no charges pending.
Street, The. Slang: The outside world; the community.
Street or Highway. A thoroughfare especially in a city, town, or village.
Street People. Drug user's slang: Ill-educated, drug-ridden youths.
Streetwalker. A prostitute, especially one who solicits business by walking the streets.
Stretch. Slang: Time served in a prison.
Strict Liability. 1. Absolute liability. 2. To hold legally liable for an injury resulting to another person, no matter what the standard of care exercised may have been.
Strike. Confidence game operator's slang: Successful completion of a con game, with the "fleecing" of the victim.
Strikebreaker. A person who aids in

breaking a labor strike by working in the place of strikers or who arranges for others to perform such work. This situation may lead to violence.

Striking a Jury. The selecting or nominating a jury of twelve men of the whole number returned as jurors on the panel.

Striking Energy. The impact energy of a projectile, usually measured in foot-pounds.

String. Slang: To deceive one through flattery or otherwise; to fool.

String Up. Slang: To hang someone.

Strings, Pull. Slang: To manipulate things so as to gain an advantage. This usually consists of using influence on those who have power to help.

Strip-Frisk. Searching a prisoner very completely by having him disrobe.

Stripper. Slang: One who does the striptease.

Strippers. Gambling slang: Cards in a deck the size (width or length) of which has been changed so they can be manipulated in dealing. 2. Entertainers who remove most or all of their clothing.

Stripping, Car. The removal of the parts of an automobile. Usually this is done to a car that has been stolen, or the parts are removed and stolen from a car that is still in the possession of the owner. The parts are stolen usually with the intent to sell them.

Strip Search. 1. A search of a crime scene, usually outdoors, where the terrain to be searched is divided into strips and searched carefully strip by strip. This should be followed by a grid search, which consists of dividing the area into strips at right angles to the lines used in the strip search. 2. A search of the person where the wearing apparel is removed, during which the clothing and body should be thoroughly searched.

Striptease. A burlesque act in which a female undresses by removing pieces of clothing one at a time, while making body movements to the accompaniment of music.

Strobe Unit. Photographic term: A device, electronic in nature, that can be used repeatedly for a flashlight source; it has the same effect as a flashbulb but can be used again without replacing the bulb or light.

Strong-Arm (Strong-Arm Man). Slang: One whose job it is to do acts of violence on people; a thug, usually working for someone else, who uses violence to accomplish his objectives.

Strong-Arm Robbery. Robbery committed without a weapon but with some actual force or threat of force.

Struck Jury. 1. A special jury. 2. A jury that is not chosen from the regular panel but from a panel drawn for a particular case.

Strung-Out. Slang: Addicted to or involved with drugs for a long period of time, resulting in a condition of mental and/or physical exhaustion.

Strychnine (*strich* nin). A poison, bitter in taste, composed of white (colorless) crystals, derived from nux vomica and certain other plants. The medical profession uses it in small quantities as a medicine.

Stuck Out. Prison slang: Said of an inmate. Not accomplishing the desired amount of work.

Students for a Democratic Society (SDS). Founded in 1962 by a small group of students at Port Huron, Michigan. It has spread and become more militant, violent, and destructive. In 1971 it had 200 to 250 chapters and membership of about 40,000. It has come under Marxist influence. Its hatred is directed against society (called the Establishment).

Student Nonviolent Coordinating Committee (SNCC). An extremist organization formed in the 1960s. It was formerly under the leadership of Stokeley Carmichael and H. Rap Brown. As of 1969 it had developed into a full-blown all-Negro revolutionary organization. Reference: Testimony of John Edgar Hoover, Director, Federal Bureau of Investigation, before the House Subcommittee on Appropriations, April 17, 1969.

Study Release (Juveniles). The release of offenders from institutions in order for the offenders to continue their formal education while still under the custody of the institution.

Stuff. 1. Slang: Heroin; narcotics in general. 2. Prison slang: Heroin, morphine, or Dilaudid.

Stun. To render unconscious or semiconscious; to become confused and mentally upset by actual force or events.

Stupid. Slow-witted; low in intelligence; not exercising normal facilities; uninteresting.

Stupor. State of mind characterized by reduced use of senses, inability to reason, and uncoordination.

Sua Ponte. Latin: Of its or his own will or motion; voluntary; without prompting or suggestion.

Subculture. A group that is set apart from the wider culture by distinctive features while still retaining the general values of the wider culture.

Subject. 1. Law enforcement term: The person under investigation or about whom information is being sought by a peace officer. 2. Moulage or casting term: The object or impression to be reproduced or cast.

Sublimation (sub le *may* shen). 1. To deflect sexual or other biological energies into socially constructive or accepted activities. 2. Unconscious substitution of goals to achieve social acceptance.

Submachine Gun (*sub* ma *sheen*). A readily portable machine gun that can be fired from the shoulder or from the hip. It can be fired full automatic or semiautomatic. It is often referred to as the "Tommy gun," which derived its name from the Thompson submachine gun.

Submission. Capitulation to social pressure.

Submit. To present for consideration; to offer.

Suborn (se *born*). To cause, persuade, or bribe a person to give false testimony (commit perjury) while under oath in a judicial matter.

Subornation of Perjury. The act of secretly procuring, preparing, or instructing a witness to give false testimony; any act that allures or disposes to perjury.

Subpoena (se *pea* na). Law: A judicial order, in writing, commanding a person to appear in court or other legally delegated places to testify. Some states provide for a subpoena to be issued at the insistance of the District Attorney or Coroner to require persons to appear before them for testimony in connection with official investigations being conducted by them. The word subpoena is sometimes used synonymously with summons, although they are not the same in many states.

Subpoena Duces Tecum. Latin: A judicial order, in writing, commanding a person to produce in court certain documents, papers, or other evidence, which are allegedly pertinent to matters being considered. The term means "under penalty you shall bring with you."

Subrogation (sub row *gay* shen). Law: The substitution of one person for another insofar as legal claims or rights are concerned.

Sub Rosa (*sub row* za). Latin: Privately or confidentially.

Substance. Essential or real part of anything; matter of which something is consisted.

Substantial. Real; true; of considerable importance or value.

Substantive Law. Laws of or consisting of legal rights and principles as distinguished by rules of form.

Subterfuge. A strategy (deceit, misrepresentation) used by a person to avoid an unpleasant or difficult situation.

Suburb. A place (settlement, village, or town) adjacent to a city.

Suburban. Of or pertaining to a suburb. Living in a suburb.

Suburbanization. The movement of the population from the center city to surrounding suburbs.

Subversion. Demolition; overthrow; destruction; a cause of destruction or overthrow, especially of a government.

Succumb (se *kum*). To yield; to give in to; to give way; to die.

Sucker. 1. Slang: A gullible person; a victim in a con game or swindle. 2. Gambler's term: Any customer of a gambling casino; an especially naive gambler.

Sucker Bet. A wager giving the hustler a high chance of winning.

Suction-Bevel Missouts. Gambling slang: Crooked dice having concave sides opposite those that are to appear most often.

Suds. Slang: Alcoholic drinks, especially beer.

Sue. To bring a lawsuit against another; to commence a legal action.

Suede. Slang: Negro.

Suffocate. To kill by depriving one from getting enough oxygen; to smother.

Suffrage. The right to vote.

Sugar. Slang: LSD. See **Hallucinogens**.

Sugar Daddy. Slang: An old man who supports a prostitute or contributes money to her.

Sugar Lump. Slang: LSD. See **Hallucinogens**.

Suicide. The act of intentionally taking one's own life.

Suicide Wounds. Aside from the hesitation marks, there is usually only one major wound causing death to the suicide victim.

Suit. Action to obtain justice in a court of law.

Sullen. Silent because of anger or emotional disturbance; gloomy.

Sullivan Act. A law of New York State making it a felony to possess firearms without legal authority.

Summart. Done without delay or ceremony; done instantly or quickly; without formality. Law: Instanter; a trial without a jury.

Summary Court Martial. The military court that is the lowest of the three grades of court martial in terms of the severity of the penalty that it can impose.

Summary Probation. Probation granted generally without supervision.

Summation. A concise statement of the facts.

Summing Up. A concise summation.

Summons. A written order for one to appear at a certain time and place. Summons are frequently issued by a police officer to a traffic violator. In some states they may be issued for any misdemeanor instead of making an arrest. They may also be issued by a judge or magistrate. A summons is not an arrest warrant, and the serving of a summons is not making an arrest.

Sunstroke. An illness caused by exposure to the sun's rays or to excessive heat. It is characterized by a sudden onset of high fever and headache. Convulsions and coma may develop. Also called "heatstroke."

Super Dropper. Gambler's term: A gambler who is crooked.

Superimpose. Put one thing on top of another.

Supersede. To discard or set aside; succeed.

Supersedeas. A writ having in general the effect of a command to stay, on good cause shown, some ordinary proceedings that ought otherwise to have proceeded.

Supervening Cause. A new effective cause that, operating independently of anything else, becomes proximate cause of the incident.

Supper Man. Slang: A burglar who steals from a residence between the hours of 7 PM and 9 PM, while the occupants are having dinner.

Supporting Evidence. Evidence that will bolster and strengthen such evidence as eyewitness testimony, transfer evidence, and statements of the accused. Supportive evidence includes such things as proof of motivation (motive), similarity of modus operandi of other crimes known to have been committed by the accused, the accused having possession of the stolen property, etc.

Suppress. To restrain from, prohibit, or prevent.

Supreme Court, State. Usually the highest court in the state judicial system.

Supreme Court of the United States. The highest court of the nation, it is the court of last resort for matters coming from both the federal and the state courts. It is headquartered in Washington, D.C., and composed of the Chief Justice and eight justices.

Sure Thing Man. Gambler's term: A gambler who is crooked.

Surname. The family name; last name.

Surplus Repression. A person denying himself bodily pleasures as a result of pressures from society.

Surprise. Law: A procedural pleading available to parties to a trial when something unexpected, unanticipated, and which could not be prevented by due diligence develops. The side that is disadvantaged by such a development may plead surprise.

Surrender. To give up or resign; act of surrendering.

Surrender of Criminals. Delivering a person accused of a crime found in one jurisdiction to the authorities of the jurisdiction in which the crime was committed.

Surreptitious (sir epp *tish* us). Secretive; "on the sly"; secretly and without authority. "He moved his car surreptitiously."

Surveillance. Observation; close watch kept on someone; "tailing"; listening, by ear or technical equipment, to what someone says. Types of surveillance; visual, audio, contact.

Surveillance, Counter–. A person who is being watched has someone watch or observe the one doing the watching. A suspect being watched by an officer may arrange for an associate to "tail" the officer.

Suspect. Person suspected of having done an unlawful act.

Suspended Sentence. The suspension of imposition or execution of sentence, after a plea of guilty or a conviction, for a reasonable and determinate period.

Suspension. To withhold temporarily a person's driver's license or any such license.

Suspicion. To suspect; impression or belief.

Sustain. Uphold validity of; to confirm.

Suture (*sue* chur). To sew or stitch together the edges of a cut or wound.

Swag. Slang: Stolen goods or money; loot; booty.

Sweat. Slang: To worry or to be concerned.

Sweatbox. A punishment chamber for prisoners, made of metal, which becomes extremely hot during the day.

Sweating. Slang: Questioning and otherwise submitting a person to such pressure as to cause him to divulge information he is thought to have; generally refers to questioning and/or other treatment of a person in custody.

Sweepstakes. A system of gambling whereby all the money bet on an event may be won by one or a few. Horse racing is an example. Except for commissions, etc., which are deducted, all the money bet goes to the winner or winners.

Sweetheart Contract. Slang: A collusion between management and a dishonest labor leader to pay low wages to members of the union.

Swindle. To defraud or cheat one of his money, property, or other things of value.

Swinger. Gambler's term: A high-rolling person; a high roller.

Swinging. Having sexual relations as a couple with at least one other individual. "Swing open" means everybody together—several couples engaging in sexual relations as a group. In "closed swinging" the couples use individual bedrooms. Reference: The American way of swinging. *Time*, Feb. 8, 1971, p. 51.

Swing Man. Narcotics slang: Retailer in narcotics.

Swing with a Gang. Juvenile slang: To be a gang member.

Swipe. Slang: To commit theft; to steal.

Switchblade Knife. A knife the blade of which will open or extrude by a mechanical device, such as a spring.

Switcher. Gambling slang: A crooked gambler who substitutes altered dice or cards into a game in order to increase his chances of winning.

Symbolic Behavior. Token actions or gestures, conforming to norms but not necessarily sincere.

Symbolic Speech. A theory that actions and objects that convey ideas in lieu of oral communication constitute symbolic speech. A person who appeared in public wearing a shirt resembling the American flag was prosecuted for mutilation and defiling the flag. He claimed his actions were symbolic speech and thus were protected by the First Amendment of the Constitution. The appellate court did not agree with this theory, and his conviction was affirmed.

Symposium (sim *po* zee em). A scholarly convocation (meeting) for discussing certain subjects or matters.

Synanon. See **Therapeutic Community**.

Syndicate (sin de kit). A name

VOCABULARY

applied to the Mafia and other organizations whose purpose is to accomplish certain unlawful or questionable objectives. It also applies to legal and legitimate organizations whose activities are joined together for business purposes. See **Mafia**.

Syndicate Acid. Slang: STP.

Syndicate-Book. Horse racing slang: Bookmakers working together under one management.

Syndicate Security. Methods used by organized crime (La Cosa Nostra) for protecting themselves, their fellow members, their secrets, and their women. Reference: Salerno, Ralph and Tomkins, John: *The Crime Confederation*. Garden City, New York, Doubleday, 1969.

Synthetic. Artificial; spurious; made artificially by using certain ingredients to make a product that approximates a thing produced by nature.

Synthetic Analgesic. A manufactured or synthesized chemical that has the pain-relieving properties of a narcotic.

Syphilis (*siff* e lis). A venereal disease caused by a microorganism. It is transmitted by direct contact or from birth. It develops through three stages: primary, where a hard chancre develops where the infection starts; secondary, where the skin and blood are affected; tertiary, where the whole system is involved. Modern medical treatment is effective against the disease.

Syphilitic Insanity. Insanity arising from contracting syphilis (a form of venereal disease).

Systematic. In an organized way; relating to the whole body, plan, etc.

System Design. Computer term: Based on systems analysis, to provide for ultimate utility (use) of the equipment to satisfy present and future (foreseeable) needs.

Systems Analysis. Computer term: The study of the operations of an agency, including its goals and purposes, so as to understand current procedures and inherent problems. The object is to improve the system performance by designing an operation that will render assistance at each stage of operation of the agency utilizing the equipment needed for the purpose.

T

T. Slang: Marijuana.
Tab. Slang: Morphine.
Tactful. Considerate; diplomatic; discreet.
Tactical Squad. A special force of law enforcement officers trained to handle a specific crime and problems associated with the crime.
Tail. Slang: Maintain a moving surveillance; to follow closely and discreetly.
Take. Slang: 1. Corruption; receiving "payoffs." 2. Gambling slang: The difference between what has been taken in from bets and the amount paid to winners; the net profit. 3. To cheat or swindle a person.
Take a Draw. Slang: Take a chance.
Take-Down Rifle. Firearms term: A rifle so made that the action and barrel can be easily taken apart, thus making it more convenient to carry.
Take Joint. Gambler's term: A crooked gambling establishment.
Taking a Main. Narcotics slang: Injecting in a vein.
Taking a Nap. Slang: Serving a short jail sentence.
Taking the Odds. Gambling term: Betting the longer odds, i.e. 5 to 3, etc.
Talesman (*talz* min). A bystander who is chosen to serve on a jury when the jury is not filled by those who had been summoned for jury duty. The person so chosen may be present in court or outside the court.
Talk-Man. Juvenile slang: Negotiator.
Talk That Noise. Juvenile slang: Continue talking; it is interesting.

Tally Sheets. Gambling term: Numbered sheets of paper used to keep records of the amount bet on each number in a numbers game.
Tamped. Slang: Badly beaten.
Tamper. To fix, bribe, meddle with, or corrupt.
Tandem Semi-Trailer. Every semi-trailer having two load-carrying axles.
Tandem Truck. Every motor-propelled single vehicle designed for the conveyance of property or things for hauling purposes and having one front or steering axle and two rear or load axles, even though one of the load axles is not permanently affixed to the frame of the vehicle and may be removed.
Tangible. That which can be touched; definite.
Tank. Slang: A room in a jail, having little or no furnishings upon which a person could injure himself, where drunks are contained until they sober up; a drunk tank.
Tanked. Slang: Drunk, intoxicated.
Tanked (Tank) Job. Crooked; prearranged.
Tanked Up. Slang: Intoxicated or under the influence of drugs.
Tap, Wire–. Electronic surveillance; connecting a listening or recording device to a telephone or telegraph line in order to hear and/or record messages transmitted on the lines. This is sometimes referred to as "electronic surveillance"; however, the latter is broader in that it includes listening to communications without necessarily physically connecting with the transmission

VOCABULARY

lines; it may also include listening to oral messages by means of microphones, etc.

Tapanoia. Slang: Fear of telephone taps.

Tapes. Gambling term: The adding machine tapes on which the day's business of gambling operation is recorded.

Tappers. Slang: Dice that have been loaded with mercury that shifts when tapped.

Taste. A small sample of a narcotic.

Tat. Slang: 1. A con game using dice with only high numbers. 2. The die itself.

Tattooing (ta *too* ing). Gunpowder patterns; the marks left on the surface of the skin of a person who has been shot at fairly close range. It is caused from the residue of unburned powder in the propellant. From little or no pattern at contact range, the design or pattern increases in size with the increase in the distance of the muzzle of the weapon from the body until a distance is reached where none of the particles reach the body. The markings caused by these particles are black or red.

TD Caps. Time-disintegrating capsules.

Tea. 1. Slang: Marijuana. 2. Horse racing term: Illegal drugs given to a horse to increase his energy.

Team Policing. A combination of line operations into a team with a leader; officers, assigned to a permanent sector or geographic area, are totally responsible for the assigned area; a form of decentralized policing.

Tear Gas. A lacrimator; a chemical that causes unusual flow of tears, with irritation of the eyes. This is a valuable aid to law enforcement in subduing an unruly group or causing persons holing up in buildings to come out. It should be used with care. Its effects will linger for long periods of time, especially in such things as fabrics, stuffed furniture, and bedding. Its fumes will also spread to other parts of a building. If tear gas shells (projectiles) are shot, care should be taken that they do not strike a person, as serious injury may occur.

Tear Me Off. Juvenile slang: Permit me to leave.

Tear-Up. A cheat appears to tear up the victim's check that covers his losses. The real check is actually being cashed at that time by someone else.

Teeth. Plural of tooth. This is an important item in recording the physical description of a person.

Teethmarks. Marks left in a solid substance that is rigid enough to maintain its shape. Teethmarks left in things such as an apple or a piece of cheese can be of significance in the identification of the person who left the teethmarks.

Telegraph. To unconsciously give away; a cheating move that will or is being made.

Telephone Calls, Abusive or Obscene. Telephone calls of an offensive, abusive, or obscene nature received by persons from callers who will not usually identify themselves.

Telephone Numbers. Slang: Large sums of money.

Telephonic Search Warrant System. A system allowing officers to obtain needed search warrants over a telephone with electronic recording equipment.

Telephoto. A lens system used in a camera, which enlarges the image of distant objects. It is useful in getting photographs of objects at a distance. The camera should be operated on a fixed base, such as a tripod, inasmuch as any movement is magnified, which may result in blurring.

Temporary Restraining Order. The temporary order is usually issued after an ex parte hearing in civil court. The court fixes a future date and a time for a hearing by the parties to determine whether the order should be made permanent.

Ten-Dash Signals. See **Signals, Ten-Dash**.

Tender. Law: To offer money in payment of a debt or in fulfillment of a contract.

Tenderloin. Slang: Red-light district; that part of a city where prostitution and other vices flourish.

Ten Points. Gambling game. See **Razzle Dazzle**.

Tension (*ten* shen). Nervous strain; mental anxiety.

Tented Arch. A pattern where the ridge lines come in from one side and go out the other side without recurve or turning back and where the "upward" thrust of the lines at or near the center of the pattern is sharp or abrupt.

Terminal. Last, final; said of an illness or condition resulting from injury from which a person is not expected to recover.

Term of Court. A duration of time that a court holds sessions and hearings.

Territorial. Belonging or pertaining to a territory or area of the U.S.

Terrorism (*ter* er izem). The use of terror for coercion.

Testamentary (test to *ment* ar ee). Having to do with a will or testament. Obtained by or through a will.

Testamentary Evidence. Evidence that is given orally; oral evidence.

Testate. Having prepared a will.

Testator (tes *tay* ter). One who makes a will prior to death; one who dies leaving a will.

Testatrix (tes *tay* tricks). A woman who dies leaving a will.

Testify. Law: To give evidence in a court of law while under oath; to give testimony.

Testimony (*tes* te mow ne). The information or statements made in testifying; evidence furnished by a witness.

Texas Tea. Slang: Marijuana.

That'll Work. Juvenile slang: To understand.

Theft. Stealing; the act of committing larceny.

Theology. The study of religious beliefs.

Theory. A set of concepts arranged to explain and/or predict possible and probable relationships between phenomena.

Therapeutic (ther a *pew* tick). Having qualities tending to heal or cure diseases.

Therapeutic Community. The name of a program engaged in rehabilitation of addicts. Centers are used for this purpose. These are called by various names, including Synanon, Kinsman Hall, Odyssey House, Phoenix House. It seems to offer promise. It operates on the principle that ex-addicts can relate to and communicate effectively with addicts.

Therapy (*ther* a pea). Disease treatment.

Thermal Burning Bar. A device used by burglars for burning safes. It consists of a steel pipe filled with small steel rods and/or rods of other metals. One end of the pipe is threaded and thus can be coupled to an oxygen supply. It is ignited at the

VOCABULARY

end with a high temperature torch. It is capable of burning through steel, other metals, and even concrete.

Thick Witted. Slang: Mentally slow; dull; deficient.

Thief. One who steals without the use of force.

Thing. Slang: Heroin.

Thing, Doing My. Slang: A term used by some modern youth to denote what they like doing or what they want.

Third Degree. Slang: Vigorous, lengthy, and sometimes brutal methods used by police to obtain information or a confession. Modern police seldom use such methods. The courts condemn them, and evidence obtained in this manner is inadmissible in court. These methods should not be used.

Thoroughbred. A high-type hustler who sells pure narcotics.

Thoroughbred Racing Protective Bureau. An organization having the function of investigating certain practices forbidden by law or regulations pertaining to racehorses and horse racing.

Thrash. To whip or beat someone.

Thread Count. The number of threads per inch in a piece of fabric. This is a factor used by the crime laboratory in the examination and comparison of fabrics (cloth or clothing).

Three-Time Loser. Slang: A third offender, sometimes facing a life sentence as a habitual offender.

Thrombosis (throm *bow* sis). Blood clot in a blood vessel or the heart. This is one of the causes of a heart attack. It can be fatal or at least very serious.

Throttling. Strangulation with the hands.

Throw. Slang: To intentionally allow an opponent to win a sports event for ulterior motive—usually money.

Throw a Cop. See **Fairbank**.

Ticker. Slang: The heart.

Ticket. 1. Slang: Summons given to one who commits a nonserious crime, such as a traffic violation. 2. Gambler slang: The ticket—the results of a horse race listing the horses as they finished the first three positions, i.e. win, place, and show, and the amount paid for each position.

Tight. 1. Slang: Close to someone; friendly with or having pull with someone. 2. Difficult to do.

Time. Slang: Serving time in prison.

Time Bet. Gambling term: Accepting a bet on the premise that the race has not started.

Time of Death. The time that a person dies. This is important in homicide investigations and at times is of importance in civil cases.

Times. Gambling term: A unit of betting used in sports wagering. One time means five dollars.

Tip. Confidential information furnished to a law enforcement officer.

Tip Off. Slang: To warn someone of an impending occurrence.

Tip On Out. Juvenile slang: Depart; leave.

Tip Sheet. Horse racing term: A list of horses allegedly most likely to win. Distributed by people who make their living from such sales.

Tipsy. Slang: Unsteady because of partial intoxication.

Tire Tread. The design on the outer surface of a vehicle rubber (or similar material) tire. The marks and impressions made by such a tire can be used to identify the tire that made it.

Title. Legal ownership of property; documentary evidence of ownership of property.

Titration (tie *tray* shun). An analytical experiment that determines the amount of reactant required to react with a volume of another reactant.

Toasty. Juvenile slang: Boy or girl from a nice neighborhood.

Toe. Juvenile slang: To get drunk.

Toilet Workers. A thief or a group of thieves working together to steal from the victim's coat while he is in a restroom or toilet. Also known as "Donnegan workers."

Toke Up. To light a marijuana cigarette.

Tolerance, Drug. The phenomenon whereby the body builds up the capacity to use more narcotics, and thus it takes larger doses of the narcotics or drugs to achieve the feeling of well-being that was previously achieved with smaller doses; the ability of the body to absorb increased amounts of drugs.

Tommy Gun. A submachine gun deriving its name from the Thompson submachine gun. See **Machine gun.**

Tone Set. An electronic device used by the telephone company to "lock in" the line of an abusive caller.

Tong. Chinese in origin. In the United States it refers to organizations, generally secret, the members of which are Chinese.

Tonk. Juvenile slang: Card game.

Tooies. Tuinal® (brand of amobarbital sodium and secobarbital sodium) capsules.

Tool. Slang: The actual pickpocket in a team of pants-pocket workers pickpockets. The other partner is called the "stall."

Tool Marks. Marks, scratches, and depressions made by a hard object on another object or substance that is softer than the tool but is rigid enough to retain the marks. A screwdriver will make tool marks on a softer piece of metal with which it forceably comes in contact.

Top. 1. The gross intake from a betting operation or game. 2. High-ranking mob or civic officials who supply protection.

Topped. Slang: Hanged; executed.

Tops and Bottoms. Gambler slang: Dice that have been altered so that only three numbers appear on each die, thus the same number will appear on opposite sides of each die. Sometimes called misspots. This makes it impossible to throw certain numbers.

Top Secret. In government service, information that is ranked of extreme importance and that, if divulged without authority, might cause irreparable harm to the nation. Such information includes that which would bring about a break in diplomatic relations with another country or cause an armed attack upon the nation or its allies, or would compromise military or defense plans or other developments vital to the national defense.

Top Ten Most Wanted Criminals. A program of the FBI whereby a group of ten (or more) persons charged with major crimes are publicized and their photographs and descriptions published. They are each the subject of an Identification Order. This program has proven effective, and many wanted persons have been identified by members of the public, which resulted in their apprehension.

Torch. Slang: One hired to set fire to property illegally. Such a person may be an expert or a professional.

VOCABULARY

Tore. Juvenile slang: Violently beaten; intoxicated.

Torn Up. Slang: Intoxicated, stoned.

Torpedo. Slang: A gunman, bodyguard, or hit man who works for a criminal boss.

Torso (*tor* soe). The main part of the body, i.e. the body minus the arms, the legs, and the head.

Tort. A civil wrong; a private offense committed against an individual; a wrongful act that subjects the person doing it to civil liability, i.e. he is obligated by law to pay for the injury or damage caused. An act or failure to act may be a tort and a crime.

Tort Feasor. The person in a civil case who has committed the wrong; the defendant.

Tortuous. Wrongful.

Torture (*tor* cher). Subject one to intense pain. Used in former times by police to force a confession from a suspect. This has been outlawed by statute and the courts in the United States for many years.

Toss. Slang: To search.

Tossed. Slang: Deserted, as by a spouse or partner.

Total Institutions. Institutions, such as a prison, that devote themselves to the total resocialization of the persons admitted to those institutions.

Totalitarianism. The ideology that holds that the government of a nation should totally control the individuals in that nation.

Tote Board. Slang: The indicator at the racetracks that shows the parimutuel odds.

Touch. Slang: Borrowing or getting money, either as a loan or gift; proceeds of a crime.

Tough. 1. A rough individual. "He is a tough one." 2. Rough or difficult situation.

Tough Enough. Juvenile slang: Good-looking; agreeable.

Tout. One who gives what purports to be secret information about a horse race, usually for a fee or price.

Town Clown. Carnival slang: A detective or policeman.

Toxic (*tok* sik). Poisonous. "It is a highly toxic chemical."

Toxicology. A study or science that pertains to toxic substances and their characteristics, effects, and antidotes.

Toy. The smallest container of prepared opium.

Traced Forgery. The forging of writings accomplished by tracing the genuine writings onto another document. This is usually done by placing the genuine document over a lighted glass or other transparent surface and tracing the writings onto a document placed over the genuine writings. A qualified document examiner can detect this type of forgery due to the wavering lines in the forged writings.

Trace Elements. Minute quantities of chemical elements present in or on objects or materials. The crime laboratory has developed techniques for finding and analyzing such small amounts of chemicals, which can be useful in identifying two or more specimens as having come from the same source.

Trace Metal Detection Technique. Based on the finding that metal that comes into contact with the skin or clothing leaves traces, a technique has been developed to detect them. Traces vary according to weight, friction, and duration of the contact. The skin or clothing is treated with a harmless chemical test solution, allowed to dry, and then examined under ultraviolet light. Metal traces then appear as fluorescent colors. Different metals produce different colors. One use of the test is to determine if a person has handled a firearm. A description of the technique can be obtained in a manual, "Trace Metal Detection Technique," from the National Institute of Law Enforcement and Criminal Justice, 633 Indiana Avenue, N.W., Washington, D.C. 20530.

Tracer (*tray* ser). A bullet coated with a chemical that lights and burns while the bullet is in flight so its path may be followed. These are helpful in night firing.

Track. 1. To follow and locate a person being sought, such as a criminal. "The police tracked down the robber." 2. Abbreviation for racetrack.

Tracked Up. Having numerous injection marks along the vein.

Tracking. The following of an individual through the entire criminal justice process; this technique is still rarely used.

Track Odds. Racing term: Odds on races established at the track by pari-mutuel machines.

Tracks. Drug user slang: Scars along veins after many injections of narcotics.

Trade Fire. Arson fires that are related to trade conditions. Also called business fires. These include burning merchandise to collect insurance or burning a competitor's business.

Traditional Authority. An authority accepted because it has been accepted in the past.

Traffic. Movement of vehicles along a roadway or other places of travel. The control of traffic and its enforcement has become one of the most important functions of law enforcement.

Traffic Control Devices. All signs, signals, markings, and devices not inconsistent with the act placed or erected by authority of a public body or official having jurisdiction, for the purpose of regulating, warning, or guiding traffic.

Traffic Control Signal. Any device, whether manually, electrically, or mechanically operated, by which traffic is alternately directed to stop and to proceed.

Trailer. One who follows and keeps another under observation; one who watches another.

Trailers. Trails of combustible materials used by arsonists to rapidly spread a fire throughout a structure or area. Materials used are usually those that burn completely, leaving little ash or residue.

Trainee (*train* ee). An officer who is receiving training. This is not restricted to a recruit.

Training Key, The. A series of short "meaty" articles on various topics related to law enforcement. There are questions, and at another place answers are given. They are printed twice monthly and sold by the Professional Standards Division of the International Association of Chiefs of Police.

Training Officer. The officer in charge of training all new officers.

Training School. State institution housing juvenile delinquents on court order; designed to offer educational and vocational training programs.

Trajectory (tre *jek* te ree). The path a projectile follows in flight.

Tramp. 1. A hobo, vagabond, or one who has no job. 2. Slang: A woman of low morals and repute.

VOCABULARY

Transceiver (tran *see* vur). Radio equipment that will transmit (send) and receive radio messages. This may be fixed or mobile. Most police cars are so equipped.

Transcript. Something that has been transcribed; a copy, especially of a record.

Transfuse. Transfer from one to another, such as transferring blood from one person to another. Transfusion—the act of transferring blood from one person to another or the act of introducing someone else's blood (donor) into the system of another.

Transient (*tran* shent). One who comes to a place for a temporary period of time and then moves on.

Transition Program. A program established by the Department of Defense in January 1968, offering to more than 800,000 enlisted men who leave the military each year "a path to more productive civilian careers." Under the program, personnel with from one to six months of service time remaining, who have not had an opportunity to develop a saleable civilian skill, are offered an opportunity to develop or upgrade the skills they will require when they return to civilian life. These services were provided in 1970 at more than 250 military installations. "Operation Police Manpower" is one of the services. For more details, contact the IACP.

Transmission Belt. A term used by the Communist Party in describing the function of the "front" organizations in getting the message of Communism to the masses of the people. See **Communist Front.**

Transparent. Allowing light to pass through and to be seen through.

Transportation Energy Center, Chemical. For information dealing with hazardous chemicals involved in transportation accidents, see **CHEMTREC.**

Transportation Thief. One who steals a motor vehicle that is used in the commission of another crime and then usually abandoned.

Transvestism (trans *ves* tizm). Sex deviation term: Sexual excitement obtained by one wearing the clothing of the opposite sex and playing the role of that sex.

Trap. 1. As used by game operators, any banking game. 2. A sucker bet.

Trap Circuit. A device used by telephone companies to locate trouble on the line. Can be used to locate the line on which abusive calls originate.

Travel Agent. A pusher of hallucinogenic drugs.

Traverse Method. A method of sketching (drawing) a scene, especially an outdoor scene, where distances, contours, and locations of objects need to be shown. It requires the use of a sketchboard, compass, and an alidade (sextant).

Treason. "Treason against the United States, shall consist only in levying war against them, or in adhering to their enemies, giving them aid and comfort. No person shall be convicted of treason unless on the testimony of two witnesses to the same overt act, or on confession in open court." Reference: United States Constitution, Art. 3, sec. 3.

Treasury Ticket. A lottery game based on the last five digits of the daily balance of the U.S. Treasury.

Trespass. In common usage it means to enter upon the property of another without the right to do so; to go beyond the limits of what is proper or correct. In law it goes much further and involves doing or not doing an act, unlawfully, that injures the property or person of another.

Trey. A three-dollar purchase.

Trial, Bench. A trial before a judge sitting without a jury.

Trial, Criminal. A judicial determination of guilt or innocence as prescribed by the law of the state or nation before a court of proper jurisdiction. (Civil trial determines rights of the parties.)

Trial, Joint. See **Joint Trial**.

Trial by Jury. Criminal law: The procedure of trying the accused before a jury. The Sixth Amendment of the Constitution provides, "In all criminal prosecutions, the accused shall enjoy the right to a speedy and public trial, by an impartial jury of the State and District wherein the crime shall have been committed. . . ." The law in some states had provided for trial by jury in felony cases and only before the court in misdemeanor cases. The Supreme Court, in Duncan v. Louisiana, 88 S.Ct. 1441 (1968), held that persons charged with serious misdemeanor violations had the right to trial before a jury. Although the court did not specifically spell it out, it talked about any crime providing a penalty in excess of six months imprisonment and a fine in excess of $500 as being considered a serious misdemeanor.

Trial by Ordeal. The early English method of determining guilt, which subjected the accused to a proof of innocence by surviving the test utilizing boiling water or hot beds of coal.

Triangulation Method (tri ang gye lay shen). A method of sketching where the positions of two points are known and the third, which may be inaccessible, is determined by use of a sketchboard, alidade, and compass.

Tribadism (*trib* a dizm). Sex deviation term: Female homosexuality; sexual act performed by one woman on another where the act of coitus is simulated by rubbing the female sex organs against one another.

Tribunal (tri *bue* nul). Place where justice is rendered; place where judge sits as a court.

Trick. Slang: A prostitute's sexual transaction with a customer. Also, an easy mark; a sucker; a fool.

Trick Bag, In a. Prison slang: To entrap; cause another person to neglect his defenses and to foolishly place himself in danger of damaging action from a third source.

Trier of Fact. One who tries judicially; a judge who tries a person or cause.

Trifurcation (try fur *kay* shun). Fingerprint term: A single ridge line that divides into three lines.

Trigger. 1. That part of a gun that, when pulled, releases the mechanism that causes the cartridge or ammunition to detonate (fire). 2. An object or event that releases a thing into action. 3. To smoke a marijuana cigarette immediately after taking LSD.

Trigger, Quick on the. Slang: Shoots quickly; alert mentally.

Trigger Happy. Slang: Shooting a firearm with little or no reason or justification; to be quick to shoot; "quick on the trigger."

Trigger Man. Slang: An assassin or hit man.

Trigger Pull. Firearms term: The amount of pull (force) required to pull the trigger to the point of release. This force is referred to in

VOCABULARY

terms of pounds—one pound, two pounds, etc. A hair trigger is one that requires very little pull to release it. Other pulls are "hard," "smooth," etc.

Trim. Slang: To cheat.

Trims. Cards gaffed by making trimmed cuts on them in certain ways.

Triolism (*try* o lizm). Sex deviation term: The desire to perform the sex act with multiple partners in the presence of people. This is a condition of exhibitionism.

Trip. Slang: An experience with or the effects of taking LSD.

Trip Dice. Gambling term: Dice on which the edges have been altered so they do not roll normally.

Tripping Out. Slang: High on psychedelics.

Trips. Slang: LSD.

Truant. Child who plays hookey from school, i.e. stays away from school without authority.

True Bill. Law: An indictment returned by a grand jury. See **Indictment**.

True Verdict. The verdict that is found by twelve impartial jurors who have not been coerced in any way.

Truck. A vehicle (as a strong automobile) designed for carrying heavy articles.

Truck Drivers. Narcotics slang: Amphetamine drugs.

Trusty (*trus* tee). A prisoner who, by good conduct, is given special privileges. Such trusties are found in jails and prisons. This word is frequently incorrectly pronounced. Trus*tee* means one who has the responsibility of looking after the property or affairs of another.

Truth Serum. A drug that produces a semiconscious condition or twilight sleep, in which a person will allegedly tell the truth. Sodium amytal is a drug recommended for this use. Some researchers state the procedure is unreliable and information so obtained would be legally inadmissible in a trial. The condition is also known as narcosis or narconalysis.

Try. Law: To determine facts in a court of law; to conduct a trial.

Turkey. 1. Juvenile slang: A person. 2. Narcotics slang: No narcotics or phony narcotics (baking powder).

Turkey Trots. Narcotics slang: Marks and scars on the body from the use of hypodermic needles.

Turned Off. Withdrawn from drugs.

Turned On. 1. Slang: Under the influence of drugs. 2. Juvenile slang: Free-spending.

Turned Out. Prison slang: To be assaulted homosexually, probably after a period of "courtship."

Turning People On. To give others drugs or to excite and interest them.

Turnkey. The person in charge of the keys, or a part of the keys, in a jail or penitentiary.

"Turn On, Tune In, Drop Out." Take LSD, learn about the "real" world, and drop out of the non-drugged world.

Turn Up. Narcotics slang: To feel the influence.

Turps. Slang: Elixir of terpin hydrate with codeine, a cough syrup.

Tussle. Grapple; wrestle; bodily conflict short of hitting.

Twenty-Five. Narcotics slang: LSD (from its original designation, LSD-25).

Twin Loop. A fingerprint pattern. See **Loop**.

Twist. Firearms term: The rate of spiral of the lands and grooves in the barrel of a rifle or pistol. The degree or rate of twist in a rifled barrel.

Twister. Juvenile slang: Key to any lock.

Two Bits. Slang: A quarter of a dollar.

Two-Faced. Insincere; deceptive; hypocritical; one who will "stab you in the back."

Two-Timed. Slang: Attacked by two persons.

Two-Way Joint. A carnival game operated honestly sometimes and crookedly other times.

Type Lines. Fingerprint term: The two innermost ridges, which start parallel, diverge, and surround the pattern area.

Typology. A classification scheme composed of two or more ideal types, which provide abstract categories in terms of which individual or group phenomena are analyzed.

Tyrant (*tie* rent). One who uses his position and power in an unjust way.

U

Ulna (*ull* nah) (ull as in pull). One of the two bones in the forearm that is opposite to the thumb.

Ulnar Loop (*ull* ner). A fingerprint pattern.

Ultimatum (ull te *may* tum). A final proposition or demand that, if not met, will result in some action, occurrence, or resort to force. "The kidnappers gave an ultimatum that the ransom must be paid by a certain day or the victim would be harmed."

Ultraviolet (ull trah *vigh* oh let). Light located in the spectrum beyond the violet end of the visible spectrum. Sometimes referred to as "black light." Used in law enforcement to detect certain fluorescent substances such as semen, invisible laundry marks, and other invisible writings. It is at the end of the spectrum opposite infrared light.

Ultra Vires (*ull* trah *vigh* rez). Latin, Law: Beyond the legal authority allowed; acts done outside of legal authority. This term is used by courts in their decisions. It would apply to a situation where an officer does an unlawful act that is beyond or outside of the authority granted him by law, such as arresting outside of his jurisdiction and where he has no authority to do so. In a tort action brought by the injured person against the officer's employing agency, the latter would claim that the acts of the officer were *ultra vires*.

Un-American. Opposed to or not conforming to the constitutional or legal usages, standards, or traditions of America. We see many allegations and apparent examples of Un-American Activities. It is a relative thing. Care should be exercised in not wrongfully accusing someone of being in this category.

Unauthorized Use of Movables. Criminal law: The intentional taking or use of any movable that belongs to another, either without the other's consent or by means of fraudulent conduct, practices, or representations, but without any intention to deprive the other of the movable permanently. The definition may vary among the states. The principal type of offense under this law is "joy riding" in automobiles.

Unbalanced (un *bal* enst). Mentally deranged; abnormal mentally; somewhat insane.

Unbiased (un *bi* est). Fair; impartial; having no bias or prejudice.

Unburden (un *bur* den). To ease one's mind by talking, particularly about one's problems or wrongdoing.

Uncle. Slang: Federal narcotics agent.

Underboss, The. The second man in control of a "family" of La Cosa Nostra. He is immediately under the Boss in power and direction of the "family." See **Boss; La Cosa Nostra**.

Undercover (un der *kuv* er). Secret and confidential operator; investigator. One who uses a "cover" name, occupation, or pretext to investigate a matter or determine situations. "The use of undercover operators in law enforcement is most helpful, particularly in crimes involving vices (gambling, prostitution, etc.)"

Undercut. Slang: The dealing of a

card from the bottom of the deck in a card game. This is done by a card sharp or manipulator.

Underground (*un* der ground). 1. A group working together, secretly and clandestinely, to free a country of a rulership to which the group is opposed. "There was a strong underground in France when it was occupied by the Germans." 2. To disappear from sight or conceal activities. "To go underground is to disappear from sight or fade away from public view and carry on operations secretly."

Underworld. That part of society in which are found criminals and their associates. Generally it is viewed as a degraded section of society. "Activities of the underworld are such that they are concealed, at least partially, from the public."

Under Wraps. A horse who is restrained from running to his full capacity.

Undeveloped Lead. A lead, clue, or investigation that remains to be done or that necessitates further investigation or inquiry. Some agencies list the undeveloped leads at the end of the investigative report.

Undue Influence. Influence exerted when one acquires such an ascendancy over another as to prevent the latter from acting on his own free will.

Uniform Crime Report. A statistical compilation of crime in the United States. The report is published annually by the Federal Bureau of Investigation. The main body of the report is limited to several selected crimes, known as index crimes.

Uniform Laws. Laws approved by the NCCUSL, of which many have been adopted in one or more jurisdictions in the U.S. and its possessions.

Union, Police. See **International Brotherhood of Police Officers**.

Union Shop. A business or company where the majority of the workmen belong to labor unions.

United States Attorney. The chief legal officer of the United States in the federal judicial district. He prosecutes violators of crimes against the United States and represents the federal government in civil matters. He acts under the direction of the United States Attorney General. There is one in each federal district. His position is appointive. He usually has one or more assistants, who have the title Assistant United States Attorney.

United States Code (U.S.C.). The criminal law of the United States.

United States Code Annotated (U.S.C.A.). An annotated version or printing of the United States Code.

United States Commissioner. A federal magistrate. His functions in the federal field are comparable to those in state matters of the Justice of the Peace. He is not a judge and does not hold court. He may issue certain warrants, act as a committing official, set bail, and bind over for trial. His functions are prescribed by statute.

United States Educational, Scientific and Cultural Organization (UNESCO). A separate but related agency of the United Nations, to work in the fields designated in its name.

United States Magistrates. Formerly, United States Commissioners. Judges who fulfill the pretrial judicial obligations of the federal district courts.

United States Marshal. A federal

law enforcement officer of the federal judicial district. He is appointed by the President and approved by the United States Senate and is under the supervision of the United States Attorney General. His duties at the federal level are somewhat comparable to that of the sheriff at the county level. They include making arrests for federal crimes, maintaining custody of federal prisoners awaiting trial, transporting federal prisoners to and from jail and the courts as well as to and from federal penal institutions, maintaining order in federal courts, and executing the orders of the federal judges. There is one in each federal judicial district. He may have one or more deputies, who bear the title Deputy United States Marshal.

Universalism. Using the same rules and applying those rules in the same way for all people.

Unkie (Unky). Slang: Morphine.

Unlawful (un *law* full). Illegal; against the law; a criminal act.

Unlawful Assembly. At common law, the meeting together of three or more persons, to the disturbance of the public peace, with the intention of cooperating in the forcible and violent execution of some unlawful enterprise. If they take steps toward the performance of their purpose, it becomes a rout, and if they put their design into actual execution, it is a riot. Any meetings of great numbers of people, with such circumstances of terror as cannot but endanger the public peace and raise fears and jealousies among the subjects of the realm. (*Black's Law Dictionary*).

Unlawful Entry. A less serious type of burglary; entering an open or unlocked building without the authority or legal right.

Unlawful Flight to Avoid Giving Testimony. A federal law making it a felony for any person to travel to another state or nation to avoid giving testimony as a material witness in a criminal proceeding in which a felony is charged under the state laws. This is also called the Fugitive Witness Act.

Unlawful Flight to Avoid Prosecution. A federal law making it a felony for any person charged by a state with violation of a felony, under the state law, to travel to another state or nation for the purpose of avoiding prosecution. It is also called the Fugitive Felon Act.

Unload. Slang: To tell what one knows about another, who may or may not be an accomplice.

Unmask. To reveal identity; to take off disguise; to show or reveal the true character.

Unnatural Act. The act of sodomy or buggery.

Unreliable. Not dependable; not reliable.

U.N.R.R.A. United Relief and Rehabilitation Administration.

Unsavory. Morally bad; unclean; distasteful.

Unscrupulous (un *screw* pyu les). Without scruples, principles, or morals; without integrity.

Unsnarl. Disentangle; untangle; straighten up and restore to order a state of confusion.

Unwritten Law. 1. Law that has not been written and adopted by legislative bodies. Conduct that has been accepted as lawful by reason of common acceptance—common law. 2. All portions of the law, observed and administered in the courts, which have not been enacted or promulgated in the form of statute or ordinance, including the unenacted portions of the common law, general, and particular customs having the force of laws, and the rules, principles, and maxims established by judicial precedents or the successive like decisions of the courts (*Black's Law Dictionary*).

Uppers. Slang: Drugs that cause one to be stimulated, pepped up, or feel "high," such as amphetamines.

Uppish. Slang: Conceited; demonstrating self-importance; inclined to be arrogant; "high hatted."

Upstairs. Juvenile slang: Outstanding; very nice.

Upstart. One raised quickly to importance, power, or influence. A newcomer in the field who has not received the respect of older persons. He is usually characterized as being arrogant and pretentious.

Uptight. Prison slang: 1. Very nervous. 2. Close association with someone.

Uptown. Slang: The elite part of town; fashionable part of a city. Something that is high class.

Uranism. Homosexuality.

Urban. Relative to towns and cities; area within towns or cities. Urban population and the attendant problems are matters of recent discussion in the field of criminal justice. The increase in urban growth has created many problems.

Urban District. The territory contiguous to and including any street that is built up with structures devoted to business, industry, or dwelling houses situated at intervals of less than 100 feet for a distance of a quarter-mile or more.

Urban Ecology. The study of the distributive patterns of residential, commercial, and industrial buildings and their interdependence.

Urban Guerilla. A term applied to terrorists who, motivated by some political idea, commit arson, bomb, kidnap, murder, and hijack airplanes.

Urbanization. The movement of the population from the rural areas to the cities.

Urban Renewal. Program to replace "run-down" urban areas with modern structures and facilities, usually with the use of public funds and directed by a local government agency.

Urgent (*er* gent). Something demanding immediate action or attention; imperative; pressing.

Urinalysis (your e *nal* e sis). Urine analysis; the analysis (laboratory examination) of a specimen (quantity) of urine.

Urolagnia (*uro* lag ne ah). Sex deviation term: The arousing of sexual emotion by the sight of a person urinating or of urine.

U.S.C. United States Code.

U.S.C.A. United States Code Annotated.

U.S. Court of Appeals. The first appellate court in the federal court system.

U.S. District Court. The level in the federal court system where felony and misdemeanor violations of federal law are tried.

User. One who uses drugs.

Usufruct (*you* so frukt). Law: The right to use property, and receive its earnings or increase, that belongs to another.

Usurer (*you* zer er). One who loans money at unlawfully high interest rates.

Usury (*you* zer ee). Lending of money at an interest rate that is uncommonly or unlawfully high.

VOCABULARY

Utilitarian Power. Power based on such material resources as personal or corporate wealth.

Utmost Resistance. To resist to the fullest extent. This is a term used in connection with the crime of rape, where the law frequently requires that the victim must have resisted to the utmost. It is a relative term.

Utter. Law: To put or send (as a forged check) into circulation (*Black's Law Dictionary*).

V

Vacate (*vay* kate). 1. To leave premises unoccupied. 2. Law: To cancel, set aside, rescind, or annul.

Vacutainer®. Trade name for a blood collection system used for collecting blood specimens for laboratory testing of blood for alcohol content.

Vag. To arrest and book a person on the charge of vagrancy.

Vagabond. A transient without employment; hobo; nomad; vagrant.

Vagrancy (*vay* gren see). Conduct or manner of living consisting of going about from place to place without visible means of support and, although able to work, not doing so and/or living on the charity of others.

Vagrant. A tramp or idle wanderer; one guilty of vagrancy; one having no fixed place of abode.

Validity (va *lid* i te). Legal sufficiency.

Value. 1. Clusters of beliefs to which attitudes have been attached. 2. Something counted worthy or desirable.

Vamoose. Slang: Get away; leave quickly.

VASCAR. Visual Average Speed Computer and Recorder. An electronic device, manually activated, that measures quantities of distance and time and computes the resultant speed.

Vault. A place of security, generally built of steel and/or concrete, for safe storage of valuables. There has been constant competition between burglars and businesses. The latter have sought to develop vaults and safes that are burglarproof, and the safe burglars have worked for ways to overcome such protective devices. The thermal burning bar is one of the latest developments used by burglars to penetrate vaults and safes. See **Thermal Burning Bar**.

Veal Cutlet. Slang: A victim.

Vegetable. A person who has lost his mental capacity (through injury or otherwise). The body functions exist, but there is a total or almost total loss of mental performance.

Vehicle (*vee* hick el). 1. A means of conveyance. The self-propelled vehicle is the one of most concern in law enforcement. See **ITSMV—Interstate Transportation of Stolen Motor Vehicles; Automobile Theft; Unauthorized Use of Motor Vehicle; Traffic**. 2. A person in illegal enterprise who is used by an undercover man to furnish information about the operation and who introduces the undercover man to other persons operating in the enterprise.

Vein (vain). A tubular blood vessel that carries blood from the capillaries to the heart; a part of the human circulatory system.

Velocity (ve *los* i tee). 1. Speed at which an object moves. 2. Firearms term: The speed of a bullet in flight.

Velvet. Money won from gambling.

Venal (*veen* el). Corruptible; susceptible to being bribed; swayed or influenced by bribery.

Vendetta (ven *det* uh). A feud in which the blood relatives of the person who has been injured or killed take action against the offender or members of his family.

Venereal Disease. A disease associated with the sexual act; a disease that is spread through sexual intercourse with an infected person. Gonorrhea and syphilis are two such diseases.

Venire (ve *nigh* ree). Law: A panel, made up of several persons, from which jurors are drawn.

Venire Facias (*fay* she es). Law: A writ, issued by the court, ordering the sheriff to summon qualified persons to serve on a jury.

Venireman (ve *nire* ee min). Law: An individual member of a jury panel (venire).

Ventral. Anatomy: The portion of the body opposite the spine; situated near the abdomen.

Venue (*ven* you). Place where a trial is held; geographical area (county, district, state) where legal action or trial should be held.

Veracity (ve *ras* e tee). Truthfulness.

Vera Institute of Justice. A non-profit organization devoted to the improvement of the administration of criminal justice. It was started in October, 1961, in New York by Louis Schweitzer as the Manhattan Bail Project.

Verbal. Oral; consisting merely of words; spoken words.

Verbatim (ver *bay* tim). The same words in the same order; word for word.

Verdict. The official decision of a jury; decision reached by a jury.

Vertical (*ver* te kul). Straight up; a line perpendicular to a level surface.

Vertical Mobility. Changing social roles, such as occupation, without changing social status (moving up or down in society).

Veterans Day. Formerly Armistice Day—November 11. The name was changed by Congress in 1954.

Vibes (Vibrations). Feelings coming from another; may be "good" or "bad" vibes.

Vicarious Murder (vi *kar* i us). See **Murder, Vicarious.**

Vice. Bad habit; a fault; having to do with such things as gambling, prostitution, etc. Name given to the segment of a police agency dealing with vice.

Vice Versa. In the opposite way; conversely.

Victim. Person who has been kidnapped, swindled, defrauded (such as by a worthless check), robbed, suffered other types of wrong by criminal acts, or injured in traffic accident.

Victimization. A specific criminal act as it affects a single victim. In criminal acts against persons, the number of victimizations is determined by the number of victims of such acts. Because more than one individual may be victimized during certain crimes against persons, the number of victimizations is somewhat higher than the number of incidents. Each criminal act against a household or commercial establishment is assumed to involve a single victim, the affected household, or establishment.

Victimization Rate. For crimes against persons, the victimization rate, a measure of occurrence among population groups at risk, is computed on the basis of victimizations per 1,000 resident population age twelve or over. For crimes against households, victimization rates are calculated on the basis of the number of incidents per 1,000 households. For crimes against commercial establishments, victimization rates are derived from the number of incidents per 1,000 establishments. Note that the victimization rate is not a ratio of number of population units victimized to number exposed to risk, nor a probability of a given person being victimized.

Victimless Crimes. Crimes that do no harm other than harm to the perpetrator.

Vigilante (vij e *lan* tee). A member of a group that undertakes to enforce the law and/or maintain morals without legal authority for such actions.

Vigorish (Viggerish; Vig). Percentage on a banking game taken by the operator, hidden in the mechanics of the game.

Villain. 1. The "bad guy" in a play or movie. 2. A bad character; scoundrel; evil person.

Vindicate (*vin* de kate). 1. To remove or clear from a charge or allegation of wrong or suspicion; avenge; exonerate; confirm. 2. To maintain a right to assert.

Violate. Break the law.

Violation. Breaking of a law, agreement, or rules.

Violator. A person who breaks a law, agreement, or rule.

Violence (*vi* o lens). Law: The unlawful exercise of physical force; actions that tend to intimidate or coerce by producing fear of bodily injury.

Violent Death. Unlike natural death, it is death resulting from the acts of other humans. It may be caused or hastened by such humans. Death resulting from unusual force.

VIP. Very important person.

Viper. Slang: A habitual opium or marijuana smoker.

Virtual Image. An image that cannot be projected onto a screen and can only be seen in a mirror or through a lens.

Visa. Approval by the government or representatives of a country for a person of a foreign country to be in the country giving the approval; approval to proceed into or through a country, stamped on the passport.

Vis A Vis (vee zah *vee*). Face to face with one another. Two people or things that face one another.

Visible Prints. Fingerprints composed of a deposit of a visible substance or stain left by soiled fingers. These may be left by blood, dirt, oil, stains, etc., being on the fingers.

Visual Acuity (eh *que* e ty). The ability to see clearly or perceive things through sight.

Visual Aid. Something to aid the teacher and benefit the student, such as photographs, motion pictures, drawings, and charts. This means the student learns through sight as well as hearing and increases learning and retention of knowledge.

Visual Surveillance. Keeping watch or observing people, places, or vehicles. These may be (1) fixed (a plant or stakeout), where the watchers are located in a stationary or semistationary place of concealment, such as a house or a parked vehicle, or (2) a moving surveillance (shadow or tail), where the person or vehicle is kept under observation by investigators, either on foot or in vehicle.

Vixen (*vick* sen). A woman who quarrels frequently and exhibits a bad temper.

Vociferous. Loud; noisy; capable of disturbing the public peace.

Voice Identification. One may become so familiar with the voice of another that the speaker can be identified. In order for testimony on voice identification to be admissible in court, a foundation must be laid by testimony that the witness has talked by phone or has otherwise heard the person speak and that the witness does recognize the person's voice when he hears it.

Voiceprint. A spectrographic record (recording) of the energy output produced by the sound of words or sounds made by a person when speaking. Allegedly it is distinctive for each person.

Void. Without effect; not binding by law; without force in law.

Voidable. Capable of being annulled, made void, or judged invalid.

Voir Dire (*vwar* dear). To speak the truth. Law: An oath given to a witness or prospective juror, to give truthful answers to questions propounded to him relative to his competence, interest, or prejudice; an examination of prospective jurors to determine competency.

Volstead Act. An act of Congress, named after Representative Andrew J. Volstead, to enforce the Eighteenth Amendment of the United States Constitution. It is also called the Prohibition Act.

Voluntary Association. Association that an individual may join entirely of his own free will or for social or economic reasons.

Voodoo. A mystic procedure or ceremony involving magic and superstition. Found in certain parts of the United States among poorly educated people.

Voyeur (voy *yur*). Sex deviation term: A "peeping tom"; a peeper; one who gets sexual gratification from seeing the sex organs of another, especially of the opposite sex, or seeing the act of sexual intercourse.

Vulgar. Reflecting lack of manners; speech that is offensive in that the words used are not good taste.

Vulnerability. As used in victimization statistics, the likelihood or risk of being victimized.

W

Wac. Women's Army Corps; a member of the Women's Army Corps.
Wacky. "Nutty"; peculiar; eccentric; mentally deranged.
Wad. Firearms term: The partition, made of a soft resilient material, placed over the powder in a shell containing shot. It generally is made of felt or a similar material. It controls the gas blast.
WAF. Women's Air Force; A member of the Women's Air Force.
Waffle. Juvenile slang: Strike someone.
Wager. A bet.
Wager Ticket. Gambling term: A written record of bets.
Wait, Lie in. To conceal one's self or stay hidden, ready to attack. The Louisiana "attempt" statute provides that lying in wait with a dangerous weapon with intent to commit a crime constitutes an attempt to commit the offense intended.
Waive. Agree to give up something that a person has a right to retain and use.
Waiver. Also called "discharge" in some states. A procedure whereby a suspect under arrest may be released by the arresting agency when his innocence becomes obvious.
Wakeups. Slang: Stimulant drugs.
Walking Line. One of the elements of the walking picture. An imaginary line that in normal and ideal walking fuses with the direction line and runs along the inner sides of both heelprints.
Walking Picture. The study of the characteristics of footprints left by a person walking. Included in this study are the direction line, the walking line, and the foot line.
Wampole. A liquid narcotic. Alcohol, quinine, and strychnine are the chief ingredients.
Wanted Notice. A flyer, bulletin, or other notice used by law enforcement agencies to let it be known that a certain person is wanted for an offense.
Wanton. Reckless; heedless; with an utter disregard of right or consequence.
War Chief. Juvenile slang: Liaison officer of a gang.
Warden. A custodian or keeper of persons confined. Usually the title of the chief administrative official of a prison or a large jail.
Warden's Box. A box or other receptacle in a prison or penitentiary into which an inmate drops notes dealing with personal problems or suggestions for the improvement of the establishment.
Warning Shot. The firing of a weapon into the air or into the ground or street as a warning to a fleeing person that unless he stops the next shots may be directed at him. The purpose is to frighten the running person so he will stop. Many police agencies have a policy against this. It seldom works in stopping the running person and may injure bystanders.
Warrant, Search. See **Search Warrant**.
Warrant of Arrest. An order, in writing, issued by and signed by a

VOCABULARY

judge or magistrate commanding that a designated person be arrested and processed according to the law; a writ ordering an arrest of a certain person.

Warrant Officer. An officer of the United States armed services, ranking below a commissioned officer and above a noncommissioned officer and who holds a warrant from the president.

Wash a Cat Away. Juvenile slang: Physically beat someone.

Washed-Up. Slang: Having failed in an undertaking; having finished a project without success. Also, withdrawn from drugs.

Waste. Juvenile slang: To kill or brutally beat someone.

Wasted. Juvenile slang: Beaten up. Also, high or drunk.

Watch and Ward. An early system of law enforcement used in England in the towns and cities. Citizens took turns serving as watchmen.

Watch Commander. The person who has full operational responsibility for all police functions during the eight- or ten-hour periods that his officers are on duty.

Watermark. A design worked into certain kinds of paper. It can be seen by holding the paper so it is viewed against a bright light. It is usually put in the paper by the manufacturer, and the manufacturer may be identified by such watermark. This is one of the factors or characteristics of paper determined by a crime laboratory examination of the paper. A lead may be obtained by tracing such paper from the manufacturer through the retailer.

WATS Line. A service offered by the telephone company whereby the subscriber, for a given monthly rate, can call any telephone within a given radius. It is abbreviation for wide area telephone service. It is attractive to bookies because of the savings in costs and the fact that records are not kept on the identity of the individual calls.

Wave. To bend the edge of a card during play for identification purposes; the bend itself.

Wavelength. The distance between crests or troughs of adjacent waves.

WAVES. Women Appointed Volunteer Emergency Service (U.S. Naval Reserve); a member of the organization.

Waylay. Lie in wait for someone.

W.C.T.U. Women's Christian Temperance Union.

Wear Drag. Slang: To wear female clothing.

Weasel. Slang: A police informant.

Weathermen. A militant faction of the Students for a Democratic Society (SDS). It splintered from SDS in June, 1969, at Ann Arbor, Michigan.

Wedding Bells. Slang: LSD.

Wedges. Small tablets of wedge (almost triangular) shape.

Weed. Slang: Tobacco cigarette; marijuana cigarette.

Weed Head. Marijuana smoker.

Weekend Habit. Irregular drug habit.

Weighing. To value, rate, rank, or otherwise compare one thing with another.

Weight. The gravitational pull upon a substance.

Weight of Evidence. The degree of importance or the significance of evidence. This is a matter for the jury to decide.

Weird. On drugs.

Welsher. One who will not pay off his gambling obligations, especially his losses.

Went Up Against. Juvenile slang: Challenged.
West Coast Turnarounds. Amphetamine tablets or capsules.
Wet, All. Slang: To be wrong concerning a matter.
What's Shaking? Juvenile slang: What's going on?
Wheel. 1. Gambler's term: Backer or owner of a policy or numbers operation. 2. Juvenile slang: Skillfully operate a car; to go in fashion.
Wheel Man. Criminal slang: The driver of a getaway car; the driver of the vehicle used in the commission of a crime.
Wheels. Slang: Motor vehicle.
Where It's At. Slang: Where (drug) action is taking place.
Where's Buster Brown? Expression meaning switch the loaded dice into the craps game.
Whipping Boy. Slang: One upon whom punishment or blame is placed whereas another should receive such; scapegoat.
Whip Shot. Gambler slang: The shooting of the dice with a spinning motion so they do not tumble when hitting the table surface, thus keeping the same sides up.
Whiskers. Federal narcotics agents.
White-Collar Crimes. Those crimes committed by persons of middle or high socioeconomic status. These crimes may be violations of regular penal laws or of special laws enacted to cover certain occupational activities. The white-collar person may be an official of a commercial organization or of lower organizational structure. Usually such a person is in a position of trust in the place where he works and takes advantage of it in his criminal activities.
White Head. Juvenile slang: Colorless whiskey.

Whites. Amphetamine tablets.
White Slave Traffic Act. A federal violation pertaining to interstate transportation of a woman or a girl for immoral purposes. Also known as the Mann Act; U.S. Code 18, 2421-24.
White Stuff. Slang: Generic name for narcotics and drugs generally, including morphine and codeine.
Whitewash. Slang: To cover up, gloss over, or ignore faults and wrongdoings of others.
Whitey. Slang: A white person. This is a term used by some members of the black race.
Whiz-Kid. Slang: A very intellectual young person.
Whore. Woman of loose morals; a prostitute.
Whorehouse. House of prostitution.
Whoremonger. A man consorting with prostitutes.
Whorl. A fingerprint pattern where one or more ridges make a complete circuit in the core of the pattern. It has two deltas. The central pocket loop, the double loop, and the accidentals are classified as whorls.
Whorl, Plain. A fingerprint pattern that has one or more ridges that make a complete circuit. It has two deltas, between which, when an imaginary line is drawn, at least one recurving ridge is cut or touched.
Wickersham Commission. A commission appointed by the President of the United States in 1929 to study crime in the United States as a national problem.
Wig Out (Wigging). See **Blow Your Mind**.
Wild-Goose Chase. Slang: A search or undertaking that is useless and fruitless.
Wild Oats, Sowing One's. Slang: Youthful escapades of questionable

character before settling down into life.

Will. A legal declaration of a person's desires as to the disposition of his property after he is dead; testament.

Willful. Done deliberately; intentional.

Windage (*win* dij). The effect of the wind in deflecting the course of a projectile (bullet); the horizontal sight adjustment necessary to compensate for wind deflection in aiming a gun.

Windbag. Slang: One who talks a great deal but most of it without substance; one who talks much and says little.

Windowpane. Narcotics slang: A dot of LSD about one eighth of an inch square attached to paper or tape.

Window Smashers. A technique of display window burglars to obtain valuables, such as jewelry. The gang will park near the victim's business, usually during business hours, break the display glass with a stone or hard object, quickly grab valuable merchandise, and escape in the waiting vehicle.

Wipe It Off. Gambler's term: To stop accepting bets on an event, fearing that the event is fixed.

Wire-Off Job. Gambling term: An illegally installed extension telephone.

Wire Room. Gambling term: Place where the bets are accepted over the phone.

Wiretap. See **Tap, Wire.**

Wiry (*wi* ree). Description of a person; slender, strong, and tough.

Withdrawal, Drug. When a drug or narcotic addict abstains from or is deprived from the use of drugs, a characteristic syndrome of symptoms develops. See **Abstinence Syndrome.**

With It. Slang: To be a member of the carnival crew.

With the Happenings. Juvenile slang: Having a knowledge of events.

Witness. 1. A person who testifies to facts in a legal proceeding. 2. A person who sees something happen.

Witness Stand. The place where a witness is positioned while testifying in court. See **Stand.**

Wobble. Firearms term: The erratic spin of a bullet in flight. The cause may be that the gun barrel does not have enough twist.

Wolf. Slang: 1. A man who readily entices or seduces. 2. An active lesbian. 3. An aggressive pederast.

Wood. Nonplayers or players who have lost all their money.

Wood Alcohol. A poisonous form of alcohol, methyl alcohol, that is made from complex cellulose; drinking it could cause death or blindness.

Woodcheck. Slang: Minor criminal or one suspected of participation in minor crimes.

Wop. Slang: Derogatory term for an Italian.

Word Association Test. A test whereby the suspect is asked to name a synonym for each of several words read to him from a list containing words not relevant to the crime interspersed with relevant words. Evaluation is based upon reaction time in answering, repetition of stimulus words, and other factors. First research on this type of test was started in 1879.

Work. 1. A place where cash and gambling records are kept. It is a part of gambling operations conducted by organized crime; the day's business in gambling. 2. Gambling slang: Altered cards or dice; the altering of gambling equipment.

Workhorse. Slang: A hard-working individual.

Workhouse. Correctional establishment for petty offenders. Work is usually required of inmates.

Working. Slang: Prostitution; hustling.

Working Points. A percentage of ownership in a casino purchased by a worker.

Work Release. Correctional programs that allow an inmate to leave the institution for the purpose of continuing regular employment during the daytime, but reporting back to lockup nights and weekends.

Works. Slang: Equipment used for injecting drugs.

Works, Give Him the. Slang: Give one the full treatment; give it all to him.

Wraps, Keep It Under. Slang: Keep it confidential.

Wrapup. Summary news item.

Wrecker. A specially built truck, usually equipped with hoist and chains, used for removing vehicles from public streets or highways. To avoid claims of collusion or favoritism, many law enforcement agencies do not recommend the wrecking service of any particular person but let the victim select the wrecker service. Others rotate the calls among the services.

Writ. A written order issued by a judicial officer commanding a person to do or not to do something described therein.

Writer. Gambling term: One who writes numbers.

Writer's Code. Gambling term: The system, including the method and form, of recording betting information.

Writ of Assistance. A form of general search warrant issued out of the Colonial courts, under the British law, in the eighteenth century. They were general in nature in that they did not have to name specific things for which the search was to be made but authorized the search to be made for "unaccustomed or otherwise illegal commodities." Such writs were widely used in the American colonies and were much resented. They are no longer allowed as constitutional.

Writ of Error. A writ issued from a court of appellate jurisdiction, directed to the judge or judges of a court of record, requiring them to remit to the appellate court the record of an action before them in which a final judgement has been entered, in order that examination may be made of certain errors alleged to have been committed, and that the judgement may be reversed, corrected, or affirmed, as the case might be.

Wrong. 1. Injustice; improper abuse of the rights of another. 2. Gambling term: Betting that the player does not make his point in a crap game.

X

X, The. Total control of all the gambling establishments in town.

X Chromosome. The female sex chromosome.

Xenophobia. Medical term: Dislike of foreigners.

X-Ray. To examine or test something with X ray. This technique is used extensively in the medical field and in some examinations conducted by the crime laboratory.

XYZ Chromosome. An abnormal arrangement of the chromosomes in the nucleus of cells, which, according to some scientists, produces antisocial behavior in persons having this abnormality. As of 1970, the National Institute of Mental Health reported that no definite conclusions had been reached as to the validity of such claims. Reference: *The Police Chief,* December, 1970, p. 54.

Y

Yaled Up. Slang: Padlocked.

Yankee. Slang: An American when referred to by people in some foreign countries; a person from the northern part of the United States when referred to by some people from the southern part of the country.

Yard. 1. Gambling term: One thousand dollars. 2. Juvenile slang: One hundred dollars.

Yard, The. 1. Slang: British-Scotland Yard or New Scotland Yard. 2. Prison slang: An area outside the cells in which prisoners are allowed to exercise. This is a critical area for a prison because of the number of prisoners intermingling.

Y Chromosome. The male sex chromosome.

Yegg. Slang: Safe burglar or any burglar.

Yellow Jacket. Slang: Nembutal® capsule; depressant drugs; barbiturates.

Yellows. Slang: Depressant drugs—barbiturates.

Yellow Sunshine. Narcotics slang: Tablets containing LSD.

Yen. Slang: A desire or craving; an addict's craving for narcotics.

Yen-Hok. A long steel needle upon which an opium pill is cooked.

Yen-Pock. A ration of opium prepared for smoking.

Yen-Pop. Marijuana.

Yen-Shee. The residue left in the opium pipe's bowl and stem after the opium has been smoked.

Yen-Shee Doy. Chinese: A Chinese drug addict.

Yen-Shee Gow. A scraper for removing yen-shee from the opium pipe.

Yen-Shee Suey. Opium wine; Yen-shee mixed with water or whiskey.

Yen Sleep. Slang: A drowsy, restless state during the withdrawal period of one on drugs.

Yesca. Spanish terminology for marijuana.

Yield. To give way to; to allow someone else to act; to surrender to.

York, Statute of. An important English statute pertaining to attorneys, witnesses, and the taking of inquests by *nisi prius*.

Youngblood. A young person using marijuana for the first time.

Youth Service Bureau. A diversion program for juvenile courts that eliminates noncriminal cases and petty first offenses from the courts' consideration by providing a resource to help a young person become less troubled or less troubling.

Yuck. Slang: A victim.

Z

Zealous Witness. An overeager witness who is so biased in favor of the side calling him that he materially reduces his effectiveness by showing his partiality.

Zero Population Growth. A state that occurs when the birth rate equals or is less than the death rate.

Zilch. Slang: Nothing; no money.

Zing It In. To bet high, especially with money won in the game.

ZIP Code. A system used by the United States Post Office Department to designate specified areas of the country. This aids in handling the mail. The number consists of five numbers and is placed after the name of the state in an address.

Zip Gun. Slang: A nonprofessionally made gun of crude materials such as a metal pipe for a barrel and a rubber band or spring to move the firing pin. They are made mostly by juveniles and are varied in construction.

Zips. Juvenile slang: Homemade weapons or firearms.

Zone Search. A method of searching a crime scene where the area to be searched is divided into sectors (squares or rectangles) and each one is carefully examined (searched). This is also called the sector search.

Zonked. Under the influence of narcotics.

Zoo. Slang: A penitentiary, prison, or lockup.

Zoot Suit. Slang: A flashy man's suit with wide padded shoulders and "peg leg" trousers.